PATERNOSTER BIBLICAL MONOGRAPHS

Jesus as the Fulfillment of the Temple in the Gospel of John

PATERNOSTER BIBLICAL MONOGRAPHS

A complete listing of all titles in this series and Paternoster Theological Monographs will be found at the close of this book.

PATERNOSTER BIBLICAL MONOGRAPHS

Jesus as the Fulfillment of the Temple in the Gospel of John

Paul M. Hoskins

Foreword by D. A. Carson

Wipf & Stock
PUBLISHERS
Eugene, Oregon

Wipf and Stock Publishers
199 W 8th Ave, Suite 3
Eugene, OR 97401

Jesus as the Fulfillment of the Temple in the Gospel of John
By Hoskins, Paul M.
Copyright©2006 Paternoster
ISBN 13: 978-1-55635-223-2
ISBN 10: 1-55635-223-9
Publication date 1/24/2007
Previously published by Paternoster, 2006

Paternoster
9 Holdom Avenue
Bletchley
Milton Keyes, MK1 1QR
Great Britain

PATERNOSTER BIBLICAL MONOGRAPHS

Series Preface

One of the major objectives of Paternoster is to serve biblical scholarship by providing a channel for the publication of theses and other monographs of high quality at affordable prices. Paternoster stands within the broad evangelical tradition of Christianity. Our authors would describe themselves as Christians who recognise the authority of the Bible, maintain the centrality of the gospel message and assent to the classical credal statements of Christian belief. There is diversity within this constituency; advances in scholarship are possible only if there is freedom for frank debate on controversial issues and for the publication of new and sometimes provocative proposals. What is offered in this series is the best of writing by committed Christians who are concerned to develop well-founded biblical scholarship in a spirit of loyalty to the historic faith.

Series Editors

I. Howard Marshall, Honorary Research Professor of New Testament, University of Aberdeen, Scotland, UK

Richard J. Bauckham, Professor of New Testament Studies and Bishop Wardlaw Professor, University of St Andrews, Scotland, UK

Craig Blomberg, Distinguished Professor of New Testament, Denver Seminary, Colorado, USA

Robert P. Gordon, Regius Professor of Hebrew, University of Cambridge, UK

Tremper Longman III, Robert H. Gundry Professor and Chair of the Department of Biblical Studies, Westmont College, Santa Barbara, California, USA

*This book is dedicated to my dear wife, Cheryl,
and our children, Hannah and Timothy*

Contents

Foreword by D. A Carson   xiii

Preface and Acknowledgements   xv

Chapter 1
Introduction   1
Background for the Current Study: Contemporary Trends in
Johannine Studies   3
Methodological Framework of the Study   5
Review of Literature   9
    Jesus as the Fulfillment or Replacement of the Temple in the
    Fourth Gospel   10
    Typology   18
Plan for the Study   37

Chapter 2
History and Significance of the Temple according to the Old Testament and Selected Jewish Literature   38
The Tabernacle: Antecedent of the Temple   39
Deuteronomy's Expectation of a 'Place that the Lord Your God
Will Choose'   45
The Establishment of the Temple as a Legitimate Replacement
for the Tabernacle   51
The Temple as the Lord's Dwelling Place in the Midst of His People   59
Prophetic Hopes for a New Temple of God   69
The Temple in the Post-Exilic Period   83
The Temple in Extra-Biblical Jewish Literature   89
Temple Replacement in the Old Testament and Jewish Literature   103

Conclusion   105

Chapter 3
Jesus as the Fulfillment and Replacement of the Temple in the Fourth Gospel: Part One   108
John 2:18-22   108
John 1:14   116
John 1:51   125
John 4:20-24   135
Conclusion   145

Chapter 4
Jesus as the Fulfillment and Replacement of the Temple in the Fourth Gospel: Part Two   147
Converging Themes: Replacement of the Temple, Glory, and Death/Resurrection/Exaltation   147
   Jesus' Lifting up or Glorification in the Fourth Gospel   148
   Background for Jesus' Lifting up and Glorification in Isaiah   152
Jesus' Fulfillment of the Temple and His Fulfillment of the Jewish Feasts   160
   Fulfillment of the Feast of Tabernacles   160
   Fulfillment of the Feast of Dedication   170
   Fulfillment of the Passover   176
Conclusion   181

Chapter 5
A Proper Understanding of Jesus' Replacement of the Temple in the Fourth Gospel   182

Chapter 6
Conclusion   194
Review of Chapters 1 to 5   194
John's Temple Typology in New Testament Perspective   197
Some Implications for Further Study and Theological Reflection   201

Bibliography   205

Author Index 241

Scripture Index 247

Index for Other Ancient Sources 263

Foreword

The burgeoning literature on the way the New Testament cites, alludes to and echoes the Old Testament is becoming increasingly specialized. Thus there is plenty of scope for a study of how one Old Testament theme or text is used in one New Testament book or corpus. Some recent works, of course, have surveyed the use of the tabernacle/temple theme in all of the New Testament (e.g. Craig R. Koester, *The Dwelling of God: The Tabernacle in the Old Testament, Intertestamental Jewish Literature, and the New Testament* [1989]; Kurt Paesler, *Das Tempelwort Jesu: Die Traditionen von Tempelzerstörung und Tempelerneuerung im Neuen Testament* [1999]) or even through all of the Bible (Greg R. Beale, *The Temple and the Church's Mission: A Biblical Theology of the Dwelling Place of God* [2004]). But several recent monographs have focused on how this theme unfolds in one Gospel, the Gospel of John—in particular, the work of Mary L. Coloe, *God Dwells with Us: Temple Symbolism in the Fourth Gospel* (2001) and the work of Alan R. Kerr, *The Temple of Jesus' Body: The Temple Theme in the Gospel of John* (2002). All of these are worth reading. What more does Paul Hoskins add?

In part, of course, this work overlaps earlier volumes. That is as it should be: even while allowing for legitimate diversity in interpretation, careful exegesis of the same texts should produce at least some things in common. And Paul Hoskins is careful: this study aims to let the texts speak, with readings that are usually understated and always clearly presented. But this volume offers something more. Hoskins is interested not only in the way John presents Jesus as the ultimate temple, and in what this might mean for Johannine theology, but also in the *nature* of the relationship between Jesus and the temple, as John presents it. In particularly, Hoskins picks up older discussions on the nature of typology, refines them in the light of more recent treatments, and probes what it might mean to describe the relationship between Jesus and the temple as typological.

Whether or not one concurs with all of the conclusions of Paul Hoskins—Does one ever entirely concur with a book of this length and depth?—it is hard to imagine how anyone could not come away without enjoying a clearer grasp of some fundamental interpretative issues that have often been overlooked. And those interested in canonical and biblical theology, not least for pastoral purposes, will appreciate this fine synthesis.

D. A. Carson
Trinity Evangelical Divinity School

Preface and Acknowledgements

This work is a revision of my doctoral dissertation, which I defended in 2002 at Trinity Evangelical Divinity School. I was privileged to devote over two years to the completion of this project and some significant time to revisions. My attention to this project has truly been a blessing for which I am grateful to God.

The opportunity to study at Trinity became meaningful due to the contributions of my teachers, fellow students, and Trinity's staff. I am thankful to all who fit in this group. I owe special thanks and deep gratitude to Dr. D. A. Carson who served as mentor for my dissertation. Dr. Carson's attention to detail, insight into the biblical text, and commitment to sound scholarly work inspired and aided my work in numerous ways. He also created room for me to work under his supervision, which means that I bear responsibility for all of the shortcomings of the project. In short, Dr. Carson's care and instruction in the dissertation phase made this phase of my education the most challenging and rewarding. I am also thankful to Dr. Robert Yarbrough who served as second reader for this project and was a valued advisor during my time at Trinity. His love for Christ and family has encouraged me to keep my sights on the important things in life. Finally, I wish to thank Dr. Willem VanGemeren, the Ph.D. program director, for his steady encouragement and helpful comments on my work. Among my fellow students, I am thankful for the continuing support and encouragement of Dr. Sigurd Grindheim. Sigurd is a true colleague whom I appreciate deeply.

My family and friends have also been instrumental in this work. I have benefited greatly from my wife's patient comments during countless hours of conversation. I learned to apply much of what I was studying due to Cheryl's input. Cheryl's actions demonstrated a commitment to this project that spoke louder than her words of support. She deserves considerable credit and recognition for its completion and for benefit that comes of it for the kingdom. My children, Hannah and Timothy, deserve recognition as well for their patience and encouragement, especially encouragement to say enough is enough. Something would be missing if I did not acknowledge my parents here. If you knew my parents, you would know how much of this work is built upon a platform that they worked on for years. My mother also came through for me in terms of spending hours on the typesetting and indexes. My dear friend, Paul Moldenhauer, walked with me through this project and listened to my growing pains.

I am thankful to Paternoster Press for accepting this manuscript as part of its Biblical Monographs Series. I am grateful for the help of Dr. Robin Parry and especially Dr. Anthony R. Cross, who helped me with issues involving typesetting.

Finally, I am thankful to my students who helped me to see where I needed to clarify my thinking. I also benefited from the editing help of Jason Maston, my teaching assistant.

It will help the reader to note that in the footnotes I have abbreviated many titles following *The SBL Handbook of Style* (1999). Rather than include a lengthy abbreviations list, I have not used abbreviations in the bibliography (or the index for ancient sources) in order to facilitate the location of the sources cited. The only abbreviation that is not clarified in this way is BAGD, which refers to the second edition of *A Greek-English Lexicon of the New Testament* by W. Bauer, W. Arndt, F. Gingrich, and W. Danker.

Paul Hoskins

CHAPTER 1

Introduction

Interpreters of the Fourth Gospel continue to seek fresh approaches to its interpretation, often seeking to demonstrate the explanatory power and usefulness of applying new methods. Alongside such efforts, interpreters continue to follow more traditional approaches and to ask traditional questions. One traditional line of questioning involves the examination of the connections between the Fourth Gospel and the Old Testament. Stephen Neill, among others, believes that the Old Testament background of the Fourth Gospel is more significant than is often appreciated:

> I am convinced that, the more carefully the Gospel is studied, the clearer it becomes that the Hellenistic elements belong to a secondary phase of interpretation, and that the deepest elements in the thought, the bony structure on which the whole Gospel is constructed, are derived from the Old Testament.[1]

John himself gives support to Neill's conviction in those passages where it is explicitly indicated that the Old Testament points to Christ (especially, 1:45, 5:39-47), justifying John's christological interpretation of the Old Testament.[2] The use of the Old Testament in the Fourth Gospel and the hermeneutical axioms by which John interpreted the Old Testament deserve ongoing study. If Neill is right, attention to these two areas will continue to produce fruitful insights for interpreters of the Fourth Gospel comparable in significance to insights gained through the application of new interpretive methods.

---

[1] Stephen Neill and Tom Wright, *The Interpretation of the New Testament 1861-1986*, 2nd ed. (New York: Oxford University Press, 1988), 346. Cf. D. A. Carson, 'John and the Johannine Epistles,' in *It Is Written: Scripture Citing Scripture: Essays in Honour of Barnabas Lindars*, eds. D. A. Carson and H. G. M. Williamson (Cambridge: Cambridge, 1988), 245. On the other hand, note the lack of enthusiasm for the OT background of the Fourth Gospel evident in D. Moody Smith's treatment of 'the history-of-religions problem' in Johannine studies (D. Moody Smith, 'Johannine Studies,' in *The New Testament and Its Modern Interpreters*, eds. Eldon J. Epp and George W. MacRae [Atlanta: Scholars Press, 1989], 276-9).
[2] Carson, 'John and the Johannine Epistles,' 252.

The following study will focus on one aspect of John's use of the Old Testament. Jesus is commonly portrayed in the Fourth Gospel as the fulfillment and replacement of those Old Testament institutions that preceded him. D. A. Carson summarizes the theological significance of this replacement when he says that Old Testament institutions 'find their true significance and real continuity in him who is the true vine, the true light, the true temple, the one of whom Moses wrote.'[3] As this quote attests, one of the Old Testament institutions fulfilled and replaced by Jesus in the Fourth Gospel is the Temple. John makes explicit the connection between Jesus and the Temple in John 2:19-22. At one time, interpreters commonly noted that John 2:19-22 suggests a typological relationship between Jesus and the Temple.[4] Recent interpreters often note that Jesus is portrayed as the replacement of the Temple, but only a few continue to suggest that a typological relationship between Jesus and the Temple lies behind Jesus' statement in 2:19.[5]

This study aims to fulfill two primary objectives: (1) to examine John's portrayal of Jesus as the fulfillment and replacement of the Temple and (2) to explore the possibility that the relationship between Jesus and the Temple may properly be described as typological. The results obtained from accomplishing these two objectives will be significant for the interpretation of the Fourth Gospel, the use of the Old Testament in the Fourth Gospel, and biblical theology.

In order to lay a suitable foundation for the work at hand, the following matters deserve some initial introductory discussion. The first area of concern

---

[3] Ibid., 256. It is important to maintain a tight connection between fulfillment and replacement in order to understand the type of replacement that is characteristic of the theology of the Fourth Gospel. As discussed later in this chapter and in chapter 5, such a connection is coherent with a traditional typological understanding of the relationship between OT institutions and their NT fulfillments.

[4] See the commentaries by Johann Bengel, E. W. Hengstenberg, John Lightfoot, and Heinrich Meyer at John 2:19-22; see also Patrick Fairbairn, *The Typology of Scripture*, vol. 2 (Grand Rapids: Zondervan, 1963), 217-8.

[5] In favor of a typological relationship are D. A. Carson, Richard Longenecker, Leon Morris, Samuel Amsler, E. Earle Ellis, Harald Sahlin, and Leonhard Goppelt (D.A. Carson, *The Gospel according to John* [Grand Rapids: Eerdmans, 1991], 182; Richard N. Longenecker, *Biblical Exegesis in the Apostolic Period* [Grand Rapids: Eerdmans, 1975], 153-4; Leon Morris, *The New Testament and the Jewish Lectionaries* [London: Tyndale Press, 1964], 71; Samuel Amsler, *L'Ancien Testament dans l'église: Essai d'herméneutique chrétienne* [Neuchâtel, Switzerland: Delachaux and Niestlé, 1960], 217-8; E. Earle Ellis, *Paul's Use of the Old Testament* [Grand Rapids: Eerdmans, 1957], 91; Harald Sahlin, *Zur Typologie des Johannesevangeliums*, UUÅ, no. 4 [Uppsala: A.-B. Lundequistska, 1950], 12-13; Leonhard Goppelt, *Typos: The Typological Interpretation of the Old Testament in the New*, trans. D. H. Madvig [Grand Rapids: Eerdmans, 1982], 191).

is how this study is related to recent emphases in Johannine studies. The second is to outline the methodological framework undergirding the study. The third is to review relevant scholarly literature on the fulfillment or replacement of the Temple in the Fourth Gospel and on typology. Finally, a chapter-by-chapter overview will lay out the plan for the work.

Background for the Current Study: Contemporary Trends in Johannine Studies

Probably the most noticeable trend in contemporary Johannine studies is the focus on literary-critical approaches.[6] R. Alan Culpepper is often given special recognition for demonstrating the promise of examining the Fourth Gospel as a literary work.[7] Culpepper's literary-critical study of the Fourth Gospel uses terminology and theory developed by academicians for use in analysis of fictional narratives.[8] Culpepper's initial work has been followed in rapid succession by numerous other works. While some have followed up on Culpepper's groundbreaking insights, others have worked more independently by adopting or adapting an impressive variety of literary theories, including reader-response and structuralism.[9] One of the positive aspects of literary-critical analyses of the Fourth Gospel has been a focus upon the text in its canonical form, diverting attention away from its sources and redaction. Although some have questioned the appropriateness and fruitfulness of literary studies, literary-critical terminology and theory continue to be prominent in recent works on the Fourth Gospel.[10]

Even so, literary-critical approaches to the Fourth Gospel do not monopolize

---

[6] Literary critical approach is here meant to describe a variety of approaches variously classified using descriptors like 'narrative criticism' or 'new literary criticism.'

[7] His groundbreaking work was *Anatomy of the Fourth Gospel: A Study in Literary Design* (Philadelphia: Fortress, 1983). Concerning the promise of Culpepper's approach, see Xavier Léon-Dufour, 'Bulletin d'exégèse du Nouveau Testament: L évangile de Jean,' *RSR* 73 (1985): 252-3.

[8] Even more narrowly, the literary theory that Culpepper draws upon was developed with respect to analysis of nineteenth-century fiction (Carson, *John*, 67; cf. Culpepper, *Anatomy of the Fourth Gospel*, 4-6, 9-11, 101-6).

[9] For a convenient summary of literary theory as it relates to biblical studies, see Anthony Thiselton, *New Horizons in Hermeneutics: The Theory and Practice of Transforming Biblical Reading* (Grand Rapids: Zondervan, 1992), 471-514.

[10] Concerning appropriateness, see Jürgen Becker, 'Das Johannesevangelium im Streit der Methoden (1980-1984),' *TRu* 51 (1986): 14-15, and Carson, *John*, 63-68; concerning fruitfulness, see John Ashton, *Studying John: Approaches to the Fourth Gospel* (Oxford: Clarendon, 1994), 156; concerning the limitations and concomitant presuppositions involved in the application of certain literary theories in biblical studies generally, see Thiselton, *New Horizons in Hermeneutics*, 471, 491, 493, 502.

the field. The methodological diversity that characterizes the current scene in Johannine studies brings with it a tendency toward exclusivity and conflict.[11] Perhaps the most unavoidable area of conflict is between those scholars who continue to pursue source-critical investigations and those who are demonstrating the usefulness of various literary-critical approaches to the study of the Fourth Gospel. The conflict stems in part from the fact that several interpreters who are studying the Fourth Gospel from a literary-critical vantage point make optimistic statements about the basic unity of the Fourth Gospel.[12] Ashton, for one, finds such statements to be at best superficial and at worst to be insulting to the proponents of source-critical hypotheses.[13] One can appreciate Ashton's complaints when one recognizes that source criticism depends upon evidence that supports the disunity of the Fourth Gospel. Source critics need to find evidence of editorial work (i.e., seams and aporias). On the other hand, literary-critical studies would benefit from establishing that the basic unity and coherence of the Fourth Gospel are evident in its canonical form.[14] This would buttress detailed studies of the Fourth Gospel's structure and plot. From this brief description, one can appreciate how the methodological diversity characteristic of contemporary Johannine studies does not always allow for peaceful coexistence of differing approaches.

In spite of points of tension, recent attempts toward more inclusive and integrative approaches to the Fourth Gospel seem to have picked up on Meir Sternberg's conviction that 'ideological, historiographic, and aesthetic' concerns all contribute to one's understanding of biblical narrative.[15] One example of a study that attempts to bring together ideological, historiographic, and aesthetic concerns is Margaret Davies's *Rhetoric and Reference in the*

---

[11] Cf. Thomas Brodie's short history of interpretive approaches to the Fourth Gospel and his observations about methodological 'totalitarianism' (*The Gospel according to John: A Literary and Theological Commentary* [New York: Oxford University, 1993], 3-10).

[12] Ashton, *Studying John*, 144-8.

[13] Ibid., 145.

[14] This requires a response to the source critics regarding the apparent seams in the narrative. One form of response involves establishing the stylistic unity of the Fourth Gospel (see E. Ruckstuhl and P. Dschulnigg, *Stilkritik und Verfasserfrage im Johannesevangelium: Die johanneischen Sprachmerkmale auf dem Hintergrund des Neuen Testaments und des zeitgenössischen hellenistischen Schrifttums*, NTOA, no. 17 [Göttingen: Vandenhoeck and Ruprecht, 1991]). Another form of response involves engagement with source-critical theorists through the study of individual passages, like Paul Anderson's study of John 6 (*The Christology of the Fourth Gospel: Its Unity and Disunity in the Light of John 6* [Valley Forge, Pa.: Trinity, 1996]).

[15] Meir Sternberg, *The Poetics of Biblical Narrative: Ideological Literature and the Drama of Reading* (Bloomington: Indiana University, 1985), 41-48. Cf. Thiselton's interpretation of Sternberg concerning this point (*New Horizons in Hermeneutics*, 484).

Fourth Gospel.[16] Davies's study is basically designed to move from aesthetic (i.e., literary) to theological to historical issues. Similarly, David Ball attempts to examine the 'I am' sayings of the Fourth Gospel, giving attention to their literary function, historical background, and theological implications.[17] A third example would be Paul Anderson's examination of John 6.[18] Anderson examines the theological and literary coherence of John 6 while giving attention to pertinent historical issues that might have influenced John's rhetoric.

The preceding discussion of contemporary trends in Johannine studies gives prominence to the emergence of literary approaches to the Fourth Gospel. While literary theory and practice appear to be almost ubiquitous in recent works on the Fourth Gospel, one should note that studies concerning the Fourth Gospel's theology, background, composition, and authorship continue to be produced. Such studies may either question specific conclusions resulting from literary studies or find contemporary literary approaches to be tangential to their concerns. They also continue to insist that it is appropriate to ask questions that many literary-critical interpreters consider to be of little significance.

Methodological Framework of the Study

Since methodological choices have become so significant in Johannine studies, one finds it necessary to discuss one's methodological choices and concomitant inclinations or presuppositions. The following study attempts to be integrative in its approach to the biblical text. It will integrate what Sternberg calls 'ideological, historiographic, and aesthetic' concerns.[19] The study's approach will differ from other contemporary integrative approaches in certain respects.[20] Its affinities to and divergences from other integrative approaches will be

---

[16] Davies mentions Sternberg's integrative approach on the first page of her introduction (*Rhetoric and Reference in the Fourth Gospel*, JSNTSup, no. 69 [Sheffield: JSOT, 1992], 12).

[17] David Mark Ball, *'I Am' in John's Gospel: Literary Function, Background and Theological Implications*, JSNTSup, no. 124 (Sheffield: JSOT, 1996).

[18] Anderson, *Christology of the Fourth Gospel*. See also the recent work by Stanley Porter where he attempts to demonstrate the benefits of integrating a traditional exegetical approach with recent literary-critical approaches to the Fourth Gospel ('Can Traditional Exegesis Enlighten Literary Analysis of the Fourth Gospel? An Examination of the Old Testament Fulfilment Motif and the Passover Theme,' in *The Gospels and the Scriptures of Israel*, eds. Craig A. Evans and W. Richard Stegner, JSNTSup, no. 104 [Sheffield: Sheffield Academic, 1994], 396-428).

[19] Sternberg, *Poetics of Biblical Narrative*, 41.

[20] See the previous section for mention of the integrative approaches of Margaret Davies, David Ball, and Paul Anderson.

discussed briefly in connection with aesthetic, historiographic, and ideological concerns.

The recent focus on the aesthetic, or literary, dimension directs attention to the structure, style, and themes of the Fourth Gospel. Of course, such literary concerns are not revolutionary, but they have sometimes been overshadowed due to a focus upon theological or historical points of interest.[21] Like recent literary studies, the following study will attempt to remain sensitive to the structure, style, and themes of the Fourth Gospel as a whole. The study will also draw attention to the interconnections that serve to strengthen the case for the basic unity of the Fourth Gospel. On the other hand, the complex methodologies characteristic of the changing landscape of literary-critical studies will not be in evidence, except in cases where a particular study is relevant to the discussion. An attempt has also been made to avoid unnecessary jargon that has entered Johannine studies along with literary-critical approaches.[22]

With regard to historiographic concerns, two deserve special mention. The first involves the source and composition criticism of the Fourth Gospel. Source and composition criticism of the Fourth Gospel is only tangentially related to the following study. Like contemporary literary studies, the study will focus upon the canonical form of the Fourth Gospel.[23] Unlike many contemporary literary studies, the rationale for such a focus is not based upon a desire to concentrate upon the interplay between the reader and the text.[24] Instead, it is based primarily upon three factors. First, the Fourth Gospel does not anywhere draw attention to its use of sources other than the Old Testament and personal testimony. Therefore one can probably assume that source criticism is not essential for understanding the Fourth Gospel. Second, source and composition theorists have not been able to agree on any rearrangement of the canonical form of the Fourth Gospel that would improve upon the current state of the text without creating further problems.[25] Third, the composition

---

[21] Brodie, in particular, stresses this point (*John*, 12).

[22] Some of which may be inappropriate or in need of redefinition when one is commenting on the Fourth Gospel or on the Bible generally (cf. Sternberg, *Poetics of Biblical Narrative*, 56-57).

[23] Cf. Maarten Menken's summary remarks regarding composition criticism of the Fourth Gospel and the move toward focusing 'primary attention' on the canonical form of the Gospel ('The Christology of the Fourth Gospel: A Survey of Recent Research,' in *From Jesus to John: Essays on Jesus and New Testament Christology in Honour of Marinus de Jonge*, ed. Martinus C. de Boer, JSNTSup, no. 84 [Sheffield: JSOT, 1993], 319).

[24] Cf. Culpepper, *Anatomy of the Fourth Gospel*, 3-5.

[25] Of course, this excludes text-critical problems, like John 7:53-8:11. On the creation of further problems, see D.A. Carson, 'Current Source Criticism of the Fourth Gospel: Some Methodological Questions,' *JBL* 97 (1978): 422-3.

critics have not produced any compelling evidence for the work of a later redactor or redactors.[26]

A second historiographic point is necessitated by the effects of the 'new hermeneutic' on historical studies and the new literary criticism on biblical studies. 'Historiography' as used to denote the writing of history is being re-examined by historians who are becoming aware that it may be unfair to judge ancient historiographic conventions by modern standards. Some are questioning whether modern values and assumptions about proper historiographic conventions have unfairly prompted the dismissal of the truth value of ancient historical accounts.[27] Sternberg is not alone in claiming that there 'are simply no universals of historical vs. fictive form.'[28] The difference between fiction and history involves questions of truth claim. 'History-writing' involves a 'discourse that claims to be a record of fact,' while 'fiction-writing' involves a 'discourse that claims freedom of invention.'[29] A similar focus upon truth claim may be noted in K. Lawson Younger's definition of history as 'a committedly true account which imposes form on the actions of men in the past.'[30]

---

[26] The problematic 'we' in John 21:24 does not necessarily point to the work of a later redactor (Carson, *John*, 683-5; cf. George R. Beasley-Murray, *John*, WBC, vol. 36 [Waco: Word Books, 1987], 413-5). Even if one allows that it does, composition theorists have not been able to develop convincing criteria for differentiating between the work of the later redactor(s) and that of the Gospel's author (Robert Kysar, *The Fourth Evangelist and His Gospel: An Examination of Contemporary Scholarship* [Minneapolis: Augsburg, 1975], 53-54).

[27] Nancy Partner, 'Historicity in an Age of Reality-Fictions,' in *A New Philosophy of History*, eds. Frank Ankersmit and Hans Kellner (Chicago: University of Chicago, 1995), 21-39.

[28] Sternberg, *Poetics of Biblical Narrative*, 30; cf. Partner, 'Historicity in an Age of Reality-Fictions,' 26-36; also, V. Philips Long, *The Art of Biblical History*, in *Foundations of Contemporary Interpretation*, ed. Moisés Silva (Grand Rapids: Zondervan, 1996), 321-2; K. Lawson Younger, Jr., *Ancient Conquest Accounts: A Study in Ancient Near Eastern and Biblical History Writing*, JSOTSup, no. 98 (Sheffield: JSOT, 1990), 30-31, 35.

[29] Sternberg, *Poetics of Biblical Narrative*, 25. See also Sternberg's criticism of Hans Frei's *The Eclipse of Biblical Narrative* based on its failure to deal adequately with 'history-likeness, history telling, and historicity' (*Poetics of Biblical Narrative*, 81-82).

[30] *Ancient Conquest Accounts*, 46. One should not be quick to invoke the intentional fallacy as an objection to such a definition of history as some biblical historians do (cf. Marc Z. Brettler, *The Creation of History in Ancient Israel* [New York: Routledge, 1995], 12). Sternberg, among others, defends interpreters of the Bible against those who would invoke the 'intentional fallacy,' since interpreters of the Bible find their clues to the author's intention in the text itself (and not from external sources) (Sternberg, *Poetics of Biblical Narrative*, 9, 69-70; cf. Tremper Longman III, *Literary Approaches to Biblical Interpretation*, in *Foundations of Contemporary Interpretation*, ed. Moisés Silva [Grand Rapids: Zondervan, 1996], 107-8).

According to such a definition, both the Old Testament historical narratives and the Fourth Gospel are historical works and not fictional ones.[31] This means that one cannot separate the literary artistry or theological concerns of the biblical authors from questions of historical reference. It also means that discussions of biblical narratives using categories and terminology that have been developed with reference to fictional works should be approached with caution. One must ask whether such categories and terminology are readily transferable to biblical, historical narratives.[32]

The preceding discussion of historiographic conventions leads naturally into a brief discussion of the term 'ideological.' Such a discussion is warranted since the term has already been used above and has become part of the vocabulary of interpreters of biblical, historical narratives.[33] 'Ideology' is often associated with a distorted view of reality.[34] Yet distortion is by no means inherent to every definition of the term. It can be defined in a neutral way that does not necessitate distortion.[35] Thus to use the term 'ideological' with reference to the biblical, historical narratives does not necessarily involve a pejorative judgment. In the following study, the term 'ideology' is avoided in most instances. Instead, the ideology of a biblical, historical narrative is assumed to be a subset of its theology.[36] In biblical studies, 'theological' is a more traditional adjective than 'ideological,' and less susceptible to misunderstanding.

The biblical theological endeavor depends upon careful reading and

---

[31] One finds textual evidence for the truth claims of the Fourth Gospel and the OT historical accounts. For the Fourth Gospel, see John 19:35, 20:30-31, 21:24. For the OT historical narratives, one could refer to specific verses, like Num 33:2, where Moses is commanded to write records pertaining to the Exodus, or 1 Chr 29:29-30, where the Chronicler acknowledges other accounts concerning the actions of King David. Or, like Sternberg, one may point to the distinctive way in which the Hebrews defined themselves 'in terms of their past' and kept their past alive (Sternberg, *Poetics of Biblical Narrative*, 31). The OT witness to a people whose present was so fundamentally anchored in its past convinces Sternberg that the OT historical sections are concerned with history and not fiction (cf. Deut 6:20-25, 8:1-20).

[32] Cf. Becker, 'Johannesevangelium im Streit der Methoden,' 14-16; also, Sternberg's discussion of 'implied author,' 'narrator,' and 'omniscience' (*Poetics of Biblical Narrative*, 74-77).

[33] Younger, *Ancient Conquest Accounts*, 47.

[34] Ibid., 47-51.

[35] Younger summarizes the 'neutral sense' of ideology like this: 'ideology embraces both normative and allegedly factual elements; and these elements are not *necessarily* distorted' (*Ancient Conquest Accounts*, 48).

[36] 'Theology' is here understood to encompass beliefs about social and supernatural states of affairs.

interpreting of biblical texts.[37] In doing so, the biblical theologian cannot ignore historical or literary issues. Margaret Davies's discussion of the theology of the Fourth Gospel provides a good model for the following study. Throughout her discussion, she draws attention to relevant historical and literary points, as well as to relevant Old Testament background. Davies is also careful to document the textual basis for her statements.[38]

A further methodological concern for the current study involves the danger of isolating its central theme, Jesus as the replacement of the Temple in the Fourth Gospel, from other, more prominent themes of the Fourth Gospel (and the Johannine corpus).[39] Isolating a minor theme from the major emphases of a book or corpus may give a distorted impression of its significance. Such isolation also misses an opportunity to benefit from the interconnectedness of the theological themes of a book or corpus. The major theological emphases of a book or corpus may provide further insight into the significance attached to a minor theme. Davies again provides a useful illustration. In her short discussion of the eschatology of the Fourth Gospel, she refers repeatedly to significant theological emphases in the Fourth Gospel that help to clarify its eschatology.[40]

The methodological framework for the study has been described above in general terms. One can expect specific methodological comments to occur in the review of literature section immediately following and at appropriate points throughout the study.

Review of Literature

The following study is directly concerned with investigating previous work on the portrayal of Jesus as the fulfillment or replacement of the Temple in the Fourth Gospel and building upon such work. The study will examine the possibility that a typological relationship proves useful for understanding how Jesus could be the fulfillment of the Temple. Given such an agenda, the following review of literature will necessarily include two sections. The first

---

[37] Two common pitfalls accompanying studies in OT and NT theology are insufficient care in interpreting biblical texts in their contexts and focusing attention upon certain passages while failing to integrate others. For the first pitfall, see the comments by Brodie regarding biblical theology (*John*, 12-13); on the second pitfall, see Grant R. Osborne, *The Hermeneutical Spiral: A Comprehensive Introduction to Biblical Interpretation* (Downers Grove, Ill.: InterVarsity, 1991), 274, 284.

[38] See especially, Davies, *Rhetoric and Reference*, 112-240.

[39] D.A. Carson warns that 'it is imperative that relatively light themes in a particular book or corpus be teased out first within the context of the major themes of that book or corpus' ('New Testament Theology,' in *Dictionary of the Later New Testament and Its Developments*, eds. Ralph P. Martin and Peter H. Davids [Downers Grove, Ill.: InterVarsity, 1997], 811).

[40] Davies, *Rhetoric and Reference*, 158-61.

will review previous work on Jesus as the fulfillment or replacement of the Temple in the Fourth Gospel. The second will discuss recent developments in the study of biblical typology, indicate the direction of the current study in relation to recent studies of biblical typology, and review recent works on the typology of the Fourth Gospel.

Jesus as the Fulfillment or Replacement of the Temple in the Fourth Gospel

Recent scholarship on Jesus as the replacement of the Temple in the Fourth Gospel makes frequent reference to several significant articles that contain some treatment of the subject.[41] Among these, François-Marie Braun provides the most thorough attempt to trace the development of this theme in the Fourth Gospel as a whole.[42] The articles of Xavier Léon-Dufour and André Marie Dubarle are often cited as important treatments of John 2:19-22.[43] C. F. D. Moule finds in John 2:19-22 crucial evidence for supersession of the Temple by Jesus and the church.[44] Oscar Cullmann and Marcel Simon point to Jesus'

---

[41] The theme under consideration is commonly identified in this section as the replacement of the Temple. This does not mean that the works associated with this theme never mention the fulfillment of the Temple as well. They also sometimes identify Jesus as the new or true Temple. Even in cases where fulfillment is mentioned, the nature of the relationship between Jesus and the Temple is given so little attention that one usually cannot tell whether replacement or fulfillment (or both) characterizes it more adequately for a given interpreter. As a result, replacement of the Temple is used here, because it seems to be the most common category invoked to characterize the relationship between Jesus and the Temple. Yet a few authors emphasize fulfillment over replacement and that is reflected below where possible (for instance, cf. Saeed Hamid-Khani, *Revelation and Concealment of Christ: A Theological Inquiry into the Elusive Language of the Fourth Gospel*, WUNT, 2nd series, no. 120 [Tübingen: Mohr Siebeck, 2000], 280-5).

[42] François-Marie Braun, 'In Spiritu et veritate,' *RevThom* 52 (1952): 245-74.

[43] Xavier Léon-Dufour, 'Le signe du temple selon saint Jean,' *RSR* 39 (1951-1952): 155-75; André Marie Dubarle, 'Le signe du temple (Jo. II, 19),' *RB* 48 (1939): 21-44. Both mention briefly how John 2:19-22 is related to the larger theme of the replacement of the Temple in the Fourth Gospel (Léon-Dufour, 'Le signe du temple selon saint Jean,' 171; Dubarle, 'Le signe du temple (Jo. II, 19),' 37). For two more recent and detailed treatments of these verses, see Johanna Rahner, *'Er aber sprach vom Tempel seines Leibes': Jesus von Nazaret als Ort der Offenbarung Gottes im vierten Evangelium*, BBB, no. 117 (Bodenheim: Philo, 1998) and Lucius Nereparampil, *Destroy This Temple: An Exegetic-Theological Study on the Meaning of Jesus' Temple-Logion in Jn 2:19* (Bangalore: Dharmaram Publications, 1978).

[44] C.F.D. Moule, 'Sanctuary and Sacrifice in the Church of the New Testament,' *JTS*, NS (1950): 29-41. Similarly, Hans Wenschkewitz places emphasis upon John 2:19-22 as evidence for the replacement of the Temple according to the teaching of Jesus (*Die*

fulfillment of the Temple in the Fourth Gospel as significant for one's understanding of early Christian thought regarding the Temple.[45]

In addition to articles, several special studies have also drawn attention to Jesus' replacement of the Temple in the Fourth Gospel.[46] Yves Congar and John Townsend, with minor variations, suggest several passages in the Fourth Gospel where the theme of Jesus as the new Temple appears. Their treatments of the theme do not differ significantly from the treatment of Braun cited above.[47] Craig Koester acknowledges the theme of Jesus' replacement of the

Spiritualisierung der Kultusbegriffe: Tempel, Priester und Opfer im Neuen Testament, Angelos, Beiheft 4 [Leipzig: Eduard Pfeiffer, 1932], 97-101).

[45] Oscar Cullmann, 'L'opposition contre le temple de Jérusalem, motif commun de la théologie johannique et du monde ambiant,' *NTS* 5 (1958-1959): 157-73; Marcel Simon, 'Retour du Christ et reconstruction du Temple dans la pensée chrétienne primitive,' in *Aux sources de la tradition chrétienne: Mélanges offerts à M. Maurice Goguel à l'occasion de son soixante-dixième anniversaire*, ed. J.-J. von Allmen (Paris: Delachaux and Niestlé, 1950), 247-57. Note that Cullmann uses the language of replacement, while Simon adamantly rejects it ('Retour du Christ et reconstruction du Temple,' 257).

[46] Yves M.-J. Congar, *The Mystery of the Temple or the Manner of God's Presence to His Creatures from Genesis to the Apocalypse*, trans. Reginald Trevett (Westminster, Md.: Newman Press, 1962), 120-50; William G. Fowler, 'The Influence of Ezekiel in the Fourth Gospel: Intertextuality and Interpretation' (Ph.D. diss., Golden Gate Baptist Theological Seminary, 1995), 116-44; Aileen Guilding, *The Fourth Gospel and Jewish Worship: A Study of the Relation of St. John's Gospel to the Ancient Jewish Lectionary System* (Oxford: Clarendon, 1960), 171-211; Craig R. Koester, *The Dwelling of God: The Tabernacle in the Old Testament, Intertestamental Jewish Literature and the New Testament*, CBQMS, no. 22 (Washington, D.C.: Catholic Biblical Association of America, 1989), 100-15; John T. Townsend, 'The Jerusalem Temple in New Testament Thought' (Th.D. diss., Harvard University, 1958), 167-217.

[47] For comparable, brief treatments, see Ulrich Busse, 'Die Tempelmetaphorik als ein Beispiel von implizitem Rekurs auf die biblische Tradition im Johannesevangelium,' in *The Scripture in the Gospels*, ed. C.M. Tuckett, BETL, no. 131 (Leuven: University Press, 1997), 395-428; Edmund P. Clowney, 'The Final Temple,' in *Studying the New Testament Today*, ed. John H. Skilton (Nutley, N.J.: Presbyterian and Reformed, 1974), 116-20; Lloyd Gaston, *No Stone on Another: Studies in the Significance of the Fall of Jerusalem in the Synoptic Gospels*, NovTSup, vol. 23 (Leiden: E. J. Brill, 1970), 205-13; Anthony T. Hanson, 'The Theme of Christ as the True Temple in the Fourth Gospel,' in *The New Testament Interpretation of Scripture* (London: SPCK, 1980), 110-121; Lars Hartman, '"He Spoke of the Temple of His Body" (Jn 2:13-22),' *SEÅ* 54 [1989]: 70-79; Lynn A. Losie, 'The Cleansing of the Temple: A History of a Gospel Tradition in Light of Its Background in the Old Testament and in Early Judaism' (Ph.D. diss., Fuller Theological Seminary, 1984), 316-22; R. J. McKelvey, *The New Temple* (Oxford: Oxford University Press, 1969), 75-84; Franz Mussner, 'Jesus und "das Haus des Vaters"–Jesus als "Tempel,"' in *Freude am Gottesdienst: Aspekte ursprünglicher Liturgie*, ed. Josef Schreiner (Stuttgart: Verlag Katholisches Bibelwerk, 1983), 270-3; Andrea Spatafora, *From the 'Temple of God' to God as the Temple: A Biblical*

Temple, but his primary interest is in the possible allusion to the Tabernacle in John 1:14. Therefore he stresses the importance of Jesus' replacement of the Tabernacle, giving it preference over Jesus' replacement of the Jerusalem Temple (2:19-22) or the Samaritan holy places (4:1-24). William Fowler makes a case for the influence of Ezekiel (especially, Ezekiel 40-47) upon John's conception of Jesus as the new Temple. Aileen Guilding's work rests upon the questionable presupposition that Jewish lectionary readings shed light upon John's concern for the new Temple theme in the early part of the Gospel.[48]

In addition, the following paragraphs highlight some significant recent contributions to the study of Jesus' replacement of the Temple in the Fourth Gospel. First, W.D. Davies's treatment of Jesus' replacement of the Temple connects Jesus' replacement of the Temple to Jesus' replacement of other holy places in the Fourth Gospel.[49] Jesus' replacement of holy places leads him to the conclusion that the 'Gospel is destined to personalize or Christify that space, or, rather, holiness is no longer to be attached to space at all.'[50] Davies also suggests that perhaps details in the Fourth Gospel related to time and geography should be given closer attention than has previously been the case.[51]

James McCaffrey attempts to expand the theme of Jesus as the replacement of the Temple. He argues that John 14:2-3 should be interpreted against the background of this Temple theme. As a result, John 14:2-3 basically teaches that Jesus is the "New Temple" (the τόπος or "place") in which the disciples begin to reside spiritually after Jesus' death and resurrection. Residing in this New Temple means that they already occupy "dwelling places" (μοναί) in the "Father's house" (the heavenly Temple), because that is where Jesus is. Then, they more fully take up residence in the heavenly Temple (the Father's house) at the time of Jesus' second coming or Parousia.[52]

Theological Study of the Temple in the Book of Revelation, TESI Gregoriana Serie Teologia, no. 27 (Rome: Editrice Pontificia Università Gregoriana, 1997), 101-16; Wilhelm Thüsing, *Die Erhöhung und Verherrlichung Jesu im Johannesevangelium*, NTAbh, vol. 21 (Westfalen: Aschendorffsche, 1960), 279-83; Camillus Umoh, 'The Temple in the Fourth Gospel,' in *Israel und seine Heilstradition im Johannesevangelium*, eds. Michael Labahn et al. (Paderborn: Ferdinand Schöningh, 2004), 314-33; and Peter W. L. Walker, *Jesus and the Holy City: New Testament Perspectives on Jerusalem* (Grand Rapids: Eerdmans, 1996), 161-74.

[48] Cf. Guilding, *Jewish Worship*, 172. Guilding's Jewish lectionary system almost certainly reflects later developments in Jewish worship (Morris, *New Testament and the Jewish Lectionaries*, 34).

[49] W.D. Davies, *The Gospel and the Land: Early Christianity and Jewish Territorial Doctrine* (Sheffield: JSOT, 1994), 289-318.

[50] Ibid., 290.

[51] Ibid., 288-9, 316-8.

[52] James McCaffrey, *The House with Many Rooms: The Temple Imagery of Jn. 14,2-3*, AnBib, no. 114 (Rome: Editrice Pontificio Instituto Biblico, 1988), 21, 247, 254-5.

McCaffrey's work has been given favorable attention by two recent works on the new Temple theme in the Fourth Gospel.[53] However, two points in McCaffrey's interpretation of John 14:2-3 are problematic. First, as McCaffrey notes, 'οἰκία is never found in the Jewish tradition to designate the temple, earthly or heavenly.'[54] Yet McCaffrey's interpretation of John 14:2-3 understands 'my Father's house' (οἰκία) as a reference to the heavenly Temple.[55] Second, most commentators interpret John 14:3 as predicting a future coming and receiving of believers with the result that they are with Jesus in the place where he is (his Father's house).[56] McCaffrey differs from them in that he insists that the coming of Jesus and his receiving of believers begin immediately after Christ's death and resurrection instead of happening only at the time of the Parousia.[57] Thus John 14:2-3 describes a spiritual union between Jesus and believers. McCaffrey's case for such an understanding of 14:2-3 is not as convincing as it seems at first.

McCaffrey finds fault with the traditional interpretation primarily based

---

[53] Walker, *Jesus and the Holy City*, 171-2; Mark Kinzer, 'Temple Christology in the Gospel of John,' *SBLSP* (1998): 447-64.

[54] McCaffrey, *House with Many Rooms*, 63. Instead, one consistently finds οἶκος (Ibid.).

[55] For McCaffrey's best defense of this interpretive step, see *House with Many Rooms*, 132-3, 177-9.

[56] See, for instance, F. F. Bruce, *The Gospel of John: Introduction, Exposition and Notes* (Grand Rapids: Eerdmans, 1983), 297-8; Carson, *John*, 488-9; Meyer, *John*, 407-9.

[57] McCaffrey, *House with Many Rooms*, 40, 192-6, 204-5, 252. It is not clear exactly what McCaffrey believes will happen at the Parousia. His interpretation of 14:2-3 makes it almost entirely applicable to the current situation of the church; he does say however that the disciples will move into a closer union with Jesus at the Parousia (*House with Many Rooms*, 205, 254). One should recall that McCaffrey's view requires one to equate Jesus' body with the New Temple where believers currently dwell in the Father's house. One problem with this view is that it ignores the distinction between two facets of the presence of Jesus with believers. One facet is Jesus' presence in the believer, presumably through the Spirit (John 14:20, 23; 15:4-6; 17:21, 26). The second facet is Jesus' identifiable, visible presence with the believer (12:26, 14:2-3, 17:24; also cf. 1:14; 14:17; 16:16, 22 [references to Jesus' presence with the first disciples]) (cf. Beasley-Murray, *John*, 250-1; Bultmann, *John*, 519, 602). The difference between these two facets is especially evident in John 17:21-24. Although Jesus already dwells in the believer (17:21, 26), he also prays for them to be with him in the place where they can actually see his glory (cf. esp. Beasley-Murray, *John*, 251). Hence one is able to see that the first facet is not dependent upon being together in the same physical location, whereas the second appears to require it. McCaffrey disagrees; he asserts that believers are already present where Jesus is (12:26, 14:2-3, 17:24) in the sense that he is spiritually in them and they are in him (*House with Many Rooms*, 247, 251). See the following note for the difficulties inherent in McCaffrey's interpretation of ὅπου εἰμὶ ἐγώ in 12:26, 14:3, 17:24.

upon his reading of the significance of παραλήμψομαι ὑμᾶς πρὸς ἐμαυτόν ('receive you to myself') and ὅπου εἰμὶ ἐγώ ('where I am'). In both instances, McCaffrey's reading is linguistically questionable. In the case of παραλήμψομαι ὑμᾶς πρὸς ἐμαυτόν, McCaffrey finds it problematic, because παραλαμβάνω 'literally' means 'to take along with.' Yet McCaffrey does not provide a clear and convincing case that παραλαμβάνω probably means 'to take along with' in 14:3.[58] As a result, this appears to be an instance of the root fallacy where the meaning of a word is 'determined by etymology' rather than from interpreting its meaning in context.[59] In the case of ὅπου εἰμὶ ἐγώ, McCaffrey's reading of 14:2-3 places a good bit of emphasis upon a rigid understanding of εἰμί as a present tense.[60] Thus McCaffrey regards ὅπου εἰμὶ ἐγώ as indicating that Jesus is 'perpetually and continually in the Father's house' even at the moment when he is speaking the words of 14:2-3 to his disciples.[61] Yet such an understanding is surely questionable here. One finds εἰμί after two verbs that McCaffrey has classified as futuristic presents (πορεύομαι and ἔρχομαι) and one verb that is future (παραλήμψομαι). If he is able to find two futuristic presents in this passage, why not a third (εἰμί)? If one is identifying futuristic presents here, then there must be indicators in the passage that one is talking about actions or states that lie in the future.[62] If so, then it is quite possible and likely that the verbs

---

[58] McCaffrey, *House with Many Rooms*, 22, 41-44. Cf. BAGD, 619, where this verb is translated simply as 'take' with reference to John 14:3.

[59] D.A. Carson, *Exegetical Fallacies*, 2nd ed. (Grand Rapids: Baker, 1996), 28. In other words, McCaffrey gets 'take' from λαμβάνω and 'along with' from παρά; then he puts these together to get the true meaning of the word. Etymology does not determine meaning nor is it the best guide to what a word means (Ibid., 28-33).

[60] He says, 'The verb εἰμί must be given its full value as a present' (*House with Many Rooms*, 44).

[61] Ibid., 45.

[62] Cf. F. Blass, A. Debrunner, and R. Funk, *A Greek Grammar of the New Testament and Other Early Christian Literature* (Chicago: University of Chicago Press, 1961), 168, section 323; A. T. Robertson, *A Grammar of the Greek New Testament in the Light of Historical Research* (Nashville: Broadman, 1934), 869-70. Contrary to McCaffrey, a futuristic present (with verbs of motion like πορεύομαι and ἔρχομαι) does not necessarily mean that the verb denotes an action 'already in the process of being realised, and at the same time still in the future' (*House with Many Rooms*, 40). Present tense verbs of motion can be used for such an action (Blass et al., *Greek Grammar*, 168), but the temporal indicators lie in the context and not in the fact that one has identified a futuristic present (cf. esp. Stanley E. Porter, *Idioms of the Greek New Testament*, 2nd ed. [Sheffield: Sheffield Academic Press, 1996], 28-29). Hence, given the context, it is also likely that Jesus is not regarding himself as already present in the Father's house at the moment when he says the words ὅπου εἰμὶ ἐγώ (14:3), and that these words therefore do not create any tension or contradiction in the passage (contra McCaffrey, *House with Many Rooms*, 22, 44-45).

πορεύομαι, ἔρχομαι, and εἰμί have to do with actions or states that begin and occur in the future rather than in the present. Given the above weaknesses, it seems more plausible to read 14:2-3 in line with the common interpretation, namely, it anticipates a time when believers will dwell with Jesus in his Father's house.[63]

If McCaffrey's attempt to read John 14:2-3 against the background of the theme of Jesus' replacement of the Temple deserves further scrutiny, so does Gunnar H. Østenstad's analysis of the structure of the Fourth Gospel.[64] Østenstad argues that the main theme of the Fourth Gospel is 'Jesus as the New Temple.' This theme 'binds the whole Gospel together in a unified composition.'[65] Østenstad's evidence for Jesus' replacement of the Temple is essentially the same as that appealed to by other interpreters. As a result, he will have difficulty convincing his readers that Jesus as the new Temple is the main theme in the Fourth Gospel, since an 'explicit presentation' of the theme is absent from the second half of the Gospel.[66]

In another recent monograph, Johannes Frühwald-König examines the complex of beliefs associated with the Temple, Jewish worship, and the critique of the Temple as it relates to four passages in the Fourth Gospel (John 2:13-22, 4:1-26, 5:1-18, 7:1-52).[67] He suggests that Jesus' cleansing of the Temple restores the Temple as a place of God's presence until Jesus' death.[68] Since rejection of Jesus is closely tied to the rejection of the Temple, it is only after Jesus' death and resurrection that he fully replaces the Temple.[69]

---

[63] According to this interpretation, 'Father's house' is a reference to the place where believers will dwell with Jesus. It therefore appears to be synonymous with the New Jerusalem in which Jesus (and the Father) dwells with believers (Rev 21:3, 22-23; 22:3-4).

[64] Gunnar H. Østenstad, *Patterns of Redemption in the Fourth Gospel: An Experiment in Structural Analysis*, Studies in the Bible and Early Christianity, vol. 38 (Lewiston, N.Y.: Edwin Mellen, 1998).

[65] Ibid., xxi.

[66] Ibid., 263. He does attempt to account for this difficulty (Ibid., 263-4).

[67] Johannes Frühwald-König, *Tempel und Kult: Ein Beitrag zur Christologie des Johannesevangeliums*, Biblische Untersuchungen, vol. 27 (Regensburg: Friedrich Pustet, 1998).

[68] Ibid., 93-96, 221-2.

[69] Ibid., 95, 126, 222. While it is true that Jesus fully replaces the Temple only after his death/resurrection/exaltation (i.e., the events of his hour; see chapters 3 and 4 below), Frühwald-König's case for this rests too heavily upon an alleged deeper meaning for ναός in 2:19 (see the interpretation of this verse in chapter 3 below). The Temple referred to here is simply the Jerusalem Temple's replacement and not the true ναός within the Jerusalem Temple (the ἱερόν of vv. 14-17). Thus it is not quite accurate to say, as Frühwald-König does, that Jews destroy the Jerusalem Temple when they crucify Jesus, because he has actually identified himself as the true ναός within the ἱερόν (Ibid., 95-96, 222). Instead, it would be more correct to say that these Jews are unwittingly

The two most substantial treatments of the fulfillment and replacement of the Temple to date came to my attention just after I completed this study. These are the works of Mary Coloe and Alan Kerr.[70] Their work is similar to this study in that they focus attention on many of the same passages and themes.[71] As seen in her title, Coloe especially emphasizes the role of the Temple as the dwelling place of God. The primacy she gives to this helps to focus her study. Kerr does not have such an integrating center. He finds a number of Temple allusions in John and does not point the reader to a clear thread of continuity that runs between them. I differ from them in that I discover the integrating center for John's Temple allusions to be the death/resurrection/exaltation of Jesus (chapter four). The other four noteworthy areas in which this study differs from Coloe and Kerr are similar enough for both works to merit discussing them together.

The second key difference is that Coloe and Kerr deal with the relationship between Jesus and the Temple differently than I do. In the beginning of her work, Coloe describes the Temple as a symbol that becomes associated with Jesus by means of a metaphor, namely, 'Jesus is the Temple.' However, she says in her conclusion, 'I have argued that the narrative of the Fourth Gospel is skillfully structured to highlight that the human flesh of Jesus fulfils and replaces Israel's Temple traditions.'[72] Coloe does not help the reader to synthesize these two descriptions of the relationship between Jesus and the

---

destroying (and helping to build) the Jerusalem Temple's replacement when they lift up Jesus on the cross. The use of both ἱερόν and ναός in John 2:13-22 is probably an instance of John's use of basically synonymous terms rather than an instance where John loads special, distinctive significance into both terms (cf. Carson, *John*, 181). Further, according to Frühwald-König's logic, Jesus only replaces the ναός and not the entire ἱερόν. John 2:20 appears to undercut this logic, because it uses ναός to refer to the Temple generally (including its courts). Surely, if Frühwald-König's understanding of ναός were correct, one would have found ἱερόν in 2:20 or a shorter number of years for the building of the ναός (since the sanctuary proper was completed first and in a short period of time) (Josephus *Ant.* 15.420-1).

[70] Mary Coloe, *God Dwells with Us: Temple Symbolism in the Fourth Gospel* (Collegeville, Minn.: Liturgical Press, 2001); Alan Kerr, *The Temple of Jesus' Body: The Temple Theme in the Gospel of John*, JSNTSup, no. 220 (Sheffield: Sheffield Academic Press, 2002). One continues to find some recent works that do not yet take these two studies into account (like Bill Salier, "The Temple in the Gospel according to John," in *Heaven on Earth*, ed. T. D. Alexander and S. Gathercole [Carlisle: Paternoster, 2004], 122-33).

[71] Coloe's table of contents lists John 1:1-18, 2:13-25, 4:1-45, 7:1-8:59 (Feast of Tabernacles), 10:22-42 (Feast of Dedication), 14:1-31, and 18:1-19:42 (Passover). Kerr lists 2:13-22, the prologue (1:1-18), 1:51, 4:16-24, the Temple Festivals, John 13 and 14, and John 17.

[72] Coloe, *God Dwells with Us*, 219. Similarly, she says that Jesus 'brings to completion the rituals and symbols of Israel's cult' (205).

Temple. The language of fulfillment and replacement does not seem to be thoroughly consistent with the Temple as symbol and metaphor.[73] Kerr finds Jesus to be the fulfillment and replacement of the Temple, but he does not provide any theological justification or analogy for Jesus, a person, to fulfill and replace an Old Testament institution, the Temple. In both works, no mention is made of typology or a typological relationship between Jesus and the Temple.

Thirdly, Coloe and Kerr do not focus as much attention on reviewing the Old Testament patterns associated with the Temple.[74] This is a general point of divergence between our works. It is especially evident in that Coloe only mentions in passing the connection between the lifting up of Jesus and Isaiah.[75] Kerr does not point out this connection. Relatedly, Coloe and Kerr do not clearly connect glory and glorification in John with the fulfillment of the Temple. I examine the significance of the lifting up and glorification of Jesus in relation to his fulfillment of the Temple starting in chapter four.

Fourthly, Coloe does not clearly tie the fulfillment of all three of the Jewish feasts to the death of Jesus, while Kerr ties all three feasts to the death of Jesus, but does not draw much attention to this significant connection. Coloe and Kerr indicate a strong connection between the Passover and the death of Jesus in the Fourth Gospel.[76] Coloe and Kerr also provide evidence in support of its connection with the Feast of Tabernacles.[77] Coloe provides a few hints pointing to its connection with the Feast of Dedication, whereas Kerr finds a connection.[78] I draw attention to the link between the feasts and the death of Jesus in chapter four.

Finally, Coloe and Kerr differ from me on their understanding of John 1:51 and John 14:2-3. Coloe just mentions the significance of 1:51 for Jesus' replacement of the Temple, while Kerr does not see 1:51 as relevant to the theme.[79] I interpret 1:51 as relevant in chapter three. Both of them are convinced that John 14:2-3 has something to do with Jesus or the Spirit

---

[73] The first has to do with a theological (or prophetic) conception of the relationship and the second with a literary conception. Is it proper to say that a member in a metaphorical relationship fulfills and replaces the other member as Coloe implies?

[74] Coloe focuses most of her third chapter on the theme of the Temple as God's dwelling place in the OT and Jewish literature (*God Dwells with Us*, 31-63). Kerr spends chapter two on Jewish responses to the destruction of the Temple in A.D. 70. He sees John as part of the Christian response to this event. Both contain references to the OT where they are relevant to their discussion.

[75] Coloe, *God Dwells with Us*, 177.

[76] Ibid., 190-211; Kerr, *Temple of Jesus' Body*, 207-226.

[77] Coloe, *God Dwells with Us*, 208-9; Kerr, *Temple of Jesus' Body*, 243-5.

[78] Coloe, *God Dwells with Us*, 202-3; Kerr, *Temple of Jesus' Body*, 254-5.

[79] On John 1:51, Coloe, *God Dwells with Us*, 73, 215; Kerr, *Temple of Jesus' Body*, 136-66.

dwelling in the church now rather than simply being a reference to believers dwelling with Jesus in heaven or the New Jerusalem. As seen in the response to McCaffrey above, such a connection is tenuous, especially because it does not deal adequately with 'where I am' (14:3, 17:24).[80]

In conclusion, both of these works are helpful treatments of Jesus' replacement of the Temple. They agree with and support significant aspects of this study. They have contributed helpful insights that have been useful in revising this study for publication.

In addition to the works mentioned above, Jesus' replacement of the Temple has, of course, been treated in commentaries.[81] Raymond Brown and Carson, in particular, pay close attention to this theme and its possible connection to other themes in John.[82] Brown notes that 'emphasis on the resurrected Jesus as the Temple is clearest in the Johannine works' (see Rev 21:22).[83] A number of other commentators mention the Fourth Gospel's presentation of Jesus as the replacement of the Temple or as the new (or true) Temple with little or no discussion of the nature, christological significance, or implications of the replacement.

Typology

Studies in biblical typology have been complicated by the use of the terms 'typology' and 'type' where no definitions of these terms are given. Ambiguity arises from the fact that 'typology' is currently being used as if only one understanding of typology is clearly associated with the term. Instead, two primary conceptions of typology continue to operate within biblical

---

[80] Coloe, *God Dwells with Us*, 157-78; Kerr, *Temple of Jesus' Body*, 308-13. Understanding 'dwellings' (μοναί) in terms of relationship with God does not appear to be a convincing equation in light of the emphasis upon location rather than upon indwelling and relationship in 14:2-3 (contra Coloe, *God Dwells with Us*, 163; Kerr, *Temple of Jesus' Body*, 301; Robert H. Gundry, '"In my Father's House are many Μοναί" (John 14:2),' *ZNW* 58 [1967]: 68-72).

[81] For treatments in commentaries, see, for example, Edwyn C. Hoskyns, *The Fourth Gospel*, ed. Francis N. Davey (London: Faber and Faber, 1947), 147-9, 196-7, 385, 392; Rudolf Schnackenburg, *The Gospel according to John*, trans. Kevin Smyth, vol. 1 (New York: Herder and Herder, 1968), 269-70, 321, 349-52, 438; Rudolf Schnackenburg, *The Gospel according to St. John*, trans. Cecily Hastings et al., vol. 2 (Tunbridge Wells, Great Britain: Burns and Oates, 1979), 154-6; Theodor Zahn, *Das Evangelium des Johannes* (Wuppertal: Brockhaus, 1983), 81-82, 175.

[82] Raymond E. Brown, *The Gospel according to John*, AB, vol. 29 (New York: Doubleday, 1966), 33-34, 90-91, 104, 120-5, 180-1, 323, 411, 754, 781, 949; Carson, *John*, 127-8, 164, 182, 399, 504, 513, 537-8, 570-1, 626, 628.

[83] Brown, *John*, 124-5.

scholarship.[84] In order to relate the current study to previous works on typology, particularly the typology of the Fourth Gospel, it will be necessary first to describe and examine the claims of the two primary conceptions of typology in biblical scholarship. Then, recent studies on the typology of the Fourth Gospel will be discussed, making reference to the understanding of typology underlying these studies.

Common points of agreement between the two primary conceptions will be noted before discussing their divergent views. Both conceptions of typology could fit within the following definition: 'Typology may be defined as the study which traces parallels or correspondences between incidents recorded in the Old Testament and their counterparts in the New Testament such that the latter can be seen to resemble the former in notable respects and yet to go beyond them.'[85] Two corollaries strengthen such a definition without making it objectionable to either conception of typology. First, the 'correspondences' involved in typology are drawn between 'persons, events, and institutions, within the framework of salvation history.'[86] Second, it is often noted that typological correspondences can already be seen in the Old Testament, especially in works of prophecy like Isaiah and Ezekiel.[87]

The above definition of typology and its corollaries clarify that typology essentially involves a significant correspondence between certain persons, events, or institutions in salvation history.[88] Most proponents of typology agree

---

[84] David L. Baker, *Two Testaments, One Bible: A Study of the Theological Relationship Between the Old & New Testaments* (Downers Grove, Ill.: InterVarsity Press, 1991), 180-1.

[85] I. Howard Marshall, 'An Assessment of Recent Developments,' in *It Is Written: Scripture Citing Scripture: Essays in Honour of Barnabas Lindars*, eds. D. A. Carson and H. G. M. Williamson (Cambridge: Cambridge, 1988), 16.

[86] Elizabeth Achtemeier, 'Typology,' in *IDBSup* (Nashville: Abingdon, 1976), 926.

[87] Walther Eichrodt, 'Is Typological Exegesis an Appropriate Method?,' trans. James Barr, in *Essays on Old Testament Hermeneutics*, ed. Claus Westermann (Richmond, Va.: John Knox, 1963), 234-5. Cf. Samuel Amsler, 'Prophétie et typologie,' *RTP* 3 (1953): 139-48; Francis Foulkes, *The Acts of God: A Study of the Basis of Typology in the Old Testament* (London: Tyndale, 1958), 23-33.

[88] Typology has often been caricatured as fanciful, because it has been practiced in a haphazard fashion. In many such instances, the interpreter's practice of typology can be faulted for failing to establish a significant correspondence between the type and antitype. A favorite example of this is the correspondence drawn by some early church fathers between the scarlet thread hung by Rahab on her house and salvation through the blood of Christ (cf. *1 Clem.* 12.7; R. T. France, *Jesus and the Old Testament: His Application of Old Testament Passages to Himself and His Mission* [London: Tyndale, 1971], 41). In post-Reformation times, use of typology without adequate attention to hermeneutical controls is often associated with Johannes Cocceius (1603-1669) (Richard Davidson, *Typology in Scripture: A Study of Hermeneutical ΤΥΠΟΣ Structures*,

that the movement from the type to the antitype normally involves a movement from a lesser entity to a greater one, that is, there is a qualitative progression or escalation from type to antitype.[89]

The mention of salvation history in connection with typology deserves special qualification.[90] Typology is often connected by interpreters with the movement of salvation history along a trajectory involving promise and fulfillment.[91] Such a movement is already evident in the Old Testament itself. In the Old Testament, God's dealings with his people were associated with certain promises. In the writings of the Old Testament prophets, God's previous dealings with his people became patterns for his future dealings with his people. Thus Old Testament prophets 'looked for a new David, a new Exodus, a new covenant, a new city of God.'[92] In doing so, they were anticipating the ultimate fulfillment of God's promises.[93] Thus the future realities anticipated by the prophets would not merely serve to repeat the past, but would be greater than the patterns or types that preceded them.[94] It is therefore not surprising that the New Testament authors, who saw in Christ and the Christ-event the fulfillment of the Old Testament prophetic hopes, made use of types or patterns found in the Old Testament in their teaching about Christ, the Christ-event, and its results.[95] Like the Old Testament prophets, the New Testament authors saw in God's previous dealings with his people patterns or types that corresponded

---

Andrews University Seminary Doctoral Dissertation Series, vol. 2 [Berrien Springs, Mich.: Andrews University, 1981], 33-36).

[89] One possible exception involves the vertical typology of Hebrews 8-9 (see the clarifying discussion of Davidson [*Typology*, 363-6]). Baker objects to such a notion of 'heightening' between type and antitype (*Two Testaments*, 192).

[90] Salvation history has become a part of several definitions of typology, especially those that intend to include some notion of OT typology in the discussion (Achtemeier, 'Typology,' 926; Grant Osborne, 'Type; Typology,' in *ISBE*, ed. G. Bromiley, vol. 4 [Grand Rapids: Eerdmans, 1988], 930; Davidson, *Typology*, 421).

[91] Goppelt, *Typos*, 16-18; Amsler, *L'Ancien Testament dans l'église*, 216; Gerhard von Rad, *Old Testament Theology*, vol. 2, *The Theology of Israel's Prophetic Traditions*, trans. D. M. G. Stalker (New York: Harper and Row, 1965), 365, 371-3; Foulkes, *Acts of God*, 23; Douglas J. Moo, 'The Problem of *Sensus Plenior*,' in *Hermeneutics, Authority, and Canon*, eds. D. A. Carson and John D. Woodbridge (Grand Rapids: Zondervan, 1986), 196; Achtemeier, 'Typology,' 927; Oscar Cullmann, *Salvation in History*, trans. Sidney G. Sowers, NTL (London: SCM, 1967), 249.

[92] Von Rad, *Old Testament Theology*, vol. 2, 322-3. Cf. Foulkes, *Acts of God*, 23-33 and the remarks about von Rad's understanding of salvation history below.

[93] Ibid., 371-4; Achtemeier, 'Typology,' 927.

[94] Eichrodt, *Typological Exegesis*, 234; Amsler, 'Prophétie et typologie,' 142-7.

[95] Von Rad, *Old Testament Theology*, vol. 2, 332-3; cf. G. W. H. Lampe's remarks about NT typology and its christological orientation ('The Reasonableness of Typology,' in *Essays on Typology*, SBT [Naperville, Ill.: Alec R. Allenson, 1957], 27-28).

to the climactic fulfillment of God's promises in Christ.[96] These few points regarding salvation history seem to represent a basic framework that would be agreeable to many proponents of the two primary conceptions of typology. More will have to be said below about the specific differences between the two conceptions with regard to salvation history.

Having granted the common ground presented briefly above, a proponent of the first, more traditional conception of typology would wish to make certain clarifications. First of all, the correspondence between type and antitype reveals a pattern in God's dealing with his people that can be attributed to 'His Lordship in moulding and using history to reveal and illumine His purpose.'[97] Further, with regard to typical events, 'Divine intent is of the essence both in their occurrence and in their inscripturation' (this holds for typical persons and institutions as well).[98] Hence an important part of traditional understandings of typology is God's sovereign plan being worked out in historical events, persons, and institutions, as well as in the recording of these events, persons, and institutions in Scripture.[99] God worked it out such that certain Old Testament events, persons, and institutions would prefigure New Testament events, persons, and institutions. As a result, one aspect of the significance of these Old Testament types is their ability to be used by God to predict their New Testament antitypes. Such an understanding of typology appears to be the understanding that expresses the New Testament writers' view of the relationship between types and antitypes.[100]

In prefiguring its New Testament antitype, the Old Testament type is anticipating its goal, consummation, or fulfillment.[101] The New Testament

---

[96] Cf. France, *Jesus and the Old Testament*, 40; Stek, 'Biblical Typology,' 162. As Craig Blomberg demonstrates in a recent article, the climactic fulfillment of God's promises in Christ does not rule out partial or incomplete fulfillment of these promises in the OT era ('Interpreting the Old Testament Prophetic Literature in Matthew: Double Fulfillment,' *TJ* NS 23 [2002]: 17-33).

[97] E. Earle Ellis, *Paul's Use of the Old Testament*, 128; cf. John H. Stek, 'Biblical Typology Yesterday and Today,' *CTJ* 5 (1970): 161.

[98] Ellis, *Paul's Use of the Old Testament*, 127. Ellis is here talking about Paul's use of the Exodus events in his warnings to the Corinthians (see especially 1 Cor 10:11); cf. Stek, 'Biblical Typology,' 162.

[99] Cf. Davidson, *Typology in Scripture*, 95.

[100] Ellis, *Paul's Use of the Old Testament*, 127-8; Davidson, *Typology in Scripture*, 397-424. This will be demonstrated with respect to John in chapter 5.

[101] Cf. G. K. Beale, 'Did Jesus and His Followers Preach the Right Doctrine from the Wrong Texts?,' in *The Right Doctrine from the Wrong Texts: Essays on the Use of the Old Testament in the New*, ed. G. K. Beale (Grand Rapids: Baker Books, 1994), 396; Davidson, *Typology in Scripture*, 95, 402-3; Goppelt, *Typos*, 199, 205; J. C. K. von Hofmann, *Interpreting the Bible*, trans. Christian Preus (Minneapolis: Augsburg, 1959), 135-6; C. F. D. Moule, 'Fulfilment-Words in the New Testament: Use and Abuse,' *NTS*

antitypes are the 'climactic and consummative realities of salvation-history' that fulfill the Old Testament types, because what 'God has done in Christ is both its [salvation-history's] climax and the guarantee of its consummation.'[102] J. C. K. von Hofmann provides a helpful statement of the view of Old Testament history and interpretation that is consistent with traditional typological thinking:

> The history recorded in the Old Testament is the history of salvation as proceeding towards its full realization. Hence the things recorded therein are to be interpreted teleologically, i.e., as aiming at their final goal, and thus as being of the same nature as the goal yet modified by their respective place in history. Since the course and the events of that history are determined by their goal, this goal will manifest itself in all important stages of its progress in a way which, though preliminary, prefigures it.[103]

The connection between this view of the Old Testament and traditional typology is straightforward: the Old Testament type prefigures and predicts its goal, the New Testament antitype.

Given such an understanding of the Old Testament type and the New Testament antitype, it is now possible to summarize the nature of the relationship between the type and antitype. First, the antitype fulfills significant patterns and predictions associated in the Old Testament with the type. This accounts for noticeable points of correspondence or similarity between them.[104] Second, as the goal and fulfillment to which the imperfect type pointed, the antitype goes beyond or surpasses the patterns and predictions associated with the type.[105] As a result, some noticeable dissimilarities exist between the type and the antitype.[106] Third, the first two points lead to the conclusion that the

---

14 (1967-68): 298-9; Milton S. Terry, *Biblical Hermeneutics: A Treatise on the Interpretation of the Old and New Testaments*, 2nd ed (Grand Rapids: Zondervan, 1974), 336.

[102] Stek, 'Biblical Typology,' 162; cf. 157.

[103] *Interpreting the Bible*, 135. Similarly, Moule describes Jesus as the 'climax of an eschatological and teleological process' ('Fulfillment-Words,' 298-9).

[104] Cf. Davidson, *Typology in Scripture*, 398; Ellis, *Paul's Use of the Old Testament*, 128.

[105] The imperfect nature of types is underlined by calling them shadows compared to the 'realities' (the antitypes) (Heb 10:1, NIV). Cf. Col 2:17. It is important to remember that a prophecy or promise is fulfilled when the things predicted or promised are carried out. Fulfilling OT types appears to mean more than merely measuring up to what was expected; it is consistent with 'fulfill' in the sense of 'complete' or 'consummate' (cf. BAGD, 671 or Moule, 'Fulfillment-Words,' 293-4).

[106] Davidson, *Typology in Scripture*, 398-9. Cf. E. Earle Ellis, *The Old Testament in Early Christianity: Canon and Interpretation in the Light of Modern Research* (Grand

New Testament antitype also fills the place of or replaces the Old Testament type. The first point anticipates this conclusion, because the antitype does what the type did and what it was supposed to do in the future. The second point anticipates it, because the antitype abundantly fills the role of the type in a way that makes the type unnecessary and effectively obsolete.[107] Of course, the type does have one important role that continues on, namely, it continues to be relevant in the divine economy as a pointer to its antitype.[108] In short, as the goal or fulfillment of the Old Testament type, the New Testament antitype fulfills and surpasses the patterns and predictions associated with the Old Testament type and in doing so takes the place of the type.

The view of typology just described creates a significant hermeneutical stumbling block for those who agree with certain accepted norms of historical critical interpretation. If Old Testament types are truly predictive of New Testament antitypes, then their predictive character creates a hermeneutical dilemma, because the Old Testament authors were not aware of what exactly they were predicting. One of the norms of historical critical hermeneutics is that Old Testament writings mean what their human authors meant or intended.[109] This would lead to difficulties with the idea that the psalmist was predicting something about Jesus as he was writing about David or David's sons in Psalm 2. How could he know that he was writing about Jesus and David at the same

---

Rapids: Baker, 1991), 108-9; Vern S. Poythress, 'Divine Meaning of Scripture' in *The Right Doctrine from the Wrong Texts: Essays on the Use of the Old Testament in the New*, ed. G. K. Beale (Grand Rapids: Baker Books, 1994), 103.

[107] Hebrews 8:13 provides a good example of this perspective with respect to the obsolescence of the old covenant. Hebrews 9-10 also demonstrates the temporary and imperfect character of the OT sacrifices (especially Heb 10:9) (George Ladd, 'Israel and the Church,' *EQ* 36 [1964]: 209-10). This article by Ladd defends the biblical character of the type of fulfillment and replacement advocated here. See also Clowney, 'Final Temple,' 124-32; David Holwerda, *Jesus and Israel: One Covenant or Two?* (Grand Rapids: Eerdmans, 1995), 74-5.

[108] The coherence between these points and John's view of the OT will be examined in chapter 5. A fulfills, surpasses, and replaces conception of typology came together as a result of meditation on some remarks by F. F. Bruce. Bruce says, 'This Gospel emphasizes in a series of presentations that the new order fulfils, surpasses, and replaces the old' and he goes on to give several examples like the 'new temple' (*John*, 43-44). As seen above, fulfilling, surpassing, and replacing are all important for understanding the relationship between types and antitypes, but fulfilling and surpassing are more intimately connected than the quote from Bruce leads one to believe.

[109] This hermeneutical thinking was held in high regard in biblical scholarship due to the influence of historical critical scholars and is still held today in some quarters, but it no longer controls the field in the way it once did due to recent emphasis upon the interaction between reader and text rather than upon the intentions of the original author (William W. Klein, C. L. Blomberg, and Robert L. Hubbard, *Introduction to Biblical Interpretation* [Nashville: Nelson, 1993], 171; Osborne, *Hermeneutical Spiral*, 368-9).

time? The root concern at stake here is admirable. It is a concern to provide norms for interpretation that insist on the primacy of the interpretation of Old Testament Scripture in its literary and historical context. The problem is that this particular norm does not provide adequate room for the inspiration of Scripture. As a result of inspiration, the human author's intention is not the only intention that is important for the interpreter. Divine intention is also important and relevant. Henri Blocher provides a helpful defense of this point:

> Why should not later expressions of the unchanging mind of the Spirit, spoken through holy men of God, clarify the meaning of older inspired words? If the meaning of the prophet and that of the Spirit coincide, better to ascertain the mind of the Spirit is better to ascertain the mind of the prophet. This involves no forcing of additional content, drawn, e.g., form the Gospels, into Isaiah's words; later revelation provides us with contextual information in the widest sense, a significant hermeneutical help in correcting mistakes. Critics who do not acknowledge the role of the Spirit as *auctor primarius* may look down on our procedure as 'unscientific,' but we have not received a spirit of timidity![110]

In light of divine intention and inspiration, the human author of an Old Testament writing may not have a full understanding of the typological import of what he is writing.[111] For example, David need not have been referring to anything other than himself and his sons when he writes about the authority of the Lord's king over all the nations (Ps 2).[112] In Psalm 2, the claims of the psalmist may appear grandiose to modern readers, but that is because modern readers know the story of the fate of the Davidic kings. For the sake of example, then, assume that David was expressing his inspired belief that the Lord had crowned the Davidic kings as the kings over all the nations (Ps 2:6-9). If this belief was only mentioned here, then perhaps it could be dismissed as idealistic. Yet similar words are spoken in other Psalms.[113] Its context widens further in the words spoken through the prophets regarding Israel's future

---

[110] 'The "Analogy of Faith" in the Study of Scripture' in *The Challenge of Evangelical Theology: Essays in Approach and Method*, ed. Nigel M. de S. Cameron (Edinburgh: Rutherford House Books, 1987), 35.

[111] For similar treatments, see Lampe, 'Reasonableness of Typology,' 29-30; Terry, *Biblical Hermeneutics*, 344; cf. Joseph Coppens, *Les Harmonies des deux Testaments: Essai sur les Divers Sens des Ecritures et sur l'Unité de la Révélation* (Paris: Casterman, 1949), 84-85; Stek, 'Biblical Typology,' 139.

[112] Cf. von Rad, who says, 'a petty Judean king was given in God's name a claim to world-wide domination and a saving office which he could not possibly fulfil' (*Old Testament Theology*, vol. 2, 374). Note that the Davidic authorship of Psalm 2 is supported by Acts 4:25 and is assumed here for the sake of argument.

[113] Pss 18:43-50, 72:8-11, 89:27.

king.[114] The authority of this future king over the nations is explicitly reaffirmed in two of these passages.[115] In addition, since the prophetic writings present David as the pattern for the future king, the beliefs of David regarding his kingship and that of his descendants could be regarded as part of the pattern for the future Davidic king.[116] Thus David's typological import becomes clear in the prophetic writings and this justifies regarding Psalm 2:6-9 as one element of the Old Testament pattern for the coming Messiah. In this case, David may have grasped some measure of the typological import of what he was writing (Ps 2:6-9), but he may not have grasped it as clearly as those who could benefit from the entire Old Testament. David's typological import takes on even further clarity in the teachings of Jesus when Jesus points out how David's experiences have anticipated his own.[117]

Given the above example and similar ones like it, proponents of a traditional conception of typology need not appeal to a divine author who hid the anticipatory import of Old Testament events, persons, and institutions from the Old Testament authors and then disclosed it to the New Testament authors.[118] Rather they can appeal to a canonical approach that views one divine author as ultimately responsible for the unity of the whole canon.[119] This divine author is a God who uses certain Old Testament events, persons, and institutions both to advance 'his saving purposes' and to anticipate 'what he is yet to do' for his people.[120] Focusing specifically upon the anticipatory import of these Old Testament events, persons, and institutions, the inspired Old Testament authors

---

[114] Isa 9:6-7 (MT vv. 5-6); 11:1-5; Jer 23:5-6, 30:9, 33:15-22; Ezek 21:27 (MT v. 32), 34:23-24, 37:24-28; Hos 3:5; Amos 9:11; Mic 5:2-4 (MT vv. 1-3); Hag 2:23; Zech 3:8, 6:11-12, 9:9, 10:4, 12:8, 13:1.

[115] Isa 9:7, Mic 5:4.

[116] Von Rad, *Old Testament Theology*, vol. 2, 323. Cf. esp. Ezek 34:23-24, 37:24-28; *Pss. Sol.* 17:23-24.

[117] John 13:18, 15:25.

[118] Such an appeal to a hidden significance, or *sensus plenior*, could lead one to regard the typological significance of an OT passage as mystical and beyond verification (cf. Moo, 'Sensus Plenior,' 201-4, 206; D. A. Carson, *Matthew 1-12*, Expositor's Bible Commentary [Grand Rapids: Zondervan, 1995], 92-93).

[119] Moo, 'Sensus Plenior,' 204-6, 209. With reference to the use of the OT in the NT, Moo defines 'canonical approach' as a focus upon 'the ultimate canonical context of any single scriptural text as the basis on which to find a "fuller" sense in that text than its human author may have been cognizant of' ('Sensus Plenior,' 204). What Moo is describing here is very similar to J. I. Packer's understanding of the 'analogy of faith' (*God Has Spoken: Revelation and the Bible*, 3rd ed. [Grand Rapids: Baker, 1993], 99). Beale and Poythress also make remarks that are very similar to Moo regarding the divine author and canonical context (Beale, 'Right Doctrine from the Wrong Texts,' 401; Poythress, 'Divine Meaning of Scripture,' 108, 112).

[120] Stek, 'Biblical Typology,' 162.

may have had some understanding of it.[121] Yet it becomes clearer to later ones in the light of further revelation; this is especially evident in the works of the Latter Prophets.[122] Then the New Testament authors, who have benefitted from both additional revelation and fulfillment in Christ, are able to shed even more light on the anticipatory import of Old Testament events, persons, and institutions. They point to the role played by certain Old Testament events, persons, and institutions in prefiguring their climactic fulfillment in Christ, the church, and the ultimate coming of God's kingdom. The New Testament authors carry on this endeavor believing that they are proclaiming one legitimate aspect of the meaning of these Old Testament events, persons, and institutions.[123]

In appealing to a canonical approach, proponents of typology are asking the reader to believe that sometimes the anticipatory import of Old Testament events, persons, and institutions is clarified by later revelation. This import is open to verification, since the texts relevant to each type and antitype are found within the canon. Typology, unlike allegory, depends upon the literal sense of the relevant Old Testament and New Testament texts to substantiate its claims.[124]

In addition to a concern for divine involvement in effectively prefiguring antitypes, the first primary conception of typology is concerned to defend typology as more than a merely literary phenomenon. It is rightfully concerned about the historicity of the Old Testament and New Testament accounts. If the Old Testament historical accounts represent unhistorical traditions, then the Old Testament types are merely inscripturated literary foreshadowings of their

---

[121] Moo, 'Sensus Plenior,' 205.

[122] Cf. Beale, 'Right Doctrine from the Wrong Texts,' 400. For specific prophetic texts regarding several typological events, persons, or institutions, see p. 71. See also Rikki Watts's summary of the Isaianic new Exodus theme and its relevance for Mark's Gospel (*Isaiah's New Exodus and Mark*, WUNT, 2nd series, no. 88 [Tübingen: Mohr Siebeck, 1997], esp. 79-90).

[123] Moo, 'Sensus Plenior,' 209.

[124] Ibid., 206; Carson, *Matthew*, 93. It follows that each appeal to typology must be substantiated with relevant biblical evidence and that the case for a given typological relationship is only as strong as the biblical evidence for it. Cf. Wilhelm Vischer, who notes, 'The proof from scripture must be susceptible of verification by intellectual methods. If Jesus is really the hidden meaning of Old Testament scripture an honest philological exegesis cannot fail to stumble across this truth; not in the sense that it directly finds Jesus there, but in the sense that it would be led to affirm that the thoughts expressed and the stories narrated in the Old Testament, as they are transmitted in the Bible, point toward the crucifixion of Jesus; that the Christ Jesus of the New Testament stands precisely at the vanishing point of Old Testament perspective' (*The Witness of the Old Testament to Christ*, trans. A. B. Crabtree [London: Lutterworth, 1949], 28).

antitypes.[125] One of the essential convictions of the first conception of typology involves the working out of God's plan in human history. With regard to the New Testament accounts, their portrayal of Jesus as the antitype to certain Old Testament types is believed to reflect the historical Jesus. Proponents of the first conception of typology would object to the notion that the New Testament authors 'felt free to modify the details of the narrative tradition' in order to conform the historical Jesus to Old Testament types.[126] If significant freedom was exercised by the New Testament authors, then one could claim that their typological correspondences were intentionally fabricated with little or no basis in historical fact at all. Thus the typological correspondences evident in the New Testament become little more than a literary phenomenon. In relation to the earlier discussion of salvation history, a traditional conception of typology defends the historicity of the salvation-historical events and the accounts of them recorded in the Bible.[127]

The above treatment of the traditional conception of typology prepares sufficiently for discussion of the second primary conception of typology. The second primary conception of typology involves an attempt to bring together elements of traditional typology with the findings of modern critical scholarship.[128] Modern critical scholarship has undermined optimism about the unity between the Old Testament and the New Testament and about the historicity of biblical, historical narratives.[129] As a result, typology is useful to modern scholars if it can be used independently of such presuppositions. Proponents of the second primary conception tend to place particular emphasis upon the biblical authors' belief in 'the constant principles of God's working.'[130] Thus typology involves a recognition that God works according to certain patterns in the Old Testament as well as in the New Testament. R. T. France provides a representative picture of the second conception:

---

[125] Cf. the discussion of historicity and salvation history by Eichrodt ('Typological Exegesis,' 236-7).

[126] Lampe, 'Reasonableness of Typology,' 19.

[127] Cf. Stek, 'Biblical Typology,' 160-1.

[128] Von Rad, one of the proponents of the second primary conception, makes it quite clear that he does not want his use of the term 'typology' to be confused with traditional uses of the term (*Old Testament Theology*, vol. 2, 367); for a similar distinction, see Samuel Amsler, 'Où en est la typologie de l'Ancien Testament?,' *ETR* 27 (1952): 78. Cf. Stek, 'Biblical Typology,' 155-7.

[129] Lampe, 'Reasonableness of Typology,' 14-17; von Rad, *Old Testament Theology*, vol. 2, 362, 366. Cf. Amsler, *L'Ancien Testament dans l'église*, 220-7; Goppelt, *Typos*, 229-33.

[130] France, *Jesus and the Old Testament*, 39; cf. Amsler, 'La typologie de l'Ancien Testament,' 78; Baker, *Two Testaments*, 198; von Rad, *Old Testament Theology*, vol. 2, 363-6.

It [typology] is essentially the recognition of a correspondence between New and Old Testament events, based on a conviction of the unchanging character of the principles of God's working, and a consequent understanding and description of the New Testament event in terms of the Old Testament model. The idea of fulfillment inherent in New Testament typology derives not from a belief that events so understood were explicitly predicted, but from the conviction that in the coming and work of Jesus the principles of God's working, already imperfectly embodied in the Old Testament, were more perfectly re-embodied, and thus brought to completion.[131]

Thus France allows that New Testament antitypes correspond to and fulfill Old Testament types, but he shows his concern about the predictive significance of types.[132]

In discussing Old Testament types and New Testament antitypes, proponents of the second primary conception of typology largely discount the prospective or predictive nature of Old Testament types. As discussed above, they claim that Old Testament types cannot be prospective (that is, have an intended 'forward reference'), because this would give Old Testament types an additional meaning that was hidden with reference to the Old Testament authors.[133] If the type of canonical approach discussed above is given due weight, an objection based upon the intent of the Old Testament author need not be decisive. The inspired Old Testament author could have written accounts with an anticipatory import that would become clearer and clearer as God's plan unfolded and the rest of the canon was written.[134] It is also important to

---

[131] France, *Jesus and the Old Testament*, 40.

[132] Later he indicates that typology and prediction are to be kept quite separate: 'Thus the decision on whether a given use of the Old Testament in the New is typological or an appeal to prediction will reduce itself to a question of Old Testament exegesis. If a forward reference was intended in the Old Testament . . . we are not concerned with typology, but with the appeal to prediction' (*Jesus and the Old Testament*, 42).

[133] France, *Jesus and the Old Testament*, 41-42; cf. Amsler, *L'Ancien Testament dans l'église*, 220-1, 225-6; Baker, *Two Testaments*, 190, 192.

[134] Moo, 'Sensus Plenior,' 206; cf. Carson, *Matthew*, 92-93; Foulkes, *Acts of God*, 38-39; Stek, 'Biblical Typology,' 139, 161. On the canonical approach, see p. 25. Of course, proponents of the second primary conception of typology do have a point in calling attention to the retrospective character of NT typology. It was only in light of further revelation that the NT authors were able to come to a fuller appreciation of the typological significance of OT types (Amsler, *L'Ancien Testament dans l'église*, 226). Even so, this does not exclude the possibility that God designed the type in order to prefigure its antitype, knowing full well that its typological significance would be gradually disclosed. Besides, NT typology has a lot in common with the typology already evident in the OT prophets. They were already seeing earlier events, persons,

add that the New Testament authors probably did not share this concern with guarding the type from having a predictive significance unforeseen by the Old Testament author.[135] As a result, France is not quite accurate when he calls his conception of typology 'New Testament typology.'[136]

Another reason for discounting the prospective nature of Old Testament types is that the Old Testament types are so different from their New Testament antitypes; that is, the Old Testament 'shadows' (types) only vaguely resemble corresponding New Testament realities (antitypes).[137] Giving adequate place to the discontinuities between Old Testament types and New Testament antitypes is important. The nature of the correspondence and the nature of the discontinuity deserve careful evaluation for each given type and antitype. On the other hand, areas of remarkable correspondence do exist and have been described by Christian exegetes up until the present day. As Eichrodt notes, Christian exegesis is distinctively Christian in that it 'believes and recognizes that the Old Testament is determined fundamentally by its directedness toward the New.'[138] Therefore discontinuities between Old Testament types and New Testament antitypes should not distract Christian exegetes from noticing genuine areas of continuity.

In addition to regarding types as only retrospective, the second primary conception of typology is distinctive in that it commonly displays less confidence in the historicity of the biblical, historical narratives.[139] For instance, von Rad's treatment of Old Testament theology rests upon a distinction between Israel's beliefs about her history and her history as it is reconstructed by historical-critical scholars.[140] Von Rad's treatment thus leaves one wondering about the historical basis for Israel's beliefs regarding the allegedly historical events of her salvation history.[141] Such an approach to Old

---

and institutions as patterns for what God was going to do for his people. The recognition of the fulfillment of these patterns is bound to be retrospective, just like the recognition of the fulfillment of other forms of prediction (pace Baker, *Two Testaments*, 190).

[135] For support, see discussion of the first conception above and chapter 5.

[136] France, *Jesus and the Old Testament*, 43. Baker presents a conception of typology similar to France's and he also acts as if this conception is the same as the one found in the Bible (Baker, *Two Testaments*, 185-88).

[137] Von Rad, *Old Testament Theology*, vol. 2, 384. Von Rad here emphasizes the discontinuity between the OT and the NT.

[138] Further, he adds, 'The task [of Christian exegesis] is to make visible this slope toward the New Testament, and typology is one of the factors which serve this purpose' ('Typological Exegesis,' 242).

[139] Von Rad claims that traditional typology was decisively undermined by critical scholarship due to a loss of 'its old connexion with historical facts' (*Old Testament Theology*, vol. 2, 366).

[140] Baker, *Two Testaments*, 158-9.

[141] Ibid., 159-60; Stek, 'Biblical Typology,' 148-9, 153.

Testament theology and interpretation essentially renders suspect the historical referents of Old Testament types. In doing so, it calls into question whether Old Testament typology is anything more than a literary phenomenon that the biblical writers used to describe Israel's past and future in terms of traditions surrounding 'a few saving institutions ordained by God.'[142] It also calls into question New Testament typology, suggesting that it is a further elaboration built on types with an uncertain historical basis.[143] It seems to be only a short step from an understanding of typology like von Rad's to other conceptions of typology that are more open about their kinship to literary studies.[144]

K. J. Woollcombe takes that short step in his discussion of typology as a method of writing.[145] He relates typological patterns to the literary artistry of the New Testament author. Woollcombe claims that typology can be described as a 'method of writing,' which he defines as 'the description of an event, person or thing in the New Testament in terms borrowed from the description of its prototypal counterpart in the Old Testament.'[146] Woollcombe is not alone in making such a move toward a merely literary conception of typology. Woollcombe's typological method of writing appears related to the 'literary patternism' or 'typological criticism' of other authors.[147] Woollcombe, Lampe,

---

[142] Von Rad, *Old Testament Theology*, vol. 2, 368.

[143] Robert W. Yarbrough questions the epistemological basis of Leonhard Goppelt's typology and finds that Goppelt's (like von Rad's) 'approach largely cuts necessary ties between biblical events and the biblical interpretations of them' ('The heilsgeschichtliche Perspective in Modern New Testament Theology' [Ph.D. diss., University of Aberdeen, 1985], 450; cf. Goppelt, *Typos*, 229-33, esp. 232). Similar remarks could be made concerning Amsler who claims that only the theological significance of the OT events is important for NT typology and that this significance is independent of the historicity of the events (*L'Ancien Testament dans l'église*, 222).

[144] Eichrodt is careful to point out that von Rad's view of typology is different from his own. He perceives von Rad's concern to be with 'structural relatedness in the experience of God in the Old and New Testaments, by virtue of which God's action in his community pursues the same goals in each case and illumines the one covenant through the other' (Eichrodt, 'Typological Exegesis,' 245). One should also note that von Rad appears to use the term 'typology' reluctantly at some points (i.e., he is not committed to calling what he is doing 'typology') (*Old Testament Theology*, vol. 2, 371, see also 363-4).

[145] Woollcombe's conception of typology as a method of writing is related to, but distinct from, the second primary conception of typology.

[146] He gives the example of Matthew and Mark describing John the Baptist 'in terms borrowed from the description of Elijah' (K. J. Woollcombe, 'The Biblical Origins and Patristic Development of Typology,' in *Essays on Typology*, SBT [Naperville, Ill.: Alec R. Allenson, 1957], 39-40).

[147] Davidson discusses the treatments of 'literary patternism' by Austin M. Farrer (*A Study in St. Mark* [New York: Oxford University, 1952]; *The Glass of Vision* [London:

Introduction

and Goulder seem to agree that the New Testament authors could 'modify the details of the narrative tradition in order to bring out the meaning which it possessed for them when it was expressed in imagery derived from the Old Testament history.'[148] Such charges of modification slight a commitment to historicity on the part of the New Testament authors.[149]

One can observe from the above discussion that each of the two primary conceptions of typology is associated with its own set of presuppositions. Proponents of both conceptions are able to bear witness to the typology that is employed by the biblical authors. Proponents of the second primary conception are attempting to revive some form of typology that would be acceptable to critical scholarship. This is done in recognition of the fact that critical scholarship has brushed aside the first, traditional conception of typology as merely 'an historical curiosity.'[150]

The most helpful recent detailed study of the typology characteristic of the New Testament authors is that of Richard Davidson. Davidson seeks to buttress the first, traditional conception of typology by giving careful attention to the hermeneutical structures associated with typology as it was understood by the New Testament authors.[151] Davidson's study also profits from its consideration of the second conception of typology and the criticisms of traditional typological studies made by proponents of the second conception.[152] Davidson provides a useful guide for further studies in biblical typology. He is alert to the

---

Dacre Press, 1948]) and the similar 'typological criticism' of Michael D. Goulder (*Type and History in Acts* [London: SPCK, 1964]) (*Typology in Scripture*, 105).

[148] This quote is from Lampe ('Reasonableness of Typology,' 19).

[149] Davidson, *Typology in Scripture*, 105; Woollcombe, 'Biblical Origins of Typology,' 40; Lampe, 'Reasonableness of Typology,' 19-20.

[150] Lampe, 'Reasonableness of Typology,' 16. Cf. Anthony T. Hanson's admission that John's understanding of the OT is distinct from that of critical scholars who do not share the NT writers' 'assumptions about the inerrancy and inspiration of Scripture' ('John's Technique in Using Scripture,' in *The New Testament Interpretation of Scripture* [London: SPCK, 1980], 175).

[151] In addition, Davidson provides useful comments upon the use of τύπος and its cognates by the NT authors (*Typology in Scripture*, 115-90, 286-90, 311-3, 333-4, 358-63, 403-4); he thus shores up the biblical basis for typological vocabulary, like 'type' and 'antitype' (cf. George W. Buchanan, *Typology and the Gospel* [New York: University Press of America, 1987], 21-27). Recently, Goppelt's (and Davidson's) understanding of τύπος has been challenged by K.-H. Ostmeyer. Ostmeyer's challenges are not as serious as he thinks, because he still finds the term associated with baptism and new creation in 1 Peter 3:21. Thus the term is still associated with fulfillment (new creation) and is therefore more closely connected to a traditional typological hermeneutic than Ostmeyer is willing to grant (K.-H. Ostmeyer, *Taufe und Typos: Elemente und Theologie der Tauftypologien in 1. Korinther 10 und 1. Petrus 3*, WUNT, 2nd series, no. 118 [Tübingen: Mohr Siebeck, 2000], 49-52, 199-200).

[152] See Davidson, *Typology in Scripture*, 422-3.

need for establishing guidelines that would result in a controlled approach to typological interpretation.[153] His focus upon the use of typology found in the New Testament itself allows him to interact with proponents of both primary conceptions of typology based upon how their conceptions of typology match up with that of the New Testament authors.

Like Davidson's study, the following study will consider previous treatments of typology based upon each of the two primary conceptions. Since its particular focus will be upon the Fourth Gospel, a brief overview of recent treatments of typology in the Fourth Gospel will examine the relevant content of such treatments. Recent studies give particular attention to Exodus typology (or, more narrowly, to Moses typology), so three attempts to see Exodus typology as a key factor in the structure of the Fourth Gospel will be examined first.[154]

First, Harald Sahlin attempts to relate the Fourth Gospel as a whole to an Old Testament pattern that extends from Moses at the burning bush to the dedication of Solomon's Temple.[155] Second, Jacob Enz thinks that one can focus on the book of Exodus alone as a 'literary pattern in the Gospel of John in which the career and place of Jesus are interpreted in the light of the ministry of Moses.'[156] Third, having noted the deficiencies of the studies by Sahlin and Enz, Robert Smith defines Exod 2:23-12:51 to be the 'most likely place where one may seek an exodus typology of major proportions in the Gospel of John.'[157] Each of these studies is built upon a mixture of credible and far-fetched parallels between the Fourth Gospel and the proposed Old Testament pattern. Smith, who works the hardest at developing methodological controls for his typology, strains to correlate Moses' miracles in Egypt with Jesus' miracles. For example, the disease of boils (Exod 9:8-12) is correlated with the healing of the lame man (John 5:2-9).[158] These three authors, especially Enz and Smith, are building upon a widely recognized parallelism between Moses and Jesus in the Fourth Gospel. Yet their attempts to expand upon recognized parallels lead them to overstate the level and significance of the correspondences between the Fourth Gospel and selected sections of the Old Testament. If the Fourth Gospel was written with a specific Old Testament literary pattern in mind, surely that pattern would be more evident than the

---

[153] Ibid., 397-408, 411-12. See John E. Alsup's appeal for a controlled approach to typology that does not ignore the concerns of historical-critical scholarship ('Typology,' in *ABD*, ed. D. N. Freedman, vol. 6 [New York: Doubleday, 1992], 685).

[154] Sahlin, *Typologie des Johannesevangeliums*; Jacob J. Enz, 'The Book of Exodus as a Literary Type for the Gospel of John,' *JBL* 76 (1957): 208-15; Robert Houston Smith, 'Exodus Typology in the Fourth Gospel,' *JBL* 81 (1962): 329-42.

[155] Sahlin, *Typologie des Johannesevangeliums*, 5, 73-74.

[156] Enz, 'Exodus as a Literary Type,' 215.

[157] Smith, 'Exodus Typology,' 333.

[158] Ibid., 338. For his methodology, see 331-3.

patterns proposed by Sahlin, Enz, and Smith.[159]

As noted above, studies of Exodus typology in the Fourth Gospel draw on some of the same evidence used to establish a correspondence between Jesus and Moses. The fact that Moses is mentioned in the Fourth Gospel eleven times (excluding John 8:5) probably has contributed to the desire to find multiple links between Moses and Jesus. Like the studies discussed above, T. F. Glasson and Marie-Émile Boismard have been criticized for finding correspondences between Moses' ministry and Jesus' ministry that appear to be based upon rather superficial similarities.[160] Wayne Meeks attempts to provide a more cautious overview of several possible correlations between Moses and Jesus.[161] Günter Reim also evaluates attempts to establish a typological relationship between Jesus and Moses.[162] Both Meeks and Reim reject a typological correlation between Moses and Jesus.[163] Meeks claims that one may assume that John regarded 'Jesus as greater than Moses' and that one who was familiar with the Moses traditions 'would recognize (1) that Jesus fulfills for the believer those functions elsewhere attributed to Moses and (2) that the Christian claims he does this in a superior and exclusive way.'[164] Meeks doubts, however, that John 'wished to depict Jesus as a "new Moses."'[165] Meeks apparently rejects a proposed typological relationship between Moses and Jesus, because the Fourth Gospel does not draw clear enough correspondences between the two.[166] He does however recognize a typological relationship between the serpent and Jesus (John 3:14).[167] Similarly, Reim points out that Moses and Christ are not parallel entities in a typological sense. Instead, the alleged types associated with Moses' ministry are related to, but quite different

---

[159] Cf. the evaluation of Sahlin, Enz, and Smith given by Günter Reim (*Studien zum alttestamentlichen Hintergrund des Johannesevangeliums*, SNTSMS, no. 22 [Cambridge: Cambridge University, 1974], 263-5).

[160] For criticism of the excesses of Glasson's *Moses in the Fourth Gospel* (SBT, Naperville, Ill.: Alec R. Allenson, 1963) see Wayne A. Meeks, *Moses Traditions and the Johannine Christology*, NovTSup, vol. 14 (Leiden: E. J. Brill, 1967), 287. For similar criticism of Boismard's *Moïse ou Jésus: Essai de christologie johannique* (BETL, no. 84, Leuven: Leuven University, 1988) see Maarten Menken, 'The Christology of the Fourth Gospel,' 316. Along similar lines, see B. P. W. Stather Hunt's attempt to relate Moses' 'sweetening of the brackish waters of Marah' (Exod 15:23-26) to Jesus' turning the water into wine (John 2:1-11) (*Some Johannine Problems* [London: Skeffington, 1958], 57-59).

[161] Meeks, *Moses Traditions*, 286-319.
[162] Reim, *Hintergrund des Johannesevangeliums*, 266-8.
[163] Meeks, *Moses Traditions*, 319; Reim, *Hintergrund des Johannesevangeliums*, 268.
[164] Meeks, *Moses Traditions*, 319.
[165] Ibid.
[166] Ibid.
[167] Ibid., 291-2.

from the antitype that they hint at, which is Christ.[168] Reim's rejection of a typological correlation between Moses and Christ appears to rest on an understanding of typology that emphasizes the correspondence between type and antitype, while de-emphasizing progression from type to antitype.[169]

In spite of their doubts about Moses–Jesus typology, Reim and Meeks both make a similar observation regarding potential instances of typology in the Fourth Gospel; that is, the movement from type to antitype involves a progression from a lesser to a greater entity.[170] Similarly, Goppelt finds that the Fourth Gospel presents Jesus as bringing about the fulfillment in 'perfect form' of 'the redemptive gifts of the Mosaic period.'[171] Goppelt places more emphasis upon typology involving 'redemptive gifts' than upon Moses–Jesus typology, without ruling out the latter.[172] Severino Pancaro also allows for both Moses–Jesus typology and typology involving the manna in relation to the bread Jesus offers (John 6).[173] In both cases, Pancaro notes that the antitype is represented as greater than the type.[174] In summary, one finds that several interpreters agree that the typology of the Fourth Gospel involves a progression between type and antitype. The antitype corresponds to the type, but is greater.

Exodus typology and Moses–Jesus typology have been given considerable attention compared to other possible typological correspondences that might be relevant to the interpretation of the Fourth Gospel.[175] Goppelt provides a brief attempt at providing many points of departure for further study of the typology of the Fourth Gospel.[176] George Buchanan attempts to develop a typological relationship between Elijah/Elisha and Jesus. Like proponents of Moses–Jesus

---

[168] Reim, *Hintergrund des Johannesevangeliums*, 267-8.
[169] Ibid.
[170] Ibid., 268; Meeks, Moses Traditions, 292.
[171] Goppelt, *Typos*, 185.
[172] Ibid., 185, 188.
[173] Severino Pancaro, *The Law in the Fourth Gospel: The Torah and the Gospel, Moses and Jesus, Judaism and Christianity according to John*, NovTSup, vol. 42 (Leiden: Brill, 1975), 471. See also his remarks about the serpent (John 3:14) as a type of Christ (p. 336).
[174] Édouard Cothenet also makes this point with regard to the manna and the bread Jesus offers ('Typologie de l'exode dans le IVe Évangile,' in *Tradició i Traducció de la Paraula: Miscel·lània Guiu Camps*, ed. Frederic Raurell et al. [Barcelona: Associació Bíblica de Catalunya, 1993], 250-1). This is the only point at which Cothenet gives any indication of his understanding of typology or the typology typical of the Fourth Gospel.
[175] Cf. Carson, 'John and the Johannine Epistles,' 255-6 and Cothenet, 'Typologie de l'exode dans le IVe Évangile,' 244. Cf. also Bertil Gärtner's attempt to understand John 6 in light of examples of Exodus/Passover typology from the early church fathers and the NT (*John 6 and the Jewish Passover*, ConBNT, no. 17 [Lund: C. W. K. Gleerup, 1959], 29-38).
[176] Goppelt, *Typos*, 179-95.

typology, Buchanan looks for evidence in the Fourth Gospel of parallels between Jesus' miracles and those of Elijah and Elisha.[177] Carson suggests the possibility that Davidic typology may help one to understand some of John's quotations from the Psalms.[178] Margaret Daly-Denton provides helpful evidence for a significant connection between David and Jesus in the Fourth Gospel.[179] In addition, A.T. Hanson has recently drawn attention to John's use of typology.[180]

A.T. Hanson's brief discussion of the typology of the Fourth Gospel mentions several possible typological relationships. His comments are pertinent to the following study in that he denies that one should think of the relationship between the Temple and Jesus as typological. He says, 'It is more accurate, for instance, to say that Jesus as the true place where the people of God should worship supersedes the Temple than to say that the Temple is a type of Christ.'[181] This is in line with Hanson's conviction that 'John is more likely to represent Jesus as superseding in his own person some person or object in the Old Testament than to present that person or object as a type of Christ.'[182] Hanson never gives clear justification for this statement. It appears that he finds examples of typology only in those instances where he is convinced that the Fourth Gospel provides good evidence for a significant correspondence between an Old Testament type and Christ. If he does not observe a significant correspondence, then he regards Christ as merely superseding the Old Testament person or object.[183] In response, the following study seeks to provide

---

[177] Buchanan's brief presentation of this typological relationship does produce points of similarity, but does not provide compelling evidence that he is observing anything more than the similarities that one might expect between any two sets of biblical miracle stories (see Buchanan, *Typology and the Gospel*, 104-11).

[178] Carson, 'John and the Johannine Epistles,' 249-50. Carson's discussion of Davidic typology is clearly aligned with the first primary conception of typology (see especially, 'John and the Johannine Epistles,' 249). Cf. also the brief discussion of Davidic typology in the Fourth Gospel by Andreas J. Köstenberger ('Jesus the Good Shepherd Who Will Also Bring Other Sheep [John 10:16]: The Old Testament Background of a Familiar Metaphor,' *BBR* 12 [2002]: 81-82).

[179] *David in the Fourth Gospel: The Johannine Reception of the Psalms*, AGJU, vol. 47 (Leiden: Brill, 2000).

[180] Anthony T. Hanson, 'John's Use of Scripture,' in *The Gospels and the Scriptures of Israel*, eds. Craig A. Evans and W. Richard Stegner, JSNTSup, no. 104 (Sheffield: Sheffield Academic, 1994), 362-4.

[181] Ibid., 362.

[182] Ibid. Hanson does find genuine typology in a few places, like the bronze serpent, the manna, and the vine (cf. also Anthony T. Hanson, *Jesus Christ in the Old Testament* [London: SPCK, 1965], 177).

[183] Although Hanson appears to regard typology and supersession as distinct categories, it is possible that he thinks of supersession as one element in a typological relationship.

convincing evidence for a significant correspondence between the Temple and Jesus in the Fourth Gospel.[184]

Besides Hanson's mention of Temple–Jesus typology, one finds direct, although brief, discussion of it by Carson, Goppelt, and Fairbairn.[185] It is also mentioned in passing by Amsler, Longenecker, Morris, and Sahlin.[186] Yet previous studies of Jesus' replacement of the Temple in the Fourth Gospel provide helpful background for the current study even if they do not mention typology. R. J. McKelvey, for instance, finds that John depicts Jesus as a 'new temple.'[187] He finds that Jesus displaces the Jerusalem Temple, 'because Christ fulfils what it stands for so magnificently that it is necessary for it to have a completely new form.'[188] Such a claim suggests that McKelvey associates Jesus' replacement of the Temple with abundant fulfilment of its purposes. Thus the Fourth Gospel depicts a relationship between Jesus and the Temple that involves both correspondence and escalation. In doing so, McKelvey provides grounds for a typological relationship between them.[189]

The preceding discussion provides an overview of recent scholarship related to the current study. The current study will seek to integrate previous work on Jesus' replacement of the Temple in the Fourth Gospel and previous work on Johannine typology. Studies in Johannine typology are clustered around Exodus typology and Moses–Jesus typology. Yet it seems that Jesus' replacement of the Temple could also involve a typological relationship that has been given insufficient attention in previous works.

Thus supersession plus something else constitutes typology. His understanding of both categories remains unclear in this article.

[184] Similarly, Ulrich Busse discounts typology and prefers to examine the Temple imagery in the Fourth Gospel using literary critical categories. It is difficult to interact with Busse, because he only makes a few terse comments about his understanding of typology and its inferiority to literary categories like intertextuality and metaphorical language. It seems that he prefers literary categories, because they free the reader from the necessity of appealing to fulfillment and supersession, which carry overtones of anti-Semitism (Busse, 'Tempelmetaphorik im Johannesevangelium,' 397-8, 427-8).

[185] Carson, *John*, 182; Goppelt, *Typos*, 191; Fairbairn, *Typology of Scripture*, vol. 2, 217-8.

[186] Amsler, *Ancien Testament dans l'église*, 217-18; Longenecker, *Biblical Exegesis in the Apostolic Period*, 153-4; Morris, *New Testament and the Jewish Lectionaries*, 71; Sahlin, *Typologie des Johannesevangeliums*, 12-13.

[187] McKelvey, *New Temple*, 77-84.

[188] Ibid., 84.

[189] It may be that McKelvey intentionally avoids any mention of typology, just like Glasson avoids it in *Moses in the Fourth Gospel*. Even though he avoids the term 'typology,' Glasson's study is repeatedly associated with it by other scholars.

Plan for the Study

The next chapter considers the history and significance of the Temple in the Old Testament and extra-biblical Jewish literature. It provides relevant background for investigating John's portrayal of Jesus as the replacement of the Temple. The third chapter examines the verses most often associated with Jesus' fulfillment and replacement of the Temple in the Fourth Gospel. The fourth chapter develops insights gained from chapter three in that it develops further the associations between the Temple and Jesus' death/resurrection/exaltation and between the Temple and Jesus' fulfillment of the Jewish feasts. The fifth chapter shows how evidence from previous chapters leads one to understand the relationship between Jesus and the Temple as typological. The final chapter summarizes the results of the study. It also relates it to the Temple typology evident in other parts of the New Testament.

CHAPTER 2

History and Significance of the Temple according to the Old Testament and Selected Jewish Literature

The story of the Temple in the Old Testament is an integral part of the story of God's dealings with his people. Although one can find precursors to the story of the Temple in Genesis, it really begins to take shape in Exodus with the revelation of the Tabernacle to Moses.[1] Like the plans for the Tabernacle, its predecessor, the plans for the Temple are revealed by God. In addition, God reveals his plans for worship at the Tabernacle and the Temple. The specificity and quantity of the laws connected with them suggest their significance as revelatory institutions. The prominent place given to them in the Old Testament is also reflected in extra-biblical Jewish literature.

The Temple is not a static institution in the Old Testament. The first, glorious days of the Temple built by Solomon do not constitute the norm for its existence. At several junctures, God corrects and refines his people's beliefs concerning the Temple and proper worship, especially through prophets in combination with historical events. Of particular importance is Ezekiel's vision in Ezekiel 40-48, which pictures a brighter, more secure future for God's people and his Temple. The following chapter will examine the beliefs and events associated with the Temple from its emergence in the form of the Tabernacle to its final destruction in A.D. 70. It will attempt to draw attention to noteworthy patterns that characterize the beliefs and events connected with the Temple as it is portrayed in the Old Testament and in selected, extra-biblical, Jewish literature.[2]

---

[1] For precursors to the Temple in Genesis, see the discussion of the Garden of Eden (pp. 64, 79, 106) and Bethel (p. 129).

[2] Since the chapter is concerned with providing background for the Fourth Gospel, the survey of extra-biblical, Jewish literature will focus on literature of the first century A.D. and earlier. It will also focus attention upon relevant OT texts and not upon critical reconstructions of the history and significance of the Temple (and Tabernacle), because it is generally acknowledged that the NT authors would have regarded the OT as trustworthy, inspired Scripture (Hanson, 'John's Technique in Using Scripture,' 175; Koester, *Dwelling of God*, 6; cf. Amsler, 'La typologie de l'Ancien Testament,' 78).

The Tabernacle: Antecedent of the Temple

As the antecedent of the Temple, the Tabernacle serves as the precedent for the Temple's structure and for its place in the worship of Israel.[3] It is introduced in Exodus 25:9 as a 'sanctuary' (מקדש) constructed by the people in order that the Lord might dwell among them.[4] In Exodus 25-31, the Lord reveals to Moses the pattern that is to govern the construction of the Tabernacle. The account of this pattern gives priority to the ark and the mercy seat, which are to be placed in the 'holy of holies' (or 'most holy place') (Exod 25:10-22, 26:33-34). The priority given to the ark and the mercy seat draws attention to the special character of these objects. Between the cherubim of the mercy seat is the designated place where the Lord will meet with his people (Exod 25:22).[5] The Lord's presence is localized at this place in a special way.[6]

In addition to the description of the Lord's presence in association with the mercy seat, the Lord's presence in the Tabernacle is also associated with two of the Hebrew terms used to refer to the Tabernacle. One Hebrew term that is often used to refer to the Tabernacle is משכן ('tabernacle' or 'dwelling place'). Since משכן is a derivative of שכן ('to dwell'), it is a fitting designation for the tent sanctuary established by God so that he might dwell among his people. It is a reminder of the primary purpose of the Tabernacle (see Exod 25:8).[7] Another designation for the Tabernacle is אהל מועד ('tent of meeting'). The noun מועד ('meeting') is derived from the verb יעד that appears in Exodus 25:22, 29:42-43 where it is translated 'meet.' In Exodus 29:42-43, the Lord makes it clear that he will meet with his people at the 'tent of meeting.' Thus this second name for the Tabernacle also is a reminder that the Tabernacle where God dwells is to be a special meeting place between God and his people. In order to meet with his people at the Tabernacle, the Lord's presence must be localized there in a

---

[3] On continuity with regard to worship, see 2 Chr 8:13; on structural continuity, see W. Shaw Caldecott and James Orr, 'Temple,' in *ISBE*, ed. J. Orr, vol. 5 (Chicago: Howard-Severance, 1915), 2931. Of course, it is not clear in Exodus that the Tabernacle is the antecedent for anything. Its character as an antecedent becomes clear through the establishment of the Temple as its divinely instituted successor (see below).

[4] It is common to find in Exod 25:8 an expression of the purpose for the Tabernacle (cf. Exod 29:45-46) (Brevard S. Childs, *The Book of Exodus: A Critical, Theological Commentary*, OTL [Philadelphia: Westminster, 1974], 540; Geerhardus Vos, *Biblical Theology: Old and New Testaments* [Grand Rapids: Eerdmans, 1954], 165).

[5] See also Num 7:89. Of course, it was not possible for the people or even the priests to look upon the presence of the Lord above the cherubim. Only one priest could enter the 'holy of holies' on the day of atonement, and even he was commanded to shield his view of the mercy seat with a cloud of incense (Lev 16:13).

[6] Cf. 1 Sam 4:4, 2 Sam 6:2 // 1 Chr 13:6, 2 Kgs 19:15. For the ark as the 'unoccupied throne of the deity,' see the evidence cited by Walther Eichrodt (*Theology of the Old Testament*, vol. 1, trans. J. A. Baker [Philadelphia: Westminster, 1961], 107-8).

[7] One finds שכן in both Exod 25:8, 29:45-46 where God's intention to dwell among his people is stated in connection with the building and consecration of the Tabernacle.

special way.⁸

A third indication of the Lord's presence in the Tabernacle can be found in its furnishings.⁹ Whatever else they may symbolize, the furnishings (including the table, the tableware, the lampstand, and the incense altar) draw attention to the nature of the Tabernacle as the Lord's residence, where he resides 'among his people' (Exod 29:45).¹⁰

In order for the Lord to be present among his people in the Tabernacle, certain preparations and safeguards need to be established. One of those safeguards involves the setting apart of holy space. Like the plan for the Temple, the plan for the Tabernacle includes the Tabernacle proper and a courtyard around it. The Tabernacle proper is divided into two parts, the 'holy place' and the 'holy of holies.' Their names, the laws governing access to them, and the materials used to construct the objects placed in them emphasize the special holiness of the 'holy place' and the 'holy of holies.'¹¹ Once the Tabernacle is built according to this plan, the next step is to sanctify it. Considerable attention is given to the sanctification of the Tabernacle, its

---

⁸ Cf. Philip P. Jenson, *Graded Holiness: A Key to the Priestly Conception of the World*, JSOTSup, no. 106 (Sheffield: JSOT Press, 1992), 113-4. Another idiomatic expression associated with the Lord's presence in the Tabernacle is the repeated use of לפני יהוה ('before the Lord' or 'in the presence of the Lord') (Exod 25:30, 27:21, etc.). The significance of this phrase as indicative of a temple or 'divine dwelling-place' has been called into question by Mervyn Fowler (for the position being opposed by Fowler, see Menahem Haran, *Temples and Temple-Service in Ancient Israel: An Inquiry into the Character of Cult Phenomena and the Historical Setting of the Priestly School* [Oxford: Clarendon, 1978], 26; for Fowler's treatment, see 'The Meaning of *lipnê* YHWH in the Old Testament,' *ZAW* 99 [1987]: 384-90). Based on Fowler's arguments, לפני יהוה (by itself) does not establish that the Tabernacle is the Lord's special dwelling place. Yet the reverse logic does appear to hold, i.e., since God is regarded as present in the Tabernacle in a special way, one is 'before the Lord' in a special way as one enters the Tabernacle (cf. Rainer Schmitt, *Zelt und Lade als Thema alttestamentlicher Wissenschaft: Eine kritische forschungsgeschichtliche Darstellung* [Gütersloh: Gütersloher Verlagshaus, 1972], 221; Ian Wilson, *Out of the Midst of the Fire: Divine Presence in Deuteronomy*, SBLDS, no. 151 [Atlanta: Scholars Press, 1995], 156-8, 194).

⁹ One common approach to the description of the Tabernacle is to find a symbolic meaning associated with each of its furnishings (see, for example, Vern S. Poythress, *The Shadow of Christ in the Law of Moses* [Brentwood, Tenn.: Wolgemuth and Hyatt, 1991], 18-25). Although the Tabernacle does appear to have a 'symbolic dimension,' the symbolic interpretation of its furnishings has produced too wide an array of possible associations for them to be given adequate consideration here (Childs, *Exodus*, 538-9; see the brief remarks by Vos, *Biblical Theology*, 168).

¹⁰ Menahem Haran, 'The Divine Presence in the Israelite Cult and the Cultic Institutions,' *Bib* 50 (1969): 255. Cf. Jenson, *Graded Holiness*, 113; U. Cassuto, *A Commentary on the Book of Exodus*, trans. Israel Abrahams (Jerusalem: Magnes, 1967), 336-8.

¹¹ Jenson, *Graded Holiness*, 89-103.

priests, and its contents (Exod 29:1-46, 30:22-33, 40:9-13; Lev 8-9). The sanctification of the Tabernacle is the point at which the completed Tabernacle is effectively set apart as God's sanctuary.[12]

After its sanctification, attention turns to maintaining the holiness of the Tabernacle. This has implications for the duties performed by the priests within the Tabernacle (for example, Exod 30:20). It also has implications for the daily life of the people. Since the Tabernacle of God is in their midst, the people of Israel must be purified from their uncleanness and their sins so that they will not defile the Tabernacle (Lev 15:31; Num 19:13). Sin offerings (also called purification offerings) are offered to atone for sins, to render unclean persons clean, and to purify God's sanctuary.[13] The concern for the purification of God's sanctuary is evident in Leviticus 4 where, depending on who sinned, blood from the sin offering is either sprinkled before the veil and applied to the horns of the incense altar in the holy place or applied to the horns of the altar of burnt offering.[14] This blood from the sin offering purifies God's sanctuary.[15]

In addition to the everyday sacrifices and rituals that are prescribed for dealing with sin and special conditions of uncleanness, one finds in Leviticus 16 the establishment of a yearly atonement ceremony. Through this ceremony, atonement is made for the Tabernacle, which means that it is re-purified and re-sanctified (Lev 16:16, 19).[16] The atonement for the Tabernacle is necessary due to the sin and uncleanness of the people. The 'atonement-day rituals' cleanse the Tabernacle in order to continue to 'permit the holy God to dwell among an unholy people.'[17]

One significant aspect of the account of the Tabernacle's construction and sanctification has been intentionally left out of the above treatment, because it deserves special treatment. After the sanctification of the Tabernacle and the priests is carried out by Moses, the stage is set for the Lord to appear to his

---

[12] The holiness word group (built on the Hebrew root קדש) is well represented in Exodus 25-40.

[13] See, in particular, Lev 4:1-6:7, 11:1-15:33; Gordon J. Wenham, *The Book of Leviticus*, NICOT (Grand Rapids: Eerdmans, 1979), 233.

[14] Ibid., 96; Jacob Milgrom, *Studies in Cultic Theology and Terminology* (Leiden: E. J. Brill, 1983), 73, 76-78; Baruch A. Levine, *In the Presence of the Lord: A Study of Cult and Some Cultic Terms in Ancient Israel* (Leiden: E. J. Brill, 1974), 104. On the significance of Lev 4 for graded sacrifices, see Jenson, *Graded Holiness*, 171-4. On the significance of blood for making atonement, see Lev 17:11.

[15] C. F. Keil and F. Delitzsch find a different significance in the blood sprinkled before the veil and applied to the altars in Lev 4. They see it as a 'preliminary and introduction to the expiation' (*The Pentateuch*, vol. 2, trans. James Martin, Biblical Commentary on the Old Testament [Grand Rapids: Eerdmans, 1966], 304). Cf. Wenham's response to this line of reasoning (*Leviticus*, 94).

[16] Wenham, *Leviticus*, 233; Milgrom, *Cultic Theology*, 78.

[17] Wenham, *Leviticus*, 233; cf. Jenson, *Graded Holiness*, 203 and Milgrom, *Cultic Theology*, 81.

people at the Tabernacle (Lev 9). Aaron is told to gather the people at the Tabernacle, for 'the Lord' is going to appear to them (Lev 9:3-4). At the gathering, Moses informs the people that 'the glory of the Lord' is going to appear to them (Lev 9:6). Thus one finds out that in this case it is by means of a visual manifestation of his glory that the Lord appears to his people.

In anticipation of the appearance of the Lord, Aaron presents a sin offering and a burnt offering for himself followed by a sin offering, burnt offering, grain offering, and peace offerings for the people. The various offerings are given considerable attention (Lev 9:2-4, 7-22), stressing their preparatory importance. Next, Aaron blesses the people and enters the tent of meeting with Moses. After Moses and Aaron exit the tent and bless the people, all the people behold the glory of the Lord. Part of the manifestation of glory is fire that comes 'from before the Lord' and consumes the offerings on the altar.[18] When the people see it, they shout and fall on their faces.

The appearance of the glory of the Lord at the Tabernacle in Leviticus 9 should be compared with its appearance in Exodus 40:34-38.[19] Leviticus 9 describes a particular occasion where the people are to make preparations for a special manifestation of the glory of the Lord at the Tabernacle. Exodus 40:34-35 simply draws attention to the fact that the cloud covers the tent of meeting, the glory of the Lord fills the Tabernacle, and Moses is therefore temporarily unable to enter the tent of meeting. It is not clear from Exodus 40:34 exactly how the glory of the Lord manifests itself in connection with the cloud. Together, the two accounts demonstrate that the Lord has now taken up residence in the midst of his people in a portable sanctuary. In addition, the appearance of the glory fulfills the Lord's promise to sanctify the Tabernacle with his glory (Exod 29:43).[20]

The accounts of the appearance of the glory of the Lord in the Tabernacle (Exod 40:34-35 and Lev 9) point to a significant correspondence between Mount Sinai and the completed Tabernacle. Prior to settling on Mount Sinai, the glory of the Lord manifested itself to the Israelites within a cloud (Exod

---

[18] Cf. Manfred Görg, *Das Zelt der Begegnung: Untersuchung zur Gestalt der sakralen Zelttraditionen Altisraels*, BBB, no. 27 (Bonn: Peter Hanstein Verlag, 1967), 64-66.

[19] Lev 9 and Exod 40:34-38 are probably describing two distinct events. Lev 9 depicts a special manifestation of the Lord's glory at the Tabernacle several days after it has been built and consecrated (cf. Num 14:10; 16:19, 42). Exod 40:34-38 is apparently referring to a manifestation of God's glory in the Tabernacle on the day of its completion and consecration (cf. Num 9:15; Exod 24:15-16).

[20] On Exod 29:43, see Cassuto, *Exodus*, 388; cf. also Léo Laberge, 'Le lieu que YHWH a choisi pour y mettre son Nom (TM, LXX, Vg et Targums). Contribution à la critique textuelle d'une formule deutéronomiste,' *EstBib* 43 (1985): 232. On the other hand, Keil and Delitzsch claim that Exod 29:43 teaches that Israel will be sanctified by God's glory (Keil, *Pentateuch*, vol. 2, 207-8).

16:10).²¹ In comparison with the cloud, the appearance of the glory of the Lord on Mount Sinai is the climactic visible and audible manifestation of the glory of the Lord. In Exodus 19:9-13, Moses is commanded to sanctify the people in preparation for the appearance of the Lord on Mount Sinai. The Lord also orders Moses to set apart Mount Sinai as a restricted, holy place (Exod 19:12-13, 23). The Lord's appearance on Mount Sinai is visibly and audibly demonstrated with thunder, lightning, a thick cloud, a loud trumpet sound, fire, smoke, and an earthquake (vv. 16, 18). The spectacle causes the people to tremble (Exod 19:16, 20:18).

One finds another instance of the appearance of the Lord on Mount Sinai in Exodus 24. In this chapter, the appearance of the Lord is perceived in a special way by Moses, Aaron, Nadab, Abihu, and seventy elders of Israel (vv. 1, 10). The preparations for this appearance include building an altar, offering sacrifices, reading the 'book of the covenant,' and sprinkling the 'blood of the covenant' on the people. As in Exodus 19:20, Moses alone is summoned to ascend to the top of the mountain (24:12). While Moses is on the mountain, the 'glory of the Lord' is visibly manifested upon it, taking the form of a fire veiled in a cloud (vv. 16-17).

The special appearances of the Lord on Mount Sinai emphasize the Lord's holiness and power. In each case, preparations are made for the Lord's appearance and access to Mount Sinai is limited, because it has been set apart as a holy place. When the Lord appears in the Tabernacle in Leviticus 9, one finds a similar pattern. The laws for sanctifying the Tabernacle, for limiting access to it, and for regulating the various offerings bring order to the preliminary rituals. After the preparatory rites, the Lord's glory manifests itself there by fire (Lev 9:23-24). At Mount Sinai and at the Tabernacle, the visual manifestation of the Lord's glory evokes reverence and fear (Exod 19:16, 20:18; Lev 9:24).²² Its manifestation in the Tabernacle acts as a reminder to the people that the God who dwells in the Tabernacle is the same God whose power and glory they beheld on Mount Sinai. He is to be held in awe and his commandments are to be obeyed.²³

After the initial appearance of God's glory in the Tabernacle, the Tabernacle becomes the locus for further special manifestations of God's glory (Num 14:10; 16:19, 42; 20:6). Three of these manifestations depict God's glory appearing to all of the people (Num 14:10; 16:19, 42). Each of these occasions involves situations where God appears in order to judge some or all of his

---

²¹ When the pillar of cloud and fire is introduced, it is said to symbolize the Lord going before them (Exod 13:21).

²² Cf. the parallel to Exod 19-20 in Deut 5.

²³ God's commandments are so important that God writes them on stone tablets and has them placed in the ark, which is placed in the 'holy of holies.'

people for significant acts of rebellion.[24] God's power is vividly demonstrated in Numbers 16 where the earth splits and swallows up the families of the rebellious Levites, and these Levites themselves are consumed with fire from the Tabernacle (Num 16:35). God's glory also apparently manifests itself privately to Moses and Aaron (Num 20:6), which is comparable to what one observes when Joshua is commissioned (Deut 31:14-15).

In addition to special manifestations of God's glory in the Tabernacle, God's presence in the Tabernacle is also suggested by the pillar of cloud, which becomes a pillar of fire at night (Exod 40:34-38; Num 9:15-23, 14:14). The pillar of cloud and fire previously symbolized the presence of the Lord leading his people (Exod 13:21-22), and the Lord's glory appeared in it during their travels (Exod 16:10).[25] A cloud and fire were also associated with the theophanies of the Lord on Mount Sinai, where God's glory was perceived as a raging fire (Exod 19:16, 18; 24:15-18). After the completion of the Tabernacle, the pillar of cloud and fire rests upon it and continues to guide Israel's movements, as it did prior to their arrival at Mount Sinai. When the pillar moves from over the Tabernacle, the people break camp and follow it until it stops.

The above treatment touches briefly upon the combination of regulations, terminology, miraculous signs, and revelatory events that establish the special character of the Tabernacle as God's dwelling place in the midst of his people. After its sanctification, the Lord is able to reside within the camp, instead of at some point outside the camp.[26] As the Lord's dwelling place, the Tabernacle becomes the central place for revelation, including visible manifestations of God's glory. In this regard, it is the successor to Mount Sinai. At the Tabernacle, God meets with particular persons or with the people in general.[27] The Tabernacle's presence within the camp, along with the entry of the priests and the people into it, means that attention must be given to the purification of the Tabernacle, the priests, and the people. The laws pertaining to sacrifices dealing with uncleanness and sins are reminders that the holy God cannot simply overlook the unholiness of his people. They are to be holy as well (Lev 19:2).

The Tabernacle is a place where the mundane and the miraculous intersect. The detailed nature of the laws for the Tabernacle's design and sanctification

---

[24] Cf. also Numbers 12 where Miriam and Aaron sin by speaking against Moses. God appears to them at the Tent of Meeting and inflicts Miriam with leprosy.

[25] Cf. Yves Congar, who points out that the cloud is 'the phenomenon in and by means of which the Glory is revealed' (*The Mystery of the Temple or the Manner of God's Presence to His Creatures from Genesis to the Apocalypse*, trans. Reginald Trevett [Westminster, Md.: Newman Press, 1962], 10).

[26] The pillar of cloud and fire, Mount Sinai, and the original Tent of Meeting were all apparently outside the camp (Exod 13:21, 16:10, 19:2, 33:7). See Numbers 2 for the placement of the tribes around the Tabernacle.

[27] See, for instance, Lev 1:1, 9:1-24.

are complemented by detailed laws pertaining to the priests, Levites, and common people. These laws refer to realities that can be measured and many of them are to be integrated into daily life. Alongside these apparently mundane realities, one observes miraculous manifestations of God's glory in the Tabernacle that are reminders of the grand significance of the Tabernacle, the priesthood, and the offerings. The Tabernacle is established by God to be a central part of the ongoing relationship between himself and his people. The privilege of being God's chosen people and of having God dwell in their midst cannot be separated from the ethical demands that accompany the covenant between God and his people.[28] The manifestations of God's glory in the Tabernacle are powerful reminders of the promise found in Exodus 29:45, 'I will dwell among the Israelites and will be their God.'[29]

Deuteronomy's Expectation of a 'Place that the Lord Your God Will Choose'

The Tabernacle's placement in the midst of the camp means that it is attached to one place only as long as the camp remains at that place. When the people are on the verge of crossing over into the promised land, Moses says that in the promised land the Lord will choose a place in the promised land for his sanctuary. In Deuteronomy, the place is consistently referred to as 'the place that the Lord your God will choose.' This phrase can stand alone or be coupled with 'to put his name there' or 'to make his name dwell there' (or both).[30] The phrase, along with its expansions, is often referred to as the 'centralization formula.'[31] As it stands in Deuteronomy, the phrase apparently means that the Lord will choose one place for the location of his sanctuary in the promised

---

[28] Cf. Lev 26.

[29] See esp. Lev 26:11-12, Ezek 37:27, Rev 21:3. For other instances where the Lord promises that he 'will be their God,' see Gen 17:8; Lev 26:45; Jer 24:7, 31:33, 32:38; Ezek 34:24, 37:23; Zech 8:8; 2 Cor 6:16; Heb 8:10 (cf. Hos 2:23). For other instances where the Lord promises that he 'will dwell among' his people, see 1 Kgs 6:13; Ezek 43:7, 9; Zech 2:10-11 (MT vv. 14-15).

[30] For the phrase without additions, see 12:18, 26; 14:25; 15:20; 16:7, 15, 16; 17:8, 10; 18:6; 31:11; with the addition of 'to put his name there,' see 12:5, 21; 14:24; with 'to make his name dwell there,' see 12:11; 14:23; 16:2, 6, 11; 26:2; for the use of all three phrases (with the last phrase altered somewhat), see Deut 12:5. Cf. Gordon J. Wenham, 'Deuteronomy and the Central Sanctuary,' *TynBul* 22 (1971): 112; Josef Schreiner, *Sion-Jerusalem Jahwes Königssitz: Theologie der Heiligen Stadt im Alten Testament* (München: Kösel Verlag, 1963), 158.

[31] For a full discussion of the 'centralization formula' and its various forms, see J. G. McConville and J. G. Millar, *Time and Place in Deuteronomy*, JSOTSup, no. 179 (Sheffield: Sheffield Academic Press, 1994), 89-123; Norbert Lohfink, 'Zur deuteronomischen Zentralisationsformel,' *Bib* 65 (1984): 297-329; Baruch Halpern, 'The Centralization Formula in Deuteronomy,' *VT* 31 (1981): 20-38.

land.[32] The people are to bring their offerings, sacrifices, and tithes to this place (Deut 12:6, 11). In addition, they are to gather at the chosen place three times a year in order to celebrate certain festivals 'before the Lord' (Deut 16).

Due to a seminal study by Gerhard von Rad, the two expansion phrases ('to put his name there' or 'to make his name dwell there') are often read as indications of a distinctive theology of the presence of God in Deuteronomy.[33] Von Rad's basic thesis is that the phrases 'to put his name there' and 'to make his name dwell there' are used in Deuteronomy as a corrective. The phrases represent an attempt to correct the 'old crude idea of Jahweh's presence and dwelling at the shrine' by replacing it with the presence of the name.[34] After von Rad, Deuteronomy's emphasis upon the connection between the sanctuary and the name is frequently interpreted as an attempt to safeguard and defend the transcendence of God.[35] If von Rad and others are right, one finds in Deuteronomy a 'name theology' that stands in conscious opposition to earlier notions, which affirmed the actual presence of God in the Tabernacle.[36] In contrast to the 'name theology' of Deuteronomy, one also finds a 'glory theology' in the Priestly document (P) that promotes a different, distinctive conception of the presence of God.[37] As a result, 'name theology' and 'glory theology' emerge as competing, incompatible theological conceptions that attempt to put forward a proper understanding of God's presence in the

---

[32] McConnville and Millar, *Time and Place in Deuteronomy*, 120-21; Jeffrey Niehaus, 'The Central Sanctuary: Where and When?,' *TynBul* 43 (1992): 4, 7; Wenham, 'Deuteronomy and the Central Sanctuary,' 110-2, 114-5. For summary and discussion of other possible interpretations, see McConville and Millar, *Time and Place in Deuteronomy*, 89-110, 117-22; J. Gordon McConville, *Law and Theology in Deuteronomy*, JSOTSup, no. 33 (Sheffield: JSOT Press, 1984), 21-29.

[33] Gerhard von Rad, 'Deuteronomy's "Name" Theology and the Priestly Document's "Kabod" Theology,' trans. David Stalker, in *Studies in Deuteronomy* (Chicago: Henry Regnery, 1953), 37-44.

[34] Ibid., 38-39.

[35] See, for example, Samuel Terrien, *The Elusive Presence: Toward a New Biblical Theology* (New York: Harper and Row, 1978), 199-201; Moshe Weinfeld, *Deuteronomy and the Deuteronomic School* (Winona Lake, Ind.: Eisenbrauns, 1992), 191-209; R. E. Clements, *God and Temple* (Philadelphia: Fortress, 1965), 94-96.

[36] F. Dumermuth even attempts to trace the development and influence of 'name theology' through the OT, as well as to isolate the place of its origin ('Zur deuteronomischen Kulttheologie und ihren Voraussetzungen,' *ZAW* 70 [1958]: 59-98).

[37] This 'glory theology' could be a further movement away from the older conception of the Lord's constant presence in the Tabernacle (see J. G. McConville, 'God's "Name" and God's "Glory,"' *TynBul* 30 [1979]: 150; Von Rad, *Old Testament Theology*, vol. 1, 238-9; Eichrodt, *Theology of the Old Testament*, vol. 1, 106-7). On the other hand, it could be taking up and developing 'corporeal' representations of the glory of God drawn from 'ancient traditions' (McConville, 'God's "Name" and "Glory,"' 150; Weinfeld, *Deuteronomy*, 204-6).

Tabernacle (and Temple).[38]

The conception of the 'name theology' developed by von Rad and others is not, however, the only way to interpret the connection between the name and the chosen place apparent in Deuteronomy's centralization formula.[39] This centralization formula occurs for the first time in Deuteronomy 12:5. In Deuteronomy 12, the Lord's placement of his name stands in marked contrast to the command to remove the 'name' of other gods from the promised land ('that place').[40] The Lord's chosen place in the promised land will only become evident after Israel has entered the land and been granted rest from its enemies (12:10). Having given the land to his people (Deut 12:1), it becomes appropriate for the Lord to select a place for his sanctuary. The phrases 'to put his name there' and 'to make his name dwell there' could both be Hebrew equivalents for an idiomatic expression found in other Ancient Near Eastern documents.[41] According to this idiom, to place or establish one's name somewhere 'is an affirmation of ownership, the equivalent of taking possession.'[42] Thus the idiom conveys the Lord's exclusive ownership of the place where he establishes his sanctuary.[43] In a land where 'places' dedicated to other gods once stood (Deut 12:2), the Lord will choose a place that will be

---

[38] For an instructive response to this attempt to define incompatible 'name' and 'glory' theologies, see McConville, 'God's "Name" and "Glory,"' 149-63. McConville finds that the incompatibility of 'name theology' and 'glory theology' as described by von Rad and others cannot be sustained in light of certain texts where elements of these conceptions appear together without apparent friction (e.g., 2 Sam 6:2, 1 Kgs 8:10-12) ('God's "Name" and "Glory,"' 151, 153). Instead, the glory of God is distinguished from the name of God in the OT in that the glory of God is closely bound up with 'dramatic, exceptional divine manifestations, or when some emphasis is laid on God's majesty' ('God's "Name" and "Glory,"' 161). The distinction between the name and glory of God in the OT is consistent with Exod 33:18-23 where Moses is able to hear God's name, but has to be 'shielded from a full view of God's glory' ('God's "Name" and "Glory,"' 154).

[39] For a summary of the other possibilities and their proponents, see Wilson, *Out of the Midst of the Fire*, 8-9. Cf. also the critical comments by James C. De Young, *Jerusalem in the New Testament: The Significance of the City in the History of Redemption and in Eschatology* (Kampen: J. H. Kok, 1960), 46-47.

[40] Deut 12:2-3; Wenham, 'Deuteronomy and the Central Sanctuary,' 113.

[41] Ibid., 113-14; Roland de Vaux, 'Le lieu que Yahvé a choisi pour y établir son nom,' in *Das ferne und nahe Wort: Festschrift Leonhard Rost*, ed. Fritz Maass (Berlin: Alfred Töpelmann, 1967), 221, 224-5; Schreiner, *Sion-Jerusalem*, 163. De Vaux thinks that these two phrases express the same thing ('Le lieu que Yahvé a choisi,' 224). Haran suggests the use of שכן in the phrase 'to make his name dwell there' may be an intentional use of terminology associated with the Tabernacle (משכן) ('Divine Presence,' 260).

[42] This is Wenham's translation of de Vaux (Wenham, 'Deuteronomy and the Central Sanctuary,' 113).

[43] It may also have conquest overtones (Ibid., 114).

associated with his name, and his name alone.[44]

In addition, if the author of Deuteronomy really had serious misgivings about the actual presence of the Lord in his chosen sanctuary, he could have made this clearer. No indication of uneasiness is given with regard to the Lord's visible and audible manifestation of his presence on Mount Sinai, nor with his ability to speak with his people from the midst of the fire.[45] It is even stated that the Lord spoke with them 'face to face at the mountain from the midst of the fire' (Deut 5:4).[46] Assuming that the actual presence of the Lord in his chosen sanctuary is objectionable to the author of Deuteronomy, why does he appear to be quite comfortable with language that would suggest the actual presence of the Lord on Mount Sinai? In addition, Deuteronomy does not qualify the expression לפני יהוה ('before the Lord'), which appears multiple times in connection with 'the place that the Lord your God will choose.' The multiple uses of לפני יהוה are further evidence that the author of Deuteronomy was not trying to avoid language that could imply the presence of the Lord in his chosen sanctuary.[47] Third, Deuteronomy 31:14-15 does not include any hint of hesitation when it describes how 'the Lord appeared' in the tent of meeting.[48]

Although the evidence for a distinctive 'name theology' in Deuteronomy is not compelling, the centralization formula does make a distinctive contribution to the theology of the Tabernacle and Temple. The repetition of 'the place that

---

[44] McConville, 'God's "Name" and "Glory,"' 162. Also, Exod 20:24, which brings together sacrifice, 'place,' and the Lord's name, is significant background for Deut 12 (de Vaux, 'Le lieu que Yahvé a choisi,' 223-35; Lohfink, 'Zur deuteronomischen Zentralisationsformel,' 318).

[45] McConville and Millar, *Time and Place in Deuteronomy*, 115; Wilson, *Out of the Midst of the Fire*, 57-60; contra Weinfeld, *Deuteronomy*, 206-8. The observation that the Lord spoke with his people 'from the midst of the fire' is represented multiple times (Deut 4:12, 15, 33, 36; 5:4, 22, 23, 24, 26; 9: 10, 21; 10:4). For a full review of the pertinent evidence, see Wilson, *Out of the Midst of the Fire*, 45-129. In its reference to the pillar of cloud and fire, Deuteronomy shows further continuity with Exodus. According to Deut 1:33, the pillar of cloud and fire is the visible manifestation of the Lord, who goes before them.

[46] See Wilson's discussion of this verse (*Out of the Midst of the Fire*, 76-78).

[47] See Deut 12:7, 12, 18; 14:23, 26; 15:20; 16:11, 16; 18:7; 26:5, 10, 13. See Wilson, *Out of the Midst of the Fire*, 152-9, 192-7; McConville and Millar, *Time and Place in Deuteronomy*, 115; McConville, 'God's "Name" and "Glory,"' 159; Jenson, *Graded Holiness*, 113. Cf. also von Rad, *Studies in Deuteronomy*, 40; Tryggve Mettinger, *The Dethronement of Sabaoth: Studies in the Shem and Kabod Theologies*, trans. Frederick H. Cryer, ConBOT, 18 (Lund: CWK Gleerup, 1982), 53.

[48] One should note, however, that Deut 31:15 is often dismissed as being '*post-deuteronomistic*' (Wilson, *Out of the Midst of the Fire*, 53). For further evidence against the 'name theology' espoused by von Rad and others that is related to the content of Deuteronomy as a whole, see McConville, 'God's "Name" and "Glory,"' 161-2; for an overview of the evidence against the 'name theology,' see Wilson, *Out of the Midst of the Fire*, 209-17.

the Lord your God will choose' gives primary emphasis to God's choice of the place where his people are to establish his sanctuary.[49] The centralization formula does not entail, however, that God will choose only one place for all time.[50] The close association between the chosen place and the Lord's name sets this place apart, that is, it belongs to the Lord.

The initial fulfillment of the centralization formula is associated with Shiloh.[51] The Tabernacle is set up at Shiloh (Josh 18:1) and it is mentioned as the site for 'annual pilgrimages' (Judg 21:19-21, 1 Sam 1:3).[52] In Jeremiah 7:12, one finds evidence of a connection between the centralization formula of Deuteronomy and Shiloh.[53] The Old Testament accounts of the Tabernacle at Shiloh have challenged the categories of scholars, because it is sometimes referred to as a היכל ('palace,' 'temple') or as the בית יהוה ('house of the Lord').[54] Such evidence does not, however, rule out the possibility that the Tabernacle constructed during the time of Moses is the structure that stood at Shiloh.[55]

---

[49] McConville and Millar, *Time and Place in Deuteronomy*, 122.
[50] Ibid.
[51] For a review of the evidence for Shechem, Gilgal, and Bethel as possible sites for the central sanctuary, see Wenham, 'Deuteronomy and the Central Sanctuary,' 105-8; McConville, *Law and Theology in Deuteronomy*, 23-27. For a survey of the evidence (from Joshua through Kings) for obedience to the centralization laws of Deuteronomy, see Niehaus, 'The Central Sanctuary,' 9-17.
[52] Wenham, 'Deuteronomy and the Central Sanctuary,' 107. In agreement with Deut 12:10, the Tabernacle is apparently set up in Shiloh at a point when Israel has been given 'rest' from its enemies (cf. Josh 18:1, 21:44, 22:4) (Roddy Braun, 'Solomon, the Chosen Temple Builder: The Significance of 1 Chronicles 22, 28, and 29 for the Theology of Chronicles,' *JBL* 95 [1976]: 584).
[53] Jer 7:12 refers to Shiloh as the 'place' where 'I made my name dwell at first,' which is clearly linked with Deuteronomy's 'place' chosen by the Lord 'to make his name dwell there.'
[54] For היכל, see 1 Sam 1:9, 3:3; for בית יהוה, see Judg 18:31; 1 Sam 1:7, 24 (also, Deut 23:18). The Tabernacle is also said to have doors and a doorpost (1 Sam 1:9, 2:22, 3:15). Cf. Clements, *God and Temple*, 38.
[55] See the discussion in Franz Delitzsch, *Biblical Commentary on the Psalms*, trans. Francis Bolton, vol. 1, Biblical Commentary on the Old Testament, vol. 12 (Grand Rapids: Eerdmans, 1971), 123-5; Haran, *Temples and Temple-Service*, 201-2; Niehaus, 'The Central Sanctuary,' 17-18; L. Whitelaw, 'Tabernacle,' in *ISBE*, ed. J. Orr, vol. 5 (Chicago: Howard-Severance, 1915), 2894. Haran notes that 'talmudic sages' noticed and sought to address this difficulty. The most significant evidence for the fact that the structure at Shiloh was a tent and not a building comes from 2 Sam 7:6. 2 Sam 7:6 affirms that the Lord's dwelling place among his people has always been a tent (*Temples and Temple-Service*, 202). Further evidence can be found in 1 Sam 2:22, where the Tent of Meeting is mentioned in reference to the same structure earlier called היכל (1:9) and בית יהוה (1:7). One can also find evidence in 2 Sam 12:20, where the author can call the

The transition from Shiloh to Jerusalem is not a smooth one. The abuses of Eli's sons bring judgment upon Eli, his sons, and his descendants (1 Sam 2:27-36, 3:11-14). In preparation for a battle with the Philistines, Eli's sons accompany the ark from the Tabernacle at Shiloh to the camp of Israel's army (4:4). During the battle, the ark is captured and Eli's sons are killed (4:11). The event is punctuated with the proclamation of Eli's daughter-in-law that the 'glory has departed from Israel, for the ark of God was taken' (4:22).[56] According to Psalm 78:56-59, Eli and his sons are not the only ones to blame for this tragic event. The people are to blame as well, for they have not been faithful to God.[57] Thus, due to the sins of Israel, the Lord has abandoned the Tabernacle at Shiloh (Ps 78:60).

The Old Testament does not clearly identify another chosen place for the Lord's dwelling in Israel until one finds such an identification in connection with the Jerusalem Temple (2 Sam 7:13). In the period after the capture of the ark and prior to the Temple dedication, the ark and the Tabernacle are never reunited. During this period, the Tabernacle apparently moves from Shiloh to Nob to Gibeon (1 Sam 21:1-6; 1 Chr 16:39, 21:29). Having been returned by the Philistines, the ark is eventually brought to Jerusalem by David (1 Sam 7:1, 2 Samuel 6). The ambiguity created by this situation is evident from the fact that the author of Kings attributes sacrifices at the high places to the absence of a 'house built for the name of the Lord' (1 Kgs 3:2, NASB).[58]

In conclusion, within Deuteronomy 12-26 one finds numerous references to 'the place that the Lord your God will choose' together with 'to put his name there' or 'to make his name dwell there.' Deuteronomy 12-26 contains laws that specify under what circumstances the Israelites are to appear before God at this place. These laws make it clear that Israel's worship of the Lord is to be centralized at the place of God's choosing. The first place chosen by God is identified in the Old Testament as Shiloh. Yet the initial choice of Shiloh is jeopardized by the unfaithfulness of Israel, and God abandons it. The Lord's departure from Shiloh emphasizes the conditional nature of the relationship between the Lord and his designated dwelling place among his people. God can abandon his chosen place if his people disregard the laws that are integral to his covenant relationship with them. He can even choose a new place for his dwelling among his people. Deuteronomy's expectation of a 'place that the Lord your God will choose' and the account of God's abandonment of Shiloh

---

tent David set up for the ark 'the house of the Lord' (see 2 Sam 6:17-18). See also Josh 6:24, Ps 78:60, and Acts 7:45-47.

[56] On the significance of 1 Sam 4:22, see Schreiner, *Sion-Jerusalem*, 30-31.

[57] See, for instance, Judg 18:31.

[58] Niehaus, 'The Central Sanctuary,' 15-16. More could be said about this period, but one finds in it more questions than answers. It is not clear why the ark and the Tabernacle are never reunited. According to 1 Chr 16, David provides for the worship of the Lord at the tent in Jerusalem where the ark is kept and at the Tabernacle in Gibeon.

are brought together in Jeremiah 7:12-15. Here, the Lord's abandonment of Shiloh is used as a warning for those who find false security in connection with the Temple in their midst. Examination of the centralization formula of Deuteronomy and the abandonment of Shiloh prepares the way for consideration of the election of Jerusalem as the site for the Temple and of the Temple's replacement of the Tabernacle.

The Establishment of the Temple as a Legitimate Replacement for the Tabernacle

In the account of the establishment of the Temple, one finds significant parallels to the account of the establishment of the Tabernacle. These parallels put forth the Temple as the legitimate replacement for the Tabernacle. Before discussing the common features of the two accounts, attention should be given to a unique element that distinguishes the introduction of the Temple from that of the Tabernacle. According to Exodus 25:1-9, the Tabernacle is initiated solely by God, not Moses. On the other hand, some initiative for the Temple can be attributed to David (2 Sam 7:2). Although God does not permit David to build a temple for him, he affirms David's request by appointing one of his sons to do so (2 Sam 7:13).

An analogy is often drawn between God's response to David's plan for building a temple and God's response to Israel's request for a king (1 Sam 8).[59] The proposal to build a temple, like the request for a king, may arise from a desire to bring Israel into conformity with the nations around it.[60] On the basis of 2 Samuel 7:5-7 and the analogy with God's response to Israel's request for a king, one might conclude that God is displeased with David's proposal to build a temple and seek to uncover the reasons for God's displeasure.[61] Yet the analogy between God's response to the people's request for a king and God's

---

[59] P. Kyle McCarter Jr, *II Samuel: A New Translation with Introduction, Notes and Commentary*, AB, vol. 9 (Garden City, N.Y.: Doubleday, 1984), 227; J. Gordon McConville, 'Jerusalem in the Old Testament,' in *Jerusalem Past and Present in the Purposes of God*, ed. Peter W. L. Walker, 2nd ed. (Grand Rapids: Baker, 1994), 29.

[60] This is clearly stated in the case of the request for a king (1 Sam 8:5). In the case of the proposal for the Temple, scholars find evidence for the close connection in Ancient Near Eastern thought 'between the establishment of a royal dynasty and the provision of a temple for the dynastic god' (McCarter, *2 Samuel*, 224; cf. Eckhard von Nordheim, 'König und Tempel: Der Hintergrund des Tempelbauverbotes in 2 Samuel vii,' *VT* 27 [1977]: 442-5). Victor Hurowitz examines relevant Ancient Near Eastern parallels to David's initiative in proposing to build a Temple and to God's response to him (*I Have Built You an Exalted House: Temple Building in the Bible in the Light of Mesopotamian and Northwest Semitic Writings*, JSOTSup, no. 115 [Sheffield: JSOT Press, 1992], 136-67).

[61] The possibilities explored by those who follow this view are well presented by McCarter (*2 Samuel*, 226-7).

response to David's proposal for building a temple is not exact enough to permit one to establish firmly such an inference. God's response to the people's request for a king is characterized by clear and emphatic reluctance (see 1 Sam 8). On the other hand, God's response to David's proposal for building a temple makes it clear that God does not require a temple (2 Sam 7:5-7), but it does not give any clear indications as to why a temple would be undesirable (cf. 1 Sam 8:11-18). Furthermore it is possible to interpret 2 Samuel 7:5-7 without finding in it evidence that God regards David's proposal as 'presumptuous.'[62]

The context of 2 Samuel 7:5-7 provides further evidence that God's response to David's proposal should not be characterized as anti-Temple. Indeed, those who would characterize 2 Samuel 7:2-16 as a clear rejection of David's proposal for a temple find it necessary to dismiss v. 13 as a later interpolation.[63] Considered in its final form, Nathan's oracle apparently approves of the building of a temple, but postpones it (2 Sam 7:13).[64] Given the final form of 2 Samuel 7, vv. 5-7 defend David's predecessors for not having built a temple and assure David that he, likewise, is not at fault for building a 'house of cedar' for himself and not for God.[65] These verses also precede and introduce God's promises to David concerning the establishment of David's 'house,' that is, his dynasty (2 Sam 7:8-16). Thus, given the context, 2 Samuel 7:5-7 may introduce a point of clarification regarding God's gracious election of David and his sons. Taken as a unit, 2 Samuel 7:2-16 affirms that God's election of David and his sons is not an honor that God gives to David for building a temple. This is in marked contrast to Mesopotamian parallels where the 'building of a temple is a favor the king does for his god and for which he expects a reward,' including divine favor during his rule and that of his sons.[66]

One finds allusions to David's initiative and God's postponement of the building of the Temple elsewhere (1 Kgs 5:3-5, 8:16-19 [// 2 Chr 6:7-9]; 1 Chr 22:7-11, 28:2-6). First Kings 8:18 (// 2 Chr 6:8) is an important addition to the

---

[62] C. F. Keil and F. Delitzsch, *The Books of Samuel*, trans. James Martin, Biblical Commentary on the Old Testament, vol. 5 (Grand Rapids: Eerdmans, 1960), 342. For the contrary view, see McCarter, *2 Samuel*, 226-7.

[63] 2 Sam 7:13 is often regarded as a 'Deuteronomistic interpolation' (McCarter, *2 Samuel*, 205-6; cf. Clements, *God and Temple*, 56 and Nordheim, 'König und Tempel,' 436).

[64] Cf. 1 Chr 17:12, 14; McCarter, *2 Samuel*, 206.

[65] Cf. 2 Sam 7:2 and 7:7; McCarter, *2 Samuel*, 227.

[66] Hurowitz, *Exalted House*, 291-9; cf. McCarter, *2 Samuel*, 224. William Riley, whose focus is the parallel text in 1 Chr 17, appeals to the same parallels in defense of the opposite view. He suggests that the dynastic promise and David's victories are blessings that result from David's concern for the ark and the cultus (William Riley, *King and Cultus in Chronicles: Worship and the Reinterpretation of History*, JSOTSup, 160 [Sheffield: JSOT, 1993], 66-76). This seems unlikely, since the Lord's blessings on David can be traced back to his youth, long before David's concern for the ark and cultus (see, for example, 2 Sam 5:10 // 1 Chr 11:9; 2 Sam 7:8-9 // 1 Chr 17:7-8).

above discussion, because it reports the Lord's approval of David's initial desire to build the Temple. Another significant addition is the role played by the ark of the covenant in providing impetus for David's desire to build a temple in Jerusalem. As reported in 2 Samuel 7:2, David's desire to build the Temple is closely linked with his transfer of the ark to Jerusalem.[67] After an initial failure, David becomes convinced to bring the ark to Jerusalem, due to the blessings associated with its presence in the house of Obed-edom (2 Sam 6:12). David places the ark in a special tent and the narrative moves immediately to David's intention to build a 'house of cedar' for it (2 Sam 7:2 // 1 Chr 17:1). According to 2 Samuel 6:2 // 1 Chronicles 13:6, the ark is closely tied to the Lord's name and presence.[68] As noted above, David senses the incongruity between his 'house of cedar' and the Lord's presence in a tent (2 Sam 7:2, 7). Thus the successful transfer of the ark to Jerusalem prepares the way for David's proposal to build the Temple. The prominence given to the ark here fits well with the prominence given to it in the pattern for the Tabernacle (Exod 25:10-22). The ark is presented as the focal point for David's aspirations to build a temple in Jerusalem.[69]

Even though David is not permitted to build a temple in Jerusalem, the Chronicler, unlike the author of Kings, gives considerable prominence to David's crucial preparatory role in the building of the Temple. First, the future site for the Temple is revealed to David in 1 Chronicles 21:18-22:1. The revelation comes as a result of the plague brought on by David's census (1 Chr 21:1). The angel of the Lord instructs David to build an altar on the threshing floor of Ornan the Jebusite to stop the plague. David buys the threshing floor and builds an altar on it (1 Chr 21:18-25). After David's burnt offerings and peace offerings are placed on the altar, David prays and the Lord answers him with 'fire from heaven' that consumes his sacrifices (1 Chr 21:26). In response to these events, David proclaims, 'Here is the house of the Lord God, and here is the altar of burnt offering for Israel' (1 Chr 22:1). Thus David regards the fire

---

[67] See 2 Samuel 6. The transfer of the ark is given more attention in 1 Chronicles (see chapters 13, 15, 16). David's reasons for the first attempt to transfer the ark to Jerusalem are not stated explicitly, although attention is drawn to past neglect of the ark (1 Chr 13:3). One does notice that in the narrative it follows soon after David becomes established as the king of Israel in Jerusalem (2 Sam 5:6-12). The transfer of the ark to Jerusalem may thus follow naturally from David's desire to establish the religious and political centrality of Jerusalem within Israel (Nordheim, 'König und Tempel,' 444; cf. Keil, *Samuel*, 326-7). Hence the election of David and the election of Jerusalem as the Lord's dwelling place are closely bound together (cf. Ben Ollenburger's strained attempts to keep the election of Zion and David separate in *Zion the City of the Great King: A Theological Symbol of the Jerusalem Cult*, JSOTSup, no. 41 [Sheffield: JSOT Press, 1987], 59-66).

[68] Cf. Schreiner, *Sion-Jerusalem*, 44-46.

[69] It also plays a prominent role in the dedication of the Temple (1 Kgs 8:4-11 // 2 Chr 5:4-14).

from heaven as a sign that the Lord has chosen this place as the site for his Temple and altar. The closest precedent for this event is found in Leviticus 9:24, where a similar, miraculous manifestation of fire consumes the sacrifices on the altar before the Tabernacle. It also foreshadows a similar event, even more reminiscent of Leviticus 9:24, that occurs at the time of the dedication of the Temple (2 Chr 7:1).[70] The Chronicler moves immediately from the choice of a site for the Temple to David's provisions for the Temple (1 Chr 22:2-5).

In 1 Chronicles 22-29, David emerges 'as a cult founder alongside Moses.'[71] Although David gives due recognition to Moses (1 Chr 22:13), he finds himself at a unique juncture where provisions need to be made to update the law of Moses, particularly with regard to the duties of the Levites who no longer need to carry the Tabernacle (1 Chr 23:26, Num 4). In addition, the priests and Levites are generally in need of re-organization due to the neglect of previous years, and David plays a significant part in this re-organization (1 Chronicles 23-26). Afterwards, David's name and authority become connected with his re-organization of the Levites (2 Chr 23:18; 29:25; 35:4, 15; Neh 12:24, 45). This is only the first in a number of parallels between Moses and David in Chronicles.

One finds several parallels between David and Moses in 1 Chronicles 28 and 29, which should be read against the background of Exodus 25 and 35.[72] Already in 1 Chronicles 22:6-19, David has commissioned the chosen Temple builder, Solomon (1 Chr 22:6-16), and enlisted the support of the leaders (1 Chr 22:17-19).[73] The commissioning of Solomon is repeated in 1 Chronicles 28. In the act of commissioning, David takes on a role analogous to Moses, while Solomon is analogous to Bezalel (Exod 31:1-5, 35:30-33).[74] The most

---

[70] H. G. M. Williamson, 'The Temple in the Books of Chronicles,' in *Templum Amicitiae: Essays on the Second Temple Presented to Ernst Bammel*, ed. William Horbury (Sheffield: JSOT, 1991), 20; Rudolf Mosis, *Untersuchungen zur Theologie des chronistischen Geschichtswerkes*, Freiburger theologische Studien, no. 92 (Freiburg: Herder, 1973), 150-2.

[71] Simon J. DeVries, 'Moses and David as Cult Founders in Chronicles,' *JBL* 107 (1988): 619; cf. Clements, *God and Temple*, 129.

[72] Roddy Braun, *1 Chronicles*, WBC, vol. 14 (Waco: Word Books, 1986), 272, 279-80; H. G. M. Williamson, *1 and 2 Chronicles*, NCB (Grand Rapids: Eerdmans, 1982), 182-3.

[73] For a comparison between David's commissioning of Solomon and Moses' commissioning of Joshua, see Braun, 'Solomon, the Chosen Temple Builder,' 586-8.

[74] Cf. Braun, *1 Chronicles*, 272, who also points out verbal parallels between 1 Chr 28:20-21 and Exodus 25-31, 35-40. The analogy between Solomon and Bezalel is further aided by the Chronicler's account of the building of the Temple. One notices in 2 Chr 3-4 that ויעש ('and he made') is used repeatedly to begin paragraphs starting with 2 Chr 3:8. It is a pattern more prevalent in 2 Chronicles 3-4 than in 1 Kings 6-7. Solomon is the implied subject of this verb, except in 2 Chr 3:11-16 (see 2 Chr 3:3, 4:18-22). One finds a similar pattern in Exod 36:8-39:32 where ויעש occurs almost forty times, with

significant parallel between David and Moses is David's role as the inspired recipient of the תבנית ('pattern') for the Temple, Temple-service, and its vessels (1 Chr 28:11-19, Exod 25:9).[75] Next, David, like Moses, asks the people to give materials for use in the construction of the Temple (1 Chr 29:1-9; Exod 25:2-7, 35:4-29).[76]

The above evidence sets David apart as the recipient of the divine revelation necessary for establishing the Temple.[77] David receives revelation concerning the Temple's location, chosen builder, design, furnishings, and patterns for worship. Thus the Chronicler's account of the establishment of the Temple provides ample evidence for the conviction that the Temple, like the Tabernacle, is established by means of explicit revelation from God. Initial divine approval for the desire to build a Temple is complemented by revelation sufficient to establish the Temple and Temple-service.[78]

The parallels between the establishment of the Tabernacle as recounted in Exodus and the Chronicler's account of the establishment of the Temple establish continuity between the two events. H. G. M. Williamson claims that the Chronicler draws attention to these parallels in order to present the Temple as 'a focus of unity for the people of Israel as a whole.'[79] As the legitimate successor to the Tabernacle, the Temple takes its place, becoming the chosen focal point for the worship of the God of Israel.

The pattern for the establishment of the Tabernacle found in Exodus is not the only pattern that lends credibility to the Temple as the Tabernacle's legitimate successor. Exodus's account of the establishment of the Tabernacle is concerned with the chosen builder, the design, the furnishings, and the

---

Bezalel as its implied subject (Exod 37:1, 38:22). On this pattern, see John Van Seters, 'The Chronicler's Account of Solomon's Temple-Building: A Continuity Theme,' in *The Chronicler as Historian*, ed. M. P. Graham, K. G. Hoglund, and S. L. McKenzie, JSOTSup, no. 238 (Sheffield: JSOT, 1997), 291-2; Williamson, *Chronicles*, 208.

[75] In 1 Chr 28:19, David says, 'All this I have in writing from the hand of the Lord upon me, and he gave me understanding in all the details of the plan.' DeVries finds the language of 1 Chr 28:19 to be the Chronicler's most noteworthy claim for the authority of revelation given to David, placing it on a par with that of Moses. He notes, 'David has received revelation equivalent in authority to that of Sinai, offered in a new 'writing' of law for the metamorphosis of the Israelite cult' (DeVries, 'Moses and David,' 626).

[76] David is distinct from Moses in that he is presented as the foremost contributor (1 Chr 29:1-5). For verbal parallels that strengthen the links between these two offerings, see Braun, *1 Chronicles*, 279-80.

[77] Note that the Chronicler sometimes qualifies God's revelation to David by making it clear that God speaks to David by means of prophets (1 Chr 21:18, 2 Chr 29:25).

[78] For divine approval, see 2 Sam 7:13 (// 1 Chr 17:12) and 1 Kgs 8:18 (// 2 Chr 6:8).

[79] Williamson, 'Temple in the Books of Chronicles,' 19; cf. Braun, *1 Chronicles*, xxxvii. By relating the site of the Temple to Mount Moriah (2 Chr 3:1), the Chronicler further establishes the legitimacy of the Temple as a special place of revelation and 'focus of unity' for Israel (Williamson, 'Temple in the Books of Chronicles,' 19-25).

patterns for worship, but it is not until Deuteronomy that Moses sets out God's plan for the establishment of his sanctuary in the promised land. One of the elements of this plan is that God will choose the place where he will dwell (Deut 12:5). Another element is that God will 'give rest' to his people, which involves security from all of their enemies (Deut 12:10).[80] The Lord first chooses Shiloh as the site for the Tabernacle, and it is set up there at a time when the Lord has granted rest to his people (Jer 7:12; Josh 11:23, 18:1, 21:44). The sin of the priests and the people brings about the capture of the ark (1 Sam 4). It is not until the reign of David that one finds once again a period when the Lord gives rest to his people from all of their enemies (2 Sam 7:1, 11).[81]

If David and Israel have been given rest from their enemies (2 Sam 7:1), then why is David not permitted to build a temple? The Chronicler, in particular, clarifies that the Lord granted rest to Solomon in a more complete and final way than he did to David (1 Chr 22:9, 1 Kgs 5:4, 8:56).[82] David is characterized as a 'man of war' (1 Chr 28:3) who has been involved in a lot of bloodshed. On the other hand, Solomon is characterized as a 'man of rest' and during his reign the Lord will give 'peace and quiet to Israel' (1 Chr 22:9).[83] Therefore the Lord chooses Solomon to build the Temple and promises that during his reign Israel will experience the rest and peace appropriate for the establishment of the Temple (1 Chr 22:9-10).

If the Deuteronomic requirement of 'rest' from enemies is satisfied during

---

[80] The hiphil of the verb נוח ('rest') and the noun מנוחה ('resting-place' or 'rest') are used in Deut 12:9-10. Apart from other uses in Deuteronomy (3:20, 25:19), one finds these words used in Joshua, 2 Samuel, and 1 Kings with regard to the 'conquest of the land by Joshua (Josh 1:13, 15; 21:44; 22:4; 23:1), the dynastic promise to David (2 Sam 7:1, 11), and the erection of the temple by Solomon (1 Kgs 5:18; 8:56)' (Braun, 'Solomon, the Chosen Temple Builder,' 583). The Chronicler uses the hiphil of נוח in contexts where 'rest' sets the stage for the building of the Temple (1 Chr 22:9, 18) and the reassignment of the Levites to new duties (1 Chr 23:25). The Temple is also presented as the בית מנוחה ('house of rest') for the ark (1 Chr 28:2). Afterwards, the hiphil of נוח is used where the Lord 'gives rest' during the reign of other kings after Solomon (2 Chr 14:6-7, 15:15, 20:30 [and perhaps 32:22]) (Braun, *1 Chronicles*, 225).

[81] One should also note that the notion of 'planting' the people of Israel makes 2 Sam 7:10 // 1 Chr 17:9 an interesting parallel to Exod 15:17 (cf. McCarter, *2 Samuel*, 202-4).

[82] Braun, 'Solomon, the Chosen Temple Builder,' 584; Sara Japhet, *1 and 2 Chronicles: A Commentary*, OTL (Louisville: Westminster/John Knox, 1993), 397; Mosis, *Theologie des chronistischen Geschichtswerkes*, 94-101. Cf. also Martin Schmidt, *Prophet und Tempel: Eine Studie zum Problem der Gottesnähe im Alten Testament* (Zürich: Evangelischer Verlag, 1948), 94, 96.

[83] In 1 Chr 22:9, the juxtaposition of the name שלמה ('Solomon') and the noun שלום ('peace') involves a play on words that draws out the association between Solomon's name and 'peace' (Japhet, *1 and 2 Chronicles*, 398; Mosis, *Theologie des chronistischen Geschichtswerkes*, 96).

the first part of Solomon's reign, so is the requirement of a chosen place.[84] After David becomes king, he brings the ark to Jerusalem and desires to build a 'house of rest' for it (1 Chr 28:2). God declares to David that he does not merely want to establish a house for himself (2 Sam 7:13). God also wants to appoint a place for his people and plant them securely in it (2 Sam 7:10-11).[85] Since the Tabernacle and Temple are designed for God to dwell in the midst of his people (Exod 25:8, 1 Kgs 6:13), it follows that when God plants his people securely in their own place then he no longer needs to dwell in a portable Tabernacle.[86] It is appropriate at that point to establish a 'house' for God to take the place of his former dwelling place, a 'tent.'[87] It is against this background that God reveals to David the proper site for the Temple (1 Chr 21:18-22:1, 2 Chr 3:1).

The Chronicler further indicates that the chosen site corresponds to Mount Moriah, where Abraham almost sacrificed Isaac (2 Chr 3:1, Genesis 22).[88] Equating the Temple site with Mount Moriah demonstrates that the site already had a special place in the history of Israel. The Chronicler's unique emphasis upon the divine election of the site for the Temple enhances its legitimacy. The Chronicler is not alone in affirming the divine election of Jerusalem or Zion. It is well-represented elsewhere, especially in the Psalms.[89] In providing additional unique historical background for the election of the Temple site, the Chronicler further establishes the legitimacy of the Temple as an appropriate 'focus of unity for the people of Israel.'[90]

As observed above, the Chronicler makes a particular point of the legitimacy of the Temple itself and its site. The preparations for building it conform to the pattern for the construction of the Tabernacle. The choice of the site and time for the construction conform to the applicable Deuteronomic pattern. These considerations set up the framework necessary for the Lord's approval of the

---

[84] The rest Solomon experiences from his enemies is short-lived due to his sinful behavior (1 Kgs 11:9-14, 23, 26).

[85] Cf. Exod 15:17; McCarter, *2 Samuel*, 202-4.

[86] Cf. 2 Sam 7:6-11.

[87] Cf. 2 Sam 7:6.

[88] Japhet, *1 and 2 Chronicles*, 551.

[89] See, for example, Pss 78:68, 132:13-14; also, 1 Kgs 8:44, 11:36. For further references and discussion, see De Young, *Jerusalem in the New Testament*, 42-44. Zion first appears in 2 Sam 5:7 where it is used synonymously with 'the city of David' and Jerusalem (v. 6) (for an overview of the use of Zion in the OT, see W. Harold Mare, 'Zion,' in *ABD*, ed. David Noel Freedman, vol. 6 [New York: Doubleday, 1992], 1096-7). Indeed, in the OT, 'any basic distinction between Zion and Jerusalem is seldom present or implied.' Where a distinction is present, Zion or Mount Zion can be used to refer to the site of the Temple within Jerusalem (De Young, *Jerusalem in the New Testament*, 32; cf. Mare, 'Zion,' 1096).

[90] Williamson, 'Temple in the Books of Chronicles,' 19-25.

Temple.[91] The Lord demonstrates his approval of the Temple by filling it with his glory.[92] In both Chronicles and Kings, the glory of the Lord fills the Temple at the time of its dedication (1 Kgs 8:10-11 // 2 Chr 5:11-14). The glory of the Lord manifests itself after the ark is placed in the 'holy of holies' and the priests come out of the 'holy place.' With the placement of the ark in the Temple, the Temple is completed.[93] When one compares this with Exod 40:33-35, one finds that the cloud and the glory of the Lord fill the Tabernacle just after Moses completes it. The focus upon the placement of the ark is not just due to its contribution to the completion of the Temple. The placement of the ark is also significant as a climactic point in the building of the Temple, because it is an important locus of continuity between the Tabernacle and the Temple. It calls attention to the covenant made with Israel at Sinai (1 Kgs 8:9 // 2 Chr 5:10) and is closely associated with the presence of God (2 Sam 6:2 // 1 Chr 13:6, Exod 25:22).[94]

The Chronicler's interest in the legitimacy of the Temple emerges again with regard to the glory of the Lord filling the Temple. He portrays a second manifestation of the glory of the Lord in the Temple after Solomon finishes praying.[95] It is parallel to the first in that the glory of the Lord fills the Temple and the priests cannot enter it (2 Chr 7:2), but it adds that fire comes down from heaven and consumes the sacrifices on the altar (v. 1). The people's response to this is also given. They prostrate themselves before the Lord and worship him (v. 3). The people's response and the fire from heaven is parallel to Leviticus 9:23-24.[96] The inability of the priests to enter the Temple is parallel to the situation of Moses in Exodus 40:34-35. The timing of the fire from heaven (just after Solomon's prayer) is particularly reminiscent of David's prayer and the Lord's response with fire from heaven (1 Chr 21:26). Thus the second manifestation of glory simultaneously brings out associations with the Tabernacle and with the revelation to David of the site for the Temple. Second Chronicles 7:1-3 gives further evidence for the legitimacy of both the Temple site and the Temple itself.

---

[91] For discussion of the Chronicler's unique elements that draw attention to the parallels between the actual building of the Temple and the building of the Tabernacle, see Van Seters, 'Chronicler's Account of Solomon's Temple-Building,' 283-300; Williamson, 'Temple in the Books of Chronicles,' 26-27.

[92] Williamson, *Chronicles*, 222.

[93] Mosis, *Theologie des chronistischen Geschichtswerkes*, 153.

[94] It is also central to the Day of Atonement ritual (Lev 16:11-17).

[95] Commentators disagree as to whether there are two manifestations of the glory of the Lord filling the Temple in 2 Chronicles or just one incident whose description is repeated (Raymond B. Dillard, *2 Chronicles*, WBC, vol. 15 [Waco: Word Books, 1987], 56). Japhet and Keil favor two separate manifestations of the glory of the Lord (Japhet, *Chronicles*, 609; C. F. Keil, *The Books of the Chronicles*, trans. Andrew Harper, Biblical Commentary on the Old Testament, vol. 7 [Grand Rapids: Eerdmans, 1966], 330-2).

[96] Mosis, *Theologie des chronistischen Geschichtswerkes*, 151-2.

As observed at several points above, the Chronicler's account contains more information relevant to the establishment of the Temple as the chosen house of the Lord than one finds in the books of Samuel and Kings. By providing additional information about the establishment of the Temple, the Chronicler strengthens the case for the legitimacy of the Temple as the Lord's chosen sanctuary. In both Kings and Chronicles, divine approval of the Temple is connected with the manifestation of the glory of the Lord at the time of its dedication. Divine approval is later confirmed by a special revelation given to Solomon (1 Kgs 9:3 // 2 Chr 7:16). As with the Tabernacle, the manifestation of the glory of the Lord is also evidence that the Lord has taken up residence in the Temple.[97] The next section will consider further the continuity between the Tabernacle and the Temple as the dwelling place of God among his people.

The Temple as the Lord's Dwelling Place in the Midst of His People

The Temple is presented in the Old Testament as the new dwelling place of God in the midst of his people. The significance of the Temple as the new dwelling place of God ties its significance to that of its predecessor, the Tabernacle. Its significance is given further clarification in the dedication speech of Solomon and in the Psalms. After its dedication and initial days of glory, the practical implications of the Temple's significance are worked out in conjunction with the peaks and valleys evident in the fortunes of the divided kingdom. The following section examines the Temple's significance from its emergence as the successor of the Tabernacle to the brink of its destruction by the Babylonians.

The same features that set apart the Tabernacle as the special dwelling place of God find parallels in the Temple. The first such feature is the ark of the covenant placed in the holy of holies.[98] Second are the common designations for the Temple. The most common designation for the Temple is בית יהוה ('house of the Lord') or בית אלהים ('house of God').[99] It 'arises from the concept of divine residence and expresses the intrinsic nature of the institution, which was primarily conceived as the god's dwelling place.'[100] Another common designation is היכל ('palace' or 'temple'), which could also be applied to the residence of a king (1 Kgs 21:1). Like בית יהוה, היכל points to the nature of the

---

[97] The second appearance of the glory of the Lord provides further evidence for this since it is a response to Solomon's prayer (see 2 Chr 6:41 // Ps 132:8) (Mosis, *Theologie des chronistischen Geschichtswerkes*, 148).

[98] It is associated with the presence of God in Exod 25:22, 2 Sam 6:2 // 1 Chr 13:6.

[99] While the Tabernacle could be figuratively referred to as a בית יהוה ('house of the Lord'), this designation is considered more suitable for a solid structure like the Temple (BDB, 108). For its application to the Tabernacle, see Judg 18:31; 1 Sam 1:7, 24.

[100] Haran, *Temple and Temple-Service*, 13.

Temple as God's dwelling place.[101] A third common feature is to be found in the furnishings of the Temple, which are patterned after those of the Tabernacle.[102] As noted in the discussion of the Tabernacle, these furnishings have symbolic significance as objects appropriate for the divine residence.

Since the Temple replaces the Tabernacle, the Mosaic laws pertaining to the Tabernacle must be applied to it.[103] Both are constructed according to the same basic pattern of 'graded holiness' with a courtyard, a 'holy place,' and a 'holy of holies.'[104] The continuity between the general layout of the Tabernacle and the Temple allows for ready application of the Mosaic laws pertaining to holy space, the duties of the priests, the sacrifices, and the festivals.[105] Thus the variations in size and quantity of furnishings that distinguish the Temple from the Tabernacle do not preclude adherence to the Mosaic law within it.[106] The sanctification of the Temple is a noteworthy point of restoration for Israel. It is finally in a position to resume the offering of appropriate sacrifices to God in a structure that contains all of the essential features of the Tabernacle, including the ark of the covenant. The Temple is accepted by God as an appropriate 'house of sacrifice' (2 Chr 7:12).

The appearance of the Lord's glory in the Temple draws attention to its unique character as the new place where the Lord dwells (1 Kgs 8:10-11 // 2 Chr 5:13-14, 2 Chr 7:1-3). It marks the Temple as the chosen dwelling place for the same God whose glory appeared in the pillar of cloud, on Mount Sinai, and in the Tabernacle. Like the Tabernacle, the final step of its sanctification is accomplished by the glory of the Lord (Exod 29:43).

The significance of the glory of the Lord, which is visibly manifested in the form of a cloud, is picked up in Solomon's first words on the occasion of the dedication of the Temple (1 Kgs 8:12-13 // 2 Chr 6:1-2). Just after the cloud fills the Temple, Solomon says, 'The Lord has said that he would dwell in a dark cloud' (1 Kgs 8:12). The Lord's words that are being referred to are probably those found in Exodus 19:9, where the Lord tells Moses that he will appear on Mount Sinai in a 'thick cloud.'[107] Solomon's first words (1 Kgs 8:12)

---

[101] As with בית יהוה, היכל could be applied figuratively to the Tabernacle (1 Sam 1:9, 3:3), but is considered more appropriate for a 'large, luxurious house' (Ibid., 14). For discussions of other designations for the Temple, see ibid., 14-15.

[102] For a discussion of the parallels between the furnishings, see Van Seters, 'Chronicler's Account of Solomon's Temple-Building,' 292-9.

[103] Cf. 1 Kgs 2:3, 1 Chr 22:13.

[104] Cf. Jenson, *Graded Holiness*, 90-92.

[105] Cf. 1 Chr 6:49; 2 Chr 8:13; 23:18; 24:6, 9; 30:16; 35:6, 12.

[106] With regard to quantity of furnishings, the ten lampstands and ten tables set in the holy place are prominent examples (1 Kgs 7:49; 2 Chr 4:7-8, 19-20).

[107] The exact word used by Solomon is ערפל ('dark cloud'), which appears in Exod 20:21; Deut 4:11, 5:22. In Exodus, the wording of Exod 19:9, בעב הענן ('in a thick cloud'), is essentially synonymous with ערפל. On the significance of ערפל in the OT, see Schreiner, *Sion-Jerusalem*, 153.

point to the continuity between the cloud in which the Lord's dwelling among his people manifested itself in the past and the cloud that fills the Temple.[108] Next, Solomon affirms that the Temple has been built as a house for the Lord so that it might be his dwelling place forever (1 Kgs 8:13 / / 2 Chr 6:2).[109]

Solomon follows up on these words by recounting the history of the Temple, highlighting David's desire to build a 'house for the name of the Lord' (1 Kgs 8:17 / / 2 Chr 6:7).[110] He sees the Temple as part of the initial fulfillment of the Lord's promises to David (1 Kgs 8:20-21 / / 2 Chr 6:10-11). Solomon prays that the Lord would also fulfill the dynastic promises he made to David (1 Kgs 8:25-26 / / 2 Chr 6:16-17).

The next section of Solomon's prayer (1 Kgs 8:27-53 / / 2 Chr 6:18-39) does not deny that the Lord dwells in the Temple (see 1 Kgs 8:12-13 / / 2 Chr 6:1-2).[111] Instead, it both qualifies and develops the significance of the Temple as the Lord's dwelling place. In 1 Kings 8:27 / / 2 Chronicles 6:18, Solomon clarifies that he does not suppose that God is a finite being who has become a resident within the Temple.[112] God is much greater than that, such that not even the heavens can contain him (1 Kgs 8:27). While God's presence in the Temple does not limit him to this one location, the Temple is not thereby robbed of significance. Solomon's prayer defines the special nature of the Temple as a locus for communication between the Lord and his people. He asks that the Lord will always be attentive to the prayers offered toward or within the Temple, even those offered by a non-Israelite.[113] Solomon's repetition of 'in this house' or 'toward this house' in connection with prayers is just as pronounced as his repetition of 'in heaven,' which denotes God's dwelling

---

[108] Williamson, *Chronicles*, 216.

[109] Cf. the similar language in 2 Sam 7:5 / / 1 Chr 17:4.

[110] This section of Solomon's speech is parallel to what one finds in 2 Sam 7:5-16 / / 1 Chr 17:4-14 (also, 1 Chr 22:7-11, 28:2-10).

[111] Contra Weinfeld, *Deuteronomy*, 195. The implications of Solomon's prayer for the dwelling of God among his people are consistent with what one finds in Exodus and Deuteronomy. In Exodus, God can be said to speak to his people 'from heaven' (20:22) and still be represented as present on Mount Sinai (19:17-24, 20:21) (cf. Exod 33:18-23, 34:5-6; McConville, *Time and Place in Deuteronomy*, 113). In Deuteronomy, one finds the juxtaposition of the belief that the Lord's dwelling place is in heaven (26:15) and the implication that he is present in a special way in his sanctuary on earth (26:5, 10) (cf. Deut 4:36, 39; Wilson, *Out of the Midst of the Fire*, 214-6; McConville, *Time and Place in Deuteronomy*, 113, 135-8).

[112] C. F. Keil, *The Books of the Kings*, trans. James Martin, Biblical Commentary on the Old Testament, vol. 6 (Grand Rapids: Eerdmans, 1950), 127. Cf. also 2 Chr 2:6 (MT v. 5).

[113] 1 Kgs 8:29-30 / / 2 Chr 6:20-21; also, 1 Kgs 8:33-48 / / 2 Chr 6:24-38. Solomon also asks that the Lord would be attentive to oaths taken before the altar of the Temple (1 Kgs 8:31-32 / / 2 Chr 6:22-23).

place.[114] Thus the people are to pray in or toward the Temple and God will answer them from heaven. In making the Temple the central locus for prayer, Solomon is affirming the special place of the Temple in the relationship between God and his people.

Later, the Lord answers Solomon's prayer with a promise that his eyes and heart will always be present at his Temple, where he has placed his name (1 Kgs 9:3 // 2 Chr 7:16).[115] The presence of the eyes and heart along with the placement of the Lord's name there 'express the intimate relation of God himself to the temple, and, hence, to the city and people of Israel.'[116] Solomon's prayer and the Lord's response to it give some clarification to the manner in which the Lord dwells among his people in the Temple. As the Lord's dwelling place (1 Kgs 8:13), the Temple does not constitute the exclusive spatial location of the Lord. Instead, it is a particular place that the Lord chooses for relating to his people.[117]

The special significance attributed to the Temple in the contents of Solomon's Temple dedication speech and prayer is also attributed to it in the Psalms. Like Solomon, the Psalmists confidently affirm that the Lord dwells in the Temple on Mount Zion.[118] At the same time, they affirm that the Lord dwells in heaven.[119] The Temple is his footstool.[120] The Lord also hears the prayers of his people that are prayed in or toward his Temple.[121] In addition, the Psalmists draw out the implications of these beliefs by means of poetic imagery.

According to the Psalmists, one of the implications of the Lord's presence

---

[114] For prayers 'in this house,' see 1 Kgs 8:33 // 2 Chr 6:24; for prayers 'toward this house' (with slight variations), see 1 Kgs 8:29-30, 35, 38, 42, 44, 47 // 2 Chr 6:20-21, 26, 29, 32, 34, 38. For 'in heaven, your dwelling place,' see 1 Kgs 8:30, 39, 43, 49 // 2 Chr 6:21, 30, 33, 39; for 'in heaven,' see 1 Kgs 8:32, 34, 36, 45 // 2 Chr 6:23, 25, 27, 35.

[115] Cf. 2 Chr 7:14-15. The phrase 'to put my name there' in 1 Kgs 9:3 corresponds to the phraseology of Deuteronomy discussed above (cf., for example, Deut 12:5).

[116] De Young, *Jerusalem in the New Testament*, 48. Cf. Martin J. Selman, 'Jerusalem in Chronicles,' in *Zion, City of Our God*, ed. Richard S. Hess and Gordon J. Wenham (Grand Rapids: Eerdmans, 1999), 50.

[117] Cf. Jon Levenson, who says, 'As the junction between heaven and earth, Zion, the Temple mount, is a preeminent locus of communication between God and man' (*Sinai and Zion: An Entry into the Jewish Bible* [San Francisco: Harper and Row, 1985], 125).

[118] For example, see Pss 11:4; 26:8; 43:3; 46:4 (MT v. 5); 63:2 (MT v. 3); 68:24 (MT v. 25); 74:2-4; 76:2 (MT v. 3); 80:1 (MT v. 2); 99:1-2, 5; 132:5, 7, 13-14; 135:21.

[119] For example, see Pss 20:6 (MT v. 7), 33:13-14, 80:14 (MT v. 15), 102:19 (MT v. 20), 103:19, 113:5, 115:3, 123:1.

[120] Pss 99:5, 132:7 (cf. 1 Chr 28:2, Lam 2:1). Cf. Haran, *Temples and Temple-Service*, 256.

[121] For example, see Pss 18:6 (MT v. 7), 20:1-9 (MT vv. 2-10), 28:2. On Ps 18:6, see Hans-Joachim Kraus, *Psalms 1-59: A Commentary*, trans. Hilton C. Oswald, CC (Minneapolis: Augsburg, 1988), 260.

among his people in the Temple is the inviolability of Jerusalem and the Temple. The Lord's people can dwell in security, because he will defend them from the attacks of their enemies.[122] Yet it should be noted that the security of the Lord's people is dependent upon their faithful obedience to the Torah.[123] Indeed a second implication of the Lord's presence in the Temple is the necessity for Israelites to commit themselves to living righteous lives. This is directly related to worship in the Temple in Psalms 15 and 24. Here the Psalmist considers the question of the qualifications necessary for standing before the Lord in the Temple (Pss 15:1, 24:3).[124] Psalms 15:2-5, 24:4 reply to the Psalmist's question with a description of the righteous person. Taken with utmost seriousness, these verses would seem to prohibit all people from entering into the Temple.[125] They present a picture of the ideal worshiper. Jon Levenson claims that these verses call worshipers who would enter the Temple to 'pledge allegiance to the ideal' portrayed in them.[126] The idealization of those who seek entry into the Temple leads quite naturally to consideration of the idealization of the Temple itself as the most desirable dwelling place for the righteous worshiper.

The Lord's presence in the Temple sets it apart from other places. As the site of the Temple, Zion becomes the 'perfection of beauty' (Ps 50:2) and 'the joy of the whole earth' (Ps 48:2). In Psalm 27:4, the Psalmist asks the Lord to permit him to dwell in the Temple all the days of his life so that he can 'gaze upon the beauty of the Lord' and 'seek him in his temple.'[127] It is a special place of refuge for him (Ps 27:5).[128] Psalm 84 also expresses an intense longing for the Temple.[129] One day spent in the Temple is better than a thousand spent elsewhere (84:10).[130]

---

[122] See especially Psalms 46, 48, 76.

[123] David experiences victory over his enemies in accordance with the Lord's promise (2 Sam 7:11 // 1 Chr 17:10), bringing security to Israel (1 Kgs 8:56, 1 Chr 22:18). Even so, according to the Torah itself, Israel's security is conditional (cf. Lev 26, Deut 28). This becomes evident in the accounts of the kings after David and Solomon. See also Pss 18:16-29 (MT vv. 17-30), 50:16-22, 81:11-16 (MT vv. 12-17). Cf. Aubrey R. Johnson, *Cultic Prophet and Israel's Psalmody* (Cardiff: University of Wales Press, 1979), 100.

[124] Kraus, *Psalms 1-59*, 227-8; Levenson, *Sinai and Zion*, 171-2.

[125] Kraus, *Psalms 1-59*, 229; Levenson, *Sinai and Zion*, 174; Peter C. Craigie, *Psalms 1-50*, WBC, vol. 19 (Waco: Word, 1983), 153.

[126] Levenson, *Sinai and Zion*, 175.

[127] Regarding 'to dwell in the house of the Lord,' Craigie notes, 'The statement should not be taken literally, as if referring to a temple servant who would actually live perpetually within the temple precincts' (*Psalms 1-50*, 232).

[128] Cf. Ps 61:4 (MT v. 5). On the Temple as the ideal place of refuge, see Hans-Joachim Kraus, *Theology of the Psalms*, trans. Keith Crim (Minneapolis: Augsburg, 1986), 159-60.

[129] Cf. Ps 63:1 (MT v. 2).

[130] Cf. Ps 26:8, 42:1-4 (MT vv. 2-5), 43:3-4.

In addition to being a place of refuge and an ideal place, the Temple is linked with the abundance of God's provision for his people. Psalm 36:7-9 presents the most vivid picture of this when it says, 'Both high and low among men find refuge in the shadow of your wings. They feast on the abundance of your house; you give them drink from your river of delights. For with you is the fountain of life; in your light we see light.' Psalm 65:4 expresses a similar sentiment.[131] In Psalms 36:7-9 and 65:4, the Psalmist links God's abundant provision for his people directly with his Temple.[132] In Psalm 36:8-9, one finds the introduction of the 'river of delights' and 'the fountain of life.' The 'river of delights' of Psalm 36:8 is particularly interesting in that 'delights' is the plural of עֶדֶן, which is the noun associated with the proper name עֵדֶן ('Eden').[133] Psalm 46:4 also describes a river in connection with the Temple.[134] The river image of Psalms 36:8, 46:4 is language of divine blessing and provision that recalls the river of Eden (Gen 2:10).[135]

Taken as a whole, the above idealizations of the Temple as a unique place draw attention to its special character. The Lord's presence in the Temple makes the Temple and Zion a special place of revelation and beauty (Pss 27:4, 50:2, 63:2). Thus the Temple is the most desirable place for the worshiper who wants to understand who God is and to communicate with him. It is also a place of refuge and blessing due to the character of the God who dwells there.[136] This does not mean that communication with God and experience of God's blessings are limited to the Temple. Instead, it means that the Temple is represented as the most ideal place for communion between God and his faithful worshiper.[137] As such, the ideal nature of the communion between God and his people in the Temple makes the Temple a beatific place comparable to the Garden of Eden.

---

[131] Ps 65:4 (MT v. 5): 'How blessed is the one whom You choose, and bring near to You, To dwell in Your courts. We will be satisfied with the goodness of Your house, Your holy temple' (NASB).

[132] The peace (or fellowship) offerings shared by God and the worshiper already point in this direction (see Lev 3) (Delitzsch, *Psalms*, vol. 2, 6; Levenson, *Sinai and Zion*, 132).

[133] BDB, 726-27; Levenson, *Sinai and Zion*, 132.

[134] Ps 46:4 (MT v. 5): 'There is a river whose streams make glad the city of God, the holy place where the Most High dwells.'

[135] Delitzsch, *Psalms*, vol. 2, 94; Kraus, *Psalms 1-59*, 399, 462-63; Kraus, *Theology of the Psalms*, 80-81; Schreiner, *Sion-Jerusalem*, 222. The Psalmist does not point out that the Gihon spring of Jerusalem (cf. 2 Chr 32:30) has the same name as one of the rivers of Eden (Gen 2:13) (Richard J. Clifford, *The Cosmic Mountain in Canaan and the Old Testament*, HSM, vol. 4 [Cambridge: Harvard University Press, 1972], 160; Levenson, *Sinai and Zion*, 131).

[136] Pss 36:5-9 (MT vv. 6-10), 61:3-4 (MT vv. 4-5), 84:10-11 (MT vv. 11-12).

[137] See Ps 42:2-4 [MT vv. 3-5] (Kraus, *Psalms 1-59*, 439); Pss 27:4, 84:1-4 (MT vv. 2-5).

This is in line with the promise expressed in Leviticus 26:12.[138] Like the language of the Psalmist, it also alludes to a more ideal time in the history of God's dealing with humankind when the Lord was able to walk in the midst of humankind in the Garden of Eden (Gen 3:8). In the Garden of Eden, God provided abundantly for Adam and Eve (Gen 2:16, 3:17-19). Similarly, the locus for God's presence in the midst of his people and God's abundant provision for his people is the Temple.[139]

Clearly, the full measure of the blessings associated with the Lord's presence in the Temple, like the Lord's guaranteed protection or deliverance, is not available to everyone. As noted above, the ideal worshiper is righteous (Pss 15:2-5, 24:4). Such a one is able to enter the Temple and is qualified to receive the Lord's blessing (Ps 24:5). In addition, the blessed nature of the life of the righteous one is described in terms of a healthy tree that is planted in the Temple (Pss 92:12-14, 52:8). This tree metaphor brings together elements of the divine blessing lavished upon the righteous one, including nearness to God, abundant provision, and longevity.[140] The Temple is thus the ideal place for the righteous person to dwell, and it is where he yearns to be more than any other place.[141]

Although the righteous ones do not literally take up permanent residence in the courts of the Temple, they are the ones most qualified to experience the blessings associated with communion with God.[142] The Temple is the designated locus for this communion and is therefore represented as the point to which the righteous one is drawn (Ps 43:3-4). The figurative language of the Psalms, and especially the tree metaphor mentioned above, suggests that the actual spatial location of the righteous person does not tell the whole story. No matter where the righteous person dwells, the Temple is central to his or her life and well-being. Such a conception is integrally related to God's presence in the Temple as promised to Solomon. God promised that his eyes and heart would

---

[138] Lev 26:12: 'I will walk among you and be your God, and you shall be my people.' Lev 26:12 follows the promise that God will establish a place to dwell in the midst of his people (v. 11).

[139] Pss 36:7-9 (MT vv. 8-10), 65:4 (MT v. 5). For further discussion of the connections between the Garden of Eden and the Temple, see Gordon J. Wenham, 'Sanctuary Symbolism in the Garden of Eden Story,' in *'I Studied Inscriptions from before the Flood': Ancient Near Eastern, Literary, and Linguistic Approaches to Genesis 1-11*, ed. Richard S. Hess and David T. Tsumura (Winona Lake, Ind.: Eisenbrauns, 1994), 399-404.

[140] Cf. Artur Weiser, *The Psalms: A Commentary*, trans. Herbert Hartwell, OTL (Philadelphia: Westminster, 1962), 616; Kraus, *Psalms 1-59*, 511; Hans-Joachim Kraus, *Psalms 60-150: A Commentary*, trans. Hilton C. Oswald (Minneapolis: Augsburg, 1989), 230.

[141] Cf. Pss 23:6, 26:8, 27:4, 36:5-9 (MT vv. 6-10), 42:1-4 (MT vv. 2-5), 43:3-4, 61:4 (MT v. 5), 63:1-5 (MT 2-6), 65:4 (MT v. 5), 84:1-12 (MT vv. 2-13).

[142] Cf. Levenson, *Sinai and Zion*, 178.

always be present in the Temple, setting it apart as a special place of communion with his people (1 Kgs 9:3 // 2 Chr 7:16).[143] As such, the Temple is the most appropriate place for God's people to seek him and to direct their prayers to him. The Psalmists go a step further by presenting the Temple as the central point out of which God's blessings flow, especially into the lives of the righteous ones among God's people.[144] According to the Psalmists, the Temple is the central hub for the lives of the righteous ones who trust in God and look to experience the beatific life. It is the place associated with the peak of human existence.

The Psalmists' emphasis upon the connection between divine blessing and human righteousness or faithfulness is an emphasis that one also finds in the historical accounts in the books of Kings and Chronicles. Just after the dedication of the Temple, God reminds Solomon that the dynastic promise made to David is conditional. David's sons must follow God faithfully like David did. If they do not, God will remove Israel from the land and will desert the Temple (1 Kgs 9:4-9 // 2 Chr 7:17-22). The king has a significant role to play in the future of Israel and of the Temple. If he is righteous, the king can expect to experience God's blessings like David did. If he is not, the king can expect God's discipline to come upon him and his people (2 Sam 7:15). According to 1 Kings 11:4-13, Solomon himself takes the first steps that lead to the ultimate destruction of the Temple. He serves other gods, departing from the faithful example of David. As a result, Solomon's son only rules over a portion of his father's kingdom (Judah), while Jeroboam is chosen as king over the northern kingdom (Israel).

The accounts of Kings and Chronicles classify the kings of Israel and Judah according to their adherence to the example of David. Among the kings of Israel, the ultimate foil to David is Jeroboam. Jeroboam is blamed for leading Israel to worship other gods and images, placing Israel on the road that leads to exile (1 Kgs 14:9-10, 15-16; 2 Kgs 17:21-23). Likewise, Manasseh is singled out as the ultimate foil to David among the kings of Judah. Like Jeroboam, his unfaithfulness to God leads his people into such idolatry and sin that their exile is basically inevitable (2 Kgs 21:11-15, 24:3-4). As the ultimate foils to David, Jeroboam and Manasseh both personally experience the Lord's judgment.[145] The punishment they experience fulfills the expectations of the Psalmists concerning the fate of the unrighteous person.[146]

---

[143] See also 2 Chr 7:12-15.

[144] Thus the righteous ones pray within or toward the Temple (Ps 18:6 [MT v. 7]) and expect their help to come from Zion (Ps 20:2 [MT v. 3], 50:2).

[145] Jeroboam's line is wiped out (1 Kgs 14:11-14). Manasseh is captured and taken to Babylon where he humbles himself (2 Chr 33:11-13). On Manasseh's exile in and return from Babylon as an anticipation of Judah's, see Mosis, *Theologie des chronistischen Geschichtswerkes*, 193.

[146] See, for example, Pss 36:1-4, 12 (MT vv. 2-5, 13); 37:7-10, 22; 50:16-23.

A significant part of their departure from the example of David is Jeroboam's and Manasseh's disregard for the Temple. Jeroboam replaces worship at the Temple with an alternative system of worship centralized at two points, Bethel and Dan.[147] Manasseh violates the sanctity of the Temple itself by setting up altars within it for other gods along with an image of Asherah (2 Kgs 21:5, 7 // 2 Chr 33:5, 7). The authors of Kings and Chronicles both point out the seriousness of setting up the image of Asherah in the Temple. In doing so, Manasseh acts in direct defiance of the dedication of the Temple as a place set apart for the Lord alone.[148]

Jeroboam and Manasseh provide direct, negative confirmation of the connection between human faithfulness and divine blessing in Kings and Chronicles. On the flip side, certain kings of Judah deserve special attention as recipients of God's blessing. Besides David and Solomon, Asa, Jehoshaphat, Hezekiah, and Josiah experience a noteworthy measure of God's blessing according to the extent of their faithfulness to God. The Chronicler explicitly connects Solomon, Asa, Jehoshaphat, and Hezekiah as kings who experienced rest from their enemies for at least part of their reigns.[149] Such rest is a prominent part of the Chronicler's theology of blessing.[150] Similarly, Josiah's zealous faithfulness to the Lord is rewarded with the delay of God's judgment until after his death (2 Kgs 22:20 // 2 Chr 34:28).

In both Kings and Chronicles, Hezekiah emerges as the king who is most like David with regard to his faithfulness to God and his experience of divine blessing.[151] Hezekiah's trust in the Lord is unique, as is his careful obedience to

---

[147] Jeroboam seeks to guarantee the loyalty of his subjects by setting up an alternative system of worship in lieu of the Temple in Jerusalem. He even appoints priests who are not from the tribe of Levi (1 Kgs 12:28-33, 2 Chr 11:13-15).

[148] See 2 Kgs 21:7-8 // 2 Chr 33:7-8. These verses summarize the Temple theology that one finds elsewhere in Kings and Chronicles (see especially 1 Kgs 9:3-9 // 2 Chr 7:16-22). They also reflect the concern for removing the name of other gods from the land expressed in Deut 12:3. Manasseh's actions are the most direct threat possible to the exaltation of the Lord's name above the names of other gods. He brings the name of another god right into the Temple, the house where the Lord placed his name. Cf. Japhet, *Chronicles*, 1007.

[149] 1 Chr 22:9, 18; 2 Chr 14:6-7 (MT vv. 5-6), 15:15, 20:30. 2 Chr 32:22 should also probably be added to this list (see Japhet, *Chronicles*, 991-2; Braun, *1 Chronicles*, 225; Edward Lewis Curtis and Albert A. Madsen, *A Critical and Exegetical Commentary on the Book of Chronicles*, ICC [New York: Charles Scribner's Sons, 1910], 490).

[150] Japhet, *Chronicles*, 991-92; Braun, *1 Chronicles*, 225. Only one occurrence of the specific, idiomatic use of 'rest' found in Chronicles appears in Kings (1 Kgs 5:4 [MT v. 18]). It applies to the first part of the reign of Solomon. In addition, it is clear that the Lord blessed Hezekiah with success against his enemies and deliverance from the king of Assyria (1 Kgs 18:7-8, 19:32-34).

[151] In both Kings and Chronicles, Josiah's faithfulness is also given ample recognition (2 Kgs 22:2; 2 Chr 34:2). Yet less attention is given to the Lord's blessings upon him due to his righteousness. Josiah stands at a significant disadvantage to Hezekiah, because his

the Mosaic law (2 Kgs 18:5-6). Hezekiah's faithfulness results in blessings for him and his people. As mentioned above, Hezekiah experiences rest from his enemies (2 Chr 32:22). At two points, Hezekiah experiences truly miraculous answers to his prayers. In response to his prayer in the Temple, God delivers him and his people from the king of Assyria (2 Kgs 19 / / 2 Chr 32:1-22). God later answers his prayers by lengthening his life (2 Kgs 20:1-11, 2 Chr 32:24). During his reign, other nations send gifts to the Lord and to Hezekiah (2 Chr 32:23), and Hezekiah becomes wealthy (2 Chr 32:27-29).[152] These blessings are consistent with the expectations expressed in the Psalms.[153]

Like David and in contrast to Jeroboam and Manasseh, Hezekiah's faithfulness to God necessitates his attentiveness to proper worship of God. Hezekiah restores proper worship in the Temple (2 Chronicles 29) and gets rid of the competing high places and idols (2 Kgs 18:4). He calls upon the Israelites to gather at Jerusalem for a Passover celebration, one which is reminiscent of the days of Solomon (2 Chr 30:26, 8:13).

The accounts in Kings and Chronicles draw the reader into a framework that sizes up each of the kings of Israel and Judah. One of the firmly established impressions left by this evaluative framework is that David is the standard for what God expects of his chosen king. The two kings who compare most favorably with David are Hezekiah and Josiah (2 Kgs 18:3, 22:2). These three kings are characterized as displaying trust in the Lord and turning the hearts of their people to the Lord. A significant area of reform undertaken by them is the re-establishment of proper worship to the Lord at the Tabernacle or the Temple. The accounts of David and Hezekiah portray most clearly the manner in which the Lord desires to bless his king and people.

Kings and Chronicles provide specific historical scenarios that draw attention to the practical implications of the Psalmists' beliefs concerning the Temple. In accordance with the Psalmists, the accounts of Kings and Chronicles demonstrate that the mere presence of the Temple does not guarantee that God's blessings will flow out from it. God's blessings will flow out from it if his king and his people are faithful to him. Righteous kings, like David and Hezekiah, derive the greatest benefit from the presence of God in the Temple. For them, the Temple is the place associated with prayer and deliverance from enemies, illness, or other hardships. They witness the power of God whose authority and reputation are associated with the Temple. Conversely, unrighteous kings, like Jeroboam and Manasseh, bring God's

---

reign follows that of Manasseh. The fate of Judah has already been sealed due to the sins committed during Manasseh's reign (2 Kgs 23:26-27). Given the circumstances, the delay of the Lord's judgment is a significant blessing granted to Josiah and his kingdom.

[152] This particular area of blessing finds its closest parallels in the Lord's blessings upon Solomon's reign (1 Kgs 10:25 / / 2 Chr 9:24) (Williamson, *Chronicles*, 385).

[153] For God's deliverance of his king from the threat of enemies, see Psalm 2; for deliverance from illness, see Psalm 116; for gifts from other nations, see Ps 72:10.

punishment upon themselves and their people. The unrighteousness of such kings and their subjects results in the exile of the northern and southern kingdoms and in the destruction of the Temple.

Prophetic Hopes for a New Temple of God

Even before the destruction of the Temple built by Solomon, prophets anticipated a new Temple.[154] Just as he had delivered them out of Egypt, God was expected to deliver his people from exile and gather them back into the promised land. He was also expected to return to his new Temple and to bless his people. In their prophecies concerning the Lord's departure from the first Temple and return to the new Temple, the prophetic books of the Old Testament give emphasis to certain well-known points of Temple theology. They also develop lesser-known points and add unique touches of their own. With regard to unique touches, Ezekiel 40-48 stands out as a fascinating crux of Temple theology. To present a full picture of the prophetic writings' contributions to Temple theology requires a two-stage approach. The first stage examines the prophetic warnings of the impending destruction of the Temple. It provides necessary background for the second stage, which considers prophetic hopes for a new Temple of God.

Among the prophetic warnings that anticipate the destruction of Jerusalem and the Temple, Jeremiah 7 and Ezekiel 8-11 are particularly significant. Jeremiah 7 addresses a false understanding of the security to be drawn from the presence of the Lord's Temple in Jerusalem.[155] The Temple itself does not guarantee unconditional deliverance from enemies. Those who continually break God's commandments (Jer 7:5-6, 9-10) and appear in the Temple are in danger of treating it like a 'robbers' den' (v. 11). According to Jeremiah 7:12-14, the Temple in Jerusalem is no more impervious to the effects of the people's sin than a prior sanctuary, the Tabernacle at Shiloh. The Lord could just as easily depart from the Temple as from the Tabernacle at Shiloh (1 Sam 4:21-22, Ps 78:60). The Lord warns the people of Judah to change their ways (Jer 7:2-3) or to witness his judgment upon the Temple and upon them (vv. 14-15).[156] The rest of Jeremiah 7 expresses the certainty that the people will not heed Jeremiah's warning and will be judged for their disobedience.

While Jeremiah 7:12-14 alludes to the departure of the Lord's glory from the

---

[154] As seen below, the degree to which this new Temple was truly something new differs from one expectation to another. In any case, expectations preserve significant continuity between the pre-exilic Temple and the new Temple of the new age.

[155] Cf. also Jer 26:1-6, a parallel passage to Jeremiah 7.

[156] Jer 7:1-15 is in accord with those Psalms that set out the character of those who are fit to worship in the Temple and to draw security from the Lord's presence in it (Pss 15:1-5, 24:1-6, 26:1-12, 52:1-9 [MT vv. 2-10], 92:7-14 [MT vv. 8-15]). It also fits well with the expectations of Lev 26:1-12, 30-33 and the perspective of Mal 2:13.

Tabernacle at Shiloh and the Temple, Ezekiel 8-11 actually portrays the departure, which Ezekiel witnesses in a vision. In these chapters, as in Jeremiah 7, the sins of God's people are to blame for the departure of the Lord from his sanctuary (Ezek 8:6). Although it does not ignore other areas of sin, Ezekiel 8-11 places particular emphasis upon their idolatry.[157] In the vision, Ezekiel watches as the Lord himself (by means of his angels) brings about judgment upon the people of Jerusalem (Ezek 9:1-10:7).[158] Yet God provides for the deliverance of those who are grieved by the sins committed in Jerusalem. He instructs one angel to mark them and instructs the other angels to spare their lives (Ezek 9:4-6).

After the visions of judgment in Ezekiel 9:1-10:7, Ezekiel sees the glory of the Lord move from the threshold of the Temple to a point above the mobile throne-chariot (10:18). The throne-chariot pauses at the eastern gate of the Temple where Ezekiel has another vision and prophesies judgment upon the leaders of Jerusalem (10:19-11:12). In addition, the Lord gives Ezekiel words of hope for the exiles. The Lord promises to be a sanctuary for them in their places of exile (11:16).[159] This means that the Lord has not deserted them. He is still with them.[160] As Ezekiel's vision shows, those who remain in Jerusalem will be deprived of their reason to boast in their nearness to God (11:15), for the glory of the Lord is going to depart from Jerusalem (11:22).

Jeremiah 7 and Ezekiel 8-11 clarify that the destruction of Jerusalem and the Temple is no accident. Their destruction reinforces the consequences of sin, namely, experience of the Lord's judgment.[161] The people's perseverance in unrighteousness eventually disqualifies them from experiencing the Lord's blessings, including the land and the Temple (Jer 7:14-15). The Temple itself cannot confer righteousness upon the unrighteous (Jer 7:4-8). On the other

---

[157] On their idolatry, see especially Ezek 8:3-17; on their acts of injustice, see 9:9, 11:7.
[158] Cf. Lev 26:28.
[159] The limitation placed upon this sanctuary by מעט ('little') can be understood adjectivally ('little sanctuary') or adverbially ('for a little while' or 'to a limited extent') (Daniel I. Block, *The Book of Ezekiel: Chapters 1-24*, NICOT [Grand Rapids: Eerdmans, 1997], 350). Given the context, 'for a little while' is appealing since Ezek 11:16 is meant to provide comfort to the exiles who are looked upon by those in Jerusalem as 'far from the Lord' (Ezek 11:15). They are also promised that the Lord will return them to the land of Israel (11:17). In the meantime, the Lord himself is their sanctuary.
[160] Cf. Carl F. Keil, *Biblical Commentary on the Prophecies of Ezekiel*, vol. 1, trans. James Martin, Biblical Commentary on the Old Testament, vol. 21 (Grand Rapids: Eerdmans, 1966), 151. Their situation is analogous to the one experienced by Israel before the construction of the Tabernacle (cf. Isa 4:5-6, a suggestive parallel).
[161] For parallels where perseverance in sin and experience of judgment are vividly connected, see Lev 26:14-39, Deut 28:15-57, Psalm 37. Daniel Block finds that 'the style and language of Ezekiel are heavily influenced' by Lev 26 and Deut 28 (*Ezekiel 1-24*, 40).

hand, the unrighteous can profane the Temple, bringing about its destruction (Jer 7:9-11, Ezek 8:6). In short, the destruction of the Temple is the direct result of the people's perseverance in sin (Jer 7). Their sin drives the Lord from the Temple (Ezek 8:6) and brings judgment upon Jerusalem (Ezek 9:4-10:6).[162]

The bleak warnings of the Temple's destruction do not stand alone. They are complemented by prophetic expectations of a new Temple of God.[163] In many passages, the expectation of a new Temple is just one significant expectation among a whole collection of seemingly intertwined expectations. The first group of related expectations anticipates the re-establishment of God's people in the promised land. Common expectations include a new or renewed covenant, a re-gathering of the scattered exiles, a new Jerusalem, and a Davidic king.[164] The second group of related expectations express various ways in which God's people will be blessed. Common blessings include fertility of the land, peace, security, wealth from the nations, and abundance of Israelite offspring.[165] Some of the prominent interconnections between the expectation of a new Temple and elements of these two groups of expectations will be

---

[162] Cf. also Mic 3, especially v. 12. Of course, this means that the exilic period brings with it a time of mourning and anguish over the destruction of Jerusalem and the Temple (see, for instance, Lamentations and Ps 137).

[163] See especially, Ps 102:16 (MT v. 17); Isa 2:2-3; 44:28; 56:6-7; 60:7, 13; 62:9; 66:18-23; Jer 31:23; 33:11; Ezek 20:40; 37:26-28; 40:1-47:12; Joel 3:17 (MT 4:17); Mic 4:1-2; Hag 2:9; Zech 1:16; 6:12-15; 8:3; 9:8; 14:16-21.

[164] On the new covenant, see Isa 54:10, 61:8; Jer 31:31-37, 32:38-41; Ezek 37:26-27; Hos 2:16-20, 23 (MT vv. 18-22, 25); Zech 9:11. On the re-gathering of the exiles, see Isa 11:12-16; 27:12-13; 43:5-7; 49:5-6; 56:8; 66:20; Jer 3:14, 18; 30:3, 10; 31:8-11; 32:37; Ezek 11:17-21; 20:41; 28:25-26; 34:11-16; 36:24-28; 37:15-23; 39:25; Mic 4:6-7; 5:3 (MT v. 2); Zeph 3:19-20; Zech 8:7-8; 10:9-12. On the new Jerusalem, see Ps 102:16 (MT v. 17); Isa 33:20-24; 44:28; 54:11-17; 62:1-12; 65:17-20; Jer 30:18; 31:38-40; 33:9-11; Ezek 45:6; 48:15-17, 30-35; Joel 3:17, 20 (MT 4:17, 20); Zech 1:16; 2:1-5 (MT 2:5-9); 8:3-5, 22; 12:1-9; 14:8-11, 16-21. On the Davidic king, see Isa 9:6-7 (MT vv. 5-6); 11:1-5; Jer 23:5-6, 30:9, 33:15-22; Ezek 21:27 (MT v. 32), 34:23-24, 37:24-28; Hos 3:5; Amos 9:11; Mic 5:2-4 (MT vv. 1-3); Hag 2:23; Zech 3:8, 6:11-12, 9:9, 10:4, 12:8.

[165] On fertility of the land, see Isa 30:23-26; 32:15; Jer 31:5, 12; Ezek 34:26-27; 36:8-12, 29-30, 35; Hos 2:22 (MT v. 24); Joel 2:19, 23-24; 3:18 (MT 4:18); Amos 9:13-15; Zech 8:12; 9:17. On peace and security, see Isa 11:6-9; 54:14-15; 62:8-9; 65:20-24; 66:12-14; Jer 33:6-9; Ezek 34:25; Hos 2:18 (MT v. 20); Joel 2:20; 3:17 (MT 4:17); Mic 5:4-6 (MT vv. 3-5); Zeph 3:13, 15; Zech 8:4-5; 9:8, 13-17; 12:1-9; 14:11. On wealth from the nations, see Isa 60:5-13; 61:6-9; Ezek 39:10; Hag 2:7-8; Zech 14:14. On the abundance of Israelite offspring, see Jer 3:16; 23:3; 30:19; Ezek 36:11, 37-38; Hos 1:10-11 (MT 2:1-2). These blessings are substantially parallel to those promised in Lev 26:3-13 and Deut 28:2-13.

considered below.[166]

As seen above, the new Temple is one significant expectation associated with God's gathering of his people from exile and his subsequent blessings upon them. A third set of expectations completes the picture. This set predicts that a time will come when the Temple mount will rise to first place among the mountains and the nations will come to the Temple (Isa 2:2, Mic 4:1). They will come in submission to the Lord and will contribute to the glorification of the Temple.[167] They will worship the Lord, pray to him, follow his commandments, and see his glory.[168] As a result, the nations also will be blessed with peace.[169] According to such expectations, the Temple will become a focal point for the nations in addition to its significance for Israel.[170]

Among the prophets, Ezekiel gives particular prominence to expectations of a new Temple. Hence Ezekiel's expectations merit special attention. Ezekiel 40-48 is a well-known crux of Temple theology. As the final section of the book, it sets forth a climactic portrayal of the bright future that awaits Israel after the exile. Ezekiel 40-48 also collects into one place several aspects of Temple theology that have been discussed in previous sections of this chapter. These aspects include the revelation of a divine pattern, the appearance of God's glory, regulations for proper Temple service, a chosen site in the land, and the locus for paradisial blessings. Ezekiel does not treat these areas comprehensively, but he does provide enough information to examine each aspect separately.

The divine pattern for the Temple itself is the principal subject of Ezekiel 40-42, giving it the first place in Ezekiel's vision. Additional, isolated elements that complete the pattern can also be found in chapters 43-46. Ezekiel's vision is temporally located in the twenty-fifth year of the exile (40:1). Its timing could therefore be connected with the Old Testament jubilee year, which would

---

[166] In particular, see the discussion of the post-exilic period, which examines the historical books (Ezra and Nehemiah) and the relevant prophetic books (Haggai, Zechariah, and Malachi).

[167] Isa 60:5-14, 66:23; Hag 2:7; Zech 14:17-19. Cf. Jer 3:17, Zech 2:11 (MT v. 15), relevant parallels where the Temple is not directly mentioned.

[168] Ps 102:15, 22 (MT vv. 16, 23); Isa 2:2-3, 56:7, 60:7, 66:18-21; Mic 4:1-2; Zech 8:20-23; Mal 1:11.

[169] Isa 2:4, Mic 4:4.

[170] OT antecedents for these expectations can be found in the reigns of certain blessed kings, including David (esp. 1 Chronicles 18-20), Solomon (1 Kgs 10:23-25 // 2 Chr 9:22-24), Jehoshaphat (2 Chr 17:10-11), and Hezekiah (2 Chr 32:23). Cf. both Ps 2 and the stories of the humbling of Nebuchadnezzar (Dan 4) and of the healing of Naaman (2 Kgs 5:1-19). It therefore seems appropriate that the future subjection of the nations is also prominent in expectations associated with the coming Davidic king (see especially, Isa 9:6-7 [MT vv. 5-6], 11:4; Mic 5:2-15 [MT vv. 1-14]; Zech 9:9-10).

be an appropriate time for the exiles to be released from their captivity.[171] Thus Ezekiel's vision occurs at a significant point for those who anticipate the coming of the exiles' release.

Ezekiel's visionary experience takes him back to Israel, placing him on 'a very high mountain' (40:2). This setting brings to mind two other mountaintop revelations. First, the site for Solomon's Temple, Mount Zion, is revealed to David as he is offering sacrifices there (1 Chr 21:26-22:1). Second, the plan for the Tabernacle is revealed to Moses on Mount Sinai (Exod 24:15-18). In what follows, Ezekiel beholds the layout for the new Temple.[172]

Ezekiel's description of the layout for the new Temple is distinct from the Old Testament descriptions of the Tabernacle and the Temple. Instead of starting with its furnishings (Exodus 25) or with the Temple building itself (1 Kings 6 / / 2 Chronicles 3), Ezekiel's angelic companion starts by measuring the wall of the outer court followed by its eastern gatehouse. Next, the angel measures the remaining five gatehouses. The foremost position given to the outer wall and the gatehouses foreshadows the concern with limited access that emerges later in the regulations for proper Temple service. As noted by Moshe Greenberg, the 'massive size of the gatehouses verges on caricature.'[173] Each one is half the size of the Temple building.[174] The gatehouses bordering on the inner court indicate that the new Temple probably differs from its predecessors in that it has an inner court and an outer court.[175] In Ezekiel 40-42, the

---

[171] A jubilee year takes place every fiftieth year and is legislated as a year of release (Lev 25:10). During this year, all Israelites are to return to their own land and family (for further details, see Lev 25). On its significance for Ezekiel, see Daniel I. Block, *The Book of Ezekiel: Chapters 25-48*, NICOT (Grand Rapids: Eerdmans, 1998), 495-6.

[172] Ezekiel avoids the term תבנית ('pattern'), which one might reasonably expect to find in Ezekiel 40-48 (cf. 1 Chr 28:11-19, Exod 25:9). Kalinda Stevenson reads this omission as one indication that Ezekiel is not providing a building plan or blueprint for a new Temple (*Vision of Transformation: The Territorial Rhetoric of Ezekiel 40-48*, SBLDS, no. 154 [Atlanta: Scholars Press, 1996], 18-19, 150). As she points out, in the most likely place where one would expect to find תבנית, one finds תכנית ('measurement' or 'proportion') (Ezek 43:10). She also objects to the frequent emendation of תכנית, replacing it with תכונתו ('its layout') (*Territorial Rhetoric of Ezekiel 40-48*, 17-18; cf. Walther Zimmerli, *Ezekiel 2: A Commentary on the Book of the Prophet Ezekiel, Chapters 25-48*, trans. James D. Martin, Hermeneia [Philadelphia: Fortress, 1983], 410).

[173] Moshe Greenberg, 'The Design and Themes of Ezekiel's Program of Restoration,' *Int* 38 (1984): 193.

[174] John Skinner, *The Book of Ezekiel*, Expositor's Bible, vol. 13 (New York: A. C. Armstrong and Son, 1908), 407. On the dimensions of the Temple, see Zimmerli, *Ezekiel 2*, 378.

[175] Skinner, *Ezekiel*, 416-7. This definitely sets it apart from the Tabernacle. The layout of the courts of Solomon's Temple is actually debatable. Even so, a clear difference between Solomon's Temple courts and those envisioned here emerges with regard to the ability of the laity and ruler to enter the inner court of the new Temple (Greenberg, 'Ezekiel's Program of Restoration,' 203). This will be discussed further below.

description of the new Temple concentrates upon its measurements. It gives little attention to details of decoration or furnishings. This sets the tone for the exhortations that will follow.

After the angel has completed the initial measuring of the new Temple, the description of the return of God's glory to the Temple begins. The glory enters through the eastern gate and fills the new Temple (Ezek 43:1-5, 44:1-4).[176] The return of God's glory is the hopeful counterpart to its departure in Ezekiel 11:23. The permanent shutting of the eastern gate through which God enters the new Temple provides a pictorial reminder of God's return to it (Ezek 44:2).[177] The return of God's glory in 43:1-5 immediately precedes God's words of clarification concerning the significance of the new Temple. The Lord tells Ezekiel that the new Temple is the location of his throne and of the soles of his feet, where he will dwell in the midst of Israel forever (43:7).[178] In agreement with other Old Testament texts concerning the nature of the Lord's dwelling in the Temple, such a statement balances both the immanence and transcendence of Israel's God.[179] God chooses the new Temple as the particular locus for his dwelling in the midst of his people, but he makes it clear that he is not spatially

---

[176] Similarly, God's glory fills the Tabernacle and the Temple as the final step in their consecration (Exod 29:43, 40:34-35; 1 Kgs 8:10-11 // 2 Chr 5:13-14; 2 Chr 7:1-3). Upon beholding the Lord's glory, Ezekiel falls upon his face, which is how the people respond to similar manifestations at the Tabernacle and the Temple (Ezek 1:28, 43:3, 44:4; Lev 9:24; 2 Chr 7:3). The dual mention of the glory of the Lord filling the Temple (Ezek 43:1-5 and 44:1-4) is parallel to what one finds with the Tabernacle (Exod 40:34-35, Lev 9:24) and the Temple (2 Chr 5:13-14, 7:1-3; in contrast, see 1 Kgs 8:10-11). In the parallels, the second appearance of the glory is associated with the consecration of the altar (Lev 9:24, 2 Chr 7:1-3), which directly precedes the glory's appearance in Ezek 44:1-4.

[177] Leslie C. Allen, *Ezekiel 20-48*, WBC, vol. 29 (Dallas: Word Books, 1990), 260.

[178] The place of the Lord's throne and the locus of his glory is elsewhere closely associated with the ark (1 Sam 4:4, 21-22; 2 Sam 6:2 // 1 Chr 13:6; 1 Kgs 8:4-11 // 2 Chr 5:5-14; 2 Kgs 19:15). Ezek 43:7 is consistent with Jer 3:16, which asserts that a time is coming when the ark will be forgotten (Carl F. Keil, *Biblical Commentary on the Prophecies of Ezekiel*, vol. 2, trans. James Martin, Biblical Commentary on the Old Testament, vol. 22 [Grand Rapids: Eerdmans, 1966], 279-80). Ezekiel's vision nowhere suggests that the presence of the ark is a necessary prerequisite for the Lord's glory to fill the Temple (cf. 1 Kgs 8:4-11 // 2 Chr 5:5-14).

[179] The placement of his throne and the promise to dwell in Israel's midst are taken as evidence of immanence (cf. Exod 25:8, 29:45; Lev 26:11; 1 Kgs 8:12-13 // 2 Chr 6:1-2; Jer 3:17, 14:21, 17:12; Ezek 37:27; cf. also Isa 66:1). The placement of the soles of his feet indicates transcendence (cf. Isa 60:13, 66:1). The reference to the soles of God's feet is commonly interpreted as equivalent to asserting that the Temple is his footstool (Zimmerli, *Ezekiel 2*, 415; cf. esp. Ps 99:5, Lam 2:1). Elsewhere, Solomon's Temple dedication speech and the Lord's response to it affirm that the Lord dwells simultaneously in heaven and in the Jerusalem Temple (1 Kgs 8:12-61, 9:3 // 2 Chr 6:1-42, 7:16).

confined to this place.

In Ezekiel 43 and 44, the return of God's glory to the Temple is closely linked with criticisms of the former actions of the Israelites that drove God from the Temple (43:7b-9, 44:5-9). God intends for Ezekiel's description of the layout of the new Temple to make Israel ashamed of past sins (Ezek 43:10, 16:61-63, 36:31-32). If the Israelites are ashamed of their sins, then Ezekiel is supposed to reveal to them the layout of the new Temple and its laws (43:11). As foreshadowed by the primacy given to the gates in Ezekiel 40, explicit references are made to the new Temple's entrances and exits in conjunction with its layout and laws (43:11, 44:5). New limitations on access constitute an important concern among the laws for the new Temple, which are found in Ezekiel 43:18-27, 44:10-31, and 45:9-46:15.

Before discussing the laws that limit access to the new Temple, attention should first be given to the emergence of Ezekiel as a new Moses, which becomes particularly evident in connection with the laws for the new Temple.[180] First of all, note that the arrangement of the sections of Ezekiel 40-48 generally parallels the sequence of the law of Moses by progressing from Temple description to Temple regulations to division of the land.[181] Within

---

[180] The following remarks assume that Ezekiel would have been aware of the Mosaic law (as recorded in the Pentateuch) and makes inspired alterations to it (see Ezek 20:10-12 which recounts the giving of God's laws after the Exodus). It is recognized that such a view is disputed (for a summary and contribution to the ongoing debate, see especially J. Gordon McConville, 'Priests and Levites in Ezekiel: A Crux in the Interpretation of Israel's History,' *TynBul* 34 [1983]: 3-31). Yet the current section is based upon the supposition that the NT authors would attribute the Mosaic law to Moses, as did Jesus and the rabbis (cf. John 1:45, Acts 26:22). Rabbinic literature attests to the recognition that laws in Ezekiel 40-48 blatantly contradict the Mosaic law (or at least appear to do so). Since the rabbis regard the Mosaic law as authoritative, one finds references to attempts to harmonize the Mosaic law with the laws for the new Temple found in Ezekiel (Levenson, *Program of Restoration of Ezekiel 40-48*, 37-38; see also, Moshe Eisemann, *Yechezkel or The Book of Ezekiel: A New Translation with a Commentary Anthologized from Talmudic, Midrashic, and Rabbinic Sources*, vol. 3, ArtScroll Tanach Series [New York: Mesorah, 1980], 695-7). In addition, Moshe Greenberg claims that enough evidence exists for critical scholars to recognize that Ezekiel is instituting 'basic changes in traditional practices' ('Ezekiel's Program of Restoration,' 208). Menahem Haran, who dates the P document before the exile, comes to a different conclusion. After pointing out the substantial parallels between P and Ezekiel's code, Haran claims that Ezekiel's code contradicts laws found in P, because they are independent of one another. By the time of Ezekiel, P has been 'pushed off-stage.' It emerges some time after the exile as is evident in the ministry of Ezra, another priest like Ezekiel ('The Law Code of Ezekiel XL-XLVIII and Its Relation to the Priestly School,' *HUCA* 50 [1979]: 59-67). For criticism of Haran's position, see Greenberg, 'Ezekiel's Program of Restoration,' 203.

[181] Yehezkel Kaufmann, *The Religion of Israel from Its Beginnings to the Babylonian Exile*, trans. and abridged Moshe Greenberg (New York: Schocken Books, 1972), 443-4.

Ezekiel 43-46, however, the regulations for the new Temple differ at numerous points from comparable laws revealed to Moses.[182] Ezekiel's revisions to the Mosaic regulations are more drastic and comprehensive than David's re-organization of the priests and Levites.[183] Still, Ezekiel's Temple regulations are 'highly selective,' which has caused considerable disagreement among interpreters about the significance of that which is omitted.[184]

Instead of focusing upon what Ezekiel's regulations omit, one should assume that they treat those particular topics where either revision or reiteration is necessary, leaving the remainder of the Mosaic legislation intact.[185] Such an approach fits well with the selectivity of Ezekiel's regulations. An analogous, smaller-scale revision occurred when David re-organized the priests and Levites.[186]

In several cases, Ezekiel's new regulations involve reminders of past sins and safeguards against similar infringements upon the holiness of God.[187] The new limitations on access to the Temple illustrate well the nature and distinctiveness of Ezekiel's regulations. First, uncircumcised foreigners are barred from entrance into the Temple (44:9). This regulation is presented as a corrective to two previous offenses, namely, permitting uncircumcised foreigners into the Temple and handing over certain Temple duties to them (44:7-8).[188] Second, only descendants of Zadok are permitted to serve as priests (44:10-16). The priesthood is strictly confined to the line of Zadok, because other potential claimants to the priesthood participated in Israel's idolatry (44:15). Third, the 'prince' is not permitted to enter the inner court, but is given

---

[182] For summaries of the differences, see Greenberg, 'Ezekiel's Program of Restoration,' 203-8; Haran, 'Law Code of Ezekiel XL-XLVIII,' 61-62; Levenson, *Program of Restoration of Ezekiel 40-48*, 37-38.

[183] Cf. Numbers 4; 1 Chronicles 23-26; 2 Chr 23:18; 29:25 (this verse clarifies that David's re-organization is the result of prophetic revelation); 35:4, 15; Neh 12:24, 45.

[184] Greenberg, 'Ezekiel's Program of Restoration,' 203, 208.

[185] Ibid. For evidence of this, see Ezek 44:24a which mentions ordinances that would clearly extend beyond those found in Ezekiel 40-48 (cf. Deut 17:8-9).

[186] Cf. McConville, 'Priests and Levites in Ezekiel,' 27-28; Greenberg, 'Ezekiel's Program of Restoration,' 208. Several of Ezekiel's revisions concern changes in small details. For example, in Ezek 43:22, a goat is offered where one would expect a bull (Exod 29:36). In Ezek 45:24, both the amount of the appropriate grain offering and the concomitant amount of oil differ from what one finds required in Num 15:6, 9. The modification of such detailed regulations tends to give added emphasis to their significance. Careful obedience to all of God's laws is necessary in order to please the God who will reside in the new Temple (cf. Ezek 36:27, 43:11, 44:5; also, Levenson, *Program of Restoration of Ezekiel 40-48*, 45-46).

[187] Clements, *God and Temple*, 106.

[188] It seems that the exact nature of each past offense referred to by Ezekiel in Ezekiel 40-48 is debated by interpreters. For the various options, see the commentaries. Even so, the basic nature of the past offense and of Ezekiel's corrective is discernible.

privileged access to its eastern gateway (44:3; 46:2, 8, 12). His limited access is to be read against the background of the past offenses committed by Israel's kings (43:7b-9, 45:8-9).[189] Fourth, the laity are apparently not allowed to enter the inner court nor to slaughter their sacrificial animals (40:39-41, 46:3, 44:11). Attention is drawn to their past sins in Ezekiel 43:7b, 9. In each case, the above limitations of access are related to past sins and provide regulations that are meant to safeguard the holiness of the new Temple. When compared with other Old Testament teaching, these regulations appear to be unique limitations, providing more stringent restrictions upon access to the new Temple.[190] The layout of the Temple along with the above restrictions protects the sanctity of the entire inner court, where God's altar is located.[191]

Concern for preserving the sanctity of the new Temple is also evident in the description of its chosen site. The entire Temple mount is to be set apart as 'most holy' (43:12, 45:3).[192] Within the land of Israel, this allotment is the apex of sacred space. In addition, the area around the Temple mount is also described as a 'most holy' area, which belongs to the priests (45:1-4, 48:9-12). Next to the priests' portion is the portion of the Levites, which is set apart as 'holy' (45:5, 48:13-14). This holy district is distinguished from the land allotted

---

[189] For a recent study of the use of the terms נשיא ('prince' or 'chief') and מלך ('king') in Ezekiel, see Iain M. Duguid, *Ezekiel and the Leaders of Israel*, VTSup, vol. 56 (New York: E. J. Brill, 1994), 18-33. He finds that, with reference to Israel's future ruler, Ezekiel uses the terms interchangeably. Ezekiel's preference for נשיא could be intended to differentiate Israel's future ruler from 'rulers of the recent past' (Ibid., 25). In addition, there is no apparent distinction between the former 'princes' (45:8-9) and the former 'kings' (43:7-9) (Ibid., 27).

[190] Greenberg, 'Ezekiel's Program of Restoration,' 206. First, in the case of the uncircumcised foreigner, the OT makes it clear that such a person cannot participate in Israel's celebration of the Passover (Exod 12:43-49). It is implied that an uncircumcised foreigner cannot offer sacrifices at all (Num 15:14-16; cf. Exod 12:49). The OT does not, however, explicitly bar uncircumcised foreigners from the Temple (Keil, *Ezekiel*, vol. 2, 306). Second, with regard to the priesthood, nowhere else is it explicitly limited to descendants of Zadok (although, cf. 1 Chr 6:12-15). For previous limitations on the priesthood, see Exod 28:1; Lev 8:2, 10:1-2; Num 18:7, 25:11-13; 1 Sam 3:12-14; Jer 33:18 (on Zadok, see especially 1 Kgs 1:32-39). Third, the restrictions on the prince should be compared to the king's previous ability to approach the altar (1 Kgs 8:22, 54 / / 2 Chr 6:12, Ps 26:6; cf. also the sacrificial misconduct of previous kings in 2 Kgs 16:10-16, 2 Chr 26:16). Finally, it appears that the laity previously had access to the area near the altar (Lev 1:3, Ps 26:6) and were allowed to slaughter their own sacrifices (for example, see Lev 1:5-6).

[191] Further concern for the sanctity of the new Temple can be observed with regard to the addition of a novel purification of the sanctuary in the first month (Ezek 45:18-20) (Greenberg, 'Ezekiel's Program of Restoration,' 206). Note its similarities to the atonement rituals legislated for the day of atonement (Lev 16).

[192] To identify the Temple mount as 'most holy' designates its 'status relative to the much larger area in which it [is] set' (Eisemann, *Ezekiel*, vol. 3, 674).

to the city. The city's land is described as a 'common' or 'non-holy' area.[193] Thus the special allotment of land set aside for the priests, Levites, and the city mirrors the graded holiness of the new Temple (45:1-6, 48:9-20).[194] One moves along a spectrum toward the apex of holiness as one progresses from the city to the Levites' allotment to the priests' allotment to the outer court of the new Temple to the inner court to the holy place within the Temple to its 'most holy' place.

When one compares Ezekiel's description of the chosen site for the new Temple with parallel accounts concerning the appropriate site for the Tabernacle or Temple, one finds that Ezekiel provides a more precise spatial layout for the site of the new Temple.[195] Such precision fits well within Ezekiel 40-48, where the boundaries of sacred space and the appropriate division of the land are significant concerns. At the same time, the 'very high mountain' of Ezekiel 40:2 is not explicitly identified (see also Ezek 17:22-23, 20:40). Similar descriptions of Mount Zion outside of Ezekiel clarify that he must be making an indirect reference to it.[196] In addition, Ezekiel 40-48 makes no mention of the proper timing for the construction of the new Temple. Evidence from the rest of Ezekiel suggests that the new Temple, like Solomon's Temple, is to be established at a time when God has granted his people security from their enemies.[197]

The establishment of the new Temple and the return of God's glory are a prelude to the advent of the miraculous river flowing from the new Temple (Ezek 47:1-12). At its source in the Temple, the river is small, but it broadens and deepens as it flows to the east (vv. 3-5). It turns most of the Dead Sea into fresh water, full of fish (vv. 8-10). In addition, it is lined by trees whose abundant fruits provide food and whose leaves bring about healing (vv. 7, 12).

---

[193] The nouns חל ('common' or 'profane' thing) and קדש ('holy' thing) are used dichotomously at several points in Ezekiel (22:26, 42:20, 44:23).

[194] The closest analogies for the layout of the site for the new Temple are found in the layout of Israel's camp in Num 2:1-31; 3:23, 29, 35, 38 (Levenson, *Program of Restoration of Ezekiel 40-48*, 118-21). There is some ambiguity as to whether the Levites' allotment borders that of the priests' allotment on the north or on the south (which would place it between the priests' allotment and the city). For arguments in favor of the northern location, see Zimmerli, *Ezekiel 2*, 534; Allen, *Ezekiel 20-48*, 284. For those in favor of the southern location, see Eisemann, *Ezekiel*, vol. 3, 708; Greenberg, 'Ezekiel's Program of Restoration,' 202, n. 37.

[195] Cf. Num 2:1-31; 3:23, 29, 35, 38; Josh 18:1; 1 Chr 22:1.

[196] Cf. Ps 48:2 (MT v. 3), Isa 2:3, Mic 4:2; Walther Eichrodt, *Ezekiel: A Commentary*, trans. Cosslett Quin, OTL (Philadelphia: Westminster, 1970), 541.

[197] Instead of making reference to 'rest from all your enemies' (cf. Deut 12:10; Josh 1:13, 15; 21:44; 22:4; 23:1; 2 Sam 7:1, 11; 1 Kgs 5:4 [MT v. 18]; 8:56; 1 Chr 22:9, 18; 23:25; 2 Chr 14:6-7; 15:15; 20:30), Ezekiel says that Israel will dwell in its land 'securely' (adverb from בטח) (Ezek 28:26; 34:25, 27, 28; 38:8, 11, 14; 39:26; cf. Lev 26:5, Deut 12:10).

Ezekiel 47:1-12 portrays a miraculous transformation of one region within Israel. If God is able to transform one region of Israel so drastically, then surely he is able to make the rest of the land fruitful as well (see Ezek 34:26-27). Ezekiel 47:1-12 demonstrates vividly God's ability to transform the land of Israel into a land that is abundantly fruitful, like the Garden of Eden (see Ezek 36:35, Isa 51:3).

According to Ezekiel 47:12, the preternatural fruitfulness of the trees along the river is directly attributable to the fact that the river flows from the sanctuary. As discussed in the previous section, the Psalmists portray the Temple as a locus for God's abundant provision for his people.[198] One aspect of their portrayal associates the Temple with a river (Pss 36:8, 46:4). Another aspect depicts the righteous person as a healthy, fruitful tree planted in the Temple (Ps 92:12-14). Both of these images idealize the Temple as a beatific place of God's provision for his people, like the Garden of Eden.[199] Ezekiel 47:1-12 provides physical, geographical counterparts to the figurative images of the Psalmists by describing a river with fruitful trees along its banks. Although the Psalmists deserve special attention for associating the Temple with God's abundant provision for his people, Ezekiel's river that brings fertility and trees that provide abundant food should also be compared with the river and trees of the Garden of Eden (Gen 2:8-10).[200] According to Genesis 2:8-10, God causes trees to grow in the Garden of Eden and to produce food. He waters the garden by means of a river. By having the river flow out of the new Temple, Ezekiel 47:1-12 similarly communicates that the God who dwells in the new Temple is the source for the miraculous transformation of part of Israel into a preternaturally productive region. It also accentuates the new Temple as the locus for God's abundant provision for his people.[201]

---

[198] Pss 36:5-9 (MT vv. 6-10), 46:4 (MT v. 5), 52:8 (MT v. 10), 65:4 (MT v. 5), 84:10-11 (MT vv. 11-12), 92:12-14 (MT vv. 13-15).

[199] As pointed out above, the word 'delights' in Ps 36:8 is the noun associated with the proper name Eden.

[200] Adalbert Peter, 'Der Segensstrom des endzeitlichen Jerusalem – Herkunft und Bedeutung eines prophetischen Symbols,' in *Miscellanea Fuldensia*, ed. Franz Scholz (Fulda: Verlag Parzeller and Co., 1966), 121-7, 129-32; Congar, *Mystery of the Temple*, 74-75; Eichrodt, *Ezekiel*, 583-4; Zimmerli, *Ezekiel 2*, 510, 515; Schmidt, *Prophet und Tempel*, 170.

[201] Other parallels to the river image of Ezek 47:1-12 include Isa 33:20-21, 35:6-7, 41:17-20, 43:19-20, 44:3-4; Jer 2:13; Joel 4:18 (MT 3:18); Zech 14:8 (on these parallels, see Peter, 'Segensstrom des endzeitlichen Jerusalem,' 110, 116-21). Also, Ezek 28:13-14 brings the Garden of Eden and the 'mount of God' into close association as places of blessing (cf. Peter, 'Segensstrom des endzeitlichen Jerusalem,' 127-32; Levenson, *Program of Restoration of Ezekiel 40-48*, 25-27). Finally, abundant water, trees, vines, and the Garden of Eden are used elsewhere in Ezekiel to depict God's providential oversight over the kingdoms of the earth, including Israel (Ezek 17:3-24, 19:10-14, 31:3-18).

One of the central difficulties for interpreters of Ezekiel 40-48 has not yet been addressed. Ezekiel 40-48 is commonly understood as a plan for a new Temple, renewed Temple-service, and re-distribution of the land to the tribes of Israel. Yet it is difficult to produce any substantial evidence that Ezekiel 40-48 had an effect upon post-exilic Israel.[202] In Ezra and Nehemiah, no mention is made of Ezekiel's laws for the new Temple. In every case where legislation relevant to the Temple is mentioned, the name of Moses appears, or the name of David.[203] Interpreters therefore struggle to account for the fact that Ezekiel 40-48 has apparently not been fulfilled. They continue to appeal to three principal options. First, Ezekiel 40-48 will be fulfilled during the millenial reign of Christ.[204] Second, Ezekiel 40-48 is idealistic, but it could have been literally fulfilled in post-exilic Israel. The sinfulness of the Israelites who returned from the exile prevented them from witnessing its fulfillment.[205] Third,

---

[202] Greenberg, 'Ezekiel's Program of Restoration,' 208. Some claim that Ezekiel's Temple plan had an effect upon the design of Herod's Temple, but this evidence is difficult to evaluate since it could also be that Herod's Temple design was influenced by features of Solomon's Temple that are not reflected in the biblical account (i.e., they might reflect a later stage of Solomon's Temple) (Ibid., 208; Eisemann, *Ezekiel*, vol. 3, 605-6).

[203] For relevant references to the law of Moses, see Ezra 3:2, 6:18; Neh 8:14. For references to David's prescriptions, see Neh 12:24, 45 (12:45 adds Solomon as well).

[204] Charles L. Feinberg, *The Prophecy of Ezekiel: The Glory of the Lord* (Chicago: Moody, 1969), 233-9; Arno C. Gaebelein, *The Prophet Ezekiel: An Analytical Exposition*, 2nd ed. (Neptune, N.J.: Loizeaux Brothers, 1972), 273; John W. Schmitt and J. Carl Laney, *Messiah's Coming Temple: Ezekiel's Prophetic Vision of the Future Temple* (Grand Rapids: Kregel, 1997), 74; Merrill F. Unger, 'The Temple Vision of Ezekiel,' *BSac* 105 (1948): 418-32; 106 (1949): 48-64, 169-77.

[205] Eisemann, *Ezekiel*, vol. 3, 606; E. Henderson, *The Book of the Prophet Ezekiel* (Andover, Mass.: Warren F. Draper, 1870), vi, 198-200; W. F. Lofthouse, *Ezekiel: Introduction, Revised Version with Notes, and Index*, Century Bible (Edinburgh: T. C. and E. C. Jack, [1900]), 289; cf. Levenson, *Program of Restoration of Ezekiel 40-48*, 44-49. The proponents of this view differ with regard to certain details. Levenson and Eisemann both anticipate further fulfillment of Ezek 40-48 in the future in the form of a rebuilt Temple. On the other hand, Henderson places Ezekiel's Temple on the same plane as Solomon's. He sees both as an OT shadow of a NT reality, that is, they lead 'the mind forward in anticipation of better things to come' (Henderson, *Ezekiel*, vi). In addition to the above works, see also Moshe Greenberg's examination of the practical side of one aspect of Ezekiel's idealism ('Idealism and Practicality in Numbers 35:4-5 and Ezekiel 48,' *JAOS* 88 [1968]: 63-66). In addition, E. W. Hengstenberg takes an approach to Ezek 40-48 that is similar to this view in that he emphasizes its literal fulfillment (*The Prophecies of the Prophet Ezekiel Elucidated*, trans. A. C. Murphy and J. G. Murphy, Clark's Foreign Theological Library, series 4, vol. 21 [Edinburgh: T. and T. Clark, 1869], 348-53). He defends the literal fulfillment of these chapters in the community that returned from exile (except 47:1-12). He thinks this view is possible if one does not press the literal fulfillment of every detail (*Ezekiel*, 349-50). As others

Ezekiel 40-48 is an idealistic vision that describes eschatological realities.[206] Options two and three both make important contributions to one's understanding of Ezekiel 40-48, while option one is less appealing unless one holds to a particular understanding of the millennium.[207]

The second option contains a significant element of truth in that it gives attention to the relevance of Ezekiel's vision for the exiles and the remnant who return from Babylon after the exile. They are right to hope that they will see the fulfillment of Ezekiel's vision. Yet the historical accounts and prophecies found in Ezra, Nehemiah, Haggai, Zechariah, and Malachi provide a good basis for speculation about the reasons why Ezekiel's Temple was not built among the returned exiles. One reason is that sin infects the remnant, as it infected their fathers before them (see the next section). God's eternal dwelling place cannot be firmly established in the midst of sinful people (Ezek 43:7-11). The presence of sin in the remnant community is an obvious symptom of the deeper problem. The root problem behind this sin is that God must act in order to cleanse his people, put his spirit within them, and cause them to walk in his ways (Ezek 36:25-28). The continuing sinfulness of the remnant shows that the new age, the age of salvation, has not yet dawned. Thus it is only partially true to say that the sinfulness of the remnant prevented them from seeing the fulfillment of Ezekiel's Temple vision. It would be more true to say that their sinfulness is evidence that the time for the fulfillment of Ezekiel's Temple vision has not yet come. Ultimately, they do not witness the fulfillment of Ezekiel's Temple vision, because its fulfillment is contingent upon a decisive act of God.[208]

---

point out, however, such a view is difficult in light of the evidence of such a small measure of fulfillment even with regard to putting Ezekiel's laws into effect (see above).

[206] G. K. Beale, *The Temple and the Church's Mission: A Biblical Theology of the Dwelling Place of God*, NSBT, vol. 17 (Downers Grove, Ill.: InterVarsity Press, 2004), 335-64; Eichrodt, *Ezekiel*, 542; Patrick Fairbairn, *An Exposition of Ezekiel* (Grand Rapids: Zondervan, 1960), 434-50; Keil, *Ezekiel*, vol. 2, 416-34; Schmidt, *Prophet und Tempel*, 162-3, 166-7, 171. See also Peter, 'Segensstrom des endzeitlichen Jerusalem,' 133-4.

[207] Unger, in particular, addresses common objections to this line of interpretation, which he describes as 'literal-futuristic' (see especially, 'Temple Vision of Ezekiel,' 169-75). The millennial fulfillment of Ezek 40-48 necessitates belief in a particular understanding of the millennium as the age in which Judaism will be 'reinstated' and ethnic Israel will be blessed (Unger, 'Temple Vision of Ezekiel,' 170-1). Thus it fits within a traditional Dispensational framework, but appears to be an unnecessary regression to those who do not buy into this framework. Once the fulfillment of the Temple has come in Christ and the church, it appears unnecessary to construct another Temple in Jerusalem (even in the millennium) (Clowney, 'Final Temple,' 131-2). This fits with Christ's fulfillment and replacement of the OT sacrificial system through his sacrificial death (see George E. Ladd, 'Israel and the Church,' *EQ* 36 [1964]: 209-10).

[208] One of the common objections to the second interpretive option is that the returning Israelites could not have been expected to possess the resources to build Ezekiel's Temple. Yet this is really only the tip of the iceberg. Ezekiel's vision in 40-48 presents a

The third option is probably closer to the mark than the second option. Its proponents recognize that a decisive act of God would be required in order to realize all of the elements of Ezekiel's Temple vision.[209] According to the Gospel of John, that decisive act of God occurs in the form of the life, death, resurrection, and exaltation of Jesus. His coming marks the beginning of the fulfillment of Ezekiel 40-48. Its final fulfillment is depicted in Revelation 21-22.[210]

As seen above, the problem of the fulfillment of Ezekiel 40-48 cannot be neatly separated from consideration of the return of the exiles.[211] In the post-exilic writings of the Old Testament, one of the major foci for the returning

---

number of elements which could not come about without a dramatic new act of God. First, Ezek 40:2 suggests that the Temple mount is more dramatic with regard to its height than would have been true of Mount Zion (see Isa 2:2, Mic 4:1, Zech 14:10). Second, the plan for the division of the land for the Temple, Jerusalem, and the tribes is clearly an ideal plan that ignores many historical and geographical precedents (Eichrodt, *Ezekiel*, 570, 590-3; Eisemann, *Ezekiel*, vol. 3, 706). It is a bold program that suggests the beginning of something new in God's dealing with his people. Third, the life-giving water flowing from the Temple can only be God's doing and is a mark elsewhere of the age of blessing or the new age (Joel 3:18 [MT 4:18], Zech 14:8). More could be said about the miraculous and idealistic elements in Ezek 40-48, but further attention to these can be found in the commentaries that hold to the third interpretive option (see especially Beale, *Temple and the Church's Mission*, 342-3).

[209] Beale, Eichrodt, Fairbairn, Keil, and Schmidt support this interpretation by emphasizing the miraculous and idealistic elements of the vision and the impossibility of a human fulfillment of the vision without a decisive act of God (see previous note).

[210] Since the initial aspect of this decisive act of God is the ministry, death, resurrection, and exaltation of Jesus, it is only after Jesus' exaltation that believers really begin to experience the salvific benefits of the new age (John 7:37-39). The final aspects of the decisive act of God are described in Rev 19-22. Thus Ezek 40-48 is describing the same eschatological realities that believers experience in part now and will experience fully in the new heaven and new earth (Rev 21-22), but it is doing so from the vantage point of OT realities. These OT realities (or types) are anticipatory and once their fulfillment comes they are fulfilled and replaced by the NT realities that they anticipated (antitypes). Hence one finds no Temple in the New Jerusalem (Rev 21:22), because the Lord God and Jesus are its Temple (see chapter 6 for further comments on the Temple in Revelation). In Rev 21:12-14, one finds a city with the names of the twelve tribes on its gates (see Ezek 48:31) and the names of the twelve apostles on its foundation stones. It is the city of the entire redeemed people of God, including Jews and Gentiles. This typological approach to Ezek 40-48 is worked out in detail by Beale (*Temple and the Church's Mission*, 346-53) and Keil (*Ezekiel*, vol. 2, 416-25). Other interpreters who support this interpretation of Ezekiel 40-48, include Fairbairn (and those he lists [*Ezekiel*, 435]) and Gregory Stevenson (*Power and Place: Temple and Identity in the Book of Revelation*, BZNW, no. 107 [Berlin: Walter de Gruyter, 2001], 270-1). In chapter 4, this approach will be worked out further with respect to John 7:37-39.

[211] Cf. Paul R. House, *Old Testament Theology* (Downers Grove, Ill.: InterVarsity, 1998), 344.

exiles is the rebuilding of the Temple.[212] The post-exilic writings round out the Old Testament portrait of the Temple. At the same time, they suggest the probable trajectory for the future of Israel. Part of this trajectory includes the continuation of hope for the complete fulfillment of prophecies anticipating a new Temple of God.

The Temple in the Post-Exilic Period

The initial return of the exiles is the first indication that God is fulfilling his promises to the remnant of his people. According to Ezra 1:1-8 and 2 Chronicles 36:22-23, king Cyrus of Persia is the Lord's chosen builder for the Temple. In fulfillment of Isaiah 44:28, he returns the Temple vessels to Sheshbazzar and makes provisions for the Temple's construction (Ezra 1:4, 6:4). So begins the post-exilic period, which is frequently identified as the restoration period. The Old Testament writings of the restoration period give first priority to the rebuilding of the Temple. Haggai and Zechariah, in particular, reinforce the connection between the rebuilt Temple and God's blessings upon his people. Why does one not find accounts of the outpouring of blessing even after the Temple is rebuilt? The writings of the period consistently point to a familiar problem, the people's sin. With regard to one's understanding of the Temple, the significance of these writings should not be underestimated. Although their contribution to the theology of the Temple lies primarily in reiteration, they provide the framework for understanding the deferment of the prophetic hopes for a new, enduring Temple of God.

After laying the Temple's foundations, the enemies of Judah and Benjamin manage to stop further work (Ezra 3:10-4:24). Haggai and Zechariah encourage the rebuilding efforts to begin again and see them through to completion (Ezra 5:1-2, 6:14; Hag 1:13-15). Their ministry comes at a time when people are saying that it is not the appropriate time to rebuild the Temple (Hag 1:2).[213]

In response to those who assert that it is not time to rebuild the Temple, Haggai asserts the opposite and proclaims what God has revealed to him concerning the current situation faced by the remnant living in the land. First, Haggai reveals that the fertility of the land has been so meager, because the Temple has not been rebuilt (Hag 1:5-11). If the people would rebuild the

---

[212] Peter R. Ackroyd, *Exile and Restoration: A Study of Hebrew Thought of the Sixth Century B.C.*, OTL (Philadelphia: Westminster, 1968), 154.

[213] The idea of an appropriate time for establishing the Temple has been discussed above (cf. Deut 12:10). First Chronicles 22:9-10, 18-19 is the most prominent example of possession of the land and rest from enemies as precursors to the building of the Temple (cf. 1 Kgs 5:4-5 [MT vv. 18-19]). It could be that Haggai and Zechariah are up against a similar view of the appropriate time for establishing the Temple (Sara Japhet, 'The Temple in the Restoration Period: Reality and Ideology,' trans. Steven Weitzman, *USQR* 44 [1991]: 232).

Temple, they would place themselves in a situation where the Lord could bless their land (Hag 2:15-19). Second, their immediate blessings are only a foretaste of what is to come. The Temple built under Zerubbabel and Joshua may not compare well with Solomon's Temple, but it is only a beginning (Hag 2:3, Ezra 3:12). The Lord promises to bring the glory of the nations into the Temple such that its glory will surpass that of the former Temple (Hag 2:6-9).[214] Similarly, Haggai ends with the ambiguous proclamation of Zerubbabel's election, which probably should be associated with earlier prophetic expectations of a future Davidic king (Hag 2:23).[215]

At several points, Zechariah's message is comparable to Haggai's. Zechariah also points to the hardships faced by the remnant and connects them with the remnant's failure to rebuild the Temple (Zech 8:9-11). A rebuilt Temple is a necessary prelude to blessings from God (Zech 8:12-13).[216] As in Haggai, it is only a beginning set in 'the day of small things' (Zech 4:10). Zechariah proclaims a brighter future ahead for Jerusalem, the land, and God's scattered people.[217] He also prophesies about the coming of a Davidic king who will lead God's people against their enemies.[218] Alongside of the brighter future for God's people, the nations will experience the Lord's judgment and will be drawn to Jerusalem and to the Temple.[219] In short, Zechariah touches upon almost every primary category of blessing included in other prophetic expectations concerned with the future of Israel after the exile.[220] Thus Zechariah continues to look forward to the fulfillment of similar expectations to those found in prophetic works of pre-exilic, exilic, and post-exilic origin. At the same time, Zechariah does not dwell exclusively upon potential blessings. Zechariah, more clearly than Haggai, clarifies that expectations of a brighter future for post-exilic Israel are contingent upon the obedience of God's people.

The potential for the people's sin to hinder the realization of the prophetic expectations for Israel is a constant element of Zechariah 1-8. It occurs first in Zechariah 1:2-6, which is parallel to Zechariah 7:8-14. In both passages, the sinful actions of Israel's forefathers, God's warnings to them, and their punishment are called to mind as a warning to the present generation.[221] In spite of their forefathers' sins, God clears the way for a promising future for the

---

[214] Cf. 2 Chr 32:23.

[215] On Hag 2:24, see David L. Petersen, *Haggai and Zechariah 1-8: A Commentary*, OTL (Philadelphia: Westminster, 1984), 102-6; Théophane Chary, *Aggée – Zacharie – Malachie*, SB (Paris: J. Gabalda and Co., 1969), 34-35.

[216] Cf. also Zech 1:16; Ackroyd, *Exile and Restoration*, 175.

[217] Zech 2:4-6 (MT vv. 8-10), 11-12 (MT vv. 15-16); 8:3-8, 14-15; 9:17; 10:8-12; 13:1, 9; 14:6-11, 20-21.

[218] Zech 9:9-16, 10:4, 12:7-9.

[219] Zech 1:19-21 (MT 2:2-4); 2:8-11 (MT vv. 12-15); 8:20-23; 12:2-9; 14:2-5, 12-19.

[220] See p. 71.

[221] Ackroyd, *Exile and Restoration*, 202, 210-1.

remnant by cleansing and commissioning Joshua (Zech 3:1-7).[222] Similarly, in Zechariah 5, God intervenes to remove sin from the land.[223] God's gracious action is complemented by calls for obedience on the part of the remnant. The first is found at the end of Zechariah 6:15, which says, 'This will happen if you diligently obey the Lord your God.'[224] Zechariah 8:16-17 reiterates the call for obedience and even sets forth specific commands for the remnant to follow.[225] Zechariah 6:15 and 8:16-17 both stand side by side with God's plans to bless the remnant. Clearly, the blessings of God are understood to be contingent upon the remnant's obedience.[226]

Ezra and Nehemiah offer further evidence for such a conviction. For example, Ezra 9:14-15 draws attention to the possibility that God will choose to wipe out the remnant due to its disobedience to his commands (see also 10:2-4). Nehemiah 1:8-9 establishes a close relationship between Israel's obedience to God's commands and the re-gathering of the exiles.[227] In addition, the remnant attributes the gravity of its current situation to sin (Neh 9:36-38) and commits itself to follow God's law (10:29). Even so, the book ends with an account of the commission of the very sins specified in Nehemiah 10:30-39.[228] Thus Ezra and Nehemiah not only affirm the contingency of God's blessings upon the remnant's obedience, but also portray the disobedient acts of the remnant that compromise God's blessing.[229]

Zechariah's, Ezra's, and Nehemiah's emphasis upon obedience is shared by

---

[222] For discussion of the significance of Joshua's cleansing, see Petersen, *Haggai and Zechariah 1-8*, 194-6.

[223] On Zech 3:1-7 and 5:1-11, see Ackroyd, *Exile and Restoration*, 183-7.

[224] This statement follows closely the phraseology of Deut 28:1. Deut 28:1 is the 'Deuteronomic charge' that introduces the blessings and curses of Deut 28. See also parallels like Exod 15:26, Lev 26:14, and Deut 11:13 (Carol L. Meyers and Eric M. Meyers, *Haggai, Zechariah 1-8: A New Translation with Introduction and Commentary*, AB, vol. 25B [New York: Doubleday, 1987], 365-6).

[225] These commands are closely related to those neglected by their forefathers (Zech 7:9-10) (Meyers, *Haggai, Zechariah 1-8*, 426).

[226] On this point, see Donald A. Carson, *Divine Sovereignty and Human Responsibility: Biblical Perspectives in Tension*, New Foundations Theological Library (Atlanta: John Knox, 1981), 21.

[227] These verses are a loose citation of Deut 30:1-4 (Wilhelm Rudolph, *Esra und Nehemia samt 3. Esra*, HAT, vol. 20 [Tübingen: J. C. B. Mohr, 1949], 105).

[228] See Neh 13:10-30. Having outlined the questions raised by scholars regarding Neh 10 and its proper placement in relation to other events in Ezra and Nehemiah, Sara Japhet claims, 'These questions notwithstanding, the general picture is sufficiently clear: the covenant [in Neh 10] testifies that the people had the intention and the obligation to establish worship in the Temple to its full extent, though the description of events suggests they did not succeed in doing this' ('Temple in the Restoration Period,' 237).

[229] Cf. J. Gordon McConville, 'Ezra-Nehemiah and the Fulfilment of Prophecy,' *VT* 36 (1986): 211-12; K. Koch, 'Ezra and the Origins of Judaism,' *JSS* 19 (1974): 188, 192, 196.

Malachi, who likewise points to the sins of the remnant and correlates them with the withholding of divine blessing. First, he calls attention to the sins of the priests who are offering blemished sacrifices and leading others astray (Mal 1:8, 2:8). Next, he turns to the sins committed by the people of Judah. They are marrying foreign wives, divorcing the wives of their youth, and robbing God by skimping on their tithes (2:11, 14; 3:8-9). The sins of the people make their sacrifices unacceptable (2:13). Their situation would be so much better if they would return to God by obeying his commandments (3:7).[230] Then they would be in a position to enjoy God's blessings (3:10-12). Yet Malachi does not end with general promises of blessing for Israel. Instead, one finds promises of a day of judgment when God will punish the wicked and preserve the righteous (3:1-5, 3:17-4:3).[231]

The force of Zechariah's, Ezra's, Nehemiah's, and Malachi's concern with the remnant's obedience is magnified when it is placed against a broader Old Testament background. For instance, according to Jeremiah 17:24-27, Israel's obedience to the Sabbath regulations would ensure a continuous placement of kings on David's throne, a lasting establishment of Jerusalem, and appropriate worship of God at the Temple.[232] Equally relevant is Jeremiah 18:1-10, which compares Israel to clay in the potter's hands. In particular, after God has announced that he will bless a certain nation, he can revoke that blessing if it disobeys him (Jer 18:9-10).[233] Psalm 37 anticipates the day when the wicked will be cut off from the land, which is the appropriate inheritance of the righteous. On that day, the curses of the Lord upon the wicked will be manifest (37:22). Therefore the psalmist exhorts his listeners to 'turn from evil and do

---

[230] Cf. Zech 1:3. On the significance of returning to God as part of an 'OT/HB paradigm for renewing covenant with Yahweh,' see Andrew E. Hill, *Malachi: A New Translation with Introduction and Commentary*, AB, vol. 25D (New York: Doubleday, 1998), 322-3, 301-2.

[231] Such a day of judgment sounds similar to what is found in Ezekiel 9 (see also Zech 13:8-9).

[232] See also Jer 22:2-5. The attention given to the Sabbath regulations in Jer 17:24 should not be overemphasized as if they were the only regulations of importance (cf. Jer 7:23, 22:3) (John A. Thompson, *The Book of Jeremiah*, NICOT [Grand Rapids: Eerdmans, 1980], 429).

[233] In the context, Jer 18:1-10 is relevant to the announcement of God's plans to bring judgment upon Judah and Jerusalem (18:11). In another passage, Jeremiah places God's action of deliverance side by side with the exiles' actions (29:10-14) (Carson, *Divine Sovereignty and Human Responsibility*, 14; Thompson, *Jeremiah*, 547-8). The exiles must seek God with all their hearts before they will be brought back from exile (note the close parallel in Deut 4:29). For other passages from the prophets that correlate God's deliverance or blessing with an appropriate human response, see Isa 59:20, 65:8-16; Jer 31:16-20; Ezek 20:39-40, 43:9.

good' (37:27).[234] Two texts from Deuteronomy are significant additions to these passages. Deuteronomy 4:29-30 and 30:2-10 emphasize the responsibility of God's exiled people for turning back to him and obeying his commands. Only then will God bring them back from exile so they can enjoy his blessings in their land (30:3-10).[235] Perhaps the most general Old Testament background for all of these texts can be found in the blessings and curses of Leviticus 26 and Deuteronomy 28. They present clearly the two paths available to God's people. The path of obedience results in God's blessing and the path of disobedience results in God's curse.[236]

If the return from exile begins with turning back to God and obedience to his commandments (Deut 30:2-5), then it is not surprising that those who return from exile are expected to continue in obedience (30:6-10). It is not possible to isolate the blessings promised to the returnees from the necessity of their obedience (Jer 18:9-10).[237] This supports the appropriateness of Ezra's strong reaction to the report of a sinful practice that was threatening the holiness of the remnant (Ezra 9:1-3). Such a practice could compromise God's 'acts of purgation and deliverance.'[238] Indeed, the united testimony of Haggai, Zechariah, Ezra, Nehemiah, and Malachi suggests that significant elements of the remnant did not manage to persevere in faithfulness to God's commands.[239] The sins portrayed in these books, especially Ezra, Nehemiah, and Malachi, include a variety of sinful practices. Just as significant are sinful attitudes that question the importance of obedience (Mal 3:13-15). Hence the holiness of the remnant was compromised and so the post-exilic age falls far short of the blessed age of restoration portrayed in Israel's prophets. Even so, this is not the end of the story of God's dealings with his people.

Given the sinful practices of the people in Ezra, Nehemiah, and Malachi, one can summarize the trajectory for the future of the post-exilic community of Israel as follows: in spite of high points and the perseverance of a faithful subgroup, the remnant's sin will not be decisively dealt with until the Lord comes in judgment, separating the righteous and the wicked (Mal 3:18-4:3).[240]

---

[234] This is an appropriate parallel to Zech 5:2-4. See also Psalm 101 and the close relationship between righteousness and blessing in the theology of Chronicles as summarized above (see p. 68).

[235] Cf. Lev 26:40-45. Also, see Ezek 20:34-38 where God promises to ensure a clean start for the remnant by keeping rebellious exiles from returning to the land.

[236] The OT passages cited in this paragraph represent a limited selection for purposes of illustration.

[237] See also Ezek 37:24b and Carson, *Divine Sovereignty and Human Responsibility*, 21.

[238] McConville, 'Ezra-Nehemiah and the Fulfilment of Prophecy,' 221.

[239] Zechariah, Ezra, Nehemiah, and Malachi do not neglect to portray the faction that does remain faithful (Zech 13:9; Ezra 9:4, 10:3; Neh 13:31; Mal 3:16-18).

[240] McConville notes that the canonical books of Ezra and Nehemiah in their canonical order clearly imply 'that, were the story of the post-exilic community to be protracted, it would continue to follow the same chequered course that it has throughout our books

Such a trajectory does not overlook the remnant's opportunity to repent of its sins and to obey God's commandments. In doing so, it would put itself in a position to enjoy God's blessings.[241] The story of its ancestors suggests, however, that periods of widespread repentance and obedience will be short-lived, as will the blessings that accompany them. Nevertheless the righteous subgroup can expect to experience some measure of God's blessings, while clinging to hopes of a more glorious future in which the full measure of God's blessings will be experienced by the righteous remnant.[242]

The futuristic hope of God's faithful people is not merely wishful thinking. The basis for their hope rests in part upon the history of God's dealing with his people. God's faithfulness, justice, and deliverance are evident throughout the Old Testament. Surely God will also display his faithfulness and deliverance to the righteous remnant. Their hope is also based upon prophetic expectations. Even during the post-exilic era, Zechariah and Malachi continue to predict a brighter future for God's righteous remnant.[243] Their prophecies continue to support a future orientation, a sense that 'Yahweh is directing history towards a goal, the salvation of Israel.'[244]

According to Zechariah, the brighter future for God's righteous remnant includes a blessed future for Jerusalem and the Temple.[245] Jerusalem will always be secure and the sanctity of the Temple will always be safeguarded (Zech 14:11, 21).[246] The nations that formerly attacked Jerusalem will make yearly pilgrimages there in order to worship the Lord and celebrate the Feast of Tabernacles.[247] Zechariah does not provide a Temple plan, but it can be

---

[Ezra and Nehemiah]' ('Ezra-Nehemiah and the Fulfilment of Prophecy,' 212). Similarly, Yehezkel Kaufmann appeals to Malachi for evidence that the remnant's failures account for the delay of the anticipated 'redemption' and set it up for judgment (*History of the Religion of Israel*, vol. 4, *From the Babylonian Captivity to the End of Prophecy*, trans. C. W. Efroymson [New York: Ktav, 1977], 466).

[241] Jer 17:24-27, 22:2-5.

[242] Ackroyd, *Exile and Restoration*, 253; Rex Mason, 'The Prophets of the Restoration,' in *Israel's Prophetic Tradition: Essays in Honour of Peter R. Ackroyd*, ed. Richard Coggins et al. (Cambridge: Cambridge University Press, 1982), 151-2; Willem A. VanGemeren, *Interpreting the Prophetic Word* (Grand Rapids: Zondervan, 1990), 209.

[243] See Zech 13:8-9, 14:1-21; Mal 3:18-4:3 (MT 3:18-21).

[244] Sigmund Mowinckel, *He That Cometh*, trans. G. W. Anderson (New York: Abingdon, 1954), 152. In addition, 'God's ultimate purpose' includes the universal 'acknowledgment of Yahweh's sovereignty' (Carol L. Meyers and Eric M. Meyers, *Zechariah 9-14: A New Translation with Introduction and Commentary*, AB, vol. 25C [New York: Doubleday, 1993], 492).

[245] See also Mal 3:2-3 which depicts the cleansing of the Levites so that they can bring acceptable offerings.

[246] On the security of Jerusalem, cf. Isa 33:20-24; 54:11-17; 62:1-12; 65:17-20; Jer 31:38-40; Ezek 37:26; 39:26; Joel 3:17, 20 (MT 4:17, 20); Zech 2:1-5 (MT 2:5-9); 8:3-5, 22; 12:1-9. On the sanctity of the Temple, cf. Ezek 44:9.

[247] Zech 14:16-19. Cf. Isa 2:2-4, Mic 4:1-3, Zech 8:20-23.

assumed that his vision is basically consistent with earlier expectations of a new Temple greater than the one built by Solomon.[248] Zechariah's picture of the final deliverance of Jerusalem sustains hope for an ideal future for Israel.[249] It is a picture that stands in stark contrast to the conditions of the post-exilic age. In Zechariah 14, God manifests his redemptive presence among his people by means of political, economic, and geographic realities. In each of these areas, the exalted place of Jerusalem and the Temple is manifest. It is the place where the 'King, the Lord Almighty' is worshiped (Zech 14:16).

The preceding section looks to post-exilic texts to account for the disparity between great prophetic expectations for the restoration period and its disappointing realities. The people's sin is consistently blamed for the incomplete and meager fulfillment of prophetic expectations. Even so, Zechariah and Malachi continue to predict a brighter future for the righteous remnant of Israel. In Zechariah 14, the futuristic scene is similar to Ezekiel 40-48 in that its apex is the Temple. Zechariah 14 provides encouragement to those still anticipating the time when God will take up permanent residence among his people and shower his blessings upon them.[250] It remains to be seen how such hopes will persevere in Jewish writings from the Greek, Maccabean, and Roman periods.

The Temple in Extra-Biblical Jewish Literature

Extra-biblical Jewish literature affirms the importance of the Temple for the Jewish people.[251] By far, the majority of the evidence supports a widespread

---

[248] The wealth needed for the Temple is supplied by the nations (Zech 14:1, 14). See Isa 60:7, 13; Hag 2:9. Some details of Zechariah's vision of the future of Jerusalem and the Temple do not fit neatly with Ezekiel 40-48. First, water flows from Jerusalem and not expressly from the Temple (Zech 14:8, Ezek 47:2). In this case, the mention of Jerusalem probably does not rule out the possibility that the source is actually the Temple (Meyers and Meyers, *Zechariah 9-14*, 436). Second, the picture in Zechariah apparently places the Temple within the city of Jerusalem (14:8, 10; Ezek 45:6, 48:15). Third, water flows out of Jerusalem both to the east and to the west (14:8, Ezek 47:8). Fourth, Zechariah gives more attention to Jerusalem as a place of pilgrimage for the nations (14:16-19, 21). Among these, the only change of real significance is probably the placement of the Temple within Jerusalem. Such a change suggests that the holiness of the Jerusalem envisioned by Zechariah will be of such a caliber that it will not endanger the holiness of the Temple. An analogy for such a step up in holiness is provided by the increased holiness of certain cooking vessels used in the Temple (Zech 14:20).

[249] Meyers and Meyers, *Zechariah 9-14*, 492-3.

[250] Cf. Ezek 34:25-31, 37:25-28.

[251] As noted at the beginning of the chapter, the survey of extra-canonical Jewish literature will focus upon literature that is from the first century A.D. and earlier. The dating for extra-canonical works will not always be indicated. Therefore it should be

concern for the Temple and Temple-service. This does not mean that there were no challenges to the legitimacy of the post-exilic Temple and the sacrifices offered in it. In each case, charges of illegitimacy do not stem from a desire to do away with the Temple, but to see the Temple established as a pure, legitimate house of God.[252] Therefore it is not surprising to find several texts anticipating a future Temple that would surpass the post-exilic Temple in greatness and would endure forever. The task at hand is to survey the textual evidence for these general points.

The first concern is to examine texts that affirm the legitimacy of the post-exilic Temple.[253] Given the significance of the Temple in 1, 2, and 3 Maccabees, it is not surprising that they apply traditional Temple theology to the Second Temple. For example, 1 Maccabees 7:37 and 2 Maccabees 14:35-36 contain variations of a prayer offered by the priests. Taken together, these verses affirm that the Temple is God's chosen house called by his name, a house of prayer for his people, and his dwelling place among them.[254] In addition to similar convictions, 3 Maccabees 2:9-16 (part of the high priest's prayer) adds that the Temple is the Lord's sanctified place on earth. It is distinct from the Lord's true dwelling place, which is the 'heaven of heavens' (2:15).[255] Beyond these beliefs, the continuity between the Second Temple and Solomon's Temple is manifest in several miraculous incidents. First, the altar fire from Solomon's Temple was hidden before its destruction. The fire was miraculously preserved in a liquid form and used to rekindle the altar fire of the Second Temple.[256] Second, God's wrath was poured out upon Gentile rulers who entered the Temple proper, defiling its sanctity.[257]

Outside of 1, 2, and 3 Maccabees, one can find evidence supporting the legitimacy of the post-exilic Temple in Josephus and Philo. Josephus reports that most people present at the dedication of the Second Temple were not disappointed by its lack of grandeur (*Ant.* 11.82). This implies that he saw no

---

assumed in each instance that cited works are generally regarded by interpreters as first century A.D. or earlier. References to rabbinic literature are the general exception to this rule. Rabbinic literature will sometimes be cited when it provides instructive parallels to other texts. Yet this is done in full recognition that such parallels cannot always be dated to the first century A.D. or earlier.

[252] The prominent exception to this general rule is found in the NT, which will be discussed in the coming chapters (cf. Elisabeth Schüssler Fiorenza, 'Cultic Language in Qumran and in the New Testament,' *CBQ* 38 [1976]: 168, 176-7).

[253] For a brief overview of this subject, see E. P. Sanders, *Judaism: Practice and Belief 63 BCE–66 CE* (Philadelphia: Trinity Press International, 1992), 53.

[254] Cf. 1 Kgs 8:13, 29-30, 43; 9:3 // 2 Chr 6:2, 20-21, 33; 7:15-16; Jer 7:10.

[255] Cf. 1 Kgs 8:27, 9:3 // 2 Chr 6:18, 7:16.

[256] 2 Macc 1:20-23, 31-34. On the significance of this event, see Jonathan A. Goldstein, *II Maccabees*, AB, vol. 41A (Garden City, N.Y.: Doubleday, 1983), 173-6.

[257] 2 Macc 3:22-40, 3 Macc 1:9-2:24. Cf. 2 Chr 26:16-23.

reason for disappointment with the Second Temple.[258] In addition, Philo gives the clear impression that he views the Temple with utmost reverence. He describes the blessings experienced by the many pilgrims who travel from the Diaspora to the Temple at festival times (*Spec. Laws* 1.68-69).[259] Jews joyously contribute to the Temple, knowing that God will bless them for doing so (*Spec. Laws* 1.77).[260]

Affirmation of the post-exilic Temple is one kind of evidence for widespread concern for the Temple and Temple-service. Another kind is provided by criticism of those in charge of the Temple-service whose actions threaten the sanctity of the Temple and bring discredit to their office.[261] The most well-documented dissidents are often called the 'Essenes.'[262] Evidence from the Dead Sea Scrolls points to the existence of two distinctive types of Essene communities.[263] One type, the Qumran community, lived at Qumran near the Dead Sea, while the other type of Essene community was established outside of Qumran. As a whole, the Essenes criticized the priests in charge of

---

[258] Cf. Sir 49:12, *Sib. Or.* 3:287-294.

[259] Philo's glowing description of the Temple is analogous to the account found in *Let. Aris.* 84-99 (Philo *Spec. Laws* 1.71-74).

[260] Interestingly, Philo criticizes those whose allegorical interpretation of the laws of the OT leads them to neglect obedience to the plain sense of the laws, including laws having to do with the Temple (*Migration* 89-93, esp. 92; Sanders, *Judaism*, 53).

[261] Regarding the sanctity of the Temple, the author of 2 Maccabees and Josephus agree that God does not deliver the Temple from defilement by Gentile leaders during periods of Jewish disobedience, especially that of their leaders (2 Macc 5:15-20; Josephus *Ant.* 11.297-301, 12.237-256, 14.69-79). On the other hand, the Temple is honored most when its leadership is pleasing to God (1 Macc 14:15, 2 Macc 3:1-3).

[262] James C. VanderKam, *The Dead Sea Scrolls Today* (Grand Rapids: Eerdmans, 1994), 71-92, esp. 91-92. As Lester Grabbe points out, the identification of the Qumran community and the related communities as Essenes is far from certain. This is due to significant unresolved questions, including questions regarding the descriptions of the Essenes in the classical sources and their correspondence to the contents of the Qumran scrolls (Lester L. Grabbe, 'The Current State of the Dead Sea Scrolls: Are There More Answers than Questions?,' in *The Scrolls and the Scriptures: Qumran Fifty Years After*, ed. Stanley Porter and Craig Evans, JSPSup, vol. 3 [Sheffield: Sheffield Academic Press, 1997], 55).

[263] Philip Davies and F. García Martínez have been significant supporters of 'more than one community being represented by the non-biblical scrolls' (Charlotte Hempel, 'Qumran Communities: Beyond the Fringes of Second Temple Society,' in *The Scrolls and the Scriptures: Qumran Fifty Years After*, ed. Stanley Porter and Craig Evans, JSPSup, vol. 3 [Sheffield: Sheffield Academic Press, 1997], 49-50). Cf. Philip Davies, 'The Ideology of the Temple in the Damascus Document,' *JJS* 33 (1982): 287, 289; Sanders, *Judaism*, 347; Emil Schürer, *The History of the Jewish People in the Age of Jesus Christ (175 B.C.–A.D. 135)*, ed. Geza Vermes, Fergus Millar, and Matthew Black, vol. 2 (Edinburgh: T. and T. Clark, 1979), 575-79.

the Temple and the Temple-service performed by them.[264]

The Essenes' disapproval of the Temple-service is a natural development given their origins and theological distinctives. A central figure in the history of the Essenes is a priest referred to as the 'Teacher of Righteousness.'[265] Two factors establish the nature of the rivalry between the Essene priesthood and the contemporaneous Temple priesthood. First, the Teacher of Righteousness had an important enemy referred to as the 'Wicked Priest.' The Wicked Priest was apparently Jerusalem's reigning high priest.[266] The Wicked Priest is even accused of pursuing the Teacher of Righteousness in an attempt to snuff him out (1QpHab XI, 4-8). Such an outward display of rivalry takes on added significance when one turns to the second factor, namely, the distinctive laws of the Essenes.[267] As the communities' authoritative exegetes of the Scriptures, the Teacher of Righteousness and the priests who followed in his stead are largely responsible for these distinctive laws.[268] According to Essene writings, the 'true Israel' consists of those who obey the law of Moses as interpreted by

---

[264] See esp. 1QpHab VIII, 8-13; IX, 9-11; XI, 4-15; XII, 7-9; consider also CD VIII, 3-13; 1QS II, 24-III, 9; V, 8-13; 4QMMT. Cf. Philip R. Davies, 'The Judaism(s) of the Damascus Document,' in *The Damascus Document: A Centennial of Discovery: Proceedings of the Third International Symposium of the Orion Center for the Study of the Dead Sea Scrolls and Associated Literature, 4-8 February, 1998*, ed. J. M. Baumgarten et al. (Leiden: Brill, 2000), 34-35; Robert A. Kugler, 'Priesthood at Qumran,' in *The Dead Sea Scrolls after Fifty Years: A Comprehensive Assessment*, ed. Peter W. Flint and James C. VanderKam, vol. 2 (Leiden: Brill, 1999), 113.

[265] Cf. CD I, 11; 4QpPs II, 19; III, 15 (Kugler, 'Priesthood at Qumran,' 105; Schürer, *History of the Jewish People*, vol. 2, 587; Sanders, *Judaism*, 342-3).

[266] The enmity between the Teacher of Righteousness and the Wicked Priest is captured vividly in 1QpHab VIII, 8-13; IX, 9-11; XI, 4-15; XII, 7-9. The profile of the Wicked Priest given by the Essene writings points to Jonathan, who became high priest in 153/2 B.C. (Schürer, *History of the Jewish People*, vol. 2, 587; James C. VanderKam, 'Identity and History of the Community,' in *The Dead Sea Scrolls after Fifty Years: A Comprehensive Assessment*, ed. Peter W. Flint and James C. Vanderkam, vol. 2 [Leiden: Brill, 1999], 511).

[267] Of course, not all of the Essenes' laws are distinctive. They adopted the Torah of Moses as the basis for their legal code. Their legal distinctiveness arises largely from their unique interpretations of the Torah (see, for example, Sanders's discussion of Qumran purity laws [*Judaism*, 359-60]). At some points, however, their distinctiveness is the result of deliberate, divinely inspired choices that set them apart from other Jews (see 1QS V, 8-12). A prominent example is the Qumran community's adherence to a solar calendar (or to a unique lunar calendar), which means that they celebrated the OT feasts on different days from other Jews (Sanders, *Judaism*, 360-1; VanderKam, *Dead Sea Scrolls*, 114-6).

[268] Martin Hengel, *Judaism and Hellenism: Studies in Their Encounter in Palestine during the Early Hellenistic Period*, trans. John Bowden, vol. 1 (Philadelphia: Fortress, 1974), 227 (also, vol. 2, 150-1); Kugler, 'Priesthood at Qumran,' 110; Schürer, *History of the Jewish People*, vol. 2, 580.

the Essenes' priests and the Teacher of Righteousness.²⁶⁹ In short, the inspired exegesis of the Essenes' priests fixed a theological and behavioral gulf between themselves and the Jerusalem priests.

The above background information sets the stage for examination of the practical outworking of the Essenes' disapproval of the Jerusalem priesthood. It appears that the Essenes of the Qumran community completely cut themselves off from the Jerusalem Temple, including offering sacrifices in it.²⁷⁰ To compensate, they developed a theology of atonement that makes their community a temporary replacement for the Temple.²⁷¹ Thus the Qumran community becomes a 'holy house' with its own 'holy of holies.'²⁷² In place of atonement through sacrifices, the community brings 'the offering of the lips.'²⁷³ Similarly, they bring 'correctness of behaviour' in place of the 'freewill

---

²⁶⁹ Davies, 'Judaism(s) of the Damascus Document,' 31; Hengel, *Judaism and Hellenism*, vol. 1, 227; Schürer, *History of the Jewish People*, vol. 2, 575-6. See also 1QS II, 24-III, 9; V, 8-13; CD I, 11; XX, 27-33.

²⁷⁰ Davies, 'Judaism(s) of the Damascus Document,' 39; Sanders, *Judaism*, 362-3; Schürer, *History of the Jewish People*, vol. 2, 575-6;

²⁷¹ Interpreters generally agree that the significant relevant passages are 1QS V, 4-7; VIII, 4-10; IX, 3-6. Disputed passages of possible relevance include 4QFlor I, 1-7 and CD III, 18-IV, 10. Cf. Davies, 'Temple in the Damascus Document,' 287-8; Fiorenza, 'Cultic Language in Qumran and in the NT,' *CBQ* 38 (1976): 164-6; Bertil Gärtner, *The Temple and the Community in Qumran and the New Testament: A Comparative Study in the Temple Symbolism of the Qumran Texts and the New Testament* (Cambridge: Cambridge University Press, 1965), 22-30; Georg Klinzing, *Die Umdeutung des Kultus in der Qumrangemeinde und im Neuen Testament*, SUNT, no. 7 (Göttingen: Vandenhoeck and Ruprecht, 1971), 50-74; McKelvey, *New Temple*, 46-50.

²⁷² 1QS VIII, 5-9 (cf. 4QS^d 2 I, 1-3; 4QS^e II, 11-16); IX, 6 (cf. 4QS^d 2 II, 6) (cf. Davies, 'Judaism[s] of the Damascus Document,' 39). The 'holy house' is alternately said to be 'for Israel' (1 QS VIII, 5) and 'for Aaron' (IX, 6). Klinzing understands 'for Israel' to be an inclusive expression denoting the entire community, while 'for Aaron' is a more specific reference to the priestly subset within the community (*Umdeutung des Kultus in der Qumrangemeinde*, 62-63 [where he also discusses the use of 'house' in these passages and in 1QS generally]). The Essenes' concern for holiness is a concern commonly evident in their legal materials (Hannah K. Harrington, 'The Halakah and Religion of Qumran,' in *Religion in the Dead Sea Scrolls*, ed. John Collins and Robert Kugler [Grand Rapids: Eerdmans, 2000], 81-88).

²⁷³ The 'offering of the lips' is understood as praise (Klinzing, *Umdeutung des Kultus in der Qumrangemeinde*, 41, 96-98) or prayer (Fiorenza, 'Cultic Language in Qumran and in the NT,' 166) or the community's worship (Markus Bockmuehl, '1QS and Salvation at Qumran,' in *The Complexities of Second Temple Judaism*, ed. D. A. Carson et al, vol. 1 of *Justification and Variegated Nomism*, WUNT, 2nd series, no. 140 [Grand Rapids: Baker, 2001], 401).

offering' (1QS IX, 4-5).[274] Their replacement of the Temple is temporary, because they anticipate that a day is coming when Jerusalem will be handed over to them. Their own priests will be in charge of the Temple in Jerusalem, offering atoning sacrifices there.[275]

It is more difficult to decipher the relationship between the non-Qumran Essenes and the Jerusalem Temple. Of particular importance is the seemingly contradictory evidence found in the *Damascus Document*. On the one hand, it contains laws regulating sacrifice at the Jerusalem Temple.[276] On the other, it apparently condemns all sacrifice at the Temple.[277] Philip Davies's solution to this contradiction is perhaps the most appealing. He concludes that CD VI, 12 contains an 'expansion' placed there by a 'glossator' who was probably a member of the Qumran community.[278] If one accepts Davies's solution, then the non-Qumran Essenes could have offered sacrifices in the Jerusalem Temple during part or all of their existence. Even so, the *Damascus Document* insinuates that other Jews, including the high priests, are guilty of defiling the Temple.[279]

---

[274] The translations given here are from F. García Martínez, *The Dead Sea Scrolls Translated: The Qumran Texts in English*, trans. Wilfred G. Watson, 2nd ed. (Leiden: E. J. Brill, 1996), 13.

[275] F. García Martínez, *Qumran and Apocalyptic: Studies on the Aramaic Texts from Qumran*, STDJ, no. 9 (New York: E. J. Brill, 1992), 206-11; Yigael Yadin, *The Temple Scroll*, vol. 1 (Jerusalem: Israel Exploration Society, 1983), 182-7, 402. In *Temple Scroll* and *New Jerusalem*, one finds additional evidence that the Essenes were not opposed to animal sacrifices as such. Both works describe animal sacrifices in the Temple (2QNJ ar 4, 11QNJ ar, 11QT^a XIII-XXIX; cf. also 1QM II, 1-6). Cf. Robert Kugler, who insists that the Qumran community does not view its activities as adequate replacements for sacrifices in the Temple (to which they expect to return) ('Rewriting Rubrics: Sacrifice and the Religion of Qumran,' in *Religion in the Dead Sea Scrolls*, ed. John Collins and Robert Kugler, Studies in the Dead Sea Scrolls and Related Literature [Grand Rapids: Eerdmans, 2000], 91-92).

[276] CD IX, 13-14; XI, 17-XII, 2; XVI, 13. Cf. Davies, 'Judaism(s) of the Damascus Document,' 34-35.

[277] CD VI, 11-14 (= 4QD^a 3 III, 4-6); cf. also Josephus, *Ant.* 18.19; Philo, *Good Person* 75.

[278] Thus a member of the Qumran community, who would have opposed sacrifice in the contemporaneous Jerusalem Temple, added the words, 'They will be the ones who close the door, as God said, 'Whoever amongst you will close its door so that you do not kindle my altar in vain' [Mal 1:10]' (CD VI, 12-14). Davies feels that proposing such an expansion is justifiable, because the text as it stands is 'simply not grammatical.' Removing the expansion leaves a passage without 'grammatical or syntactical difficulties' (Davies, 'Temple in the Damascus Document,' 296-7). Cf. Davies, 'Judaism(s) of the Damascus Document,' 35.

[279] CD IV, 17; V, 6-7; VIII, 3-13; XX, 22-23; cf. Davies, 'Temple in the Damascus Document,' 289-90 and on the high priests, see Sanders's remarks on VIII, 11 (*Judaism*, 343).

The Essenes were not the only dissidents to point out the deficiencies of the Temple-service conducted in the post-exilic Temple. According to *1 Enoch* 89:73, the sacrifices offered in the Second Temple were always 'polluted.'[280] Similarly, *Testament of Levi* 17:10-11 makes general comments about the sinfulness of the priests who come after the reconstruction of the Temple.[281] These general criticisms are also complemented by others whose specific targets can be identified more clearly. While criticizing Israel's leaders for polluting the Temple, *Testament of Moses* 5:1-6:1 makes a specific reference to the 'great impiety' performed in the 'Holy of Holies' by the Hasmonean rulers.[282] Likewise, *Psalms of Solomon* blames the sins of the people and of the Hasmonean rulers for Pompey's conquest of Jerusalem and profanation of the Temple.[283] In each of these cases, criticisms of the priests and Temple-service do not indicate a desire to do away with the priesthood, the Temple-service, or the Temple itself.[284] Instead, they indicate a desire for a pure priesthood, proper Temple-service, and a holy Temple.[285] The texts themselves provide the proof for such an assertion. Each anticipates the coming of pure priests or the establishment of a holy Temple.[286] Thus the deficiencies of the post-exilic

---

[280] Patrick A. Tiller, *A Commentary on the Animal Apocalypse of 1 Enoch*, SBLEJL, no. 4 (Atlanta: Scholars Press, 1993), 336, 340.

[281] See also *T. Levi* 14, a description of the eschatological sins of the priests.

[282] J. Priest, 'Testament of Moses: A New Translation and Introduction,' in *OTP*, ed. James H. Charlesworth, vol. 1 (New York: Doubleday, 1983), 930.

[283] *Pss. Sol.* 2:3-13, 8:8-22, 17:5-10. Cf. Josephus, *Ant.* 14.69-79. It is important to remember that the Hasmonean rulers were high priests (1 Macc 14:30, 41). On *Pss. Sol.* 2, 8, and 17, see George W. E. Nickelsburg, *Jewish Literature between the Bible and the Mishnah: A Historical and Literary Introduction* (Philadelphia: Fortress, 1981), 205-7; Schürer, *History of the Jewish People*, vol. 3.1, 193-4.

[284] Some interpreters find a desire to do away with the Temple in *Sib. Or.* 4:6-11, 27-30 (see Sanders, *Judaism*, 54). The significance of these verses is debatable. It is difficult to figure out whether (or to what extent) the polemic against pagan temples and sacrifices (4:6-11, 27-30) also implies criticism of 'the great Temple of God' (4:116) (Andrew Chester, 'The Sibyl and the Temple,' in *Templum Amicitiae: Essays on the Second Temple Presented to Ernst Bammel*, ed. William Horbury, JSNTSup, no. 48 [Sheffield: Sheffield Academic Press, 1991], 62-67; Schürer, *History of the Jewish People*, vol. 3.1, 642).

[285] Sanders, *Judaism*, esp. 54, also 182-9, 292-3.

[286] For the coming of pure priests, see *T. Levi* 18 and *T. Mos.* 9:1-10:10. For the establishment of a holy Temple, see *1 En.* 90:29 and *Pss. Sol.* 17:21-44 (esp. 30-2). The significance of *1 En.* 90:29 is disputed by Tiller (*Animal Apocalypse of 1 Enoch*, 36-51 [esp. 46], 376). Most interpreters identify the 'house' of *1 En.* 89:36 as the Tabernacle (i.e., God's dwelling place in the midst of his people [see 89:40]) (Tiller, *Animal Apocalypse of 1 Enoch*, 41). The 'tower' that is built on the house appears to represent the Temple building proper (see 89:50, 73 where the Lord's table is placed before the tower). The absence of the tower from 90:29 is taken by Tiller as an indication that the New Jerusalem has no Temple (*Animal Apocalypse of 1 Enoch*, 46, 376). Tiller's

Temple and Temple-service led these critics to forecast a brighter future for the Temple of God.

Critics of the post-exilic Temple were not the only ones to anticipate a brighter future for the Temple of God. A glorified Temple was a common element of Jewish hopes for the future even before the Temple was destroyed by the Romans in A.D. 70.[287] This is not surprising given the place of the Temple in Old Testament prophecies and continuing hope that these prophecies would be completely fulfilled.[288] As observed above, the Old Testament prophetic writings often present expectations concerning the future of the Temple right alongside other expectations for the future of God's people.[289] As a result, the future of the Temple appears to be vitally connected with other aspects of the social and political future of Israel. This connection is affirmed in extra-biblical Jewish sources.[290] For instance, in Tobit 14:5-7, the hope for a future, glorious Temple is part of a composite picture that also includes the conversion of the nations and the return of all faithful Israelites to the land of Israel.[291] Similar elements are found in *Psalms of Solomon* 17:21-42 where particular emphasis is placed on a Davidic king who will deliver God's people from their enemies, ushering in the future age of blessing.[292] Also, the composite picture found in *Sibylline Oracles* 3:657-795 touches upon a number of the elements of Israel's future hope that were proclaimed by the Old

---

argument is unconvincing for two reasons. First, the tower is closely associated with the house starting at 89:50 (see 89:54, 56, 67, 72-73; in 89:72-3, the tower appears to be regarded as part of the house). Even so, in 89:51, only the abandonment of the house is mentioned, while the concomitant abandonment of the tower is implied (see 89:54). Second, the absence of the tower from 90:29 is just as notable as its absence from 90:28. It is not mentioned as part of the 'old house' that is destroyed. Since a precedence already exists for mentioning the house and assuming the presence of the tower within it (89:51), the same is probably the case in 89:28-29 (cf. Matthew Black, *The Book of Enoch or I Enoch: A New English Edition*, SVTP, no. 7 [Leiden: E. J. Brill, 1985], 278). Cf. also *1 En.* 91:13; 4QEn^g ar IV, 18.

[287] Nickelsburg, *Jewish Literature*, 18; C. C. Rowland, 'The Second Temple: Focus of Ideological Struggle?,' in *Templum Amicitiae: Essays on the Second Temple Presented to Ernst Bammel*, ed. William Horbury, JSNTSup, no. 48 (Sheffield: Sheffield Academic Press, 1991), 179, 183-9; E. P. Sanders, *Jesus and Judaism* (London: SCM Press, 1985), 77-88; Sanders, *Judaism*, 290-4; Schürer, *History of the Jewish People*, vol. 2, 529-30, 535.

[288] Tob 14:4-7; Sir 36:20-21; see also McKelvey, *New Temple*, 22-24.

[289] See p. 71.

[290] See esp. the close connection drawn between the fate of the nation and that of the 'holy place' in 2 Macc 5:19-20.

[291] Cf. Tob 13, where the same elements are present. Similarly, Sir 36:16-19 asks God to gather his people, Israel, and to manifest his glory in Zion and the Temple (cf. *Jub.* 1:15-17, *T. Benj.* 9:2).

[292] Likewise, 4 Ezra 13:32-50 focuses particular attention upon the deliverance of God's people by means of his son, the man from the sea.

Testament prophets.²⁹³ These passages, and their parallels, provide evidence for the ongoing significance of the Temple as a common element in Jewish hopes for the future.²⁹⁴

The Jewish hope for a future, glorified Temple was apparently assisted by the inadequacies of the post-exilic Temple. Even while the post-exilic Temple was standing, Tobit 14:5 says that the Temple will not be rebuilt 'like the first one until the period when the times of fulfillment shall come' (NRSV). The inadequacies of the Temple's structure, which Herod sought to remedy, could not make up for its other deficiencies.²⁹⁵ Even 2 Maccabees, which elsewhere affirms the legitimacy of the post-exilic Temple, allows for its deficiencies. It did not contain the Tabernacle or the ark, nor was its consecration completed by the miraculous appearance of God's glory in a cloud (2 Macc 2:4-8).²⁹⁶ Instead, the ark, the Tabernacle, and the incense altar were hidden by Jeremiah before the destruction of the first Temple (2 Macc 2:4-5). When 'God gathers his people together again and shows them mercy,' these hidden objects will be revealed and God's glory will appear in a cloud as in the times of Moses and Solomon (2:7-8).²⁹⁷ Apparently, one specific hope for the future, glorified

---

²⁹³ It includes a messianic king (3:652-656), a well-decorated Temple (657-658), fertile land (659-660, 744-755), final assault of the nations on the Temple (661-668), divine judgment upon the nations (669-697), secure existence of God's people around the Temple (701-709), worship of the nations at the Temple (710-724, 772-775), and an age of general peace (751-755, 780-795). Cf. the similar, less inclusive presentation of *Sib. Or.* 5:247-285, 414-434.

²⁹⁴ For a more detailed survey and systematization of the elements of Jewish hopes for the future (excluding rabbinic writings), see Schürer, *History of the Jewish People*, vol. 2, 497-547.

²⁹⁵ Josephus, *Ant.* 15.380-387.

²⁹⁶ In spite of Jer 3:16, the ark was not forgotten. Regarding the glory, Ezekiel, in particular, anticipates the appearance of God's glory in the new Temple (43:2-4, 44:4; see also Ps 102:16 [MT v. 17]; Zech 2:5 [MT v. 9]; Isa 66:18-19).

²⁹⁷ See the similar account in *2 Bar.* 6:5-9 where an angel takes holy objects from the Temple along with those from the Tabernacle and deposits them in the earth for safekeeping. They are hidden until the final, eternal restoration of Jerusalem (cf. 32:4; similarly, *Num. Rab.* 15.10). Four passages from rabbinic writings give a list of things missing from the Second Temple. None of the lists is exactly the same. The most well-known list is probably from *b. Yoma* 21b: ark, ark-cover, cherubim, fire, Shechinah, Holy Spirit, and Urim and Thummim. In the other lists, one also finds anointing oil, candlestick, jar of manna, jar of sprinkling water (Num 19:9), Aaron's staff, and gift from the Philistines (1 Sam 6:8) (*b. Yoma* 52b, *Cant. Rab.* 8.9.3, *Num. Rab.* 15.10). The mention of the Holy Spirit should probably be connected with the 'theory of the cessation of prophecy in the time of the second Temple' (J. Abelson, *The Immanence of God in Rabbinical Literature* [London: Macmillan, 1912], 260-1). The list from *b. Yoma* 21b is often cited by scholars, because it is the only list to include the Shechinah, implying the absence of the divine presence from the Second Temple. As G. I. Davies points out, however, one can also find texts that challenge such an implication (see esp.

Temple was that it would not be marred by the deficiencies of the post-exilic Temple. What else can be said about the future Temple?

With one or two notable exceptions, texts that mention a future Temple provide few details about it.[298] It is commonly described as God's eternal dwelling place among his people.[299] Additional noteworthy claims made about the future Temple include: (1) the nations will come to it to worship the God of Israel, (2) it will be greater than Solomon's Temple, and (3) God will protect it from harm.[300] A disputed point concerns the identity of the builder of the future Temple. The builder is variously identified as human beings generally, the Messiah, or God.[301] An important point to keep in mind is that the Old Testament presents both Solomon (1 Kgs 6:2) and God (Ps 78:69) as the builders of Solomon's Temple without noting any conflict between the two

---

Ps 135:21; Matt 23:21; Josephus, *J.W.* 6.299; *m. Sukk.* 5:4) ('The Presence of God in the Second Temple and Rabbinic Doctrine,' in *Templum Amicitiae: Essays on the Second Temple Presented to Ernst Bammel*, ed. William Horbury, JSNTSup, no. 48 [Sheffield: Sheffield Academic Press, 1991], 33-36). Deficiencies of the Second Temple are also mentioned in *2 Bar.* 68:5-6 and *1 En.* 89:73.

[298] The following survey is based upon Tob 13:10-11; 14:5-7; *1 En.* 90:28-36; 91:13; *Jub.* 1:17, 26-29; *Sib. Or.* 3:657-673, 702-704, 718-720, 772-775; 5:247-255, 397-434; *T. Benj.* 9:2; *Pss. Sol.* 17:30-31; *2 Bar.* 32:3-4; 4QFlor I, 1-7; *New Jerusalem*; 11QT^a XXIX, 7-9. Cf. *Apoc. Ab.* 29:17-18 and the following texts concerning the future Jerusalem where the Temple is not explicitly mentioned: *2 Bar.* 4:2-7; *4 Ezra* 7:26; 8:52; 10:27, 41-55; 13:36; *T. Dan* 5:12-13; 11QPs^a XXII, 1-5. The dates of *Sib. Or.* 5, *2 Baruch*, and *4 Ezra* could be slightly later than the first century A.D., but probably not much later (Nickelsburg, *Jewish Literature*, 287; Chester, 'Sibyl and the Temple,' 61). In addition, assigning a date to *The Testaments of the Twelve Patriarchs* is notoriously difficult (H. W. Hollander and M. de Jonge, *The Testaments of the Twelve Patriarchs: A Commentary*, SVTP, no. 8 [Leiden: E. J. Brill, 1985], 82-5).

[299] For the Temple as God's eternal dwelling, see *Jub.* 1:17, 26-29; *Sib. Or.* 3:773-775, 785-787. For the future Temple as eternal, see *1 En.* 91:13; *2 Bar.* 32:3-4; 11QT^a XXIX, 7-9 and 4QFlor I, 4-6 (where God's presence in the eternal Temple is implied). For OT parallels, see Ezek 37:26-28, 43:9; also, Joel 3:17 (MT 4:17), Zech 8:3.

[300] On the first claim, see Tob 13:11 (cf. 14:6-7); *Sib. Or.* 3:715-720, 772-773; *Pss. Sol.* 17:31 (OT parallels: Isa 2:2-3, 56:6-7, 60:7, 66:18-23; Mic 4:1-3; Zech 14:16). On the second, see Tob 14:5; *1 En.* 90:29; *T. Benj.* 9:2 (OT parallel: Hag 2:9). On the third, see *Sib. Or.* 3:657-672; 4QFlor I, 5 (OT parallels: Joel 3:17 [MT 4:17]; Zech 9:8; also Psalm 76).

[301] Human builders are implied in Tob 14:5. The Messiah (or a messianic figure) is the builder in *Sib. Or.* 5:414-434 (also, *Tg. Zech.* 6:12, *Tg. Isa.* 53:5) (see Chester, 'Sibyl and the Temple,' 50-3). God is apparently the builder in *1 En.* 90:29; *Jub.* 1:17; 11QT^a XXIX, 9. One could also add *4 Ezra* 7:26; 8:52; 10:27, 41-55; 13:36 where the entire new Jerusalem is hidden with God (its builder [10:54]) until it appears on earth (cf. *2 Bar.* 4:2-7).

notions.[302] Similarly, it appears that the author of *Sibylline Oracles* 5:414-34 attributes the responsibility for construction of a future Temple to a messianic figure and to God.[303] Thus to present God as the builder of the Temple does not necessarily deny all human agency. As in Psalm 78:69, it may simply represent one perspective. It is therefore too simplistic to assume that a reference to God as the builder of the future Temple means that it will descend from heaven already built or that all human participation is excluded.[304]

In general, the above expectations concerning the future Temple are consistent with the hopes for a new Temple found in the Old Testament. A desire to witness the fulfillment of prophetic hopes concerning the Temple is especially evident in Tobit 14:5 and Sirach 36:20. Yet a basic continuity with Old Testament prophetic expectations does not necessarily mean that Jewish hopes for a future Temple did not contain unique elements. This point is best illustrated by two exceptional texts from Qumran: the *Temple Scroll* and the *New Jerusalem*.[305] The *Temple Scroll* presents itself as the revealed plan for the Jerusalem Temple. This plan was purportedly revealed to Moses on Mount Sinai. As the normative plan for the Temple, it should have been followed by Solomon when he built the first Temple.[306] In spite of its claims, the *Temple*

---

[302] Cf. Exod 15:17 (quoted in 4QFlor I, 3). For reflections on this, see Levenson, *Sinai and Zion*, 106.

[303] Chester, 'Sibyl and the Temple,' 50.

[304] For the influence of such assumptions on the interpretation of *1 En.* 90:29, see McKelvey, *New Temple*, 30; Andrea Spatafora, *Temple in the Book of Revelation*, 64. For the clearest evidence of a new Jerusalem built solely by God and appearing on earth during the eschatological age of salvation, see *4 Ezra* 7:26; 8:52; 10:27, 41-55; 13:36; *2 Bar.* 4:2-7 (Rowland, 'Second Temple,' 186-9; Schürer, *History of the Jewish People*, vol. 2, 529-30). By extension, these texts are used as evidence for a divinely built Temple, whose presence in the eschatological Jerusalem may be indicated by *4 Ezra* 10:46 (McKelvey, *New Temple*, 32-4; Rowland, 'Second Temple,' 189). These two texts are definitely written after A.D. 70, which makes them later than Tobit, *1 Enoch*, *Jubilees*, and the *Temple Scroll* (Nickelsburg, *Jewish Literature*, 287). The dating of *4 Ezra* and *2 Baruch* suggests that it is dangerous to impose their view of the future of Jerusalem on earlier texts. Both texts could have been influenced by Revelation 21, where the New Jerusalem descends to earth already built.

[305] They are probably writings of the Essenes (García Martínez, *Qumran and Apocalyptic*, 204, 212-3; cf. Davies, 'Judaism[s] of the Damascus Document,' 41).

[306] Johann Maier, *The Temple Scroll: An Introduction, Translation and Commentary*, trans. Richard T. White, JSOTSup, no. 34 (Sheffield: JSOT, 1985), 59; Yadin, *Temple Scroll*, vol. 1, 82-83, 182-3. Some interpreters disagree with such a characterization of the *Temple Scroll*. They feel that it describes an eschatological Temple (B. E. Thiering, '*Mebaqqer* and *Episkopos* in the Light of the Temple Scroll,' *JBL* 100 [1981]: 60-61; Ben Zion Wacholder, *The Dawn of Qumran: The Sectarian Torah and the Teacher of Righteousness*, HUCM, no. 8 [Cincinnati: Hebrew Union College Press, 1983], 22-24). The key text is 11QT^a XXIX, 7-9. According to Yadin and Maier, the text means that the Temple described in the *Temple Scroll* is envisioned as temporary. It will endure 'until

Scroll appears to be a creation of the Essenes. Like Ezekiel, it provides some unique legislation regarding the details of the Temple plan and Temple-service. Even so, the *Temple Scroll*'s legislation is generally a blend of traditional and unique elements.[307] This is what one would expect from a writing of the Essenes given their emphasis upon both the Old Testament's authority and its inspired interpretation by their priests.[308] Even though the *Temple Scroll* describes an ideal Temple and not a future Temple, it provides evidence for disagreement about what the Temple and Temple-service should look like. Such disagreement would surely lead to a distinctive vision for the future Temple.

Whereas the *Temple Scroll* is apparently concerned with the ideal Temple plan, the *New Jerusalem* has a greater chance of being concerned with the future Temple and holy city.[309] Like the *Temple Scroll*, it presents its own picture of the Temple, Temple-service, and holy city, while demonstrating continuity with Old Testament laws and expectations. For instance, *New Jerusalem* differs from Ezekiel in that it places the Temple within the holy city.[310] The city is also quite large compared to the city found in Ezekiel.[311] On

---

the day of creation,' at which time it will be replaced by another Temple (Maier, *Temple Scroll*, 86; Yadin, *Temple Scroll*, vol. 1, 183, 412). This reading of 11QT^a XXIX, 7-9 appeals to many interpreters. It suits the context and is strengthened by consideration of the closely related parallel in *Jub.* 1:26-29 (Yadin, *Temple Scroll*, vol. 1, 183-4). The appeal of Wacholder's reading is hampered by its reliance upon an unusual sense for עד in XXIX, 9 (García Martínez, *Qumran and Apocalyptic*, 205). Thiering's reading does not fit as well in the context. It understands 'my sanctuary' in XXIX, 8 as a reference to Solomon's Temple and the Second Temple. Given the context, such a reference does not seem probable and is not defended adequately by Thiering.

[307] For a diagram of its Temple plan, see Yadin, *Temple Scroll*, vol. 1, 252. For a traditional element, compare Ezek 46:3 and 11QT^a XXXV, 1-9. Both make the inner court entirely off-limits to the laity. Such a limitation on the access of the laity is more extreme than what is reflected in historical accounts of the Temple (Maier, *Temple Scroll*, 92-93). On the other hand, the *Temple Scroll* describes three Temple courts. The large outer court has no counterpart in Ezekiel's Temple plan (11QT^a XL, 5-8; Yadin, *Temple Scroll*, vol. 1, 191). Its size and limitations on access also distinguish it from analogous courts in Herod's Temple plan (Maier, *Temple Scroll*, 110). For a comparable example concerned with the Temple-service, see Yadin's discussion of the *Temple Scroll*'s laws for the Day of Atonement (*Temple Scroll*, vol. 1, 131-4).

[308] 1QS I, 2-3; V, 8-10.

[309] García Martínez, *Qumran and Apocalyptic*, 209-11. García Martínez believes that the paragraph referring to the Kittim, Edom, Moab, and sons of Ammon is concerned with the final war described in the *War Scroll* (cf. 4QNJ^a ar 2 III, 16-18; 1QM I, 1-2). If so, then *New Jerusalem* could be describing the Temple that will exist during the final conflict (1QM II, 1-6) (García Martínez, *Qumran and Apocalyptic*, 210). Of course, the fragmentary nature of *New Jerusalem* makes certainty impossible.

[310] Cf. Ezek 45:6, 48:15 and 4QNJ^a ar 1 II, 18; 5QNJ ar 1 I, 3-4; also see 11QT^a XLVI, 9-12.

the other hand, the *New Jerusalem* contains clear parallels to Ezekiel 40-48.[312] The narrator has a guide who leads him around and measures the city and Temple. The wall of the city has twelve gates, three on each side, and each one is identified by the name of one of the tribes of Israel.[313]

The sequence of the gates' names in *New Jerusalem* is especially noteworthy. It differs from Ezekiel and other possible Old Testament analogies, but is identical to the sequence of names found on the gates of the Temple in the *Temple Scroll*.[314] Interestingly, Levi is the name placed upon the central eastern gate, the most significant position in this arrangement.[315] The prominent position of Levi's gate agrees with the prominence assigned to priests and Levites within the Essenes' writings.[316] It provides a specific example of the contribution of the Essenes' distinctive theological beliefs to their conception of the ideal Temple and eschatological holy city.

The *Temple Scroll* and the *New Jerusalem* suggest the possibility that

---

[311] According to Ezek 48:16, the city itself is a 4,500 cubit square (1.3 miles or 1.9 kilometers). The city's entire possession is only 25,000 by 5,000 cubits (7.1 by 1.4 miles or 11.4 by 2.1 kilometers) (48:15). By contrast the city of the *New Jerusalem* is 140 by 100 stadia (16.1 by 11.5 miles or 25.9 by 18.5 kilometers) (Michael Chyutin, *The New Jerusalem Scroll from Qumran: A Comprehensive Resonstruction*, JSPSup, no. 25 [Sheffield: Sheffield Academic Press, 1997], 76; García Martínez, *Qumran and Apocalyptic*, 188; F. García Martínez, 'L'interprétation de la Torah d'Ézéchiel dans les mss. de Qumran,' *RevQ* 13 [1988]: 449-50). Given these measurements, the city of *New Jerusalem* covers an area over 100 times larger than that of Ezekiel.

[312] See also the parallel between the description of the walls of Jerusalem in Isa 54:12 and 4QNJ^a ar 2 II, 13-15 (García Martínez, *Qumran and Apocalyptic*, 199).

[313] Cf. Ezek 48:31-34 and 4QNJ^a ar 1 I, 12-II, 11. The descriptions of the Temple-service demonstrate a similar trend. Some of its ceremonies appear to be completely different from those described in other sources (Chyutin, *New Jerusalem Scroll*, 48-56). Others are familiar. An interesting combination of familiar and novel elements occurs in the placing of the showbread. Its placement follows Lev 24:5-9. Afterward, *New Jerusalem* goes on to give a unique account of the division of the old bread among the priests (2QNJ ar 4; 11QNJ ar 13) (Chyutin, *New Jerusalem Scroll*, 59-62).

[314] Yadin, *Temple Scroll*, vol. 1, 255-6; Chyutin, *New Jerusalem Scroll*, 79-81. Both may depend upon a 'independent tradition,' since the same sequence for the names of the Temple gates apparently occurs in 4QRP^{b,c} 28 II, 1-4 (García Martínez, *Qumran and Apocalyptic*, 180, 185). It is also possible that the Temple in *New Jerusalem* has twelve gates, probably with the same names (11QNJ ar 18 I, 3) (Chyutin, *New Jerusalem Scroll*, 18).

[315] Chyutin, *New Jerusalem Scroll*, 80; Maier, *Temple Scroll*, 112. In Ezekiel's plan, the most significant gate is the central northern gate, because the Temple lies to the north of the city. It is assigned to Judah (Ezek 48:31).

[316] Cf. the above discussion of the priestly influence on the Essenes and 1QS II, 19-20; CD XIV, 5-6. According to 4QpIsa^a 8-10 III, 25, the 'royal messiah must defer to priestly authority' (John J. Collins, *The Scepter and the Star: The Messiahs of the Dead Sea Scrolls and Other Ancient Literature*, ABRL [New York: Doubleday, 1995], 76).

distinctive theological perspectives within Judaism could contribute to distinctive conceptions of the future Temple. Unfortunately, the fragments of *New Jerusalem* stand alone. They provide the most detailed conception of the future Temple and city that can be reliably dated to the first century A.D. or earlier. After *New Jerusalem*, the Mishnah provides the only other Jewish Temple plan that could have been intended for the future Temple.[317]

New Jerusalem, along with other texts that anticipate a future Temple, adds to the impression that extra-biblical Jewish literature generally affirms a widespread concern for the Temple and Temple-service.[318] If the Temple was largely irrelevant, then why would texts like *New Jerusalem* include it in their idealistic expectations regarding the future of Israel? Thus like affirmations and criticisms of the Second Temple, expectations of a future Temple support the abiding significance of the Temple in Jewish theology.[319] The question that remains is what sort of evidence exists in the Old Testament and Jewish literature to anticipate the replacement of the Temple that is proclaimed in the New Testament.

---

[317] Over half of the Mishnah (completed around A.D. 200) is concerned with the Temple and Temple-service. Yet its motives for such concern are unclear. It could be 'because the Mishnah is confidently awaiting the time of their restoration, or because the temple cult had been ordained by God and the study of its regulations was now the equivalent of their implementation, or because the rabbis were attempting to create in their minds an ideal and perfect world to which they could escape from the imperfect world around them' (Shaye J. D. Cohen, *From the Maccabees to the Mishnah*, LEC [Philadelphia: Westminster, 1987], 219). T. Busink supports the view that the Temple plan found in tractate *Middot* was intended as a plan for the future Temple (*Der Tempel von Jerusalem von Salomo bis Herodes: Ein archäologisch-historische Studie unter Berücksichtigung des westsemitischen Tempelbaus*, vol. 2, *Von Ezechiel bis Middot* [Leiden: E. J. Brill, 1980], 1538). For further comments on the Mishnah as a pattern for the future Temple, see Eisemann, *Ezekiel*, vol. 3, 605-6.

[318] Contra Julius Scott who claims that 'Intertestamental Judaism' commonly regarded the Temple as 'largely symbolic and sentimental.' He goes on to say that the 'temple as a spiritual center was an anachronism to both Judaism and Christianity' (J. Julius Scott Jr., *Customs and Controversies: Intertestamental Jewish Backgrounds of the New Testament* [Grand Rapids: Baker, 1995], 155). Scott's low estimation of the significance of the Temple in Intertestamental Judaism appears to be closely related to his claim that 'the center of Judaism had moved from temple and ceremony to morals and ethics' (Ibid., 123, 155). The validity of this dichotomy (temple and ceremony vs. morals and ethics) is dubious, as is the priority Scott places on morals and ethics (cf. Cohen, *From the Maccabees to the Mishnah*, 77-78).

[319] In his survey of rabbinic writings, Shaye Cohen finds that the future of the Temple is never in doubt. It is an irreplaceable part of the age to come (Shaye J. D. Cohen, 'The Temple and the Synagogue,' in *The Temple in Antiquity: Ancient Records and Modern Perspectives*, ed. Truman G. Madsen [Provo, UT: Brigham Young University, 1984], 169-71). By contrast, one strand of rabbinic thought anticipates that the sacrificial cult of the future Temple will be replaced by rabbinic piety (Ibid., 167-8).

Temple Replacement in the Old Testament and Jewish Literature

The Old Testament and Jewish literature contain several pieces of evidence that point to the limitations of the Jerusalem Temple and hint at its potential for replacement. First, it can only be said to be God's dwelling place in a qualified sense. Even so, God can abandon it as a special place of his presence when he chooses to. Second, God himself is able to be the sanctuary for his people during their exile in Babylon. Thus he does not require a Temple in order to dwell among his people. Third, one finds the suggestion in the Old Testament that it is the true people of God, and not the Temple, that is the most significant locus for the presence of God. Developing these points will demonstrate what kind of case the Old Testament makes for the replacement of the Temple.

The limitations of the Temple as God's dwelling place are proclaimed in several places in the Old Testament. It is God's chosen dwelling place in the midst of his people, but it does not place spatial constraints upon God whose dwelling place is more properly described as 'heaven.'[320] The Temple's limited ability to serve as a dwelling place for God may already suggest that it is not the ultimate dwelling place of God in the midst of his people. This impression is intensified by the instances in which God abandons the Tabernacle and the Temple.[321] Clearly, a new act of God has to take place to safeguard the Temple of the new age from being abandoned.[322]

Even though the Temple is God's chosen dwelling place in the midst of his people, God makes it clear that he can be a sanctuary for his people during their time of exile (Ezek 11:16). Hence they should not listen to the taunts of those who are in Jerusalem and who see the exiles as 'far from the Lord' (11:15). Like the Temple's limited ability to serve as a dwelling place for God, perhaps this temporary replacement of the Temple also suggests that it might not be the ultimate dwelling place of God in the midst of his people.[323]

The limitations of the Temple and the most significant dwelling place for God are two issues that appear to come together in Isaiah 66:1-2. Isaiah 66:1 points out the inability of any human building to serve as an adequate house for God. As seen above, this sentiment has already been expressed by Solomon and the psalmists. The added dimension here is the attention to the proper locus for God's favor and presence. The essential prerequisites for experience of God's presence and favor are to possess a humble, contrite spirit and to obey the word

---

[320] See, for instance, 1 Kgs 8:27, 9:3 // 2 Chr 6:18, 7:16; Pss 20:6 (MT v. 7), 33:13-14, 80:14 (MT v. 15), 102:19 (MT v. 20), 103:19, 113:5, 115:3, 123:1; Isa 66:1; 3 Macc 2:15.

[321] 1 Sam 4:21-22; Ps 78:60; Jer 7:12-14; Ezek 10:18-19, 11:22-23.

[322] For the Temple of the new age as God's eternal dwelling place, see Ezek 37:26, 43:9. On God's new work to produce an obedient people, see Ezek 36:25-27 (cf. the close parallel in 1 QS IV, 20-22).

[323] Cf. Beale, *Temple and the Church's Mission*, 347.

of God. Without a right spirit, the Temple is of no benefit.[324] As a result, Isaiah 66:2, like Ezekiel 11:16, places particular emphasis on God's righteous people as the proper locus for his favor and presence.[325]

In light of the preceding evidence, it is possible to see in the Old Testament and Jewish literature some hints that the Temple may not be the ultimate dwelling place of God in the midst of his people.[326] The priority for the locus of God's presence is his people rather than the Jerusalem Temple.

---

[324] Cf. Isa 57:15; John N. Oswalt, *The Book of Isaiah: Chapters 40-66*, NICOT (Grand Rapids: Eerdmans, 1998), 607-8; Brevard S. Childs, *Isaiah*, OTL (Louisville, Ky.: Westminster John Knox, 2001), 540; Japhet, 'Temple in the Restoration Period,' 235; Edward J. Young, *The Book of Isaiah*, vol. 3, NICOT (Grand Rapids: Eerdmans, 1972), 518-9. Since sacrifices also are given second place to righteous living or a right spirit (or heart) in Ps 51:14-17, Isa 66:3, Jer 7:21-23, Hos 6:6, Amos 5:21-25 (Oswalt, *Isaiah*, vol. 2, 668), it follows that God's work within a person to produce such a humble and contrite spirit takes precedence over the Temple and offering sacrifices. God's work in the hearts of his people would prepare them to experience his presence and to offer acceptable sacrifices. It is not surprising, therefore, that the decisive work of God through Christ turns out to be his work in cleansing the believer and creating a new spirit within (John 3:5-6 and its background in Ezek 36:25-27). See also the ideal in the Psalms for proper worship at the Temple (Psalms 15, 24). The righteous worshiper is the one who is able to benefit from the presence of God in the midst of his people (Ps 24:4-5). One finds interesting parallels to such thinking in the Qumran writings regarding the community's temporary replacement of the Temple (1QS V, 4-7; VIII, 4-10; IX, 3-6). Their replacement of the Temple is possible due to their righteous behavior. Their righteous acts are spiritual sacrifices that set them apart as a 'holy house for Aaron' (1 QS IX, 3-6; García Martínez, *Dead Sea Scrolls*, 13). Their righteousness shows that they are a fitting dwelling place for God even though they have no Temple building.

[325] Oswalt, *Isaiah*, vol. 2, 667-8; Ellis, *Paul's Use of the Old Testament*, 90. Cf. Exod 29:45, Lev 26:11-12, Ezek 37:26-27, 2 Cor 6:16. Some support for this point may also be found in the psalmists' desire to be a permanent fixture in the Temple (for example, 27:4) or idealization of the righteous as a permanent fixture in the Temple (52:8, 92:12-14). In this way, the psalmists picture the Temple as the ideal place for the righteous person to live, because it is the place where God dwells and the ideal place to experience his provision. Hence the locus of God's presence (i.e., the Temple) and the place where his righteous ones are would ideally be the same. Such an ideal position remained an ideal until Jesus made it possible for his people to draw near to God (Heb 10:19-22), which reaches its culmination in the new Jerusalem (Rev 3:12, 21:1-22:5).

[326] It is also possible to come to the same conclusion if one reads the OT like the author of Hebrews does. If the OT contains hints of the coming of a more perfect priest, a more perfect covenant, and a more perfect sacrifice (Heb 7-10), then this points to the need for a more perfect Temple as well, because this priest will surely serve in a more perfect Temple (8:1-6; 9:1-14, 23-25) rather than in the Jerusalem Temple (This line of reasoning was suggested to me by D. A. Carson; cf. George E. Ladd, 'Israel and the Church,' *EQ* 36 [1964]: 209-10).

Conclusion

Over the course of the Old Testament, the Temple becomes associated with certain patterns. These patterns develop through the repetition of comparable revelatory statements and events. They link Solomon's Temple with its predecessor, the Tabernacle, and with its anticipated replacement, the new Temple. These patterns converge, establishing four points. First, the Temple is God's chosen dwelling place among his people. Second, it is an ideal place closely associated with the immanence of God, his majesty, and experience of his abundant provision. Third, a new, eternal Temple is a prominent part of prophetic hopes for the future of Israel. Fourth, in spite of the Temple's greatness, the Old Testament does recognize its limitations. A review of the patterns that establish these points will demonstrate the Old Testament basis for each point, as well as its reiteration in extra-biblical Jewish literature.

From the beginning, the Old Testament characterization of the Temple sets it apart as God's chosen dwelling place among his people. In Exod 25:8, God tells Moses that the Tabernacle is to be established as the place for him to dwell among his people, Israel. At several points, God expresses the same or comparable sentiments with regard to the Temple.[327] They are therefore fitting places for God to meet with his people and speak with them.[328] Furthermore God demonstrates that he is present in the Tabernacle and the Temple in a special way by consecrating them with visible manifestations of his glory.[329]

God's glorious consecration of the Temple is the end of a process that begins with divine election. His glory appears in the Tabernacle and the Temple, because he has chosen them as his approved sanctuaries.[330] They are the result of a series of revealed choices, including the choice of the builder, plan, priesthood, sacrificial procedure, and location.[331] The Tabernacle and the Temple are essentially God's handiwork executed by human builders.[332] Even so, God is under no obligation to dwell in them, which he demonstrates by abandoning them at certain points due to Israel's sins.[333]

As God's chosen dwelling place among his people, the Temple is a special

---

[327] 1 Kgs 6:12-13; 8:12-13 (// 2 Chr 6:1-2); 9:3 (// 2 Chr 7:16); Ezek 37:26-28; 43:7, 9. Cf. 2 Macc 14:35; *Jub.* 1:17, 26-29; *Sib. Or.* 3:785-787.

[328] Exod 25:22; 29:42-43; Lev 1:1; Num 14:10-35; 16:19-24, 42-44; 20:6-8; Deut 31:14-21; Isaiah 6; Ezekiel 43-48 [esp., 43:2-6]; cf. Ps 27:4 and Luke 1:8-20.

[329] Exod 29:43, 40:34-35; Lev 9:23-24; 1 Kgs 8:10-13 (// 2 Chr 5:13-6:2); 2 Chr 7:1-2; Ps 102:16 (MT v. 17); Ezek 43:2-4, 44:4; 2 Macc 2:8; 11QT^a XXIX, 8. Cf. Isa 66:18-19 and the appearance of the Lord's glory in a cloud (Exod 16:10) and on Mount Sinai (Exod 24:16-17).

[330] Cf. Deut 12:5-6, 2 Chr 7:12.

[331] Exod 25-31; Deut 12:5; 1 Chr 22:1; 28:6, 10-21; 2 Chr 6:6; Ezekiel 40-46.

[332] The OT presents both Solomon (1 Kgs 6:2) and God (Ps 78:69) as the builders of the Temple.

[333] 1 Sam 4:21-22; Ps 78:60; Jer 7:12-14; Ezek 10:18-19, 11:22-23.

place of divine immanence. Consequently, it is idealized as the preeminent place to behold the majesty of God and to experience God's abundant provision. The majesty of God is evident in Jerusalem, because the Temple is the earthly place of God's throne.[334] As such, the Temple and Jerusalem are magnificent to behold and secure from the attacks of enemy forces.[335] Also, the Temple is the best place to approach the sovereign God in worship and prayer.[336] Those who do so 'with clean hands and a pure heart' (Ps 24:4) are able to experience God's abundant provision for them in their daily lives. The Psalmists develop this idea by idealizing the Temple as the locus for God's abundant provision for his people.[337] One aspect of their portrayal associates the Temple with a river (Pss 36:8, 46:4). Another aspect depicts the righteous person as a healthy, fruitful tree planted in the Temple (Ps 92:12-14). Both of these images idealize the Temple as a beatific place of God's provision for his people, like the Garden of Eden. It is therefore the ideal place for the righteous person to dwell and it is where he or she yearns to be more than any other place.[338]

The Psalmists' idealizations of the Temple fit well with prophetic expectations for a new, eternal Temple of God.[339] The new Temple is expected to be more magnificent and glorious than its predecessors.[340] It will always be secure from the attacks of the nations, who will actually come to the Temple in submission.[341] As in the Psalms, God's abundant provision for his people is symbolized by a river that flows out of the Temple (Ezek 47:1-12, Joel 3:18, Zech 14:8). This river connects the Temple with God's transformation of the land of Israel into a fertile region, like the Garden of Eden (Ezek 36:35, Isa 51:3).

At the same time, the Old Testament does not gloss over the limitations of the Temple. For all of its greatness, it can only be said to be God's dwelling place in a qualified sense, because God cannot be contained by a human

---

[334] Jer 3:17, Ezek 43:7. Similarly, the Temple is called God's footstool, which preserves a connection between the Temple and the rule of God while emphasizing transcendence (Ps 99:5, Lam 2:1).

[335] On the beauty of the Temple and Jerusalem, see Pss 48:1-2 (MT vv. 3-4), 50:2; on the security of Jerusalem, see Psalms 46, 48, 76.

[336] Deut 12:5-7; Pss 5:7 (MT v. 8); 18:6 (MT v. 7); 20:1-9 (MT vv. 2-10); 27:4; 28:2; 84:4 (MT v. 5); 99:5, 9; 132:7; 138:2; Isa 27:13; 56:7; 66:23; Jer 7:2; 26:2; Ezek 46:2, 3, 9; Zech 14:16-17; 1 Macc 7:37.

[337] Pss 36:5-9 (MT vv. 6-10), 46:4 (MT v. 5), 52:8 (MT v. 10), 65:4 (MT v. 5), 84:10-11 (MT vv. 11-12), 92:12-14 (MT vv. 13-15). Cf. Hag 2:18-19, Zech 8:9-12.

[338] Pss 23:6, 26:8, 27:4, 36:5-9 (MT vv. 6-10), 42:1-4 (MT vv. 2-5), 43:3-4, 61:4 (MT v. 5), 63:1-5 (MT 2-6), 65:4 (MT v. 5), 84:1-12 (MT vv. 2-13).

[339] On the eternal nature of the new Temple, see p. 98.

[340] Isaiah 60; Hag 2:9, Tob 14:5, *1 En.* 90:29, *T. Benj.* 9:2.

[341] See pp. 72, 98.

building.[342] In addition, another emphasis sometimes takes priority over the Temple as God's dwelling place, namely, God's presence and favor may be found where his righteous worshipers are (Isa 66:2). This is true even in cases where they are distant from the Temple (Ezek 11:16).

In conclusion, the Temple is a divinely established institution whose significance for Israel is developed and reiterated from Exodus to Malachi. The persistence of expectations for a new, eternal Temple preserves a special place for the Temple in Israel's hopes for the future.

---

[342] God's true dwelling place is described as 'heaven.' See, for instance, 1 Kgs 8:27, 9:3 // 2 Chr 6:18, 7:16; Pss 20:6 (MT v. 7), 33:13-14, 80:14 (MT v. 15), 102:19 (MT v. 20), 103:19, 113:5, 115:3, 123:1; Isa 66:1; 3 Macc 2:15.

CHAPTER 3

Jesus as the Fulfillment and Replacement of the Temple in the Fourth Gospel: Part One

A number of interpreters agree that the Fourth Gospel presents Jesus as the replacement of the Temple. The four texts most frequently cited in connection with this theme are 1:14, 1:51, 2:18-22, and 4:20-24. From among these, John 2:18-22 emerges as the most explicit passage where John correlates Jesus' body and the Temple. As such, its contribution to the theme is considered first. Besides providing a reliable starting point for examining Jesus' replacement of the Temple, John 2:18-22 contributes to a proper understanding of 1:14, 1:51, and 4:20-24. John 1:14, 1:51, and 4:20-24 clarify that Jesus is not only the replacement of the Temple, but also of other Old Testament holy places. The combined evidence from 1:14, 1:51, 2:18-22, and 4:20-24 suggests that the coming of Jesus inaugurates a new phase in the relationship between God and his people. In these verses, Jesus fulfills and surpasses prophecies and patterns associated with the Temple. In doing so, Jesus appears to be the fulfillment of the Temple who has come to take its place.[1]

John 2:18-22

John 2:18-22 occurs at the end of the Temple cleansing pericope that begins in 2:13. A proper understanding of the significance of John 2:18-22 requires attention to its immediate context (2:13-17), to the Fourth Gospel's unique presentation of misunderstandings, and to its relevance for important themes of the Fourth Gospel. Therefore the first two steps in the following treatment of 2:18-22 are (1) to clarify the contribution of 2:13-17 to 2:18-22 and (2) to interpret 2:18-22 in light of the special character of the Fourth Gospel's misunderstandings. Then it will be possible to consider how John 2:18-22

---

[1] It is important to remember that a prophecy or promise is fulfilled when the things anticipated come into being. On the other hand, fulfilling OT types appears to mean more than merely measuring up to what was expected; it is consistent with 'fulfill' in the sense of 'complete' or 'consummate' (cf. BAGD, 671 or Moule, 'Fulfillment-Words,' 293-4). As a result, NT antitypes will be greater than the OT types that anticipated them. For more on this, see the discussion of typology in chapters one and five.

contributes to important themes of the Fourth Gospel, especially Jesus' relationship to the Temple.

John 2:13 places Jesus in the Temple at Passover, the first of three (2:13, 6:4, 11:55) or possibly four (5:1) reported in the Fourth Gospel.[2] Jesus' action in the Temple disrupts the work of the moneychangers and the sale of animals for sacrifice. His action is coupled with a saying (2:16) that is addressed to those selling doves, but is relevant to his entire action.[3] The saying of Jesus clarifies that his action in the Temple is a protest against the misuse of the Temple precincts.[4] The activities of the moneychangers and animal vendors do not belong in the Temple. They are in danger of turning the Temple into a 'market' (2:16).[5] It is possible that Jesus' action and saying would have called

---

[2] The Fourth Gospel's chronology places Jesus' cleansing of the Temple two or three years before the cleansing reported in the Synoptics. Interpreters account for the discrepancy in three ways: (1) Jesus performed two cleansings; (2) for theological reasons, John placed the cleansing of the Temple earlier than the correct date given in the Synoptics; and (3) since the Synoptics' portrayal of Jesus' ministry creates only one possible placement for the cleansing of the Temple (i.e., only one visit to Jerusalem), John's date is preferable (for the history of interpretation, see François-Marie Braun, 'L'expulsion des vendeurs du temple [Mt., XXI, 12-17, 23-27; Mc., XI, 15-19, 27-33; Lc., XIX, 45-XX, 8; Jo., II, 13-22],' *RB* 38 [1929]: 178-9; Larry J. Kreitzer, 'The Temple Incident in John 2.13-25: A Preview of What Is to Come,' in *Understanding, Studying and Reading: New Testament Essays in Honour of John Ashton*, ed. Christopher Rowland and Crispin Fletcher-Louis, JSNTSup, no. 153 [Sheffield: Sheffield Academic Press, 1998], 94-95). Although contemporary interpreters tend to prefer option two, the reasons advanced for their preference are not decisive (for an appealing defense of option two, see R. T. France, 'Chronological Aspects of "Gospel Harmony,"' *VE* 16 [1986]: 41-42). Option one seems preferable to two or three. It respects the differences between the Temple cleansings in the Synoptics and the Fourth Gospel (including the chronological notices) (Carson, *John*, 177-8). It is also possible to account for the absence of two cleansings in any one Gospel (Meyer, *John*, 111).

[3] Jesus says, 'Get these out of here! How dare you turn my Father's house into a market!' (2:16 NIV). On the relevance of this saying to the entire Temple action, see Ernst Haenchen, *John 1: A Commentary on the Gospel of John Chapters 1-6*, trans. Robert W. Funk, Hermeneia (Philadelphia: Fortress, 1984), 183.

[4] Jesus' cleansing of the Temple can be understood as a cleansing action as long as one remembers its limited scope. It results in a symbolic disruption of trade in the Temple rather than the successful abolition of it (cf. Richard Bauckham, 'Jesus' Demonstration in the Temple,' in *Law and Religion: Essays on the Place of the Law in Israel and Early Christianity*, ed. Barnabas Lindars [Cambridge: James Clarke and Co., 1988], 72).

[5] Interpreters continue to debate the significance of Jesus' action in the Temple. They often appeal to two explanations for the Temple cleansings: (1) They are Jesus' reaction to the unjust or corrupt nature of the business practices evident in the Temple (Ibid., 78-79; Craig A. Evans, 'Jesus' Action in the Temple: Cleansing or Portent of Destruction?,' *CBQ* 51 [1989]: 270) or (2) Jesus is opposed to the use of the Temple precincts for commercial purposes (Bruce Chilton, '[ὡς] φραγέλλιον ἐκ σχοινίων [John 2:15],' in

to mind relevant expectations from the Old Testament, especially the prophets. Interestingly, the Old Testament text associated with the event by the disciples is not drawn from the list of relevant texts often suggested by interpreters.[6]

John 2:17, and its citation of Psalm 69:9, makes an important contribution to a proper understanding of the relationship between Jesus and the Temple in the Fourth Gospel.[7] First, if Jesus is zealous for the Lord's house, the Temple, then it is difficult to maintain that Jesus is simply anti-Temple or anti-sacrifice, a point already hinted at by the use of 'my Father's house' in 2:16.[8] Second, the relevance of Psalm 69 to Jesus probably runs deeper than merely analogous suffering.[9] The connection between the psalmist and Jesus takes on added

---

Templum Amicitiae: Essays on the Second Temple Presented to Ernst Bammel, ed. William Horbury, JSNTSup, no. 48 [Sheffield: Sheffield Academic Press, 1991], 338-42; William L. Lane, *The Gospel according to Mark*, NICNT [Grand Rapids: Eerdmans, 1974], 403-7; Morris, *John*, 195). There is probably a good bit of truth in each of these explanations. The second option is more relevant for interpreting Jesus' actions and words in 2:15-16. Note that Jesus' action involves expulsion of the vendors, bringing trade in the Temple to a standstill. Although the Temple was a convenient place for selling sacrificial animals and exchanging money, it was certainly not necessary to carry on such activities there. For instance, there is evidence that sacrificial animals were sold at markets on the Mount of Olives (*y. Ta'anit* 4:5; Victor Eppstein, 'The Historicity of the Gospel Account of the Cleansing of the Temple,' *ZNW* 55 [1964]: 49). Indeed, it may have been a recent innovation to sell sacrificial animals in the Temple precincts (Evans, 'Jesus' Action in the Temple,' 267).

[6] Interpreters often cite Zech 14:21b, which can be read 'there will no longer be a merchant in the house of the Lord,' where 'merchant' is the translation for כנעני (more literally translated 'Canaanite' [see LXX]). This understanding of Zech 14:21b is common in rabbinic literature and could have been current in Jesus' day (Cecil Roth, 'The Cleansing of the Temple and Zechariah xiv 21,' *NovT* 4 [1960]: 170-80). It is also common to link the Temple cleansing with Mal 3:1-5, which prophesies that after sending his messenger ahead of him, the Lord will come to his Temple bringing judgment upon the Levites and the people (cf. 4:5-6 [MT 3:23-24]) (Richard H. Hiers, 'Purification of the Temple: Preparation for the Kingdom of God,' *JBL* 90 [1971]: 87-88). Similarly, Jesus' action in the Temple could have pointed to his identity as the Messiah, who was expected to cleanse Jerusalem according to *Pss. Sol.* 17:30b (cf. 18:5) (Evans, 'Jesus' Action in the Temple,' 254-6).

[7] According to John 2:17, at some unspecified point (probably after the resurrection as in 2:22), the 'disciples remembered that it is written: "Zeal for your house will consume me"' (Ps 69:9 [MT v. 10]).

[8] Contra Haenchen, *John 1*, 184. Cf. Étienne Trocmé's suggestion that zeal for the Mosaic law prompted Jesus to cleanse the Temple ('L'expulsion des marchands du Temple,' *NTS* 15 [1968]: 18-19).

[9] Psalm 69 is often quoted or alluded to in connection with Jesus' suffering (Barnabas Lindars, *The Gospel of John*, NCB [Grand Rapids: Eerdmans, 1972], 140). See Matt 27:34, Luke 23:36, John 19:28 (Ps 69:21 [MT v. 22]); John 15:25 (Ps 69:4 [MT v. 5]); Rom 15:3 (Ps 69:9b [MT v. 10b]); cf. Acts 1:20 (Ps 69:25 [MT v. 26]) though its

significance when one recognizes that a typological relationship provides the link between them. As the Messiah (John 1:41, 49), Jesus is identified as 'great David's greater Son.'[10] The New Testament authors, including John, indicate that David is more than an analogy for the coming Messiah. Rather, some of David's experiences constitute the pattern for the experiences of the Messiah.[11] In the case of Psalm 69:9 and John 2:17, David's consuming zeal for the Temple prefigures that of Christ.[12] In other words, Christ's zeal for the Temple fulfills the pattern set forth in the experience of David. The significance of the above points on John 2:17 will become evident in the following examination of 2:18-22.

The Jews respond to Jesus' Temple cleansing with a request for a sign (2:18). Jesus' response (2:19) is enigmatic; it is so enigmatic that the Jews and even his own disciples do not grasp its significance at the time.[13] The Jews think Jesus is referring to the Jerusalem Temple, which leads them to dismiss his proposed sign as completely absurd (2:20). After Jesus' resurrection, the disciples remember Jesus' saying (2:19), understand it correctly (2:21), and accept it as true (2:22). Thus they understand that when Jesus says, 'Destroy

---

relevance is less clear (Bruce G. Schuchard, *Scripture within Scripture: The Interrelationship of Form and Function in the Explicit Old Testament Citations in the Gospel of John*, SBLDS, no. 133 [Atlanta: Scholars Press, 1992], 20).

[10] Carson, *John*, 180.

[11] See especially John 13:18, 15:25, 19:24-25a. Also, see Carson, 'John and the Johannine Epistles,' 249; idem, *John*, 180, 527; Douglas J. Moo, *The Old Testament in the Gospel Passion Narratives* (Sheffield: Almond, 1983), 299-300. Cf. Frédéric L. Godet, *Commentary on the Gospel of John*, trans. Timothy Dwight (Grand Rapids: Zondervan, 1969), 364 (vol. 1), 304 (vol. 2); Köstenberger, 'Jesus the Good Shepherd,' 81-82; Maarten Menken, *Old Testament Quotations in the Fourth Gospel: Studies in Textual Form*, CBET, no. 15 (Kampen: Kok Pharos, 1996), 44, 132; Mowinckel, *He That Cometh*, 12.

[12] John Calvin, *The Gospel according to St. John 1-10*, trans. T. Parker (Grand Rapids: Eerdmans, 1959), 53-54. It is possible that a typological interpretation of Ps 69:9 accounts for John's future tense (καταφάγεται) in place of the LXX's aorist. Thus John sees Ps 69:9 as a typological prediction that is fulfilled in Jesus' cleansing of the Temple (when zeal for the Temple consumes him). Changing the verb to a future tense 'was useful in facilitating a prophetic [i.e., predictive] interpretation of the Psalm' (Barrett, *John*, 165; cf. Edwin D. Freed, *Old Testament Quotations in the Gospel of John*, NovTSup, vol. 11 [Leiden: E. J. Brill, 1965], 9-10). Alternatively, it could be that the future tense (καταφάγεται) in 2:17 directs the reader toward the point when Jesus' zeal for his Father's house will result in his death (Menken, *Old Testament Quotations in the Fourth Gospel*, 40-41). It is difficult to decide which of these views is preferable, since John does not feel the need to make this change elsewhere (Ibid., 40).

[13] John 2:19: 'Jesus answered them, "Destroy this temple, and I will raise it again in three days."' See also the enigmatic 'sign of Jonah' in Matt 12:39-40 (Charles L'Eplattenier, *L'Évangile de Jean* [Geneva: Labor et Fides, 1993], 75-76).

this Temple, and I will raise it up in three days' (2:19), he is actually referring to his body as the Temple and not to the Jerusalem Temple at all (2:21).[14]

The preceding synopsis of John 2:18-22 requires an affirmative answer to a significant interpretive question: Is it possible that John 2:21 provides the correct interpretation of Jesus' saying (2:19)? Although many modern interpreters answer this question negatively, a credible case can be made for an affirmative answer. The first step toward an answer to this question requires attention to a significant aspect of the Fourth Gospel, its handling of misunderstanding or lack of understanding.[15] Misunderstanding or lack of understanding on the part of Jesus' auditors is a pervasive feature of the Fourth Gospel.[16] Misunderstandings are sometimes resolved immediately by an explanation from Jesus (4:31-34). On the other hand, one common category of misunderstandings is only resolved with the passage of time.[17] In most of these cases, the misunderstanding (or lack of understanding) persists until 'Jesus' death/resurrection/exaltation, perceived as a unified event, turns a corner in salvation history and constitutes the ground on which the Spirit is bequeathed.'[18] Thus the pervasive misunderstandings of the Fourth Gospel are more than a peculiar characteristic of John's narrative. They show that, according to John, a complete understanding of Jesus' words and deeds is not possible (even for disciples) until after his death/resurrection/exaltation and the sending of the Spirit.[19] At that point, the disciples' understanding of Jesus' words and deeds takes a giant step forward. Thus John provides a credible scenario whereby the disciples who misunderstand or fail to understand one of Jesus' sayings before the resurrection could understand it clearly afterward.

Looking at John 2:20, the initial misunderstanding of Jesus' saying fits into

---

[14] This is the common understanding of John 2:18-22 from patristic times (see Ign. *Smyr.* 2). Modern interpreters (starting with Herder) tend to interpret 2:21-22 as a 'post-resurrectional amplification' of 2:19 (Brown, *John*, 123; on the history of interpretation, see Meyer, *John*, 113).

[15] For a complete discussion of this aspect of the Fourth Gospel, see Donald A. Carson, 'Understanding Misunderstandings in the Fourth Gospel,' *TynBul* 33 (1982): 59-91. See especially the chart on p. 91 with its list of instances of misunderstanding or lack of understanding. For Synoptic analogies to the Fourth Gospel's misunderstandings, see ibid., 78-79.

[16] Barrett, *John*, 166; Brown, *John*, cxxxv-cxxxvi; Bultmann, *John*, 127, n. 1.

[17] According to Carson's chart, 31 cases of faulty understanding are cleared up with the passage of time ('Understanding Misunderstandings in the Fourth Gospel,' 91).

[18] Ibid., 83; Carson, *John*, 183.

[19] Carson, 'Understanding Misunderstandings in the Fourth Gospel,' 84-85. On the role of the Spirit, see 14:20, 26; 16:7, 12-15 (ibid., 81; cf. Udo Schnelle, 'Die Tempelreinigung und die Christologie des Johannesevangeliums,' *NTS* 42 [1996]: 362).

a common pattern of misunderstanding on the part of the Jews.[20] Neither their interpretation of Jesus' saying nor the setting in which Jesus speaks should have a decisive bearing upon the interpretation of 2:19.[21] It is possible that the Jews completely misunderstand what Jesus means by 'this Temple.'[22]

John 2:21 and 2:22 also have analogies in the Fourth Gospel. John uses asides in 2:21, 7:39, 12:33, 21:19, and 21:23 to provide the reader with the proper interpretation of Jesus' words.[23] Similarly, the asides found in 2:22, 12:16, 13:28-29, and 20:9 alert the reader to a misunderstanding or lack of understanding on the part of the disciples. In 2:22 and 12:16, it is explicitly stated that the disciples' lack of understanding is cleared up after Jesus' resurrection or glorification. The remembering involved in 2:22 and 12:16 links the disciples' later understanding to the activity of the Spirit (14:26).[24] Thus, in 2:21-22, John combines his explanation of Jesus' saying with a note about the moment when the disciples remember it and believe it. When the disciples remember Jesus' saying (2:19), they are able to interpret it correctly in light of his death (destruction) and resurrection (rising again in three days).[25] They are also able to see that the Jews completely misunderstood Jesus' saying.[26]

As seen above, evidence from the Fourth Gospel supports the possibility that 2:21 is the correct interpretation of Jesus' saying in 2:19. The Jews' response to Jesus' saying comes at a time when even the disciples do not understand the

---

[20] Carson, 'Understanding Misunderstandings in the Fourth Gospel,' 91 (col. 13 in table).

[21] With regard to the setting, see the comparable misunderstanding that occurs at the well with the Samaritan woman (4:10-15).

[22] Cf. John 7:33-36; Coloe, *God Dwells with Us*, 78; Culpepper, *Anatomy of the Fourth Gospel*, 155; Frühwald-König, *Tempel und Kult*, 95. Contra J. H. Bernard, *A Critical and Exegetical Commentary on the Gospel according to St. John*, ICC, vol. 29, pt. 1 (Edinburgh: T and T Clark, 1928), 97; Dubarle, 'Le signe du temple,' 25; Godet, *John*, vol. 1, 365.

[23] Cf. 11:51-52, where an aside is used to indicate the true significance of the high priest's words (Léon-Dufour, 'Le signe du temple selon saint Jean,' 157).

[24] In 2:22 and 12:16 (and 2:17), one finds identical forms of the verb μιμνήσκομαι ('remember'), which is clearly related to ὑπομιμνήσκω ('remind') (14:26) (Andreas Obermann, *Die christologische Erfüllung der Schrift im Johannesevangelium: Eine Untersuchung zur johanneischen Hermeneutik anhand der Schriftzitate*, WUNT, 2nd series, no. 83 [Tübingen: J.C.B. Mohr, 1996], 120-1).

[25] Cf. Barrett, *John*, 166-7; Hoskyns, *Fourth Gospel*, 195-6; Wenschkewitz, *Spiritualisierung der Kultusbegriffe*, 100-1.

[26] It seems clear that the reader is expected to understand 2:21 as the correct interpretation of Jesus' saying, and not as an additional, deeper meaning that John later discovered in it (Coloe, *God Dwells with Us*, 78; contra Léon-Dufour, 'Le signe du temple selon saint Jean,' 170, 173; Beasley-Murray, *John*, 40-41; Schnackenburg, *John*, vol. 1, 350).

meaning of Jesus' words.²⁷ It is therefore highly unlikely that the Jews understand it correctly. Besides, does it make sense that Jesus would cleanse the Temple, his Father's house, and afterward challenge the Jews to destroy it?

Further evidence for the credibility of 2:21 as the correct interpretation of 2:19 emerges from examination of the statement itself and parallels in the Synoptics. First, in John 2:19, the antecedent of the personal pronoun αὐτός ('it') is ναός ('Temple'). It makes good grammatical sense that αὐτός and ναός refer to the same Temple.²⁸ This fits with John's interpretative statement in 2:21 whereby John indicates that the Temple of 2:19 refers exclusively to Jesus' body. Second, 2:19 contains two clues that solidify its connection with Jesus' resurrection: The verb ἐγείρω ('raise up') and the reference to three days are common elements of Jesus' passion predictions.²⁹ Third, it is interesting

---

²⁷ Cf. Mark 9:32 where the disciples do not even understand Jesus' straightforward passion prediction.

²⁸ Cf. Meyer, *John*, 114. Contra Dubarle, 'Le signe du temple,' 25. This grammatical point also undermines the interpretation of 2:19 by Godet and Zahn. They give a double reference to ναός (i.e., Jesus' body and the Jerusalem Temple) and a single reference to αὐτός (i.e., Jesus' body) (Godet, *John*, vol. 1, 366; Theodor Zahn, *Das Evangelium des Johannes* [Wuppertal: Brockhaus, 1983], 175). Similarly, it rules out the possibility that 'the Temple of his body' in 2:21 is a reference to the church (contra Charles H. Dodd, *The Interpretation of the Fourth Gospel* [Cambridge: Cambridge University Press, 1953], 302-3). The church was not destroyed and raised up after three days (Carson, *John*, 182).

²⁹ For the use of the verb ἐγείρω, see Matt 16:21, 17:23, 20:19, 27:63; Luke 9:22. In each of these cases ἐγείρω is passive instead of active as in John 2:19. This makes 2:19 unique, but not impossible (note the use of the passive in 2:22; Meyer, *John*, 114). For the use of three days in Jesus' passion predictions, see Mark 8:31, 9:31, 10:34, and parallels. Interpreters often note that John's ἐν τρισὶν ἡμέραις ('in three days') (2:19; cf. Matt 27:40, Mark 15:29) is different from the usual reference to the resurrection τῇ τρίτῃ ἡμέρᾳ ('on the third day') (Matt 16:21; 17:23; 20:19; Luke 9:22; 18:33; 24:7, 46; Acts 10:40; 1 Cor 15:4) or μετὰ τρεῖς ἡμέρας ('after three days') (Matt 27:63; Mark 8:31, 9:31, 10:34) (cf. Brown, *John*, 120). For the sake of completion, two of the parallels to John 2:19 use διὰ τριῶν ἡμερῶν ('within three days') (Matt 26:61, Mark 14:58). All of these expressions share the basic notion of three days. The flexible nature of the phraseology is especially evident in Matthew, where all the expressions occur in addition to an enigmatic reference to the resurrection with no preposition (12:40). It seems best to allow for diverse phraseology rather than to insist that only one or two of these phrases contains a reference to the resurrection (Donald Juel, *Messiah and Temple: The Trial of Jesus in the Gospel of Mark*, SBLDS, no. 31 [Missoula, Mont.: Scholars Press, 1977], 144; contra Brown, *John*, 120). Interpreters who object to understanding 'three days' in connection with Jesus' resurrection often attempt to understand 'three days' as an idiom for 'a short time.' They often cite Luke 13:32 and Hos 6:2 as parallels. Yet neither of these parallels contains a bare reference to three days or a third day. Each also refers to some activity on a first day, second day, or both. Therefore they

that the Synoptic parallels to John 2:19 all contain the reference to three days (Matt 26:61, 27:40; Mark 14:58, 15:29). By preserving the reference to three days, the false witnesses and those who use their testimony to taunt the crucified Jesus are unknowingly predicting Jesus' resurrection.[30] Therefore it appears that Matthew and Mark agree that the testimony of the witnesses at Jesus' trial has something to do with the resurrection.[31] In doing so, they support the possibility that Jesus said something ambiguous about the destruction of the Temple that was actually a veiled prediction of his death and resurrection in three days.[32] In other words, they support the possibility that John has correctly understood Jesus' saying in 2:19 as an enigmatic reference to his own body, which he raises up in three days.

To sum up, it appears that evidence from the Fourth Gospel and from Synoptic parallels allows one to build a credible case for understanding John 2:21 as the necessary clue to a correct understanding of Jesus' saying in 2:19.[33] When Jesus' saying in John 2:19 is interpreted in light of the interpretive clue given in 2:21, it becomes clear that the Jews fulfill Jesus' challenge by bringing about his death.[34] Thus Jesus responds to their request for a sign (2:18) with an enigmatic prediction of his death and resurrection (2:19), like Matthew 12:39-

---

give very limited support to the contention that a bare reference to a three-day time period would be understood idiomatically. It seems much more likely that 'three days' should be read in light of the various passion predictions where it refers to the timing of the resurrection (Bernard, *John*, vol. 1, 94).

[30] Juel, *Messiah and Temple*, 144; Lindars, *John*, 142; John Paul Heil, 'The Narrative Strategy and Pragmatics of the Temple Theme in Mark,' *CBQ* 59 (1997): 97-98.

[31] It is possible to carry the argument further. The testimony of the witnesses at Jesus' trial could have been based upon their misunderstanding of a saying of Jesus that Matthew and Mark do not report (like the one in John 2:19) (Meyer, *John*, 113; Wenschkewitz, *Spiritualisierung der Kultusbegriffe*, 99-101; cf. Jerome, *Commentariorum in Matheum*, 4.1385 [on Matt 26:61]). It is possible that Matthew and Mark were aware of the saying of Jesus that John reports and also understood it as a prediction of his death and resurrection in three days. Thus, by phrasing the testimony of the false witnesses the way they did, Matthew and Mark preserved both the misunderstanding of the Jews and the true reference of the saying of Jesus, i.e., his resurrection in three days. A similar case is made by Alan Cole (*The New Temple: A Study in the Origins of the Catechetical 'Form' of the Church in the New Testament* [London: Tyndale, 1950], 5, 21, 27-28, 52). A major difference is that Cole uses Mark 14:58 to justify finding a double reference (Jesus' own body and the church) in John 2:19.

[32] Note the use of ἐν τρισὶν ἡμέραις ('in three days') in two of the parallels (Matt 27:40, Mark 15:29) and in John 2:19, 20.

[33] In any case, John 2:21 definitely represents John's understanding of Jesus' saying and is therefore useful for establishing John's theology of the Temple.

[34] On the use of the imperative (λύσατε) in 2:19, see Edwin A. Abbott, *Johannine Grammar*, vol. 1 (London: Adam and Charles Black, 1906), 321-2.

40. After the resurrection, the disciples remember Jesus' saying and interpret it correctly (2:21-22). Consequently they are able to affirm the truth of the Scripture and of Jesus' saying (2:22).[35]

As seen above, the significance of Jesus' saying in 2:19 reaches beyond its anticipation of his death and resurrection. Along with 2:21-22, it fits into John's portrayal of the process by which Jesus' disciples remember and understand his words and deeds. Furthermore John 2:19, 21-22 has several additional implications for Johannine Christology.[36] First, according to John 2:19, 21, Jesus refers to his own body as Temple while standing in the Jerusalem Temple. This suggests that Jesus' body is the replacement for the Jerusalem Temple, whose days are numbered as the special locus for the presence of God and for true worship (4:20-24).[37] Second, Jesus' body is the Temple of God that will be destroyed and raised up within three days. It will therefore be important to look for further links between Jesus' death/resurrection/exaltation and his replacement of the Temple. Third, it is possible that John sees a typological relationship between Jesus and the Temple analogous to the typological relationship between David and Jesus.[38] Further evidence for the first and third points will emerge from the following examination of John 1:14, 1:51, 4:20-24.[39]

John 1:14

John 1:14 occurs in the Fourth Gospel's prologue, which provides an introduction to and anticipation of the Fourth Gospel's presentation of Jesus.[40] Therefore, if interpreters are right in connecting 1:14 with Jesus' replacement of the Temple, then this theme is one of a number of themes introduced and anticipated by the prologue. The following section examines the evidence for the connection between Jesus' replacement of the Temple and John 1:14. Then it considers what John 1:14 might lead one to anticipate about the development of this theme in the Fourth Gospel.

The first piece of evidence for connecting 1:14 with Jesus' replacement of

---

[35] The significance of the reference to 'the Scripture' is taken up at the end of chapter five along with some final comments on 2:13-22 (p. 191).

[36] Cf. Schnelle, 'Tempelreinigung und die Christologie des Johannesevangeliums,' 366-71; Hartman, 'He Spoke of the Temple of His Body,' 70-71, 76-78.

[37] Coloe, *God Dwells with Us*, 81. Johanna Rahner points out that when the Jews crucify Jesus they are actually participating in the replacement of their Temple. Thus they are bringing about the end of the Jerusalem Temple with respect to its 'salvation-historical and soteriological' functions (*'Er aber sprach vom Tempel seines Leibes,'* 305, 310-1).

[38] See the above discussion of John 2:17.

[39] Consideration of the second point will be taken up in the next chapter.

[40] Herman N. Ridderbos, *The Gospel according to John: A Theological Commentary*, trans. John Vriend (Grand Rapids: Eerdmans, 1997), 17.

the Temple is the verb ἐσκήνωσεν ('dwelt,' from σκηνόω). It is an unusual verb found only here in the Fourth Gospel and elsewhere in the New Testament only in Revelation.[41] Craig Koester finds that John's use of σκηνόω is appropriate, because it creates a unique link between 'flesh' (1:14a) and 'glory' (1:14c-d).[42] This is so, because two nouns from the σκην root, σκῆνος ('tent') and σκήνωμα ('tent'), are used metaphorically in the New Testament in reference to the human body.[43] So it is possible for John's use of σκηνόω to suggest an analogy between Jesus' flesh and a tent. Furthermore Old Testament terms for the Tabernacle are frequently translated in the Septuagint using σκηνή ('tent').[44] The Tabernacle is designed by God so that he might dwell in the midst of his people and is a prominent place where God manifests his glory to Moses and the people.[45] According to John 1:14, human flesh becomes the locus where comparable events take place. The Word dwells on earth in the form of human flesh, that is, Jesus' body.[46] Eyewitnesses like John see Jesus'

---

[41] Rev 7:15, 12:12, 13:6, 21:3. The related verb κατασκηνόω occurs in Mark 4:32, Matt 13:32, Luke 13:19, Acts 2:26.

[42] Koester, *Dwelling of God*, 102. John 1:14 (in Greek): (a) Καὶ ὁ λόγος σὰρξ ἐγένετο (b) καὶ ἐσκήνωσεν ἐν ἡμῖν, (c) καὶ ἐθεασάμεθα τὴν δόξαν αὐτοῦ, (d) δόξαν ὡς μονογενοῦς παρὰ πατρός, (e) πλήρης χάριτος καὶ ἀληθείας.
Translation of John 1:14: (a) 'The Word became flesh (b) and made his dwelling among us. (c) We have seen his glory, (d) the glory of the One and Only, who came from the Father, (e) full of grace and truth.'

[43] Ibid. For σκῆνος, see 2 Cor 5:1, 4; for σκήνωμα, see 2 Pet 1:13-14. Cf. Zahn, *Johannes*, 80.

[44] Since the basic sense of σκηνή is 'tent,' it is regularly used in the LXX translation of the expression אהל מועד ('Tent of Meeting'), one of the common designations for the Tabernacle. In addition, it is the favored LXX translation for another common designation for the Tabernacle, משכן (also translated 17 times by σκήνωμα). The attractiveness of σκηνή as a translation for משכן is heightened by their analogous consonants (*s, k, n*). The evidence for these points is drawn from Wilhelm Michaelis, 'σκηνή,' trans. G. Bromiley, in *TDNT*, vol. 7, (Grand Rapids: Eerdmans, 1971), 369 and D. Kellermann, 'משכן,' trans. David E. Green, in *TDOT*, vol. 9 (Grand Rapids: Eerdmans, 1998), 64.

[45] Exod 25:8; 29:45; 40:34-38; Lev 9; Num 14:10; 16:19, 42; 20:6. Cf. Marie-Émile Boismard, *St. John's Prologue*, trans. Carisbrooke Dominicans (Westminster, Md.: Newman, 1957), 48; Bernard, *John*, vol. 1, 21; Zahn, *Johannes*, 81. Of course, the Tabernacle has its predecessors in the pillar of cloud and fire, Mt. Sinai, and a temporary 'tent of meeting' where Moses speaks with God (Exod 33:7-11). God's glory appears in the pillar and on Mt. Sinai (Exod 16:10, 33:12-34:9). Yet the Tabernacle is presented in Exodus as the culmination of God's desire for a dwelling place in the midst of his people and the book ends with the dramatic manifestation of God's glory in the completed Tabernacle (40:34-38).

[46] On the use of σάρξ in 1:14, see William J. Dumbrell, 'Grace and Truth: The Progress of the Argument of the Prologue of John's Gospel,' in *Doing Theology for the People of*

glory (1:14c), and the Father's glory as well, since Jesus' glory is given to him by the Father (1:14d; 17:22). The point is this: When the Word becomes flesh, God's dwelling place among his people takes on a new form, a human body.[47]

In addition to inviting a comparison between Jesus and the Tabernacle, John's phrase ἐσκήνωσεν ἐν ἡμῖν ('dwelt among us') should be connected with God's promise to dwell among his people in a new Temple.[48] In the Septuagint of Zechariah 2:14 and Ezekiel 43:9, one finds an appealing linguistic parallel to John 1:14b: κατασκηνώσω ἐν μέσῳ ('I will dwell among').[49] Examination of the Hebrew Old Testament (MT) clarifies that Zechariah 2:10 and Ezekiel 43:7, 9 actually duplicate the wording of God's initial promise to dwell among the people of Israel in the consecrated Tabernacle (Exod 29:45).[50] This promise is later repeated with reference to the Jerusalem Temple (1 Kgs 6:13). It is therefore not surprising that identical language is used when the promise is picked up again in Zechariah 2:10 and Ezekiel 43:7, 9 with reference to the new Temple of God to be established on Mount Zion.[51] The repetition of this promise indicates that dwelling among his

---

God: Studies in Honor of J. I. Packer, ed. Donald Lewis and Alister McGrath (Downers Grove, Ill.: InterVarsity, 1996), 112.

[47] On the divinity of the Word, see John 1:1. It is also common to connect John's use of σκηνόω in 1:14 with the Shekinah found in rabbinic writings. In spite of the parallels between John 1:14 and the rabbinic portrait of the Shekinah, the Shekinah is probably not a factor in the background to John 1:14 for two reasons. First, although the rabbinic portrait of the Shekinah could have begun to take shape in the first century, it is impossible to trace its early development with any precision. Consequently, John may never have come into contact with it. Second, John does not expect his readers to understand Hebrew or Aramaic terms elsewhere (1:38, 41-42; 9:7; 20:16). This makes it unlikely that he intended them to pick up on a 'veiled reference' to שכינה when he uses σκηνόω (Koester, *Dwelling of God*, 106, 72).

[48] The promise is found in the OT at Zech 2:10 (MT, LXX v. 14); Ezek 37:27; 43:7, 9. Bernard, *John*, vol. 1, 21; Boismard, *St. John's Prologue*, 49; Brown, *John*, 32-33; Evans, *Word and Glory*, 82; André Feuillet, *Le prologue du quatrième évangile: étude de théologie johannique* (Paris: Desclée de Brouwer, 1968), 100; Koester, *Dwelling of God*, 104; Meyer, *John*, 62; Schlatter, *Johannes*, 23; Zahn, *Johannes*, 81.

[49] The appeal of the parallel is enhanced when one factors in the LXX preference for translating שכן with κατασκηνόω instead of σκηνόω (Wilhelm Michaelis, 'κατασκηνόω,' trans. G. Bromiley, in *TDNT*, vol. 7, [Grand Rapids: Eerdmans, 1971], 387). Like ἐν μέσῳ, the preposition ἐν can sometimes mean 'among' (J. Louw and E. Nida, *Greek-English Lexicon of the NT*, section 83.9). Cf. Ezek 37:27 in the LXX: ἔσται ἡ κατασκήνωσίς μου ἐν αὐτοῖς.

[50] Cf. Exod 25:8. The continuity between these promises is obscured in the LXX, but see the translation of Exod 25:8, 29:45 ('and I will dwell among') by Aquila (among others) (Zahn, *Johannes*, 81). Two more interesting parallels to Exod 29:45 are found in legal sections of Numbers (5:3, 35:34).

[51] Cf. Joel 3:17 [MT 4:17], Zech 8:3.

people is a consistent aspect of God's dealings with them. Furthermore, the expression of the promise with reference to the new Temple gives it a place within Israel's hopes for the future. Consequently two significant points follow from the allusion to this promise in John 1:14b. First, John 1:14b suggests that the incarnation of the Word is an event that fulfills God's repeated promise to dwell among his people.[52] Second, in doing so, the incarnate Word is fulfilling a promise whose most recent prophetic expression anticipated its fulfillment within a new Temple building.

Next, in John 1:14c-d, John provides further evidence that the incarnation of the Word fulfills prophetic hopes associated with the dwelling of God among his people.[53] The prophets, particularly Ezekiel, expected that God would manifest his glory in the new Temple like he had in the Tabernacle and Solomon's Temple.[54] The manifestations of God's glory in the Tabernacle and the Temple are powerful reminders that the God who dwells there is the same God whose glory descended upon Mount Sinai (Exod 24:16-17). The anticipated display of God's glory did not appear in the Second Temple (2 Macc 2:7-8). At least some Jews continued to anticipate a day when God's glory would appear in his Temple on Mount Zion.[55] Against this background, John 1:14c-d points to the manifestation of the glory of God in connection with the dwelling of the incarnate Word upon the earth. Hence one implication of 1:14c-d is that Jesus' glory is the anticipated manifestation of God's glory. Thus, like 1:14b, 1:14c-d suggests that the incarnate Word fulfills an expectation whose fulfillment was expected to occur in the new Temple.

The implications of John 1:14b-d for Jesus' fulfillment and replacement of the Temple gain clarity from the context, particularly 1:16-17. Indeed, John links 1:14 and 1:16-17 together by repeating vocabulary from 1:14e in 1:16-17. The content and language of 1:16 affirm that it is an explanation of 1:14 rather than 1:15.[56] John 1:14e deserves some attention, because its contribution to 1:14 prepares the way for discussion of 1:16-17.

As the link between 1:14 and 1:16-17, 1:14e appears to be connected with the glory of the Word (1:14c-d). The strength of the connection depends upon one's decision about which noun πλήρης ('full') modifies. If it modifies δόξαν

---

[52] Cf. Brown, *John*, 33.

[53] Braun, 'In Spiritu et veritate,' 248; Brown, *John*, 34; Feuillet, *Prologue du quatrième évangile*, 111; Hoskyns, *Fourth Gospel*, 148-9.

[54] On the appearance of God's glory in the Tabernacle, see the beginning of this section (p. 117); see also 1 Kgs 8:10-11 // 2 Chr 5:13-14; 2 Chr 7:1-3 (in Solomon's Temple) and Ezek 43:2-4, 44:4 (cf. Isa 66:18-19; Zech 2:5; Ps 102:16 [MT v. 17]) (in the new Temple).

[55] Sir 36:19; 2 Macc 2:7-8; 4QFlor I, 5.

[56] Note that v. 16 begins with ὅτι ('for' or 'because'). The chiastic structure proposed by R. Alan Culpepper accounts for the placement of 1:15 between vv. 14 and 16 ('The Pivot of John's Prologue,' *NTS* 27 [1980-1981]: 12-13).

('glory'), then 1:14e is basically a further comment upon the glory of the Word and its allusion to Exod 34:6 enhances its appropriateness.[57] If 1:14e modifies λόγος ('word'), αὐτοῦ ('his'), or μονογενοῦς ('One and Only'), then 1:14e is a further comment on the Word that is connected to his glory indirectly due to its allusion to Exod 34:6.[58] The allusion to Exod 34:6 is uncertain due to John's word choice.[59] Its plausibility increases once one sees that it does not merely depend upon a verbal parallel. It is supported by thematic parallels to Exod 33:18-34:7 located in John 1:14, 17-18: (1) seeing God's glory (Exod 33:18-19, 34:5-7; John 1:14c-d), (2) seeing God (Exod 33:20-23, John 1:18a), and (3) the giving of the Law to Moses (Exod 34:1-4, John 1:17a).[60] In short, the allusion to Exod 34:6 in John 1:14e lies at least within the realm of possibility. If one accepts this allusion, then each phrase in John 1:14b-e suggests some measure of continuity between the revelation of God in the form of the incarnate Word and previous revelation in the Old Testament.[61]

Moving from 1:14e to 1:16, one finds an explanatory comment linked to 1:14e by means of two key words, πλήρωμα ('fullness') and χάρις ('grace'). The first part of 1:16 is straightforward: 'For from his fullness we all have received.' The significance of the last part of the verse is debated. Central to the debate is the preposition ἀντί. Many interpreters prefer to view the ἀντί of 1:16 as synonymous with ἐπί ('upon'). In doing so, they give ἀντί a sense that is certainly unusual and probably unparalleled.[62] When one reads ἀντί

---

[57] In this case, πλήρης is regarded as indeclinable (BAGD, 670). Carson takes this position and notes that it strengthens the case for an allusion to Exod 34:6 (*John*, 129). Cf. Brown, *John*, 14.

[58] This is the most common preference. Those who regard πλήρης as declinable choose λόγος (Schlatter, *Johannes*, 27); those who do not opt for one of the other choices (Barrett, *John*, 139; Boismard, *St. John's Prologue*, 54; Feuillet, *Prologue du quatrième évangile*, 114; Ridderbos, *John*, 54).

[59] The allusion is accepted by many commentators (see the list in Evans, *Word and Glory*, 81, n. 2). The problem is that πλήρης χάριτος καὶ ἀληθείας is John's unique rendering of the Hebrew רב־חסד ואמת. In particular, it is often pointed out that ἔλεος rather than χάρις would be the expected translation for חסד. This is based upon the LXX where χάρις is only used once (Esth 2:9) to translate חסד. John's unique rendering of רב־חסד ואמת is certainly a possible translation, even if it is not the most obvious one (Brown, *John*, 14; Feuillet, *Prologue du quatrième évangile*, 114; Lindars, *John*, 95). It is also significant that the phrase רב־חסד ואמת is found only in Exod 34:6 (elsewhere one finds just חסד ואמת) (Koester, *Dwelling of God*, 104).

[60] Anthony T. Hanson, 'John I. 14-18 and Exodus XXXIV,' *NTS* 23 (1977): 95. On the evaluation of allusions, see Jon Paulien, 'Elusive Allusions: The Problematic Use of the Old Testament in Revelation,' *BR* 33 (1988): 37-53.

[61] Cf. Koester, *Dwelling of God*, 104.

[62] To justify reading ἀντί this way, interpreters commonly appeal to a parallel in Philo (*Post.* 145). Even so, the parallel from Philo does not provide irrefutable confirmation that ἀντί sometimes carries the required significance (i.e., 'upon') (Ruth B. Edwards,

this way, the phrase χάριν ἀντὶ χάριτος ('grace upon grace') indicates that believers receive an abundant supply of grace that is never depleted.[63] A second interpretive possibility that merits attention allows ἀντί one of its common senses, namely, 'instead of' or 'in place of.'[64] In this case, 'grace in place of grace' indicates the replacement of one grace by another.[65] The nature of the two graces becomes clear in 1:17.[66]

Like 1:16, John 1:17 begins with ὅτι ('for' or 'because'). Its content affirms that it picks up and clarifies the thought of 1:16. Interpreters who disagree about the significance of ἀντί in 1:16 also tend to disagree about the significance of 1:17a in relation to 1:17b. First, those who read ἀντί as 'upon' generally regard 1:17a as antithetical to 1:17b, that is, the Law was given through Moses, but grace and truth came through Jesus Christ.[67] Second, those who read ἀντί as 'in place of' regard 1:17a and 1:17b as identifying the successive graces of 1:16, that is, the Law given through Moses was the initial grace that was superseded by the second grace, the fullness of grace and truth revealed through Jesus Christ.[68] In both cases, the grace and truth revealed in Jesus Christ ushers in something new. The major point of dispute is the

---

'Χάριν ἀντὶ χάριτος [John 1:16]: Grace and the Law in the Johannine Prologue,' *JSNT* 32 [1988]: 5-6; Abbott, *Johannine Grammar*, vol. 1, 226).

[63] For a representative sampling, see Barrett, *John*, 140; Godet, *John*, vol. 1, 278; Lindars, *John*, 97; Ridderbos, *John*, 56; Schnackenburg, *John*, vol. 1, 275.

[64] Edwards, 'Χάριν ἀντὶ χάριτος (John 1:16),' 3, 6-9; BAGD, 73; Abbott, *Johannine Grammar*, vol. 1, 225-6.

[65] Boismard, *St. John's Prologue*, 60-61; Carson, *John*, 132; Edwards, 'Χάριν ἀντὶ χάριτος (John 1:16),' 6-9; Evans, *Word and Glory*, 80; Feuillet, *Prologue du quatrième évangile*, 124; J. N. Sanders, *A Commentary on the Gospel according to St. John*, ed. B. A. Mastin, HNTC (New York: Harper and Row, 1968), 84-85; Zahn, *Johannes*, 93. Cf. Chrysostom, *Hom. Jo.* 14; Cyril of Alexandria, *Commentary on the Gospel according to St. John*, trans. members of the English church, Library of Fathers of the Holy Catholic Church, vol. 1 (Oxford: James Parker and Co., 1874), 118-9.

[66] A third, less common interpretation of ἀντί regards it as indicating correspondence, i.e., the 'grace that constitutes our share corresponds to the grace of the Word' (Brown, *John*, 16). This interpretation, like the first one mentioned above, requires one to give an unusual, probably unparalleled sense to the preposition ἀντί (Edwards, 'Χάριν ἀντὶ χάριτος [John 1:16],' 5). Feuillet objects to the subtlety of this interpretation (*Prologue du quatrième évangile*, 124).

[67] Barrett, *John*, 140-1; Bultmann, *John*, 78-79; Calvin, *John*, vol. 1, 24; Godet, *John*, vol. 1, 278; Meyer, *John*, 68; Pancaro, *Law in the Fourth Gospel*, 537, 539-40. Lindars and Schnackenburg are the exceptions. Although they agree with the general line of thinking represented by this position, they think that it is possible to communicate this by synthetic parallelism (Lindars, *John*, 98; Schnackenburg, *John*, vol. 1, 276-7).

[68] Carson, *John*, 132. Cf. Abbott, *Johannine Grammar*, vol. 1, 226; Brown, *John*, 35-36; Chrysostom, *Hom. Jo.* 14; Cyril of Alexandria, *John*, vol. 1, 118; Feuillet, *Prologue du quatrième évangile*, 124-5.

propriety of referring to the Law as χάρις ('grace' or 'gracious gift').

Many supporters of the first position want to maintain a rigid distinction between the Law and grace. The Law given through Moses was unable to impart grace and it is therefore inappropriate to identify it as grace.[69] This disallows the possibility of a correspondence between the Law of 1:17a and the grace of 1:16b. The problem with this view is that it does not recognize the distinction between the Law's ability to impart grace and the nature of the Law itself. One can maintain that the Law is unable to impart grace and still affirm that it would be appropriate to think of the Law itself as χάρις in the sense of a 'gracious gift' from God.[70] In fact, the Old Testament and the New Testament suggest that the Law was a gracious gift of God to his people.[71] These considerations support the viability of the second position.

The second position moves from viable to preferable when one considers that it does not require the interpreter to assign an unusual sense to the ἀντί of 1:16. In addition, it allows for an understanding of John 1:14e, 16-18 that progresses smoothly, at least as smoothly as the flow of thought created by other interpretations of 1:16-17. Thus John 1:14e describes the Word's glory or the Word itself as 'full of grace and truth.' Then, 1:16 carries forward the thought of 1:14e with the affirmation that all believers have received a gracious gift from the fullness of the Word. They have received one gracious gift in place of another. John 1:17 clarifies that the first gracious gift was the Law given through Moses. The Law was replaced by the second gracious gift, namely, the grace and truth that came through Jesus Christ. Finally, John 1:18 brings the passage to a close by proclaiming that a unique revelatory event occurred when the μονογενής ('only one' or 'unique one') explained the Father. When one reads John 1:14e, 16-18 this way, these verses, especially 1:16-17, introduce a significant aspect of John's approach to the relationship between the Old Testament and the New Testament.

According to John 1:16-17, the Law given through Moses, which was an essential element of the old covenant, is replaced by the grace and truth that

---

[69] See, in particular, Barrett, *John*, 140-1; Bultmann, *John*, 79; Meyer, *John*, 68. Categories from Pauline theology are often the driving motivation for the rigid distinction (cf. Rom 6:14; Bultmann, *John*, 79; Meyer, *John*, 68). Barrett's reference to the distinction between 'Law and Gospel' suggests that he is being influenced by similar thinking (*John*, 141).

[70] Cf. BAGD, 877-8 (section 3); Zahn, *Johannes*, 94. Similarly, John Chrysostom calls the revelation of the Law 'the work of grace' (*Commentary on Saint John the Apostle and Evangelist: Homilies 1-47*, trans. Sister Thomas Aquinas Goggin, FC, vol. 33 [New York: Fathers of the Church, Inc., 1957], 136).

[71] Deut 4:8; Ps 147:19-20; Rom 3:2, 9:4 (Douglas J. Moo, *The Epistle to the Romans*, NICNT [Grand Rapids: Eerdmans, 1996], 181-3).

came through Jesus Christ, which is an essential element of the new covenant.[72] This replacement does not negate continuity between the Law and the grace and truth. A significant measure of continuity is suggested by their shared source, the fullness of the Word, and by the fact that both are referred to as 'grace' (1:16b). Other passages from the Fourth Gospel demonstrate that the continuity between the Law and the grace and truth is quite significant.[73] Indeed, a correct understanding of the Law anticipates and prepares the way for belief in Jesus and his words (5:38-47).[74] Thus, although the Law contains a significant measure of truth, its truth is not complete in and of itself. It anticipates further revelation. This anticipatory or 'prophetic' function is the primary role played by the Law in the Fourth Gospel.[75] As a result, when John 1:16-17 proclaims that the Law has been replaced by the grace and truth, he surely intends to indicate that the Law has been replaced by the fuller, more complete revelation that it anticipated. This means that the Law has abiding significance as a pointer to the grace and truth that it anticipated.[76]

The replacement of the Law by the grace and truth sets the stage for many analogous, smaller-scale replacements. John repeatedly presents Jesus as the one who fulfills and replaces Old Testament 'institutions, events and themes that have anticipated him.'[77] In doing so, John indicates that the abiding significance of these Old Testament institutions, events, and themes lies in their ability to point to Jesus.[78]

A fine example of John's presentation of Jesus as the fulfillment and replacement of Old Testament institutions is found in John 1:14. As discussed above, John 1:14 presents Jesus as the dwelling place of God among his people. In doing so, John presents Jesus as the fulfillment of and replacement for the

---

[72] On the Law, grace and truth, and covenant in the Fourth Gospel, see John W. Pryor, 'Covenant and Community in John's Gospel,' *RTR* 47 (1988): 47-49; John W. Pryor, *John: Evangelist of the Covenant People: The Narrative and Themes of the Fourth Gospel* (Downers Grove, Ill.: InterVarsity, 1992), 123. On the use of νόμος in John, see Pancaro, *Law in the Fourth Gospel*, 515-7

[73] Especially, John 5:31-47. Cf. John 1:45 and Pancaro, *Law in the Fourth Gospel*, 508-9.

[74] Carson, 'John and the Johannine Epistles,' 252, 255-6; Pancaro, *Law in the Fourth Gospel*, 228, 261-2, 329-31, 508-9. Cf. Braun, 'In Spiritu et veritate,' 252, 265; Dodd, *Interpretation of the Fourth Gospel*, 82-83.

[75] Pancaro, *Law in the Fourth Gospel*, 329. Cf. Kerr, *Temple of Jesus' Body*, 131; Meeks, *Prophet-King*, 288-9.

[76] Carson, *John*, 133; Pancaro, *Law in the Fourth Gospel*, 228. Cf. D. Moody Smith Jr., 'John,' in *Early Christian Thought in Its Jewish Context*, ed. John Barclay and John Sweet (Cambridge: Cambridge University Press, 1996), 107.

[77] Carson, 'John and the Johannine Epistles,' 155-6. Cf. Goppelt, *Typos*, 192; Bruce, *John*, 43-44; Brown, *John*, 201-4; Braun, 'In Spiritu et veritate,' 252.

[78] For more on this, see chapter five.

Tabernacle and its successor, the Temple.[79] On the one hand, this means that Jesus fills the role of the Tabernacle and the Temple: He is the dwelling place of God in the midst of his people, which is verified by Jesus' ability to reveal God's glory (1:14b-d). The net effect is that John presents Jesus as the fulfillment of patterns and prophecies associated with the Tabernacle, Temple, and new Temple. These patterns and prophecies anticipated Jesus and he fulfills them. However, when Jesus fulfills the patterns and prophecies associated with the Tabernacle and the Temple, he does not merely recapitulate that which preceded him. He brings a new and unexpected twist to the dwelling of God among his people. God makes himself accessible to people in an unprecedented form, a body.[80] The same God who dwelt on Mount Sinai in a 'thick cloud' and then in the most restricted area of the Tabernacle and the Temple, the holy of holies, has now come to dwell among his people as the incarnate Word.[81]

The impression that the Tabernacle and Temple are surpassed by their replacement is supported by John 1:18. In 1:18, the prologue ends with the recognition that a unique revelatory event took place when the μονογενής ('only one' or 'unique one') explained the Father. This revelatory event surpasses all previous revelatory events.[82] Previously, no human being had ever seen God (1:18a). Even when God's glory appeared to Moses on Mount Sinai, Moses was only permitted a partial view of it (Exod 33:19-23).[83] Jesus, however, has not only seen the Father (6:46), but is himself God (1:1, 18).[84] Consequently he is uniquely qualified to enable humans to see and hear the Father (John 14:9-10, 3:34).[85] In short, John presents the revelation that comes through Jesus Christ as the pre-eminent revelation of God and God's glory. It surpasses the revelation that was granted through previous events, persons, and

---

[79] Cf. Braun, 'In Spiritu et veritate,' 248; Brown, *John*, 34; Hoskyns, *Fourth Gospel*, 148; Koester, *Dwelling of God*, 108; Schlatter, *Johannes*, 23.

[80] Ridderbos, *John*, 51.

[81] Cf. Exod 19:9, 20:21; Deut 4:11, 5:22; Lev 16:12-14; 1 Kgs 8:12-13 // 2 Chr 6:1-2. Although John 1:14 is concerned with Jesus' dwelling with his disciples during his ministry, one should also keep in mind that it is connected with the larger theme of Jesus' dwelling with believers. Jesus continues to dwell with believers after he has gone to the Father either through the Spirit (14:23) or when they join him where he is (14:2-3). See chapter 1, note on p. 13.

[82] Dumbrell, 'Prologue of John's Gospel,' 119; Sanders, *John*, 86; Schnackenburg, *John*, vol. 1, 278.

[83] Ridderbos, *John*, 58-59. Cf. Brown, *John*, 36; Feuillet, *Prologue du quatrième évangile*, 127; Zahn, *Johannes*, 95.

[84] Although there is a good basis for regarding the reading μονογενὴς θεός (1:18b) as original, the removal of θεός from 1:18 does not alter the fact that the Word is referred to as 'God' in 1:1 (Barrett, *John*, 141).

[85] Cf. Pancaro, *Law in the Fourth Gospel*, 91.

institutions. This includes Moses, the Law, the Tabernacle, and the Temple.[86]

In conclusion, examination of John 1:14 in its context affirms that it introduces Jesus' fulfillment and replacement of the Temple. When John 1:14 says that the Word 'made his dwelling among us,' it uses language that alludes to the Word's fulfillment of a primary purpose ascribed to the Tabernacle, the Temple, and the new Temple.[87] Further, the glory of the Word (1:14c-d) verifies that he takes the place of the Tabernacle and the Temple as the locus for the manifestation of the glory of God to his people.[88] If 1:14 points to Jesus' replacement of the Tabernacle and Temple, 1:16-17 presents an analogous, larger-scale replacement; that is, the grace and truth that came through Jesus Christ replace the Law given through Moses. The introduction of a large-scale replacement in 1:16-17 provides contextual warrant for interpreting 1:14 as a subtler presentation of an analogous replacement.

As the introduction to Jesus' fulfillment and replacement of the Temple, John 1:14 anticipates the development of this theme in the Fourth Gospel. John 1:14 also suggests that its development will be linked with the manifestation of Jesus' glory (1:14c-d) and with his role as the revealer (1:14e, 16-18). While the next chapter will examine further links between Jesus' replacement of the Temple and his glory, John 1:51 and 4:20-24 both provide additional evidence for the connection between Jesus' role as the revealer and his replacement of the Temple.

John 1:51

In John 1:51, Jesus promises his disciples, especially Nathanael, that they 'will see heaven opened, and the angels of God ascending and descending upon the Son of Man.' While interpreters often disagree about the exact significance of Jesus' promise, there is widespread agreement concerning its allusion to

---

[86] God intended the Tabernacle to be a place for him to meet with his people and speak to them (Exod 25:22, 29:42-43); he validates this role in specific instances (Lev 1:1; Num 14:10-35; 16:19-24, 42-44; 20:6-8; Deut 31:14-21). There is also evidence that the Temple plays the same role (Isa 6, Ezek 43-48 [esp., 43:2-6]; cf. Ps 27:4, Luke 1:8-20). Note how many of these examples are connected with the appearance of God's glory (explicitly, Num 14:10, 16:19, 20:6; Ezek 43:4, 44:4; implicitly, Deut 31:15, Isa 6:1-2 [cf. LXX and John 12:41]). Cf. Raymond F. Collins, *These Things Have Been Written: Studies on the Fourth Gospel* (Grand Rapids: Eerdmans, 1990), 204-5.

[87] Exod 25:8, 29:45; 1 Kgs 6:13; Zech 2:10 (MT, LXX v. 14); Ezek 43:7, 9. Significant parallels to these verses include Num 5:3, 35:34; Lev 26:11; 1 Kgs 8:13 / / 2 Chr 6:2; Ezek 37:27.

[88] See especially Exod 29:43.

Genesis 28:12 and its basic import.[89] Its basic import is to indicate that the Son of Man is the true link between God in heaven and human beings on earth.[90] By implication, the Son of Man is the true locus for the revelation of God to his people.[91] As such, he is the fulfillment and replacement of those places where God revealed himself to his people, including Bethel, the Tabernacle, and the Temple.[92] Given the assortment of interpretive options for John 1:51, the following section demonstrates that the basic import commonly attributed to 1:51 is in line with the two most viable interpretive options. Then, it examines the contribution of 1:51 to Jesus' replacement of the Temple.

En route to establishing the basic import of John 1:51, it is important to establish the probability of the allusion to Genesis 28:12, because the allusion helps to clarify the location of the Son of Man and the source of the angelic ascent-descent imagery. First, the allusion to Genesis 28:12 is not the only allusion to the story of Jacob in John 1:45-51. The first allusion occurs when Jesus says that Nathanael is 'an Israelite in whom there is no deceit' (1:47). This is the only use of the term Israelite in the Fourth Gospel, where the preferred term is Jew. Also, 'Israel' is used twice in the first chapter (1:31, 49) and only twice more in the rest of the Gospel (3:10, 12:13). It is the new name given to Jacob after he wrestles with God (Gen 32:28), and is repeated during Jacob's second encounter with God at Bethel (35:10). The renaming of Jacob is significant for John 1:47 in that the name Jacob is associated with 'deceit' in Genesis 27:35-36.[93] On the other hand, Israel is the name associated with the

---

[89] The well-known exception is Wilhelm Michaelis ('Joh. 1,51, Gen. 28,12 und das Menschensohn-Problem,' *TLZ* 85 [1960]: 561-78). Interpreters generally reject his attempt to dismiss the allusion to Gen 28:12.

[90] Brown, *John*, 91; Bruce, *John*, 62; Lindars, *John*, 122; Michèle Morgen, 'La promesse de Jésus à Nathanaël (Jn 1,51) éclairée par la hagaddah de Jacob-Israel,' *RSR* 67, no. 3 (1993): 16; Schnackenburg, *John*, vol. 1, 320; Stephen S. Smalley, 'Johannes 1,51 und die Einleitung zum vierten Evangelium,' trans. August Berz, in *Jesus und der Menschensohn: Für Anton Vögtle*, ed. R. Pesch and R. Schnackenburg (Freiburg: Herder, 1975), 312.

[91] Francis J. Moloney, *The Johannine Son of Man*, Biblioteca di Scienze Religiose, no. 14 (Rome: Libreria Ateneo Salesiano, 1976), 31-32; cf. Cullmann, 'Opposition contre le Temple,' 170; Davies, *Gospel and the Land*, 298; Irénée Fritsch, '"...videbitis ...angelos Dei ascendentes et descendentes super Filium hominis" (Io. 1,51),' *VD* 37 (1959): 8-9; Hanson, 'Christ as the True Temple in the Fourth Gospel,' 114; Hoskyns, *Fourth Gospel*, 183; Morgen, 'Promesse de Jésus à Nathanaël,' 16; Pancaro, *Law in the Fourth Gospel*, 304; Schnackenburg, *John*, vol. 1, 320.

[92] Brown, *John*, 90-91; Cullmann, 'Opposition contre le Temple,' 170; Davies, *Gospel and the Land*, 296; Hoskyns, *Fourth Gospel*, 183.

[93] The Greek word δόλος ('deceit') is found in John 1:47 and the LXX of Gen 27:35. Also, in the MT of Hos 12:1 (ET 11:12), the 'house of Israel' is accused of acting 'with deceit' just like their father Jacob was in Gen 27:35. Hosea 11:12-12:14 (MT 12:1-15) includes several comparisons between the patriarch Jacob/Israel and the nation of Israel.

Lord's blessing (32:26-29); it is the positive counterpart to Jacob.[94] Consequently when Jesus calls Nathanael 'an Israelite in whom there is no deceit,' he is placing Nathanael within a certain subset of Israelites.[95] He is an Israelite with a commendable character trait that sets him apart from the young Jacob and makes him a worthy descendant of the mature Israel.[96] Thus John 1:47 alludes to two aspects of the Jacob story: the association of the name Jacob with deceit and God's removal of this association by giving Jacob a new name, Israel.[97] Certainly, the allusion to the Jacob story in John 1:47 is subtle and becomes clearer after one has recognized the more obvious allusion in 1:51. Once one recognizes the allusion in 1:51, it is possible to see how 1:47 is the first hint that Jesus is inviting a comparison between his disciples and Jacob/Israel.

In 1:51, Jesus promises the disciples that they will see 'heaven opened and the angels of God ascending and descending on the Son of Man.'[98] The

---

[94] On Jacob's name change, see Victor P. Hamilton, *The Book of Genesis: Chapters 18-50*, NICOT (Grand Rapids: Eerdmans, 1995), 333-5, 380-1.

[95] Ridderbos, *John*, 90.

[96] Bruce, *John*, 60-61. Some interpreters contend that Jesus is doing more than simply drawing attention to a commendable aspect of Nathanael's character. They regard 'Israelite,' especially in conjunction with ἀληθῶς ('truly'), as a term that designates Nathanael as a believer, a member of the 'true Israel' (for instance, see Pancaro, *Law in the Fourth Gospel*, 292-302). This view reads too much into 'Israelite,' which need not be any more than a self-designation of Palestinian Jews. In addition, it strains ἀληθῶς to read it adjectivally ('true') when it is clearly an adverb ('truly'). If John had intended to designate Nathanael as a 'true Israelite,' surely he would have used ἀληθινός (cf. 15:1) (J. Painter, 'Christ and the Church in John 1,45-51,' in *L' Évangile de Jean: Sources, rédaction, théologie*, ed. M. de Jonge, BETL, no. 44 [Leuven: University Press, 1977], 359-60).

[97] A number of commentators recognize the allusion to the Jacob story in 1:47. For example, see Barrett, *John*, 154; Brown, *John*, 87; Pancaro, *Law in the Fourth Gospel*, 303.

[98] Some interpreters claim that 1:51 does not fit in its present context (Brown, *John*, 88-89; Jerome H. Neyrey, 'The Jacob Allusions in John 1:51,' *CBQ* 44 [1982]: 586-605). Of particular relevance to the discussion at hand is the seemingly abrupt change from speaking with Nathanael (1:50 and 1:51a) to a saying addressed to disciples generally (1:51b). The awkwardness of the change need not be amplified. Surely it is possible for Jesus to 'strengthen Nathanael's faith with a promise applicable also to other disciples' (Carson, *John*, 165). In fact, it is no more difficult to explain the transition from singular to plural in 1:51 than it is to explain the transitions from singular 'you' to plural 'you' in 3:7, 11-12 (ibid.; Michaelis, 'Joh. 1,51, Gen. 28,12 und das Menschensohn-Problem,' 563). These transitions do not give Brown any trouble (*John*, 131). The remaining reasons for isolating 1:51 from its context can be given reasonable explanations (Carson, *John*, 165-6). Other interpreters find that 1:51 is a fitting end to the first chapter and

opening of heaven is a motif found in Ezekiel 1:1, extra-biblical Jewish literature, and the New Testament.[99] As in Ezekiel 1:1, it is elsewhere used to introduce a vision or revelation from God, and is therefore followed by a description of the vision. This is the case in John 1:51. The opening of heaven anticipates the vision of the ascending and descending angels, which alludes to Jacob's vision in Genesis 28:12. The textual basis for the allusion is promising, since the end of John 1:51 nearly duplicates the Septuagint of Genesis 28:12.[100] The plausibility of the allusion increases dramatically when one considers that Genesis 28:12 is the only text in the Old Testament where angels are pictured ascending and descending.[101] In all of the extra-biblical parallels where a similar scene is pictured, it is inevitably a re-telling of Jacob's vision at Bethel.[102] It is therefore reasonably certain that the vision of the ascending and descending angels in John 1:51 alludes to Jacob's vision at Bethel. This means that Jesus is promising his disciples a vision analogous to Jacob's.

If John 1:51 alludes to Genesis 28:12, then the allusion should provide some assistance in interpreting 1:51.[103] The allusion to Genesis 28:12 leads one to expect that the ascent and descent of the angels involves movement between heaven and earth. The Johannine motif of the ascent and descent of the Son of Man supports the appropriateness of these destinations. The Son of Man descends to earth and ascends back to heaven.[104] Similarly, the angels ascend

---

anticipation of the rest of the Gospel (Moloney, *Johannine Son of Man*, 36-41; Smalley, 'Johannes 1,51,' 313).

[99] *2 Bar.* 22:1; *T. Levi* 2:8; 3 Macc 6:18; Matt 3:16 // Luke 3:21 (cf. Mark 1:10); Acts 7:56, 10:11; Rev 19:11. The opening of heaven appears to be closely related to the opening of the 'gates' (3 Macc 6:18, *T. Levi* 5:1) or 'door' (Rev 4:1) of heaven. In each of these cases, the opening prepares the way for a divine revelation (cf. David E. Aune, *Revelation 17-22*, WBC, vol. 52c [Nashville: Thomas Nelson, 1998], 1052; Allen, *Ezekiel 1-19*, 22).

[100] Gen 28:12 (LXX): καὶ οἱ ἄγγελοι τοῦ θεοῦ ἀνέβαινον καὶ κατέβαινον ἐπ' αὐτῆς and John 1:51: καὶ τοὺς ἀγγέλους τοῦ θεοῦ ἀναβαίνοντας καὶ καταβαίνοντας ἐπὶ τὸν υἱὸν τοῦ ἀνθρώπου. Until one gets to αὐτῆς, the differences between the two can be accounted for in two ways. First, they could all simply be changes that adapt the clause from Gen 28:12 (LXX) to fit within its new context in John 1:51. Second, the appropriateness of the participles, ἀναβαίνοντας and καταβαίνοντας, could have been suggested by the MT, which also uses participles when describing the angels in Gen 28:12. John therefore could have been working directly from the MT (at least to some extent) or a different Greek translation.

[101] Cf. Michaelis, 'Joh. 1,51, Gen. 28,12 und das Menschensohn-Problem,' 569.

[102] See especially *Jub.* 27:21. This is also true of rabbinic parallels, which will be discussed below.

[103] Cf. Paulien, 'Elusive Allusions,' 41.

[104] See John 3:13, 6:53-62. Cf. 20:17.

to heaven and descend to earth.[105] The order of the ascent and descent is different, but the destinations are the same.

The allusion to Genesis 28:12 also suggests certain expectations about the significance of the ascending and descending angels. When one looks at Genesis 28:12 in its context, the narrative in Genesis moves immediately from the vision of the angels (28:12) to the words of the Lord to Jacob (28:13-15). The Hebrew Old Testament (MT) of Genesis 28:13a could indicate that the Lord speaks to Jacob while standing above the ladder or over Jacob. Contrary to the Septuagint and other ancient versions, it appears more likely that the Lord is standing over Jacob rather than above the ladder.[106] Wherever the Lord is standing, the net effect of the experience creates for Jacob the sense that 'the Lord is in this place' (28:16) so much so that it deserves the designations 'house of God' (Bethel) and 'gate of heaven' (28:17). In spite of this, both accounts of Jacob's meetings with God at Bethel give very little attention to God's appearance.[107] The emphasis is upon God's words (28:13-15, 35:10-12).[108] This is consistent with Jacob's vision of the ascending and descending angels; his vision introduces Bethel as a place of 'communication between

---

[105] Some interpreters claim that the ascent and descent of the angels is only within heaven (Jerome H. Neyrey, 'The Jacob Allusions in John 1:51,' *CBQ* 44 [1982]: 597-8; William Loader, 'John 1:50-51 and the "Greater Things" of Johannine Christology,' in *Anfänge der Christologie: Festschrift für Ferdinand Hahn zum 65. Geburtstag*, ed. C. Breytenbach and H. Paulsen [Göttingen: Vandenhoeck and Ruprecht, 1991], 271-2; Gilles Quispel, 'Nathanael und der Menschensohn [Joh 1:51],' *ZNW* 47 [1956]: 281-3). This view uses the imagery from Jacob's dream 'loosely' (Loader, 'John 1:50-51,' 271). Its main difficulty is that the angels both ascend and descend upon the Son of Man. While it is possible to envision the angels ascending into or within heaven with the Son of Man as their destination, it is difficult to understand why they would also be descending upon the Son of Man. Naturally, Neyrey concentrates on the ascent ('John 1:51,' 597-8), and Quispel mysteriously claims that the angels descend upon Nathanael ('Nathanael und der Menschensohn,' 283). In short, the mention of the descent appears superfluous and is accounted for more naturally by an ascent-descent schema that involves movement between heaven and earth as in Jacob's dream.

[106] Hamilton, *Genesis 18-50*, 240-1; C. Houtman, 'What Did Jacob See in His Dream at Bethel? *Some Remarks on Genesis xxviii 10-22*,' *VT* 27 (1977): 348-9. This interpretation is supported by Gen 35:13 where God's second meeting with Jacob at Bethel ends with 'God went up from him.' The LXX here follows the MT (ἀνέβη δὲ ὁ θεὸς ἀπ' αὐτοῦ). Cf. Carson, *John*, 163.

[107] This is also true of other meetings between God and the patriarchs in Genesis (Gen 18, 32:24-30 [MT vv. 25-31]).

[108] Houtman, 'What Did Jacob See at Bethel?,' 349-50. Cf. Genesis 18, 32:24-30. Hosea 12:4 also presents Bethel as the place where God communicates with Jacob (Morgen, 'Promesse de Jésus à Nathanaël,' 17).

heaven and earth.'[109] In conclusion, examination of Genesis 28:12 in its context leads one to expect that the ascending and descending angels of John 1:51 symbolize communication between heaven and earth. This supports the viability of two interpretive options.

Two interpretative options agree that the basic import of the vision in John 1:51 involves communication between heaven and earth. They disagree over how John has understood the ambiguous בו ('on him' or 'on it') at the end of Genesis 28:12. It could signify that the angels descended on Jacob or on the ladder.[110]

If one thinks that John 1:51 presumes that the ב of Genesis 28:12 should be read 'on him,' then it follows that the angels are ascending and descending on the Son of Man just as they once did on Jacob at Bethel. This presents the Son of Man as the one with whom God speaks. By implication, the new event, God speaking with the Son of Man, fulfills and replaces the old, God speaking with Jacob at Bethel. The initial event, God speaking with Jacob/Israel at Bethel (which means 'house of God'), initiates and anticipates a pattern whereby God speaks to his people at the house of God.[111] The culmination of the pattern

---

[109] Houtman, 'What Did Jacob See at Bethel?,' 350. Given such an understanding of Jacob's experiences at Bethel, it misses the point to place too much stock in clever rabbinic solutions to the problem of the ascending angels (cf. Morgen, 'Promesse de Jésus à Nathanaël,' 13-15; Hugo Odeberg, *The Fourth Gospel Interpreted in Its Relation to Contemporaneous Religious Currents in Palestine and the Hellenistic Oriental World* [Uppsala: Almquist and Wiksell, 1929], 33-36). For instance, one commonly-cited rabbinic interpretation has angels ascend into heaven in order to encourage other angels to descend and look at Jacob. They do so, 'for by looking at Jacob the angels can see the features of one whose form is found on the throne of glory' (Christopher Rowland, 'John 1.51, Jewish Apocalyptic and Targumic Tradition,' *NTS* 30 [1984]: 501-3; cf. Neyrey, 'John 1:51,' 601-2). The point of Gen 28:12-17 is the revelation of God to Jacob, not the revelation of Jacob to the angels (cf. Morgen, 'Promesse de Jésus à Nathanaël,' 15).

[110] The pronoun governed by the preposition (ב) is masculine in gender. Both Jacob and the ladder are masculine. Given the context, they are the most likely antecedents (Dodd, *Interpretation of the Fourth Gospel*, 245). A rabbinic discussion found in *Gen. Rab.* 68:12 is often cited as evidence for the ambiguity. It names one rabbi who supports the reading 'on Jacob,' and another who supports the reading 'on the ladder' (Odeberg, *Fourth Gospel*, 33-35; Morgen, 'Promesse de Jésus à Nathanaël,' 12-13).

[111] The MT of Hos 12:5 (ET v. 4) suggests that when God spoke to Jacob/Israel at Bethel, he was also speaking to 'us,' i.e., Jacob's descendants (Israel) (Walter C. Kaiser Jr., 'Inner Biblical Exegesis as a Model for Bridging the 'Then' And 'Now' Gap: Hos 12:1-6,' *JETS* 28 [1985]: 42-43; Morgen, 'Promesse de Jésus à Nathanaël,' 17). For instances where God speaks to his people at the 'house of God' (a title that is used in the OT in reference to both the Tabernacle and the Temple), see note on p. 125. Bethel is also viewed as the 'pre-figuration' of the Temple in rabbinic texts (Joshua Schwartz, 'Jubilees, Bethel and the Temple of Jacob,' *HUCA* 56 [1985]: 82-83). Further, it is

comes when the Father in heaven speaks to the Son of Man on earth who is both the true Jacob/Israel and the true house of God.[112] The new event, the Father speaking with the Son of Man, surpasses the old in that it involves communication between the Father and his unique Son. The Son is uniquely able to hear the Father, since he descended from heaven and is not limited by an earthly perspective (3:13, 31).[113] Hence he is uniquely able to speak the words of God (3:34, 8:26-28, 12:49, 17:8). If the preceding view of John 1:51 is correct, then the vision promised to the disciples in 1:51 is a promise that they will witness a new event, God speaking with the Son of Man.

Having examined the implications of reading the בו of Genesis 28:12 as 'on him,' it is important to note the primary difficulty that limits the appeal of this line of interpretation.[114] The difficulty is syntactical and is reflected in the history of interpretation. In Genesis 28:12 and John 1:51, 'ascending' and 'descending' both modify angels.[115] It also appears syntactically logical and preferable to allow the prepositional phrase ('on him' or 'on it') to modify both participles. This means that the angels are ascending on Jacob and descending on Jacob, or they are ascending on the ladder and descending on the ladder. The idea of ascending on Jacob appears to be less comprehensible than the idea of ascending on the ladder. Consequently the history of interpretation shows that the vast majority of interpreters understand the phrase to mean that the angels are 'ascending and descending on it.'[116] In Genesis 28:12 or John 1:51, clear

---

curious that God's covenant with Jacob at Bethel is mentioned in connection with the eternal Temple of the Temple Scroll (11QT^a XXIX, 9).

[112] Jesus is presented as the locus of the true Israel in 15:1 and as the true Temple in 1:14, 2:19-21. He is also explicitly compared to Jacob in John 4.

[113] Evidence for the Son's unique ability to hear and see the Father is found in John 1:18; 3:11, 31-34; 6:46; 8:26, 38, 40; 12:49-50; 14:10 (Pancaro, *Law in the Fourth Gospel*, 91).

[114] Some interpreters object to this interpretation on other grounds. They think that one must choose between two options: the disciples are like Jacob (as the recipients of the vision) or the Son of Man replaces Jacob (as the destination of the descent of the angels) (Neyrey, 'John 1:51,' 589; Delbert Burkett, *The Son of the Man in the Gospel of John*, JSNTSup, no. 56 [Sheffield: Sheffield Academic Press, 1993], 116). On the contrary, it does not seem overly complex for the disciples to have a vision like Jacob's and to see the true Jacob/Israel in the vision (cf. George J. Brooke, 'The Temple Scroll and the New Testament,' in *Temple Scroll Studies: Papers presented at the International Symposium on the Temple Scroll*, ed. George J. Brooke, JSPSup, no. 7 [Sheffield: Sheffield Academic Press, 1989], 189). The objection is therefore less significant than some interpreters make it.

[115] In the LXX of Gen 28:12, the subject of both finite verbs is 'angels.'

[116] This is true of modern commentators (cf. Hamilton, *Genesis 18-50*, 240; Houtman, 'What Did Jacob See in His Dream at Bethel,' 337; Claus Westermann, *Genesis 12-36: A Commentary*, trans. John J. Scullion [Minneapolis: Augsburg, 1981], 454). It is also reflected in the LXX. Even in *Gen. Rab.* 68:12 (the famous source for the ambiguity),

syntactical alternatives exist that would allow the angels to descend on Jacob and avoid the implication that they were also ascending on him.[117] Rowland makes the best case for taking 'on him' with 'descending' and not 'ascending.' He finds an analogy for doing so in John 14:28.[118] Even so, the way of least resistance is to adopt the position that 'ascending and descending' are both modified by 'on it.'

If one allows the בו of Genesis 28:12 to modify both 'ascending and descending,' then it makes sense to translate בו as 'on it,' that is 'on the ladder.' Then, in John 1:51, the Son of Man fulfills the ladder.[119] When the Son of Man replaces the ladder, he also fulfills its purpose. He becomes the means by which the angels ascend to heaven and descend to earth. This signifies that the Son of Man makes communication between heaven and earth possible. By implication, the location of the Son of Man is the best place to hear the words of God.[120] His location on earth therefore becomes the true Bethel ('house of God') and the true gate of heaven (Gen 28:17). It fulfills and replaces Bethel, and all other places worthy of the title 'house of God,' as the designated place where God speaks to his people.[121] Furthermore, when Jesus fulfills and replaces the ladder, he also ushers in something greater. When the Father speaks to Jesus' disciples through the Son of Man, he communicates to them the grace and truth

---

the preference is for 'ascending and descending on the ladder' (Dodd, *Interpretation of the Fourth Gospel*, 245). Of the three targumic renderings where Jacob is clearly the destination of the descent, only two Targumim preserve the phrase 'ascending and descending;' they clarify that Jacob is the destination by adding the phrase 'and looking on him' (Rowland, 'John 1.51, Jewish Apocalyptic and Targumic Tradition,' 502).

[117] For instance, it would have been possible to describe the angels as 'ascending to heaven and descending on him.' Analogous examples from the Fourth Gospel are collected by Rowland ('John 1.51, Jewish Apocalyptic and Targumic Tradition,' 505). The three targumic renderings where Jacob is clearly the destination of the descent all give some indication of the destination of the ascent ('to the high heavens' or 'on high') (Rowland, 'John 1.51, Jewish Apocalyptic and Targumic Tradition,' 502; cf. *Gen Rab.* 68:12 right after the quote from Isa 49:3). Another possibility is to describe the angels as 'descending on him and ascending' (from him is then understood). This is analogous to Prov 30:4, which says, 'Who has ascended into heaven and descended?' (cf. MT and LXX).

[118] Rowland, 'John 1.51, Jewish Apocalyptic and Targumic Tradition,' 505.

[119] Cf. Barrett, *John*, 156; Burkett, 'Son of the Man in the Gospel of John,' 117-8; Cullmann, 'Opposition contre le Temple,' 170; Lindars, *John*, 122; Ridderbos, *John*, 94. Augustine was the first to point out a typological relationship between Christ and the ladder (Bernard, *John*, vol. 1, 71).

[120] This is confirmed by Jesus' unique ability to speak the words of God (3:34, 8:26-28, 12:49, 17:8). Cf. Kerr, *Temple of Jesus' Body*, 164.

[121] Of course, this includes the Tabernacle and the Temple. For OT texts related to the Taberrnacle and Temple as the designated place where God speaks to his people, see note on p. 125.

that fulfills and surpasses all previous revelation.[122] In short, this line of interpretation makes John 1:51 a promise that the disciples will recognize Jesus as the climactic means by which God in heaven reveals himself to human beings on earth.

Like all other interpretations of John 1:51, the above interpretation is not without its difficulties. The most obvious objection is that the ladder is not even mentioned in John 1:51.[123] The objection is significant, but it is probably not decisive. In reply, one can point to the essentially word-for-word agreement between John 1:51 and the Septuagint of Genesis 28:12.[124] The agreement ends at the pronoun ($\alpha\dot{\upsilon}\tau\hat{\eta}\varsigma$), which refers back to the ladder. John 1:51 replaces this pronoun with 'the Son of Man.'[125] Since the overwhelming majority of interpreters ancient and modern agree with the Septuagint that this pronoun's antecedent is the ladder and not Jacob, it seems reasonable to put forth the possibility that Jesus' saying in John 1:51 is meant to be read in light of the most popular interpretation of Genesis 28:12. If so, then it is possible to regard the Son of Man as the replacement for the ladder of Jacob's vision. Further, the absence of the ladder from John 1:51 could be attributed to the fact that anyone who recognizes the allusion back to Genesis 28:12 would immediately remember that an essential element of Jacob's vision is the ladder.[126] Its absence from John 1:51 may therefore be intentional, not incidental.[127] Where one expects to find the ladder, one finds the Son of Man instead. In the final analysis, it seems that the most defensible interpretation of John 1:51 understands Jesus as the replacement of the ladder in Jacob's vision. On the other hand, the ambiguity of 1:51 does not allow one to rule out the other viable option, Jesus' replacement of Jacob/Israel.

As seen above, the two viable interpretations of John 1:51 share a common element, communication between heaven and earth. In both cases, the Son of

---

[122] After all, Jesus is the incarnate Word (John 1:14). See the above discussion of John 1:14-18.

[123] Neyrey, 'John 1:51,' 589.

[124] Burkett, *Son of the Man in the Gospel of John*, 118. The verses are compared in a footnote above.

[125] Cf. Barrett, *John*, 156.

[126] The ladder appears in every subsequent reference to the vision (cf. *Jub.* 28:20-21; for the relevant parallels from rabbinic literature and Philo, see Morgen, 'Promesse de Jésus à Nathanaël,' 17 and Rowland, 'John 1.51, Jewish Apocalyptic and Targumic Tradition,' 501-3). One of the real mysteries of the vision is why angels need a ladder (or stairway) at all (Hamilton, *Genesis 18-50*, 239).

[127] If the Son of Man replaces the ladder instead of Jacob, it strengthens the case for a symbolic interpretation of the vision promised by Jesus in John 1:51. This undermines the complaint of Hans Windisch who wants to see John 1:51 as a promise of a literal angelophany ('Angelophanien um den Menschensohn auf Erden. Ein Kommentar zu Joh 1,51,' *ZNW* 30 [1931]: 223-8).

Man is an essential figure who makes the communication possible. As the recipient of the communication (like Jacob), he reveals the words of God to others. As the means of communication (like the ladder), the Son of Man allows God in heaven to speak to his people on earth. Either way, one of the implications of John 1:51 is that the location of the Son of Man on earth is the place where God speaks to his people.[128] This place therefore fulfills the pattern initiated and anticipated by Bethel (the first 'house of God') whereby God speaks to his people at his house. If the location of the Son of Man is able to fulfill this particular role of the 'house of God,' then John 1:51 suggests that the location of the Son of Man is a suitable replacement for Bethel and all other holy places worthy of the title 'house of God.'

Interpreters who regard the Son of Man as the place of communication between heaven and earth tend to generalize the import of John 1:51. As a result, the Son of Man becomes the place of God's revelation.[129] This generalization is acceptable and appropriate, because it clarifies that words are not the only means by which God speaks to people through the Son of Man. The works of the Son of Man are also powerful communicators.[130] They affirm the truth of Jesus' claims about himself (John 14:10-11).[131] If this generalization is permitted, then the vision promised in John 1:51 is a symbolic vision that is realized when the disciples see Jesus' words and works for what they really are, namely, revelation from God.[132]

A significant element of the vision promised by Jesus in John 1:51 is its reference to 'the Son of Man.' When Jesus refers to himself as 'the Son of Man,' he is using a title that is distinct from the titles used by the disciples in the preceding narrative. These include Messiah (1:41), Son of God (1:49), and King of Israel (1:49). Compared to such titles, 'the Son of Man' is more ambiguous, ambiguous enough to require clarification.[133] As it has been interpreted above, John 1:51 anticipates an important aspect of the Johannine

---

[128] Cf. Moloney, *Johannine Son of Man*, 31-32.

[129] Ibid., 31; Culpepper, *Anatomy of the Fourth Gospel*, 64; Hoskyns, *Fourth Gospel*, 183; Schnackenburg, *John*, vol. 1, 320, 531. Cf. Dodd, *Interpretation of the Fourth Gospel*, 294; Lindars, *John*, 122.

[130] As Nathanael already can attest (John 1:48-50).

[131] Bultmann, *John*, 106; Ridderbos, *John*, 94; cf. Schlatter, *Johannes*, 64. Some interpreters go too far, however, in that they relate the fulfillment of John 1:51 almost exclusively to Jesus' miracles (Godet, *John*, vol. 1, 337; Ludger Schenke, *Johannes Kommentar* [Düsseldorf: Patmos Verlag, 1998], 50; Zahn, *Johannes*, 144; cf. Meyer, *John*, 93-94).

[132] Similarly, if the Son of Man is described as the place of God's revelation, it is possible to relate him to those instances where the revelation of God to his people at the Tabernacle or the Temple is described in general terms, including light, truth, and glory (Pss 27:4, 36:9 [MT v. 10], 43:3; Isa 2:2-5, 66:18-24; Mic 4:1-4).

[133] Stephen S. Smalley, 'The Johannine Son of Man Sayings,' *NTS* 15 (1968-1969): 299.

picture of the Son of Man.[134] The Son of Man emerges in the Fourth Gospel as both 'the revealer and the revelation of God among men.'[135] The judgment exercised by the Son of Man is based upon people's response to him as revealer and revelation (3:13-19, 5:24-27, 12:31-36).[136] John 1:51, the first Son of Man saying in the Fourth Gospel, provides the initial hint that the Son of Man is the one who is able to reveal the Father in heaven to people on earth.[137] In addition, the mention of the Son of Man in 1:51 suggests that Jesus' replacement of the Temple could be associated with his death/resurrection/exaltation, which is the climax of the Son of Man's role as revealer and revelation.[138]

When John 1:51 presents the Son of Man as the instrument and locus of divine revelation, it is possible to see the affinity between the Son of Man of 1:51 and the incarnate Word of the prologue (1:14, 16-18). In these verses, Jesus emerges as the one who is able to reveal the Father in heaven and as the locus of divine revelation. Their presentation of Jesus as the locus of divine revelation suggests that he brings about the climax of the pattern whereby God speaks to his people at the 'house of God.'[139] Jesus therefore fulfills a purpose associated with Bethel, the Tabernacle, and the Temple. By implication, he is a suitable replacement for these holy places. John 1:51, like 1:14 and 2:18-22, anticipates 4:20-24, the moment when Jesus most clearly announces the replacement of the Temple.

John 4:20-24

Jesus' replacement of the Temple is a theme that grows in clarity from the first

---

[134] Barnabas Lindars, 'The Son of Man in the Johannine Christology,' in *Christ and Spirit in the New Testament*, ed. B. Lindars and S. Smalley (Cambridge: Cambridge University Press, 1973), 46; Smalley, 'Johannes 1,51,' 313.

[135] Moloney, *Johannine Son of Man*, 216. The Son of Man emerges as the revealer and revelation in connection with his descent from heaven (3:13, 6:62), his ability to speak the words of God (8:28), and his role as the light of the world (3:19-21; 9:5, 35, 39; 12:34-36).

[136] Ibid., 84, 215; Lindars, 'Son of Man in the Johannine Christology,' 56-57.

[137] Hence the above interpretation of John 1:51 does not 'make it too much *sui generis*' (contra Robert Maddox, 'The Function of the Son of Man in the Gospel of John,' in *Reconciliation and Hope: New Testament Essays on Atonement and Eschatology*, ed. Robert Banks [Grand Rapids: Eerdmans, 1974], 190). If the Son of Man is the ladder, then 1:51 also hints at the supernatural character of the Son of Man. If mere mortals cannot even ascend into heaven (3:13), surely it is beyond them to be the link between heaven and earth.

[138] John 3:14-15; 8:28; 12:23, 32-34; 13:31-32; Moloney, *Johannine Son of Man*, 202, 83. This will be pursued in the next chapter.

[139] Cf. especially Collins, *These Things Have Been Written*, 204-5.

initial hints in 1:14, 51 to the more obvious claims in 2:18-22 and 4:20-24. John 4:20-24 goes further than 1:14, 51 and 2:18-22 in that it provides the clearest evidence for the Temple's obsolescence and replacement. The issue that lies at the heart of John 4:20-24 is how to worship the Father.[140] Having predicted the obsolescence of the Jerusalem Temple as the special locus for true worship (4:21), Jesus proclaims the advent of worship 'in spirit and truth' (4:23-24). One is to understand by this that the true worship 'in spirit and truth' fulfills and replaces worship at the Jerusalem Temple.[141] The introduction of this true worship fits with the trend already noted in 1:14, 51. When Jesus replaces the Temple, he also abundantly fulfills the patterns associated with the Temple that prefigure him and the salvation that he brings. The goal of the following section is to substantiate these points by examining 4:20-24 in light of the Fourth Gospel, the Old Testament, and extra-biblical Jewish parallels.

Although John 4:20 is the beginning of the discussion of true worship, it is the consequence of the Samaritan woman's recognition that Jesus is a Jewish prophet (4:19). She attributes this title to Jesus, because of his miraculous knowledge of her past (4:18).[142] Her identification of Jesus as a prophet and their location near Mount Gerizim provide sufficient grounds for her transition to the proper place to worship (4:20).[143]

In 4:20, the Samaritan woman's statement introduces the topic of the proper place to worship with two opposing views that are given unequal justification. First, in presenting the Samaritan view, she says, 'Our fathers worshiped on this mountain' (4:20a).[144] Her statement implies that Mount Gerizim is the appropriate place to worship. This view rests upon historical precedent, the practice of the woman's ancestors. It has some persuasive force even for a Jew,

---

[140] I. de la Potterie, '"Nous adorons, nous, ce que nous connaissons, car le salut vient des Juifs": Histoire de l'exégèse et interprétation de Jn 4,22,' *Bib* 64 (1983): 76.

[141] Barrett, *John*, 199; Bruce, *John*, 43-44; Hoskyns, *Fourth Gospel*, 244; Schnackenburg, *John*, vol. 1, 438.

[142] Jesus' miraculous knowledge begins to call into question the woman's skepticism about his superiority to 'our father Jacob' (4:12). The woman's question in 4:12 is introduced by μή, indicating that she expects a negative reply. It is a widely 'recognized instance of Johannine irony' (Gail R. O'Day, *Revelation in the Fourth Gospel: Narrative Mode and Theological Claim* [Philadelphia: Fortress, 1986], 62). It is interesting to note the obvious parallels between this passage (4:5-19) and the calling of Nathanael (1:45-51): the reference to Jacob, the woman's skepticism, and Jesus' demonstration of miraculous knowledge. Like Nathanael, the Samaritan woman is quite impressed with Jesus' supernatural knowledge (1:49; 4:19, 29, 39), but she is more tentative about affirming him as 'the Christ' (4:29).

[143] O'Day, *Revelation in the Fourth Gospel*, 68.

[144] Josephus records an incident in which Samaritans and Jews were carried into exile in Egypt. On account of the traditions handed down to them by their fathers, the Samaritans sent sacrifices back to Mount Gerizim (*Ant.* 12.10).

since the Samaritan woman could back up her claim by appealing to the fact that Jacob and Abraham built altars at Shechem (Gen 12:6, 33:19-20).[145] Also, Mount Gerizim was the site identified with the blessing spoken after Israel's entry into the promised land (Deut 11:29, 27:12).[146] Second, in presenting the Jewish view, the woman says, 'You (Jews) say that in Jerusalem is the place where one must worship.' In presenting the Jewish view, the Samaritan woman simply states the view and leaves out its justification.[147] The basic issue, the proper place to worship, is really a dispute over the proper site for the Temple.[148] Of course, the tension between Jews and Samaritans over this issue escalated after John Hyrcanus destroyed the Temple on Mount Gerizim in 129 BC. It 'was apparently still there in a ruined state in New Testament times.'[149] These observations prepare the way for considering Jesus' response in 4:21-24.

In 4:21, Jesus begins his reply with a claim that relativizes the competing views presented by the Samaritan woman in 4:20. He suggests that the

---

[145] Shechem is near Mount Gerizim. Bruce, *John*, 108; John Macdonald, *The Theology of the Samaritans* (Philadelphia: Westminster, 1964), 329; Jerome H. Neyrey, 'Jacob Traditions and the Interpretation of John 4:10-26,' *CBQ* 41 (1979): 428.

[146] Cf. Josh 8:33-34. The woman could buttress her position by appealing to Samaritan traditions. For instance, in the Samaritan Bible (which is their unique version of the Pentateuch), the tenth commandment specifically ordains the construction of an altar on Mount Gerizim following entry into the promised land (for the text, see Bruce, *John*, 108-9). This commandment is based upon Deut 11:30, 27:2-7, but differs from these verses mainly in its replacement of the MT's 'Ebal' (Deut 27:4) with 'Gerizim.' Markah, a Samaritan teacher who postdates the NT, applies thirteen biblical names to Mount Gerizim, including Bethel (Macdonald, *Theology of the Samaritans*, 328). Markah thus provides examples of passages that Samaritans in the time of Jesus could have read in relation to Gerizim.

[147] Of course, the Jewish claim for Jerusalem as the proper place to worship rests upon revelation to one of their ancestors, David. Since the Samaritans only regard their version of the Pentateuch as Scripture, the Samaritan woman would have no reason to regard God's revelation to David as authoritative. This may be why she reports the Jewish claim for Jerusalem as their opinion, that is, she either does not know or does not choose to recognize the basis for the Jewish claim.

[148] The idea that God chooses the appropriate site for the Temple goes back to Deut 12, where one finds the first references to 'the place [LXX τόπος] which the Lord your God shall choose' (vv. 5, 11, 14, 18, 21). This is the designated place for offering sacrifices and for worshiping before the Lord (Deut 12:5-6, 26:10). By implication, it is the designated site for the Tabernacle or Temple (cf. 2 Chr 6:5-6, Jer 7:12-14). Therefore the Samaritan woman's use of τόπος in 4:20 naturally includes a reference to the place and the Temple located there (cf. John 11:48, 3 Macc 2:9-16, Davies, *Gospel and the Land*, 301-2). In addition, Josephus provides evidence for the disagreement between Jews and Samaritans regarding the superiority of their respective Temples in Jerusalem and on Mount Gerizim (*Ant.* 12.10; 13.74-79; cf. 18.29-30, 85-87).

[149] Macdonald, *Theology of the Samaritans*, 330.

Samaritan woman's concern for the proper place to worship will soon be irrelevant, for 'an hour is coming when you will worship the Father neither on this mountain nor in Jerusalem' (4:21).[150] Such a claim would be equally surprising to a Jewish auditor, since his Scriptures present the Jerusalem Temple as the central place of worship from its inception, and eschatological prophecies predict that it will continue to play this role.[151] Before developing his initial claim further in 4:23-24, Jesus addresses the Samaritan woman's assurance that the fathers of her people are appropriate guides for her in the area of proper worship.

The aim of 4:22 is to disclose the danger of assuming that Samaritan worship traditions are superior to those of the Jews. When Jesus says, 'You (Samaritans) worship what you do not know,' he is confronting the Samaritan woman's confidence in the worship traditions of her fathers. The Jewish Scriptures, particularly 2 Kings 17:24-41, reveal the extent to which her confidence is misplaced.[152] A number of her ancestors came to Samaria in total ignorance of the proper way to worship the God of Israel (2 Kgs 17:24-26). Their experience of the wrath of God resulted in the appointment of an Israelite priest to instruct them in proper worship (2 Kgs 17:26-28).[153] The value of this appointment is undercut by the dubious credentials of Israelite priests whose worship practices were informed by the misguided policies of Jeroboam (1 Kgs 13:28-33, 2 Kgs 17:7-20). As one might have expected, the Samaritans, like the exiled Israelites whose lands they occupied, tainted their worship of the God of Israel by worshiping him as one God among many (2 Kgs 17:32-41). Given this background, it is clear that the Samaritan woman would be foolish to rely on her ancestors as proper guides to the correct worship of the God of Israel. Instead, she should look to the Jews for instruction on how to worship the God of Israel. Jesus points her in this direction when he says, 'We (Jews) worship what we know' (4:22). His statement suggests that, in contrast to the Samaritans, the worship of the Jews rests upon revelation that teaches them

---

[150] Cf. Hendrikus Boers, *Neither on This Mountain nor in Jerusalem: A Study of John 4*, SBLMS, vol. 35 (Atlanta: Scholars Press, 1988), 52.

[151] Pss 5:7 (MT v. 8); 99:5, 9; 132:7; 138:2; Jer 7:2; 26:2; for eschatological prophecies, see Isa 27:13, 66:23; Ezek 46:2, 3, 9; Zech 14:16-17.

[152] Otto Betz, '"To Worship God in Spirit and Truth": Reflections on John 4:20-26,' trans. Nora Quigley et al., in *Jesus der Messias Israels: Aufsätze zur biblischen Theologie*, WUNT, no. 42 (Tübingen: J. C. B. Mohr [Paul Siebeck], 1987), 423-5; cf. Chrysostom, *Hom. Jo.* 33. As indicated above, the Samaritans would not recognize 2 Kgs 17:24-41 as Scripture, but a Jew, like Jesus, would recognize this passage as a challenge to the woman's confidence in the worship traditions handed down from her fathers.

[153] According to Josephus, this brought 'salvation' (σωτήριον) from the plague that the Samaritans were experiencing (*Ant.* 9.289) (Betz, 'To Worship God in Spirit and Truth,' 424).

how to worship God correctly. Consequently the worship of the Samaritans is only a trustworthy guide to proper worship in those cases where it is in line with Jewish worship.[154]

Jesus next gives a reason to believe that the Jews worship what they know, namely, 'salvation is from the Jews' (4:22b). The appropriateness of this reason is supported by 2 Kings 17:39, which is the last verse in a section that summarizes the essential elements of acceptable worship (17:35-39). In 2 Kings 17:39, the Lord exhorts his people to worship him exclusively, because he is the one who will save them from their enemies.[155] Thus if the Jews worship God correctly, one would expect God to save them from their enemies. Further, one would expect them to be able to teach others to worship God correctly so that they could experience God's salvation.[156] When one examines John 4:22 alongside of 2 Kings 17:39, it is possible to understand the logic of the jump from worship to salvation. By worshiping God correctly, the Jews place themselves in a position to experience God's salvation. When their salvation occurs, it vindicates the authenticity of their worship. Consequently the claim that salvation is from the Jews is suitable supporting evidence for the previous claim that the Jews worship what they know. The Jews possess the knowledge of God that can lead to proper worship and salvation. The Samaritans do not, so the wise course of action is to learn from the Jews.

Of course, it is difficult not to see further significance in Jesus' claim that salvation is from the Jews. First, the worship of the Jews anticipates and even prefigures the salvific gifts that Jesus brings. For instance, the Feast of Tabernacles anticipates the living water and the light that Jesus brings (7:37-39, 8:12).[157] Such worship should lead to belief in Jesus, who brings its fulfillment (5:46). Second, Jesus is himself a Jew (4:9) who is about to teach the Samaritan woman about true worship and to be revealed to the Samaritans as 'the savior of the world' (4:42).[158] As the divine Son of God, Jesus is uniquely able to

---

[154] For instance, when the Samaritan woman claims Jacob as her father (4:12), she is acknowledging an ancestor that a Jew would also acknowledge. Her non-Jewish ancestors could have established worthy patterns for worshiping God correctly if they had followed the example of Jacob rather than the example of the exiled Israelites. Even Jacob recognized the discord between worshiping God and idols simultaneously (Gen 35:2-4; Josh 24:4, 14). Cf. Betz, 'To Worship God in Spirit and Truth,' 426-7.

[155] 2 Kgs 17:39 says, 'But you shall worship the LORD your God; he will deliver you out of the hand of all your enemies' (NRSV).

[156] The context of 2 Kgs 17:39 suggests that the Samaritans could have learned to worship God correctly, which would have placed them in a position to experience God's deliverance (see esp. 17:34). Cf. Isa 2:2-4; Hoskyns, *Fourth Gospel*, 244; Zahn, *Johannes*, 247.

[157] Cf. 4:10-14. These verses will be discussed further in the next chapter.

[158] Cf. Potterie, 'Nous adorons, nous, ce que nous connaissons,' 85, 92; Ferdinand Hahn, "Das Heil kommt von den Juden': Erwägungen zu Joh 4,22b,' in *Wort und*

instruct the Samaritan woman in proper worship that is consistent with God's plan of salvation. Giving adequate weight to the above points clarifies the contribution of 4:22 to Jesus' discussion of true worship. This verse is a reminder that proper worship is guided by knowledge and those who worship God correctly can hope to experience God's salvation and to pass on the same hope to others. In preparation for 4:23-24, John 4:22b highlights the ultimate significance of proper worship.[159]

Having emphasized the significance of proper worship, Jesus' teaching in 4:23 follows up on 4:21. The time when his instructions will have their fullest significance is marked by the coming of 'an hour' (4:21, 23). The Fourth Gospel enables one to define this hour as the time of Jesus' death, resurrection, and exaltation.[160] Although this hour inaugurates the true worship that Jesus describes, the true worship has its roots and beginnings in the presence and teaching of Jesus. Hence it is possible for Jesus to say that the hour is both coming and present now (4:23).[161]

The topic of 4:21, 23-24 is how to worship the Father in light of the new situation that is brought about by the coming of Jesus. The use of the adjective ἀληθινοί ('true,' 'genuine') to describe the worshipers that the Father seeks (4:23) distinguishes these worshipers from all others. Their worship, like the worship of the Jews before them (4:22), provides the pattern for worship that is sanctioned by the Father.[162] One of its distinguishing characteristics is that it is not tied to the Jerusalem Temple (4:21).[163] The phrase 'in spirit and truth'

Wirklichkeit: Studien zur Afrikanistik und Orientalistik, vol. 1, *Geschichte und Religionswissenschaft: Bibliographie*, ed. B. Benzing, O. Böcher, and G. Mayer (Meisenheim: Verlag Anton Hain, 1976), 76.

[159] Those who regard 4:22b as an editorial gloss are convinced that it contradicts John's portrayal of 'the Jews' elsewhere in the Fourth Gospel (Bultmann, *John*, 189-90, n. 6; J. Eugene Botha, *Jesus and the Samaritan Woman: A Speech Act Reading of John 4:1-42*, NovTSup, vol. 65 [Leiden: E. J. Brill, 1991], 146). The strength of such a view dissipates if one takes into account that John's portrayal of the Jews is not entirely negative. Some Jews do believe (8:31, 11:45) (Culpepper, *Anatomy of the Fourth Gospel*, 130). For further discussion, see O'Day, *Revelation in the Fourth Gospel*, 70; Potterie, 'Nous adorons, nous, ce que nous connaissons,' 85-86, n. 21.

[160] Brown, *John*, 517; Lindars, *John*, 188.

[161] Brown, *John*, 518; O'Day, *Revelation in the Fourth Gospel*, 71; Felix Porsch, *Pneuma und Wort: Ein exegetischer Beitrag zur Pneumatologie des Johannesevangeliums* (Frankfurt: Josef Knecht, 1974), 147; Potterie, 'Nous adorons, nous, ce que nous connaissons,' 88-89. Cf. John 5:25.

[162] Barrett, *John*, 199; Bultmann, *John*, 191; André Feuillet, *The Priesthood of Christ and His Ministers*, trans. Matthew J. O'Connell (Garden City, N.Y.: Doubleday, 1975), 150; George E. Ladd, *A Theology of the New Testament*, rev. ed. (Grand Rapids: Eerdmans, 1993), 303.

[163] This already suggests that it is distinct from Jewish worship. Contra Edwin Freed who finds no distinction between the worship 'in spirit and truth' and the worship that

provides the clue to its other distinguishing characteristics.

The key to understanding the phrase 'in spirit and truth' lies in the short phrase 'God is spirit' (4:24).[164] Not only does it stand between the repetition of 'in spirit and truth' in vv. 23 and 24, it also provides a basis for the assertion that those who worship the Father must worship in spirit and truth (4:24b). 'God is spirit' is not an ontological definition of God, but a description of the nature of God as he reveals himself to human beings.[165] It has a threefold significance in 4:23-24. First, if God is spirit, then the nature of God does not place inherent limitations upon where and when one can worship him. Worship of God need not be limited to Mount Gerizim or Jerusalem.[166] Second, God is the appropriate source of the 'spirit' that enables them to worship 'in spirit' (3:5-6). Third, he is also the best source of knowledge about what the requisite 'spirit' is and how to receive it.[167] As a result, only God can enable human beings to worship 'in spirit and truth.'[168] While a close reading of John 4:20-24 in its context establishes the significance of the first point, the significance of the next two points is established by evidence that is provided in the subsequent discussion. It is now possible to define more exactly what is meant by worship 'in spirit and truth.'

A proper understanding of worship in spirit and truth must consider both the unique contributions and collective significance of spirit and truth in the Fourth Gospel.[169] Regarding spirit, Jesus has already been presented as the one who possesses the Spirit (1:32, 3:34) and baptizes in the Holy Spirit (1:33). Jesus also teaches Nicodemus that entry into the kingdom of God requires a birth of water and spirit (3:5). He adds that flesh begets flesh while Spirit begets spirit

---

'was already present in Judaism' ('The Manner of Worship in John 4:23f.,' in *Search the Scriptures: New Testament Studies in Honor of Raymond T. Stamm* [Leiden: E. J. Brill, 1969], 47). Cf. also Brown, *John*, 181.

[164] Ladd, *Theology of the New Testament*, 328; Porsch, *Pneuma und Wort*, 149-52.

[165] Porsch, *Pneuma und Wort*, 150. Cf. Isa 31:3. Also, see 1 John 1:5; 4:8, 16 where God is characterized as light and love.

[166] This is already intimated in passages like Isa 66:1-2 and Ezek 11:15-16 where the location of the Temple is considered less important than the location of those who are truly God's people.

[167] On these last two points, cf. O'Day, *Revelation in the Fourth Gospel*, 71.

[168] Braun, 'In Spiritu et veritate,' 271.

[169] The nature of the Fourth Gospel provides the warrant for looking to the wider context for clarification. John frequently introduces themes that require further clarification and then develops them over the course of the Gospel (Brown, *John*, 181). A good example is the water that Jesus offers to the Samaritan woman in 4:14. Further clarification comes in 7:37-39, but even there the water is linked to two larger themes, the giving of the Spirit and the glorification of Jesus. These themes make a noteworthy contribution to a proper understanding of 4:14 and 7:37-39, but this contribution only emerges after further development.

(3:6). Additional teaching on the Spirit is found in 4:14; 6:63; 7:37-39; 14:16-17, 26; 15:26; 16:7-15; and 20:22. Taken as a whole, these verses make three claims relevant to the interpretation of worship in spirit: (1) the Spirit is present and active in the ministry of Jesus (1:32, 3:34, 6:63, 14:17); (2) Jesus (or the Father) will send the Spirit after his ascension (7:39, 14:17, 16:7); and (3) at that point, the Spirit plays two significant roles, namely, it infuses believers with 'spirit' (3:5-6) and reveals truth to Jesus' disciples (14:26, 16:13). Looking at 4:23-24, the first point clarifies why worship in spirit begins 'now.' The activity of the Spirit in the ministry of Jesus lays the foundation for worship in spirit.[170] The second and third points clarify why worship in spirit is fully possible only in the future. Only after Jesus' ascension does the Spirit come and take up residence within believers, infusing them with spirit (3:5-6, 14:17).[171] The infusion of spirit is part of the new birth that sets believers apart as God's children who immediately begin to enjoy the benefits of eternal life. In other words, when believers receive spirit, they enter into the new age, the kingdom of God (3:5).[172] Compared to non-believers, this makes believers uniquely alive and allows them to experience unique communion with Jesus and the

---

[170] Cf. John 14:17. See also 6:63, where Jesus' words are called 'spirit,' that is, they 'are the product of the life-giving Spirit' (Carson, *John*, 301-2; cf. Lindars, *John*, 274). Further, it is appropriate to call Jesus' words 'spirit,' because accepting them leads to belief in Jesus, which is the prerequisite for receiving the Holy Spirit (7:37-39). Thus the work of the Spirit in Jesus' ministry prepares the way for the further work of the Spirit in Jesus' disciples after his ascension (Brown, *John*, 300; Carson, *John*, 196). This also explains Jesus' offer of living water to the Samaritan woman in 4:10-14. He is able to offer living water to her, because her belief in him would guarantee that she would receive the living water that comes with the sending of the Spirit.

[171] The believer's need for an infusion of 'spirit' is made clear in John 3:5. It is misleading to capitalize 'spirit' in John 3:5, because 'the focus is upon the impartation of God's nature as "spirit" [*cf.* 4:24], not on the Holy Spirit as such' (Carson, *John*, 195; cf. J. Terence Forestell, *The Word of the Cross: Salvation as Revelation in the Fourth Gospel*, AnBib, no. 57 [Rome: Biblical Institute Press, 1974], 124; Francis J. McCool, 'Living Water in John,' in *The Bible in Current Catholic Thought*, ed. John L. McKenzie [New York: Herder and Herder, 1962], 231). John 3:6 clarifies that the source of 'spirit' in 3:5 must be the Holy Spirit. In parallels to John 3:5-6, one finds similar recognition of the human need for an act of God that cleanses from sin, creates a new spirit within, or imparts God's spirit to his people (Ezek 37:14; Ps 51:7-12 [MT vv. 8-15]; *Jub.* 1:23; 1QS IV, 18-26; cf. Schnackenburg, *John*, vol. 1, 370-1, 437). All three of these elements are present in Ezek 36:25-27.

[172] John 1:12-13; 3:5, 16, 36; 4:10-14; 5:25; 11:26; 14:16-23; 17:3; Barrett, *John*, 179; Brown, *John*, 507; David Holwerda, *The Holy Spirit and Eschatology in the Gospel of John: A Critique of Rudolf Bultmann's Present Eschatology* (Kampen: Kok, 1959), 83; Schnackenburg, *John*, vol. 1, 438 and vol. 2., 352-3. The presentation of eternal life in the Fourth Gospel illustrates well its emphasis upon realized eschatology (Brown, *John*, cxvii-cxviii; Ladd, *Theology of the New Testament*, 293-5).

Father.[173]

The contribution of truth to proper worship is more straightforward than that of spirit. The Fourth Gospel presents Jesus as the one who both teaches the truth and is the truth.[174] The truth that he reveals is anticipated by the Old Testament, but perfects and goes beyond the teaching found in it.[175] It is the 'supreme revelation of God' to human beings.[176] Once this truth has been revealed, it makes sense that true worship must conform to it (4:24).[177] Further, those who believe in the truth, which Jesus reveals and is, are the same ones who receive the infusion of spirit.[178]

Given the above treatment of spirit and truth, what is the significance of bringing the two terms together in John 4:23-24? The combination of spirit and truth delineates a mode of worship that is only fully possible for those who believe in Jesus. Only believers receive the requisite gift of spirit and are capable of a full knowledge of the truth.[179] This is because belief in Jesus, who is the truth and teaches the truth, is the basic prerequisite for receiving the Spirit (7:37-39).[180] Those who receive the Spirit become equipped to worship the Father in spirit and truth, since the Spirit infuses them with spirit and teaches them the truth.[181]

It is now possible to consider how worship in spirit and truth fulfills, surpasses, and replaces worship at the Jerusalem Temple, that is, worship under the old covenant. In the first place, worship in spirit and truth fulfills a fundamental pattern associated with proper worship under the old covenant: The worship that God desires can only be offered by those who are truly his people. Under the old covenant, membership in the true people of God requires

---

[173] John 8:24, 31-36; 14:17-23; 15:14-15; Holwerda, *Holy Spirit and Eschatology*, 61, 83; Ignace de la Potterie, *La vérité dans Saint Jean*, vol. 2, AnBib, no. 74 (Rome: Biblical Institute Press, 1977), 701, 705-6.

[174] John 1:14, 17-18; 8:31-32; 14:6; 16:12-15. Cf. Barrett, *John*, 139; Brown, *John*, 180; Pancaro, *Law in the Fourth Gospel*, 538; Potterie, *La vérité dans Saint Jean*, 678-9, 701.

[175] Pancaro, *Law in the Fourth Gospel*, 538, 83, 87, 116, 287; Potterie, *La vérité dans Saint Jean*, 705. Cf. John 1:17-18, 5:37-47, 6:45.

[176] Carson, *John*, 491; cf. John 8:31-36; Ladd, *Theology of the New Testament*, 328; Schnackenburg, *John*, vol. 2, 228.

[177] As with spirit, the truth is available to some extent during Jesus' ministry, but becomes available to its fullest extent only after Jesus departs and sends the Spirit of truth (John 16:7, 12-15).

[178] John 3:36, 7:37-39, 8:12, 14:17; Gary M. Burge, *The Anointed Community: The Holy Spirit in the Johannine Tradition* (Grand Rapids: Eerdmans, 1987), 169-70.

[179] John 1:12-13, 3:5-6, 8:31-36, 14:17. Cf. Porsch, *Pneuma und Wort*, 153, 159-60; Potterie, *La vérité dans Saint Jean*, 705; Eduard Schweizer, '$\pi\nu\epsilon\hat{u}\mu\alpha$,' trans. G. Bromiley, in *TDNT*, ed. G. Friedrich, vol. 6 (Grand Rapids: Eerdmans, 1968), 439.

[180] Burge, *Anointed Community*, 170.

[181] Cf. Potterie, *La vérité dans Saint Jean*, 682, 704.

faithful obedience to the Torah, including its prescriptions for worship.[182] Only the worship of righteous, obedient believers is pleasing to God; the unrighteous are merely going through the motions of worshiping him.[183] Then, with the coming of Jesus, the decisive mark of the true people of God becomes belief in Jesus and conformity to the truth that he reveals. Those who do not believe in Jesus show by their unbelief that they do not really know God or understand what he requires of them.[184] Their worship falls short of the true worship of those who believe in Jesus.

Worship in spirit and truth is also the worship of those who are already able to enjoy some of the benefits of eternal life, that is, the new age. When the Old Testament predicts the new age, one element in its description is the outpouring of God's Spirit upon his people.[185] This outpouring plays a decisive role in re-creating God's people, restoring them to a position where they can benefit from the blessings associated with being the people of God.[186] In fulfillment of these expectations, Jesus indicates that the Spirit plays a decisive role in creating the people of God in the new age. Those who enter into this people of God do so by means of a new birth that is brought about by the Spirit. As a result of the new birth, they begin to experience the blessings that are reserved for the people of God in the new age.[187] Like the new age and the new birth, the blessings to be experienced by the people of God are anticipated in the Old Testament. At the same time, the clearest picture of the life that is characteristic of the new age is provided by the truth that Jesus reveals to his followers.[188]

---

[182] See, for example, Exod 24:3-8; Lev 26:1-3; Deut 28:1; Neh 9:34; 2 Kgs 23:25; Dan 9:4-11; Ezek 36:25-27.

[183] See, for example, Pss 15, 24:3-6; Jeremiah 7; Isa 1:10-20, 66:1-6; Amos 5:21-24; cf. Levenson, *Sinai and Zion*, 165-74. As discussed above, this is where Samaritan worship falls short of proper worship. They disobey God by persisting in idolatry (2 Kgs 17:34-41).

[184] Cf. John 5:37-47. Thus Jews who do not believe in Jesus are just as incapable of proper worship as Samaritan unbelievers.

[185] Isa 32:15-17, 44:3-5; Ezek 36:25-27, 37:14, 39:29; Joel 2:28-29 [MT 3:1-2] (cf. Num 11:25-29); cf. Goppelt, *Typos*, 182-3; Wilf Hildebrandt, *An Old Testament Theology of the Spirit of God* (Peabody, Mass.: Hendrickson, 1995), 91-103; Willem A. VanGemeren, 'The Spirit of Restoration,' *WTJ* 50 (1988): 81-102. This outpouring is an expression of the work of God's Spirit as 'the animating principle of life' (Hildebrandt, *Old Testament Theology of the Spirit*, 196-7; cf. Gen 1:2; Ps 104:30; Job 33:4, 34:14-15).

[186] VanGemeren, 'Spirit of Restoration,' 96.

[187] John 4:10-14, 6:63, 7:37-39.

[188] See the above treatment of truth in the Fourth Gospel. The close relationship between truth (or Jesus' word) and life in the Fourth Gospel leads one to conclude that those who remain in Jesus' word are already able to experience the life of the new age more fully than any faithful believers under the old covenant (see esp. 5:24-25; 6:63; 8:21-36; 17:2-3).

In conclusion, it appears that worship in spirit and truth surpasses and replaces worship at the Jerusalem Temple in that it is worship based upon fuller experience of God's abundant provision ('spirit') and fuller revelation ('truth'). Indeed this fuller revelation indicates that the Jerusalem Temple is no longer necessary as the special locus for proper worship (4:21). Yet worship at the Jerusalem Temple is obviously important for the Fourth Gospel, where Jesus' teaching in the Temple occurs at three (or perhaps four) Passovers, the Feast of Tabernacles, and the Feast of Dedication.[189] As demonstrated in the next chapter, close inspection of the passages relevant to the celebration of each feast reveals that the worship of the Jews anticipates and even prefigures the salvific gifts brought by Jesus. When one reads John 4:20-24 alongside of this concern for the fulfillment of the Jewish feasts, it becomes clear that worship at the Jerusalem Temple is not merely replaced. It is also fulfilled by that to which it pointed. More specifically, it becomes evident that the salvific gifts that flow out from Jesus point to Jesus as the locus of God's abundant provision for his people. As such, he fulfills and replaces the Temple.[190]

Within the Fourth Gospel, the unique contribution of John 4:20-24 involves both resumption and anticipation. It resumes the theme of Jesus' replacement of the Temple introduced in 1:14, 1:51, and 2:18-22. In doing so, John 4:20-24 provides another instance where a function of the Jerusalem Temple appears to be fulfilled, surpassed, and replaced (as in 1:14, 51). The Fourth Gospel affirms this impression when it treats the fulfillment of the Jewish feasts.

Conclusion

Based on the verses of the Fourth Gospel that are most commonly associated with Jesus' replacement of the Temple, it is possible to outline some preliminary conclusions about the relationship between Jesus and the Temple. John 1:14 and 1:51 provide the first subtle pointers to Jesus' fulfillment and replacement of the Temple. They suggest that Jesus' replacement of the Temple encompasses the replacement of its predecessors, namely, Bethel and the Tabernacle. According to 1:14, Jesus is presented as the fulfillment and replacement of the Tabernacle and the Temple as the place where God dwells among his people and manifests his glory to them. John 1:51 makes a similar point: Jesus fulfills and replaces Bethel, the Tabernacle, and the Temple as the place where God reveals himself to his people. It is important to emphasize that

---

[189] John 2:13, 6:4, 11:55 (perhaps 5:1) (Passover); 7:2 (Feast of Tabernacles); and 10:22 (Feast of Dedication).

[190] Among these gifts, two of the most prominent are spirit and truth. In the next chapter, consideration of 7:37-39 demonstrates the significance of the Spirit as the central blessing that proceeds from Jesus, the true Temple, and enriches believers with other blessings like spirit and truth.

John 1:14 and 1:51 do not present Jesus as merely analogous to the holy places that preceded him; rather, he fulfills these holy places as the greater Temple to which they pointed.

John 1:14 and 1:51 anticipate 4:20-24. In 4:20-24, Jesus describes the true worship that pleases the Father. First, it is not tied to the Jerusalem Temple (4:21). Second, it is worship in spirit and truth. Examining John's treatment of spirit, truth, and Jewish feasts reveals that the true worship also fulfills worship at the Jerusalem Temple. The cumulative evidence from 1:14, 1:51, and 4:20-24 leads one to posit that Jesus fulfills and replaces the Temple.

Notably absent from the above remarks is John 2:18-22. These verses support the implication that Jesus replaces the Temple, but their full significance cannot be worked out in isolation from Jesus' death/resurrection/exaltation. Similarly, the relationship between worship in spirit and truth and worship at the Jerusalem Temple (4:20-24) becomes clearer in light of the Fourth Gospel's treatment of the Jewish feasts. John 2:18-22 and 4:20-24 indicate that Jesus' replacement of the Temple reaches beyond the four texts examined in this chapter. It is therefore necessary to follow up on the pointers suggested by these verses before coming to any definite conclusions about the relationship between Jesus and the Temple in the Fourth Gospel.

CHAPTER 4

Jesus as the Fulfillment and Replacement of the Temple in the Fourth Gospel: Part Two

As seen in chapter three, study of John 1:14, 1:51, 2:18-22, and 4:20-24 demonstrates that Jesus' fulfillment and replacement of the Temple is not an isolated theme. It is linked with other themes like death/resurrection/exaltation, glory, revelation, and fulfillment of Jewish worship. A number of interpreters discuss the relevance of Jesus' replacement of the Temple to his fulfillment of Jewish feasts. In doing so, they sometimes touch on aspects of the significance of his replacement of the Temple for his death/resurrection/exaltation. On the other hand, one finds few attempts to draw out the relevance of Jesus' replacement of the Temple for the themes of glory and revelation. As the first section of this chapter shows, a significant connection does appear to exist between the themes of glory, replacement of the Temple, and death/resurrection/exaltation. The section also brings out the relevance of the theme of revelation to this connection. Then, the second section of the chapter treats the relevance of Jesus' fulfillment and replacement of the Temple to another theme closely related to his death/resurrection/exaltation, namely, his fulfillment of Jewish feasts.

Converging Themes: Replacement of the Temple, Glory, and Death/Resurrection/Exaltation

Right from the start, the Fourth Gospel directs the reader to its climax, the death, resurrection, and exaltation of Jesus. Along the way, it also presents a unique perspective upon these three events; that is, Jesus' death, resurrection, and exaltation are essential components of a single unified event, his lifting up or glorification.[1] Interpreters commonly find the Old Testament background for Jesus' lifting up or glorification in the Septuagint of Isaiah 52:13.[2] Although

---

[1] Even though Jesus' death/resurrection/exaltation is presented as a 'theological unity,' John does not obscure the fact that the death, resurrection, and exaltation are historically distinct (Carson, *Divine Sovereignty and Human Responsibility*, 142).

[2] For example, see Hyacinthe-M. Dion, 'Quelques traits originaux de la conception johannique du Fils de l'Homme,' *ScEccl* 19 (1967): 52; Margaret Pamment, 'The

this is one significant background text, the suffering servant is not the only entity in Isaiah that is lifted up and glorified. Indeed Jesus' replacement of the Temple points to another significant Isaianic background, the lifting up and glorification of the Temple.³ As shown below, the lifting up or glorification of Jesus is another instance in which the Fourth Gospel presents Jesus as the one who fulfills expectations previously associated with the Temple.

Jesus' Lifting up or Glorification in the Fourth Gospel

Establishing the appropriateness of the proposed Isaianic background requires a basic appreciation for John's unique presentation of Jesus' lifting up or glorification. To begin with, the unity and significance of Jesus' death, resurrection, and exaltation are closely associated with three terms, ὥρα ('hour'), ὑψόω ('lift up,' 'exalt'), and δοξάζω ('glorify'). The most straightforward of these terms is ὥρα. By frequent repetition, John uses this term to direct attention to the Gospel's climax, namely, the death, resurrection, and exaltation of Jesus.⁴ Since Jesus' 'hour' appears to embrace all three events, it is an initial indicator that the three events belong together.⁵

The second significant term is ὑψόω. One finds it in three sayings of Jesus (3:14, 8:28, 12:32) and one saying attributed to Jesus by the crowd (12:34). This verb has a double meaning that makes it uniquely suitable for implying the unity between Jesus' death on the cross, his ascension into heaven, and his exaltation.⁶ Its literal meaning ('lift up') allows it to refer to Jesus' death on the cross (12:33) or to be understood as a reference to his ascension into heaven (12:34). Its figurative meaning ('exalt') allows it to refer to Jesus' exaltation,

---

Meaning of *Doxa* in the Fourth Gospel,' *ZNW* 74 (1983): 16; Thüsing, *Erhöhung und Verherrlichung Jesu im Johannesevangelium*, 36-37.

³ See Isa 2:1-5, 12-22; 60:7, 13.

⁴ John 2:4; 4:21, 23; 5:25, 28-29; 7:30; 8:20; 12:23, 27; 13:1; 16:2, 25, 32; 17:1; Brown, *John*, 517-8. This special use of ὥρα in reference to Jesus' hour and its effects is distinct from the use of ὥρα in reference to a particular time of day (1:39; 4:6, 52-53; 19:14, 27).

⁵ The 'hour' begins with the events that lead to Jesus' death (when his climactic glorification begins) (12:23, 13:31, 17:1) and ends when his glorification ends, i.e., when he returns to the Father and is glorified with the glory he had with the Father before the creation of the world (17:4-5, 13:32) (cf. Brown, *John*, 517-8). Therefore the hour must also include Jesus' resurrection (cf. 20:17). Glorification is explained further below.

⁶ This is widely recognized (Godfrey C. Nicholson, *Death as Departure: The Johannine Descent-Ascent Schema*, SBLDS, no. 63 [Chico, Cal.: Scholars Press, 1983], 141). For a helpful summary of Greek and Semitic-language parallels to John's use of ὑψόω, see Wayne A. Meeks, 'The Man from Heaven in Johannine Sectarianism,' *JBL* 91 (1972): 62.

which ultimately involves his return to and glorification by the Father.[7] Although some interpreters continue to debate whether the literal or the metaphorical is really the primary sense, it seems preferable to recognize that the double meaning is a significant element in the interpretation of each of the lifting up sayings.[8] In 3:14, the lifting up of the serpent creates an image that corresponds to the crucifixion, but the gift of eternal life proceeds from the exalted Jesus through the gift of the Spirit (3:15, 4:10-14, 7:37-39).[9] Similarly, in 8:28, the lifting up of the Son of Man by the Jews clearly refers to the crucifixion, since they cannot possibly exalt him to the right hand of the Father. Yet it is the resurrection and exaltation of Jesus that dramatically verify all of his claims about himself and demonstrate that he is who he claims to be. Then, in 12:33, John spells out the fact that the lifting up involves Jesus' death.[10] This verse complements 12:32, which anticipates that Jesus will be lifted up from the earth and draw all people to himself. It is the exalted Jesus who draws all people to himself rather than the crucified Jesus. Clearly, the lifting up of Jesus on the cross must be bound up with his exaltation. As demonstrated further below, it is a necessary part of his exaltation to glory. It appears, then, that John's use of ὑψόω points to the unity of Jesus' death, resurrection, and exaltation, which are all part of his lifting up/exaltation. In particular, it points to the unity of Jesus' death on the cross and his exaltation, which is an emphasis unique to the Fourth Gospel.[11]

---

[7] Cf. the use of ὑψόω in Acts 2:33, 5:31; William Loader, *The Christology of the Fourth Gospel: Structure and Issues*, 2nd ed. (New York: Peter Lang, 1992), 116-7; A. Vergote, 'L'exaltation du Christ en croix selon le quatrième Evangile,' *ETL* 28 (1952): 7-8. It is significant to note that in the LXX one finds several instances where it appears that ὑψόω and δοξάζω are used synonymously (Exod 15:2; Ps 36:20; Isa 4:2, 5:16, 10:15, 33:10, 52:13; Sir 43:30; cf. Pamment, '*Doxa* in the Fourth Gospel,' 15).

[8] Some interpreters stress the primacy of the literal sense over the metaphorical, while others stress the primacy of the metaphorical sense over the literal (cf., respectively, Martinus C. de Boer, *Johannine Perspectives on the Death of Jesus* [Kampen: Kok Pharos, 1996], 170; Godfrey C. Nicholson, *Death as Departure: The Johannine Descent-Ascent Schema*, SBLDS, no. 63 [Chico, Cal.: Scholars Press, 1983], 141-2). On the other hand, Holwerda gives a balanced assessment: 'In a given context one event may stand in the foreground– in this context [12:32] it is the crucifixion– but the references can not be restricted to this single event' (*Holy Spirit and Eschatology in the Gospel of John*, 9; cf. Schnackenburg, *John*, vol. 2, 399-401).

[9] Eugen Ruckstuhl, 'Abstieg und Erhöhung des johanneischen Menschensohns,' in *Jesus und der Menschensohn: Für Anton Vögtle*, ed. R. Pesch and R. Schnackenburg (Freiburg: Herder, 1975), 331-2; Schnackenburg, *John*, vol. 2, 403; Vergote, 'L'exaltation du Christ en croix selon le quatrième Evangile,' 7, 12.

[10] Cf. John 12:35-36.

[11] Josef Blank, *Krisis: Untersuchungen zur johanneischen Christologie und Eschatologie* (Freiburg: Lambertus Verlag, 1964), 84; Dion, 'Quelques traits originaux de la conception johannique du Fils de l'Homme,' 57.

The significance of δοξάζω ('glorify,' 'display glory,' or 'clothe in glory') for Jesus' death, resurrection, and exaltation is closely related to that of ὑψόω.[12] Yet its significance in relation to his death, resurrection, and exaltation cannot be fully appreciated apart from its significance in relation to his entire saving work. This is because John's use of the verb δοξάζω and the noun δόξα ('glory') suggests that John regards all of Jesus' saving work as contributing to his glorification.[13] At the same time, his glorification is composed of two primary stages. Summarizing these stages will clarify the climactic contribution of death, resurrection, and exaltation to Jesus' glorification.

The first stage in Jesus' saving work is his ministry on earth prior to his 'hour.' During this stage, he performs the works that the Father has set out for him (5:36). Obediently performing these works is the means by which the Son glorifies, or displays the glory of, the Father.[14] The works themselves are significant, because they display the glory of the Son.[15] This initial glorification of the Son provides evidence that Jesus' claims about himself are true.[16] It simultaneously incites conflict, which Jesus attributes to a conflict between two opposed commitments, commitment to worldly glory and commitment to the glory of God.[17] The conflict reaches its climax in Jesus' 'hour,' when the Jews set into motion their plan to kill Jesus. Thus the initial glorification of the Son through his works incites the conflict that leads to the next, climactic stage in his glorification.

The second stage in Jesus' glorification is the moment of truth, when the world tries to extinguish the glory that is on display in the ministry of Jesus.[18] Its attempt to do so is doomed to failure, because Jesus' death is actually a

---

[12] On the meaning of δοξάζω in John, see G. B. Caird, 'The Glory of God in the Fourth Gospel: An Exercise in Biblical Semantics,' *NTS* 15 (1969): 270-3; Joseph H. Thayer, *Greek-English Lexicon of the New Testament* (Grand Rapids: Baker Book House, 1977), 157.

[13] Schnackenburg, *John*, vol. 2, 402.

[14] John 7:18, 8:49 (uses 'honor,' which is closely related to 'glorify'), 17:4; cf. Loader, *Christology of the Fourth Gospel*, 107.

[15] Two works in particular are called 'signs' that display the Son's glory (2:11; 11:4, 40; 12:18; cf. 1:14, 8:54). John 11:4, 40 explicitly connects the display of the glory of God and the Son's glorification. The full significance of this link becomes clear when one realizes that raising Lazarus from the dead is the decisive display of the Father's and the Son's glory that leads to the next stage in Jesus' glorification, i.e., death/resurrection/exaltation (11:46-53).

[16] John 5:36; 10:25, 37-38; 14:11; cf. Nicholson, *Death as Departure: The Johannine Descent-Ascent Schema*, 149.

[17] John 5:41-44; 8:49-50, 54 (cf. 12:43).

[18] Loader, *Christology of the Fourth Gospel*, 104.

necessary part of his glorification.[19] His death on the cross is the climactic part of the work that Jesus completes in obedience to the Father.[20] It is part of the work for which he came to earth, but not the final goal. Instead, his work reaches its goal through his death, resurrection, and exaltation.[21] They are the climactic display of the Son's and the Father's glory.[22] Theologically, they constitute one unified event, Jesus' definitive glorification.[23] The final aspect of this unified event is the completion of Jesus' exaltation or glorification, which is the moment when Jesus is re-clothed with the glory he had with the Father before the creation of the world (John 17:5, 13:32).[24] This re-clothing in glory is the definitive glory that the Son seeks and asks for (8:54, 17:5). It is a return to glory that recognizes and rewards him for his obedience to the Father, especially for obediently dying on the cross.[25] Yet the unified event is in some sense incomplete without the sending of the Spirit, since it is a 'direct

---

[19] John 12:23-24, 13:21-31; cf. Blank, *Krisis: Untersuchungen zur johanneischen Christologie und Eschatologie*, 273, 275; de Boer, *Johannine Perspectives on the Death of Jesus*, 182.

[20] John 5:36, 12:27-28.

[21] John 17:4-5; Brown, *John*, 742; Blank, *Krisis: Untersuchungen zur johanneischen Christologie und Eschatologie*, 273; Carson, *John*, 557.

[22] Dodd, *Interpretation of the Fourth Gospel*, 207-8; Forestell, *Word of the Cross*, 71-74; Schnackenburg, *John*, vol. 2, 402.

[23] Cf. Blank, *Krisis: Untersuchungen zur johanneischen Christologie und Eschatologie*, 272.

[24] Loader, *Christology of the Fourth Gospel*, 108; Moloney, *Johannine Son of Man*, 198. According to 13:31-32 and 17:1-5, Jesus' death, resurrection, and exaltation involve glorification of the Son and the Father. Although each one glorifies the other, the nature of the Son's glorification is not always identical to that of the Father. This is because the glorification of the Father is only revelatory, i.e., it is a revelation or display of his glory in the world through the words and works of Jesus or the disciples (11:4, 40; 12:28; 13:31-32; 14:13; 15:8; 17:1, 4, 22; 21:19). The glorification of the Son usually displays his glory (1:14; 2:11; 11:4; 12:23; 13:31; 16:14; 17:10, 22), but his glorification through the events of his hour is more than just revelatory. It is also the means by which he is clothed in glory, i.e., he is re-invested with the glory he had with the Father before the incarnation (7:39; 13:32; 17:5, 24; cf. Carson, *John*, 557; Haenchen, *John 2*, 151-2). In contrast, the Father has no need to be clothed in glory, since he remains clothed in glory and is thus able to re-clothe the Son in glory. Thus it is possible to spell out the significance of the glorification of the Father in the following paraphrases: 'God displays his glory in him' (13:31-32), 'that the Son might display your glory' (17:1), and 'I have displayed your glory upon the earth' (17:4) (cf. Caird, 'Glory of God in the Fourth Gospel,' 270-3; Brooke F. Westcott, *The Gospel according to St. John: The Authorized Version with Introduction and Notes* [Grand Rapids: Eerdmans, 1971], 238, 241).

[25] John 8:54-55, 17:5, 7:18; cf. Carson, *John*, 570.

consequence of Jesus' glorification.'[26]

It is now possible to integrate the preceding treatments of δοξάζω, ὥρα, and ὑψόω. The significance of the three terms overlaps at the point where they are referring to Jesus' death, resurrection, and exaltation. All three support the impression that the death, resurrection, and exaltation are to be seen as one unified event. This event is the climactic moment (ὥρα) when Jesus is lifted up (ὑψόω) or glorified (δοξάζω). At this point, there is considerable overlap between the significance of ὑψόω and δοξάζω. First, John uses both terms to suggest a vital relationship between the cross and exaltation, so that the cross is an essential aspect of Jesus' exaltation. In addition, since both terms usually refer to the same unified event, Jesus' lifting up or exaltation (ὑψόω) is also usually his glorification (δοξάζω).[27] Even so, the two verbs are more than mere synonyms. They belong to the same semantic field, but John uses each verb to make a unique contribution.[28] The verb ὑψόω lends itself to the play on words that John uses to create the clearest impression of the unity between Jesus' death, resurrection, and exaltation. The verb δοξάζω also has a unique unifying function; along with δόξα, it associates all of Jesus' saving work with the glorification of the Father and the Son.

Background for Jesus' Lifting up and Glorification in Isaiah

Examination of Jesus' lifting up and glorification prepares the way for consideration of a likely Isaianic background for them. Others have already noted that ὑψόω and δοξάζω occur together several times in the Septuagint of Isaiah.[29] L. H. Brockington has also traced out two correlations: first, the Septuagint of Isaiah tends to associate δόξα and its cognates with visible manifestations of God; and second, it correlates δόξα and σωτηρία ('salvation').[30] These observations hint at a broader Isaianic background for Jesus' lifting up and glorification. A closer look at Isaiah, especially in the Septuagint, demonstrates that the lifting up, exaltation, and glorification of God are significant elements in the theology of the book.

---

[26] Carson, *Divine Sovereignty and Human Responsibility*, 142. Cf. John 7:39. After the sending of the Spirit, the glorification of Jesus continues through the work of the Spirit (16:14). The glorification of the Father continues through Jesus' response to the prayers of believers and believers' fruit-bearing (14:13, 15:8).

[27] Loader, *Christology of the Fourth Gospel*, 116-9; cf. D. Moody Smith Jr., *The Theology of the Gospel of John* (Cambridge: Cambridge University Press, 1995), 119; contra Thüsing, *Erhöhung und Verherrlichung Jesu im Johannesevangelium*, 33.

[28] Cf. de Boer, *Johannine Perspectives on the Death of Jesus*, 176-7.

[29] Caird, 'Glory of God in the Fourth Gospel,' 274-5; Loader, *Christology of the Fourth Gospel*, 116.

[30] L. H. Brockington, 'The Greek Translator of Isaiah and His Interest in ΔΟΞΑ,' *VT* 1 (1951): 26-31.

Jesus as the Fulfillment of the Temple in the Fourth Gospel: Part 2 153

In the Septuagint of Isaiah, one finds in several places a basic thematic pattern in association with ὑψόω, δόξα, and δοξάζω. One finds the first expression of this pattern in Isaiah 2, an eschatological prophecy. The pattern has two basic elements: judgment and salvation. In Isaiah 2:6-22, one finds a picture of judgment that begins with the house of Jacob and extends to all peoples. The purpose of the judgment is to humble humanity by consuming its material reasons for pride and its idols.[31] It humbles those who exalt themselves or idols rather than the Lord. The means of judgment is God's own action; that is, he arises and displays the glory (δόξα) of his strength.[32] The result of judgment is that God alone displays his exalted nature (ὑψωθήσεται).[33] Yet

---

[31] J. Alec Motyer, *The Prophecy of Isaiah: An Introduction and Commentary* (Downers Grove, Ill.: InterVarsity, 1993), 56-58.

[32] Isa 2:10 (LXX): Καὶ νῦν εἰσέλθετε εἰς τὰς πέτρας καὶ κρύπτεσθε εἰς τὴν γῆν *ἀπὸ προσώπου τοῦ φόβου κυρίου καὶ ἀπὸ τῆς δόξης τῆς ἰσχύος αὐτοῦ, ὅταν ἀναστῇ θραῦσαι τὴν γῆν*. The italicized portion is repeated in the LXX of 2:19 and 2:21. One finds similar repetition in the MT, but its version of 2:10 omits the final clause.

[33] Isa 2:11 (LXX): Οἱ γὰρ ὀφθαλμοὶ κυρίου ὑψηλοί, ὁ δὲ ἄνθρωπος ταπεινός, καὶ ταπεινωθήσεται τὸ ὕψος τῶν ἀνθρώπων, *καὶ ὑψωθήσεται κύριος μόνος ἐν τῇ ἡμέρᾳ ἐκείνῃ*. The italicized portion is repeated in 2:17. Given the possibility that the last verb (niphal of שׂגב) could have a reflexive sense in the MT and given the independent nature of the Lord's action in judgment, it is possible that the LXX is here intending one to assign a reflexive sense to the future passive of ὑψόω (cf. Caird, 'Glory of God in the Fourth Gospel,' 273-5; F.C. Conybeare and G. Stock, *Grammar of Septuagint Greek with Selected Readings from the Septuagint according to the Text of Swete* [Peabody, Mass.: Hendrickson, 1988], 75-76; Franz Delitzsch, *Biblical Commentary on the Prophecies of Isaiah*, trans. J. Martin, vol. 1 [Grand Rapids: Eerdmans, 1960], 121). Thus the unexpressed agent of ὑψωθήσεται could be God himself and this verb might not be a true passive. As a result, a possible translation for the last clause of 2:11 is 'the Lord alone will display his exalted nature in that day' (cf. Caird, 'Glory of God in the Fourth Gospel,' 274). This understanding of ὑψωθήσεται has little significance in and of itself. Yet it appears to be the first instance of a pattern in the LXX of Isaiah. The context and MT (where available) could imply a reflexive force for passive forms of ὑψόω in 2:11, 17; 5:16; 10:15; 12:6; 30:18; 33:10 and of δοξάζω in 5:16, 10:15, 24:23, 33:10, 49:3. Closer inspection of the MT and the context for these passive forms provides good support for a reflexive sense of both verbs in 5:16, 10:15 (where God is not the subject), 33:10 and of δοξάζω in 49:3. Almost as convincing is the support for a reflexive sense of ὑψόω in 2:11, 17; 30:18. The remaining instances have less support, but are potential candidates. Of course, Isaiah is not the only place in the LXX where one finds passive forms of ὑψόω and δοξάζω that appear to have a reflexive sense. Other examples are listed below (for each verb, the list progresses from more convincing to less convincing examples, but respects canonical order for comparable ones): ὑψόω in Pss 7:6; 20:13; 93:2; Dan 11:36; Pss 36:20; 56:5, 11; 88:13; 12:2; 65:7; δοξάζω in 1 Macc 3:14; Lev 10:3; 2 Kgs 6:20, 22; Exod 15:1, 6, 11, 21; Ps 36:20; 1 Macc 2:64; ἐνδοξάζω in Exod 14:4, 17, 18; 4 Kgs 14:10; Ezek

judgment is only part of the story. The predictions of judgment stand in stark contrast to the predictions of salvation in Isaiah 2:2-4.[34] Examination of the two sets of predictions suggests that judgment precedes salvation. The best evidence for this is the exalted position of the Temple mount and the Temple itself above all competing mountains, hills, and temples. The exalted position of the Temple mount appears to be a logical consequence of the acts of judgment described in 2:9-21, because the acts of judgment humble all competing mountains and hills (2:14) so that only the Lord is exalted (2:11, 17). It is significant to note that the Septuagint differs from the Hebrew Old Testament (MT) in two respects. First, it says that the Temple itself will be exalted rather than the Temple mount. Second, the Septuagint uses the same verb, ὑψόω, for the exaltation of the Temple (2:1) and of God (2:11, 17).[35]

The thematic pattern observed in Isaiah 2 is also found in a second passage, Isaiah 33. Isaiah 33 is not clearly eschatological from start to finish, but its picture of God's judgment and salvation fits with other eschatological prophecies.[36] At the time of judgment, God arises, displays his glory, and displays his exalted nature (33:10).[37] As in Isaiah 2, God's judgment humbles human pride, especially that of rulers, and even Zion is not a refuge for sinners.

28:22; 38:23; Hag 1:8 (possible). From this list, it is clear that Isaiah is unique in that it is the place where one finds a concentration of the reflexive sense of both verbs.

[34] Brevard S. Childs, *Isaiah*, OTL (Louisville, Ky.: Westminster John Knox, 2001), 32. It is well known that Mic 4:1-4 is a close parallel to Isa 2:2-4. There is no conclusive evidence for the priority of either passage. As Childs notes, even if Isa 2:2-4 is not an original contribution of Isaiah, it 'has been shaped editorially to function specifically within the book of Isaiah' (*Isaiah*, 28-29). This is even more true of the LXX. Cf. especially Isa 2:2 and Mic 4:1 in light of the comments on ὑψόω below.

[35] Isa 2:1 (LXX): Ὅτι ἔσται ἐν ταῖς ἐσχάταις ἡμέραις ἐμφανὲς τὸ ὄρος κυρίου καὶ ὁ οἶκος τοῦ θεοῦ ἐπ' ἄκρων τῶν ὀρέων καὶ ὑψωθήσεται ὑπεράνω τῶν βουνῶν, καὶ ἥξουσιν ἐπ' αὐτὸ πάντα τὰ ἔθνη. It is also worthy of mention that the LXX uses the adjective, ὑψηλός, to describe the mountains and the hills in 2:14. This adjective and ὑψόω are cognates. Its use in 2:14 therefore strengthens the connection between the exalted Temple (2:2) and its unworthy competitors.

[36] Cf. Isaiah 2, 66:7-24; Motyer, *Isaiah*, 262, 264; Childs, *Isaiah*, 248.

[37] Isa 33:10 (LXX): Νῦν ἀναστήσομαι, λέγει κύριος, νῦν δοξασθήσομαι, νῦν ὑψωθήσομαι ('Now I will arise,' says the Lord, 'now I will display my glory, now I will display my exalted nature'). In Isaiah 2 (LXX), the first and last verbs are already associated with the Lord's judgment (2:10-11, 17, 19, 21). The verb δοξάζω is absent from Isaiah 2, but judgment is there associated with the Lord's δόξα. Since God's judgment appears to be quite independent of human involvement, it makes sense that the unexpressed agent of δοξασθήσομαι and ὑψωθήσομαι is God himself. This fits with the MT as well, where the corresponding verbs are hithpolal and niphal forms with a reflexive sense (BDB, 671, 927). As a result, δοξασθήσομαι and ὑψωθήσομαι are probably future passive forms with a reflexive sense. In both the MT and LXX of Isa 33:10, these two verbs depict the same action.

Yet the righteous people of God have nothing to fear, for judgment of the nations ushers in a time of salvation and blessing for Zion.

In Isaiah 2 and 33, one finds ὑψόω and δοξάζω (or δόξα) associated with God's revelation of himself in both judgment and salvation. It is also possible to point to passages where one or both of these terms occur in connection with judgment or salvation. For instance, one finds both ὑψόω and δοξάζω in Isaiah 5:16 where God displays his exalted nature and his glory through exercising judgment on his people.[38] On the other hand, in Isaiah 49:3 God displays his glory in his servant; the context makes it clear that the salvation of God's people is in view.[39]

The above evidence suggests that the Septuagint of Isaiah commonly associates ὑψόω, δόξα, and δοξάζω with God's revelation of himself in judgment and salvation. It also appears that judgment of the unrighteous precedes and prepares the way for the salvation of God's righteous people. In the Septuagint, the close connection between judgment and salvation is maintained by using the same verbs for God's display of his glory and exalted nature in judgment and for his subsequent display of these attributes in salvation.[40] The pattern seems to be that God manifests his glory and his exalted nature first in acts of judgment; then, he manifests them in acts of salvation. As part of the acts of salvation, God displays his glory and exalted nature by glorifying and exalting his servant, the remnant, and the Temple.[41]

The proposed Isaianic background prepares the reader for John's presentation of the exaltation and glorification of Jesus. God displays his glory in the entire work of Jesus with the climactic display of glory in the hour of Jesus' lifting up or glorification.[42] As in Isaiah, the display of God's glory and

---

[38] Isa 5:16 (LXX): Καὶ ὑψωθήσεται κύριος σαβαωθ ἐν κρίματι, καὶ ὁ θεὸς ὁ ἅγιος δοξασθήσεται ἐν δικαιοσύνῃ. Isaiah 5:16 is not found in an eschatological passage. It is fulfilled in the exile. Cf. Isa 24:23 where the Lord displays his glory in judgment, but the judgment has an eschatological character.

[39] In Isa 49:3, manuscripts differ as to whether the final verb is δοξάζω or ἐνδοξάζω. Cf. Isa 30:18 where God displays his exalted nature (ὑψωθήσεται) in order to show mercy to his people; similarly, in Isa 12:6 his display of his exalted nature in Zion is associated with the salvation of his people.

[40] The verbs are ὑψόω and δοξάζω. In the MT, the connection is maintained (albeit less clearly) through the use of the same or synonymous verbs that express the display of God's exalted nature (for example, Isa 2:1, 11, 17; 33:10; 52:13).

[41] Cf. Isa 49:5; 52:13 (servant); 4:2 (LXX, remnant; MT, branch and remnant); 2:2; 60:7, 13 (Temple). In addition, God glorifies his messianic king (55:5, MT of 4:2). In the LXX, it is less clear than in the MT that God himself is the key agent in the glorification of his Temple (60:7, 13). It appears that God's agency is assumed in the LXX (cf. 60:7 and 60:17). This is also true in the case of the servant (cf. 52:13 and 53:11-12).

[42] John 1:14; 2:11; 11:40; 13:31-32; 17:1, 4.

exalted nature means judgment for those who seek their own glory rather than the glory of God.[43] On the other hand, it means salvation for those who obey his word.[44] There is, however, a significant difference between Isaiah and the Fourth Gospel at this point. In Isaiah, God displays his glory in distinguishable acts of judgment and acts of salvation; in the Fourth Gospel, God's display of glory in Jesus' work is simultaneously an act of judgment and salvation depending upon how people respond to it.[45]

Focusing upon God's revelation of his glory for salvation, several parallels exist between the glorification and exaltation of the suffering servant and of Jesus. The most commonly cited example is Isaiah 52:13, according to which the servant is exalted and glorified.[46] A second example is that God manifests his glory in the servant and in Jesus, the Son of Man (Isa 49:3, John 13:31-32).[47] Thirdly, the servant and Jesus are both given the task of gathering God's people (Isa 49:5-6, John 11:52).[48] Although these parallels are certainly significant, they should not be allowed to crowd out the parallels between the Temple and Jesus.

When God reveals his glory for salvation, his Temple is both lifted up and glorified (Isa 2:2; 60:7, 13).[49] The lifting up and glorification of the Temple is relevant background for the Fourth Gospel's presentation of Jesus in several passages. First of all, God glorifies Jesus through the events of Jesus' hour (John 13:31-32; 17:1, 5). This presents Jesus as the fulfillment of expectations previously associated with the Temple (Isa 60:7, 13). This fulfillment in Jesus also surpasses the Isaianic expectations in that God clothes Jesus with the eternal glory of God, rather than with glory gathered from the nations (John 13:32; 17:5, 24).[50]

---

[43] Cf. Isa 2:7-22; 10:15; 14:4-20; John 3:18-21; 5:22-30, 41-44; 12:31, 37-49. In both Isaiah and John, this is especially true for rulers. In fact, it appears that the ruler whose fall is described in Isa 14:4-20 anticipates the ruler of this world (i.e., the devil) in John 12:31.

[44] Isa 2:3-5, 33:15-16, 66:2; John 5:24, 8:31-32, 17:1-3.

[45] John 3:18; cf. Moloney, *Johannine Son of Man*, 84-85.

[46] Isa 52:13 (LXX): Ἰδοὺ συνήσει ὁ παῖς μου καὶ ὑψωθήσεται καὶ δοξασθήσεται σφόδρα. See note on p. 147.

[47] Isa 49:3 (LXX): Καὶ εἶπέν μοι Δοῦλός μου εἶ σύ, Ισραηλ, καὶ ἐν σοὶ δοξασθήσομαι. John 13:31: Νῦν ἐδοξάσθη ὁ υἱὸς τοῦ ἀνθρώπου καὶ ὁ θεὸς ἐδοξάσθη ἐν αὐτῷ. Cf. Isa 33:10 with its three occurrences of νῦν.

[48] On the last two examples, see Dodd, *Fourth Gospel*, 246-7; Forestell, *Word of the Cross*, 66.

[49] On the lifting up of the Temple and Jerusalem, see also Ezek 40:2, Zech 14:10 (in Aquila, Symmachus, and Theodotion rather than in the LXX).

[50] On the glorification of the Temple, see especially 3 Macc 2:9 where God is said to glorify the Temple by his 'magnificent manifestation' (NRSV). See also 2 Chr 3:6; Hag 2:7-9; Tob 13:11; 1 Esd 8:25, 67; 2 Esd 7:27, 8:36; *Sib. Or.* 3:772-773. On the

The lifting up of the Temple supports the claims of Jesus in John 4:21-24. The lifting up of the Temple in the last days exalts it above all other temples (Isa 2:2). This demonstrates the unworthiness of all competing temples. Likewise, the lifting up of Jesus exalts him above all other temples, including the Jerusalem Temple. He therefore replaces the Jerusalem Temple as the proper locus for true worship (John 4:21, Isa 66:23).[51] As such, he becomes the place where the nations come to be instructed in the way of the Lord (Isa 2:3). As a result, they can worship 'in truth' (John 4:22-24).[52]

John 12:31-32 is another passage where the lifting up and glorification of the Temple appears relevant. John 12:23, 31 correlate the hour of Jesus' exaltation and glorification with the judgment of the world and its ruler. This corresponds to the Isaianic pattern of God's manifestation of his glory and exalted nature in judgment. John 12:32 moves on to the consequences of Jesus' lifting up for the salvation of all people.[53] Like 12:31, it conforms to an Isaianic pattern; that is, all the nations come to God's Temple, which is lifted up in the last days.[54] Furthermore, according to Isaiah 56:6-8, God brings them there. Similarly, in John 12:32, the exalted Jesus draws all people to himself.[55] 'All people' is intended to include Gentiles and Jews.[56] For Jesus to draw people 'to himself,' simultaneously means drawing them to God and his true Temple.[57]

---

glorification of Jesus as the true Temple, see McCaffrey, *House with Many Rooms*, 239-40; Rev 21:22-23.

[51] The Jerusalem Temple was the special locus for true worship before the coming of Jesus (especially his death/resurrection/exaltation). When Jesus comes, he fulfills and replaces worship at the Temple.

[52] Hoskyns cites Isa 2:2-3 as a relevant parallel to John 4:21-24 (*Fourth Gospel*, 244); Zahn cites Isa 2:1-5 as a parallel to John 4:22 (*Johannes*, 247).

[53] John 12:32: 'But I, when I am lifted up from the earth, will draw all men to myself.'

[54] Isa 2:2-4, 56:6-8, 66:23; cf. Coloe, *God Dwells with Us*, 177; McCaffrey, *House with Many Rooms*, 201-2. For parallels to Isa 2:2-4, see Mic 4:1-3; Zech 14:16; Tob 14:6-7; *Sib. Or.* 3:715-720, 772-773.

[55] As mentioned already, the servant is a light for the nations who gathers people to the Lord (Isa 49:5-6; cf. 42:6). In another passage, the nations come to David (55:5). Even in this case, the real attraction is the glory of the Lord and David appears to be performing the same role as the servant in 49:5-6, i.e., he is gathering people to the Lord (Childs, *Isaiah*, 436). It appears that Jesus fulfills this role of the suffering servant and David (John 11:52), but he also 'transcends it' since he is the Lord himself gathering his people (John 1:1, 12:32; cf. Isa 11:12, 40:11, 43:5, 56:8) (Carson, *John*, 482).

[56] Bruce, *John*, 267. Of course, 'all people' is significant in the context, because the coming of some Greeks to see Jesus apparently prompts him to announce that his hour is at hand (12:20-23).

[57] Cf. John 6:44-45, where the Father draws people to Jesus. Cf. also Craig A. Evans, 'Obduracy and the Lord's Servant: Some Observations on the Use of the Old Testament in the Fourth Gospel,' in *Early Jewish and Christian Exegesis: Studies in Memory of William Hugh Brownless*, ed. C.A. Evans and W.F. Stinespring (Atlanta: Scholars Press,

The lifting up and glorification of Jesus as the true Temple is also anticipated by two other themes associated with Jesus' fulfillment of the Temple, that is, glory and revelation. Glory and revelation are both associated with replacement of the Temple in 1:14; revelation and replacement of the Temple are linked again in John 1:51. When Jesus displays his glory and is reclothed in glory through the events of his hour, his disciples are given the climactic view of his glory and of the Father's glory in him. This display of glory is the climax of the glory and revelation anticipated by John 1:14 and 1:51.[58] It simultaneously fulfills at least three Old Testament expectations regarding the Temple: (1) God will fill his Temple with his glory, (2) God will reveal himself to his people at his Temple, and (3) God will clothe his Temple in glory.[59] Since John 1:14 and 1:51 both anticipate Jesus' glorification and make significant contributions to the theme of Jesus' replacement of the Temple, they add to the impression that Jesus' glorification and his replacement of the Temple are connected. At the same time, one can see how Jesus' fulfillment of the Temple is bound up with his role as revealer and with his glory.

Given the relevance of Jesus' lifting up and glorification for John 1:14, 1:51, and 4:20-24, it is not surprising that John 2:13-22 should also be understood in light of his lifting up and glorification. To begin with, as seen above, Jesus' lifting up and glorification are primarily accomplished through the unified event comprised of his death, resurrection, and exaltation. Consequently, if Jesus' death and resurrection are relevant to his cleansing of the Temple (2:18-22), then his lifting up and glorification are probably in view. His death and resurrection clearly display the Father's glory in him on earth. They are also the first two steps in Jesus' return to the Father to be clothed in glory, which validates that his actions were done in obedience to the Father. Otherwise, the Father would not have exalted him and glorified him. Therefore, the appropriateness of Jesus' promised sign (2:18-19) can only be appreciated once

---

1987), 232-6. Evans points out several parallels between John 12 and Isaiah 52:7-53:12. On the relevance of John 11:52 and 12:32 to Jesus' replacement of the Temple, see François-Marie Braun, 'Quatre 'signes' johanniques de l'unité chrétienne,' NTS 9 (1962-63): 149-50; Collins, *These Things Have Been Written*, 208.

[58] Bernard, *John*, vol. 1, 22; Thomas L. Brodie, *The Gospel according to John: A Literary and Theological Commentary* (New York: Oxford University, 1993), 143; Lindars, 'Son of Man in the Johannine Christology,' 46; Moloney, *Johannine Son of Man*, 39-40; Schlatter, *Johannes*, 26-27.

[59] The OT background for points one and two has been discussed in chapters two and three (see especially chapter three's treatment of John 1:14 and 1:51, respectively). Point three relies on the current section. One finds at least some support for all three points in the LXX of Isaiah (cf. 6:1-13, 60:7).

he rises from the dead and his glorification is evident.[60] Like his other works, his cleansing of the Temple is a work completed in obedience to the Father (5:19). This makes it an act of judgment in which God is displaying his glory in Jesus (8:50, 54-55; 17:4). It is works like cleansing the Temple that incite opposition to Jesus and bring about his death (and glorification). Once the glorification and exaltation of Jesus climactically demonstrate that he fulfills and replaces the Temple, it becomes obvious that he was imminently qualified to reveal where human judgment was polluting the Temple, hindering its ability to point to him.

The Isaianic background for Jesus' glorification is not the only Temple glorification pattern that one should connect with 2:19-22. As seen in chapter two, God's glory, and thus his presence, departs from the Jerusalem Temple prior to its destruction.[61] It later returns to the new, eternal Temple in Ezekiel 43:2-4, 44:4 and will not depart from it (37:26-27). In the case of Jesus, he fulfills this pattern in that God's glory and presence depart from his body at the moment of his death (19:30). God's presence and glory return to his resurrected, eternal body.[62] Consequently the departure and return of God's presence demonstrate that Jesus is truly the eternal Temple which God is glorifying through his death, resurrection, and exaltation. It will not be replaced by another. Instead, as predicted in Isaiah, it will be adorned with glory.[63]

In conclusion, the passages reviewed above provide noteworthy evidence in favor of the lifting up and glorification of the Temple as a background for Jesus' lifting up and glorification in the Fourth Gospel. It appears likely that in this respect the lifting up and glorification of the Temple should not be overshadowed by the lifting up and glorification of the suffering servant. In fact, given the Isaianic background, one would expect the lifting up and glorification of the servant, the remnant, and the Temple to take place in concomitant acts of salvation. The display of God's glory and exalted nature in acts of salvation is an Isaianic background that ties in with the Fourth Gospel's presentation of Jesus as the one who fulfills the Jewish feasts.[64] When Jesus fulfills these feasts, he does so as the one who provides the salvific gifts that are anticipated by them and by the prophets, including Isaiah.

---

[60] This means that his sign will continue to be an enigma to Jews who persist in unbelief and therefore also reject belief in his exaltation and glorification.

[61] See especially Ezek 10:18-19, 11:22-23; cf. also 1 Sam 4:21-22; Ps 78:60; Jer 7:12-14.

[62] Even though the resurrected Jesus is able to come and go as he wishes, John is careful to portray him as having a physical body that is recognizable as the body of the crucified Jesus (20:18-29, 21:7-14; cf. 16:16, 19-22). This is also what one would expect from 2:19-22, which predicts that Jews will destroy Jesus' body and he will raise up essentially the same body after three days.

[63] Isa 60:7, 13, 19; John 17:5, 24.

[64] Cf. especially Isa 30:18, 23-25; 33:10, 16, 21; 49:3, 10; John 6:35, 7:37-39.

Jesus' Fulfillment of the Temple and His Fulfillment of the Jewish Feasts

The Jewish feasts are one of the distinguishing elements of the Fourth Gospel. It specifically mentions the Passover, Feast of Tabernacles, and Feast of Dedication.[65] The mention of these feasts is more than incidental. John's interest in them appears to be connected with his presentation of Jesus as the fulfillment of Jewish institutions and history.[66] In sometimes subtle ways, Jesus is put forward as the fulfillment of all three feasts. At several points, his fulfillment of the feasts simultaneously involves fulfillment of other Jewish institutions or significant historical events.[67] One such case of overlap involves Jesus' fulfillment and replacement of the Temple. While interpreters commonly link his fulfillment of the Temple and of the Feast of Tabernacles, some interpreters also find that his fulfillment of the Temple is pertinent to his fulfillment of the Passover and Feast of Dedication.[68] In order to substantiate its link with all three feasts, the first goal of this section is to present and evaluate the evidence for a connection between the fulfillment of the Temple and the fulfillment of each feast. In support of the link with all three feasts, there appears to be a common thread that binds together the three feasts and the Temple: They are all associated with God's abundant provision for his people. Thus the second goal of the section is to show how the proposed thread binds together the fulfillment of all three feasts and the Temple. Consequently the combined evidence from Jesus' fulfillment of the three feasts creates the impression that Jesus fulfills the Temple as the locus of God's abundant provision for his people.

Fulfillment of the Feast of Tabernacles

Since the Feast of Tabernacles is commonly associated with Jesus' replacement of the Temple, it provides a suitable point of entry into the topic at hand. In the Fourth Gospel, the fulfillment of the feast is bound up with the fulfillment of two of its unique rituals, that is, the water libations and the lighting of candelabra in the Temple precincts (7:37-39, 8:12). In the case of both water and light, some Old Testament passages link God's provision of water and light with the Temple or the Tabernacle. Against this Old Testament background, it is possible that Jesus' fulfillment of the Feast of Tabernacles simultaneously

---

[65] John 2:13, 23; 6:4; 11:55; 12:1; 13:1; 18:28, 39; 19:14 (perhaps 5:1) (Passover); 7:2 (Feast of Tabernacles); and 10:22 (Feast of Dedication). Cf. Richard N. Longenecker, *Biblical Exegesis in the Apostolic Period*, 152.

[66] Ibid., 152; Morris, *New Testament and the Jewish Lectionaries*, 70.

[67] Longenecker, *Biblical Exegesis in the Apostolic Period*, 153-4.

[68] Braun, 'In Spiritu et veritate,' 255-66; Kerr, *Temple of Jesus' Body*, 226-45; Léon-Dufour, 'Le signe du temple selon saint Jean,' 171-3. Cf. also Coloe, *God Dwells with Us*, 130-4; McCaffrey, *House with Many Rooms*, 230-5.

supports his fulfillment of the Temple. The case for a connection between these two fulfillments is examined below.

Interpreters who connect Jesus' fulfillment of the Temple and of the Feast of Tabernacles do so most often in relation to John 7:37-39.[69] Interpreters commonly agree that these verses present Jesus as the fulfillment of the water libations of the Feast of Tabernacles.[70] On the other hand, there is considerable disagreement over the immediate source of the living water and the Old Testament source for 7:38c.[71] Each of these points has a bearing upon the significance of 7:37-39 for Jesus' replacement of the Temple and therefore requires attention.

According to John 7:38c, the immediate source of the living water is either Jesus' or the believer's κοιλία ('belly' or 'heart').[72] In defense of Jesus' κοιλία as the immediate source, interpreters often appeal to the following three points. First, if one places a full stop after ἐμέ ('me') instead of after πινέτω ('let him drink'), then Jesus' saying in 7:37b-38a appears to assume an appealing parallel structure.[73] This punctuation makes it easier to read 7:38c as a reference to living water flowing directly from Jesus' κοιλία. Second, 7:38c appears to make Jesus or the believer the source of living water for others. Nowhere else is the believer presented as the source of living water for others, but Jesus is

---

[69] This is particularly true of those who understand the end of 7:38 to mean that the rivers of living water flow directly out of Jesus rather than from within the believer.

[70] The water libation ritual of the Feast of Tabernacles is not mentioned in the OT, but interpreters commonly agree with Barrett that 'there is no reason to doubt that it was carried out before the destruction of the Temple' (*John*, 270). Cf. Craig S. Keener, *The Spirit in the Gospels and Acts: Divine Purity and Power* (Peabody, Mass.: Hendrickson, 1997), 157; Gale A. Yee, *Jewish Feasts and the Gospel of John* (Wilmington, Del.: Michael Glazier, 1989), 74.

[71] John 7:38: (a) ὁ πιστεύων εἰς ἐμέ ('Whoever believes in me'), (b) καθὼς εἶπεν ἡ γραφή ('as the Scripture has said'), (c) ποταμοὶ ἐκ τῆς κοιλίας αὐτοῦ ῥεύσουσιν ὕδατος ζῶντος ('rivers of living water will flow from within him'). A sizeable body of literature exists on the interpretation of John 7:37-39. The main options for interpreting these verses are summarized in a recent dissertation by C. Scott Shidemantle ('The Use of the Old Testament in John 7:37-39,' Ph.D. diss., Trinity Evangelical Divinity School, 2001).

[72] The term κοιλία is difficult for all interpretations of 7:38. Evidence from the LXX and elsewhere suggests that κοιλία and καρδία ('heart') can be used synonymously (BAGD, 437; Schnackenburg, *John*, vol. 2, 156). This supports the preference of those translations that render κοιλία as 'heart' in this case (cf. NRSV); 'heart' evokes a pleasant image and is less awkward than 'innermost being' (NASB).

[73] Menken, *Old Testament Quotations in the Fourth Gospel*, 190. Accordingly, Jesus' statement could be translated as follows: 'If anyone is thirsty let him come to me, and let him drink who believes in me' (7:37b-38a).

(4:10-14, 19:34).⁷⁴ Third, the image of the water flowing directly from Jesus' κοιλία appears to fit with two possible Old Testament backgrounds, the water flowing from the rock or from the eschatological Temple.⁷⁵ Having the water flow directly from Jesus' κοιλία certainly creates an appealing image. It especially appeals to many interpreters who treat Jesus' replacement of the Temple.⁷⁶

If one accepts Jesus' κοιλία as the immediate source of the living water, then it seems easier to relate the image created by 7:38c to the outpouring of water from the eschatological Temple. At the same time, much can be said in favor of the believer's κοιλία as the immediate source of the living water. First, it appears more likely that 'the one who believes in me' should begin a new sentence rather than be appended to the end of 7:37. In the Fourth Gospel, these or similar words always occur at the beginning of a clause.⁷⁷ Second, it is not necessarily the case that 7:38c makes the believer the source of living water for others.⁷⁸ This makes 4:10-14 a helpful parallel for interpreting 7:38. Third, if the believer is not the source of living water for others, then the same Old Testament background applies equally well to 7:38c under both interpretations. This is so, because in both cases Jesus is the definitive source of the living water. He is the one who gives living water to those who believe (4:14). Hence

---

⁷⁴ For example, see André Feuillet, 'Les fleuves d'eau vive de Jo., 7, 38: Contribution à l'étude des rapports entre Quatrième Évangile et Apocalypse,' in *Parole de Dieu et sacerdoce*, ed. E. Fischer and L. Bouyer (New York: Desclée et Cie, 1962), 108.
⁷⁵ Schnackenburg, *John*, vol. 2, 154.
⁷⁶ Cf. Léon-Dufour, 'Le signe du temple selon saint Jean,' 171; McCaffrey, *House with Many Rooms*, 230-2.
⁷⁷ There are 41 comparable instances (Brown, *John*, 321). For other grammatical arguments, see Juan B. Cortés, 'Yet Another Look at Jn 7,37-38,' *CBQ* 29 (1967): 78-79. Another significant argument along this same vein is that the full stop after ἐμέ goes against Johannine logic. Looking at John 4:10-14, 6:35, the believer is the one who already possesses the true, satisfying, never-failing drink. It would therefore not cohere with Johannine logic for Jesus to invite believers to come and drink some more. Clearly, it makes sense that Jesus' invitation in 7:37 is addressed to unbelievers. As a result, the full stop rightly belongs after πινέτω (Cortés, 'Yet Another Look at Jn 7,37-38,' 82-83; Menken, *Old Testament Quotations in the Fourth Gospel*, 190-1). One should also note that the punctuation issue may incline one to favor the second interpretation, but may not be decisive evidence for it. Menken and Schnackenburg defend the possibility that one can place a full stop after πινέτω and still regard Jesus as the antecedent for the αὐτοῦ of 7:38c (Menken, *Old Testament Quotations in the Fourth Gospel*, 193; Schnackenburg, *John*, vol. 2, 154).
⁷⁸ John 7:38 can be understood this way, but such an understanding is not required. This verse can simply mean that living water will flow from within the believer, supplying him with a plentiful supply of water such that he never lacks its benefits (Cortés, 'Yet Another Look at Jn 7,37-38,' 76-77). Cf. Glenn Balfour, 'The Jewishness of John's Use of the Scriptures in John 6:31 and 7:37-38,' *TynBul* 46 (1995): 374, n. 75.

it is still possible for the water of John 19:34 to be a symbolic anticipation of the outpouring of the Spirit.[79] Based upon the above considerations, it seems preferable to regard the believer's κοιλία as the immediate source of the living water. Yet it is important to reiterate that the necessary source of the living water is Jesus even if the believer's κοιλία is in view in 7:38c.[80]

The intense disagreement over the immediate source of the living water provides a preview to the lack of consensus regarding the Old Testament source for 7:38c. Two key points allow for an acceptable solution to this quandary. First, in this case γραφή ('Scripture') probably does not refer to one Old Testament passage.[81] Second, the water libations of the Feast of Tabernacles can be associated with two Old Testament typologies, the water from the rock and the water from the eschatological Temple.[82] In turn, both typologies could stand behind 7:38c.

Beginning with the water from the rock, one can adduce several reasons that establish it as a suitable background for 7:38c. The provision of water from the rock is a prominent aspect of God's provision for Israel in the wilderness.[83] Since the Feast of Tabernacles commemorates Israel's wilderness experiences, it makes sense that the Feast's water libations would recall God's provision of water from the rock.[84] Yet the water from the rock is not merely a celebrated image from Israel's past. It is also an image that Isaiah associates with the blessings of the new age when Israel will once again experience God's acts of

---

[79] On this verse, see Edward Malatesta, 'Blood and Water from the Pierced Side of Christ (Jn 19,34),' in *Segni e sacramenti nel Vangelo di Giovanni*, ed. P.R. Tragan, Studia Anselmiana, no. 66 (Rome: Editrice Anselmiana, 1977), 165-81.

[80] Interpreters are right to insist that the symbolism of 7:38c-39 requires Jesus to be the source of the living water. In light of 7:39, most agree that the living water symbolizes the Spirit here; Jesus is elsewhere represented as the source of the Spirit for believers (1:33, 4:10-14, 6:63, 15:26, 16:7, 20:22).

[81] The best Johannine analogy for such a use of γραφή is probably 20:9, where the resurrection is in view (cf. 2:22) (Schnackenburg, *John*, vol. 2, 155). This is not the only analogy however. For instance, 19:36 could involve a conflation of two passages (Pierre Grelot, 'Jean VII, 38: eau du rocher ou source du Temple,' *RB* 70 [1963]: 50; Lindars, *John*, 590). Closer at hand, one can also see that the crowd refers to several Scripture passages using ἡ γραφή εἶπεν (7:42).

[82] See especially, Grelot, 'Jean VII, 38: eau du rocher ou source du Temple,' 45-50.

[83] Exod 17:1-7; Num 20:2-13; 21:16-18; Deut 8:15; Neh 9:15, 20; Pss 78:16, 20; 105:41.

[84] Note especially that the gifts of the Law, the Spirit, the manna, and the water from the rock are closely associated in Neh 9:14-15, 20. This chapter of Nehemiah belongs to a covenant renewal ceremony that probably takes place two days after a post-exilic Feast of Tabernacles celebration (Håkan Ulfgard, *The Story of Sukkot: The Setting, Shaping, and Sequel of the Biblical Feast of Tabernacles*, BGBE, no. 34 [Tübingen: J.C.B. Mohr, 1998], 129-31). Cf. Carson, *John*, 326-7.

salvation (48:20-21).[85] Isaiah's explicit reference to the water from the rock is a significant clue that his anticipation of abundant water in the new age is rooted in Exodus typology.[86] Of course, Isaiah is not the only prophet who anticipates abundant water in the new age.[87] Isaiah's unique contribution is his frequent mention of this blessing and the clarity with which he links this abundant water with the outpouring of the Spirit in the new age.[88] Thirst, water, hunger, bread, light, and Spirit are all significant elements in Isaiah's Exodus typology, which anticipates the new age.[89] These elements make Isaiah's expectation of abundant water in the new age a likely bridge between the events of the Exodus and the rivers of water that Jesus offers in John 7:37-39.[90] Based on this evidence alone, it is possible to see how the water libations of the Feast of Tabernacles could recall the historical incidents of water from the rock while anticipating God's future deliverance of his people.[91] If one accepts this set of associations as significant Old Testament source material for John 7:37-39,

---

[85] Edward J. Young, *The Book of Isaiah: The English Text, with Introduction, Exposition, and Notes,* vol. 3, NICOT (Grand Rapids: Eerdmans, 1972), 264.

[86] Watts, *Isaiah's New Exodus and Mark,* 80-81.

[87] Ezek 47:1-12, Joel 3:18 [MT 4:18]; Zech 13:1, 14:8.

[88] The expectation of abundant water in the new age is common in Isaiah (12:3; 30:23-25; 33:16, 21; 35:6-7; 41:17-20; 43:19-21; 44:3-4; 49:10; 55:1; 58:11). The outpouring of the Spirit on Israel is closely linked with plentiful water and blessing in 44:3-4 (cf. the LXX of 44:3 where water, thirst, and Spirit all come together). The outpouring of the Spirit is also clearly related to the anticipated fertility of the land in 32:15. Cf. Hildebrandt, *Old Testament Theology of the Spirit of God,* 60, 65-66. Also, cf. Joel 2:28 [MT 3:1], 3:18 [MT 4:18].

[89] Thirst and water occur in the verses listed in the previous note. The passages or their context sometimes make reference to hunger or bread (30:23, 33:16, 49:10, 55:2, 58:10; cf. 51:14), light (30:26; 49:6; 58:10; cf. 2:5; 4:5; 9:2; 26:9 [LXX]; 42:6; 50:10; 51:4; 51:5 [LXX]; 53:11 [LXX]; 60:1, 3, 19-20; 62:1), or Spirit (44:3, cf. 11:2, 32:15, 42:1, 59:21, 61:1). In addition, the sole passage where Moses and his leadership are mentioned also mentions the work of the Holy Spirit (63:8-14). Thirst, water, hunger, bread, and light are all common elements of those passages that look back on the Exodus (Pss 78:9-33, 105:25-45; Neh 9:9-31). Spirit is found in Neh 9:20 (cf. 9:30).

[90] As Watts notes, one must be careful to 'allow for the prophetic transformation of that founding moment [the Exodus] into the future hope of a NE [New Exodus]'; that is, 'Israel's future lay in no mere repetition of her founding moment, but in the more glorious prophetic vision of a greater and more portentous NE' (*Isaiah's New Exodus and Mark,* 49).

[91] Cf. Menken, *Old Testament Quotations in the Fourth Gospel,* 194-5. In *y. Sukkah* 5:1, one finds a connection between the water libations of the Feast of Tabernacles, the Holy Spirit, and Isa 12:3. Similarly, in *t. Sukkah* 3:6-8, one finds Ezek 47:5 interpreted in terms of an analogous water passage in Isaiah (33:21); one also finds three OT citations referring to the original water-from-the-rock incidents (Num 21:17-18; Pss 78:20, 105:41).

then the key verse that anchors such associations is probably Isaiah 48:21.[92]

Having looked at the water-from-the-rock passages, it might seem superfluous to probe further. Yet the water-from-the-rock passages do not fully satisfy some interpreters, because there is a more explicit background for 'living water.'[93] Another set of passages connected with the water libations of the Feast of Tabernacles makes a significant contribution to the 'living' aspect of the water. Of primary importance is Zechariah 14:8, which occurs in a chapter where the Feast of Tabernacles is mentioned (14:16-19).[94] According to the Septuagint of Zechariah 14:8, living water (ὕδωρ ζῶν) will continually flow out of Jerusalem in the new age. The imagery of Zechariah 14:8 tends to recall the imagery of a parallel passage, Ezekiel 47:1-12.[95] This is especially true in association with the Feast of Tabernacles.[96] Several rabbinic texts associate the water gate of the Temple, the water libations of the Feast, and Ezekiel 47:1-2.[97] Further evidence for a relevant connection between Zechariah 14:8 and Ezekiel 47:1-12 can be found in the Fourth Gospel. When Jesus offers living water to the Samaritan woman (4:10-14), he is not merely talking about running water versus still water. The living water that he offers is also 'life-giving.'[98] This double meaning for living water is suggested by reading Zechariah 14:8 in light of Ezekiel 47:1-12 where the river of water that flows out of the Temple brings life to all in its path.[99] Thus the background for living water in 4:10-14 and for

---

[92] Isa 48:21 (LXX): Καὶ ἐὰν διψήσωσιν, δι' ἐρήμου ἄξει αὐτούς, ὕδωρ ἐκ πέτρας ἐξάξει αὐτοῖς, σχισθήσεται πέτρα, καὶ ῥυήσεται ὕδωρ, καὶ πίεται ὁ λαός μου (Brenton's translation: 'And if they shall thirst, he shall lead them through the desert; he shall bring forth water to them out of the rock: the rock shall be cloven, and the water shall flow forth, and my people shall drink.').

[93] Grelot notes that 'living water' is not explicitly mentioned in passages concerned with the water from the rock ('Jean VII, 38: eau du rocher ou source du Temple,' 48). Cf. Barrett, *John*, 195; Menken, *Old Testament Quotations in the Fourth Gospel*, 196-7.

[94] Also, one finds quotes from Zechariah in John 12:15 (Zech 9:9) and 19:37 (Zech 12:10).

[95] In both passages, the water flows into the sea (two seas in Zechariah). Another significant parallel is Joel 3:18 (MT 4:18) where the water flows from the Temple as in Ezek 47:1-12. Cf. also Zech 13:1.

[96] In *t. Sukkah* 3:3-8, Ezek 47 and Zech 14:8 are both cited in connection with the water libations of the Feast of Tabernacles (see also Zech 14:17-18 in *t. Sukkah* 3:18).

[97] See *m. Šeqal.* 6:3, *m. Mid.* 2:6, *t. Sukkah* 3:3 (Menken, *Old Testament Quotations in the Fourth Gospel*, 197).

[98] Birger Olsson, *Structure and Meaning in the Fourth Gospel: A Text-Linguistic Analysis of John 2:1-11 and 4:1-42*, trans. Jean Gray, ConBNT, no. 6 (Lund: CWK Gleerup, 1974), 213.

[99] Ibid.; Carson, *John*, 327. See especially the LXX of Ezek 47:9 where one finds three instances of ζήσεται ('will live'). Cf. Feuillet's discussion of the possibility that Ezek

the water libations of the Feast of Tabernacles points to an association between Zechariah 14:8 and Ezekiel 47:1-12. The likelihood that these verses play at least some part in the background to 7:38 is also supported by John's interest in Jesus' replacement of the Temple.[100]

Having surveyed the possible source texts, it appears likely that both the water from the rock and the water from the eschatological Temple stand behind Jesus' reference to Scripture in John 7:38c.[101] Consequently, when Jesus offers water to people in John 7:37, he does so as the one who fulfills the expectations of water from the rock and from the eschatological Temple. Thus one finds another instance where Jesus fulfills prophetic expectations associated with the Temple.[102]

It is also significant that Jesus' replacement of the Temple and the gift of the Spirit are linked in both John 4:10-24 and 7:37-39. According to 4:10-14 and 7:37-39, the living water which Jesus offers can only be appropriated by

---

47 is a significant source for both the rivers of living water in John 7:38 and the river of the water of life in Rev 22:1-2 ('Les fleuves d'eau vive de Jo., 7, 38,' 110-12).

[100] Menken, *Old Testament Quotations in the Fourth Gospel*, 197. The wisdom background that is preferred by some interpreters is less promising than either of the backgrounds considered here (pace Lindars, *John*, 299-301). One finds no clear links between these proposed source texts and the Feast of Tabernacles or its rites.

[101] So François-Marie Braun, 'Avoir soif et boire (Jn 4,10-14; 7,37-39),' in *Mélanges bibliques en hommage au R. P. Béda Rigaux*, ed. A. Descamps and A. De Halleux (Gembloux: Duculot, 1970), 253-4; Brown, *John*, 323; Grelot, 'Jean VII, 38: eau du rocher ou source du Temple,' 47-51; Yu Ibuki, *Die Wahrheit im Johannesevangelium*, BBB, vol. 38 (Bonn: Peter Hanstein Verlag, 1972), 316-7; Keener, *Spirit in the Gospels and Acts*, 159; Olsson, *Fourth Gospel*, 216-7; Schlatter, *Johannes*, 200-1; Schnackenburg, *John*, vol. 2, 155-6; Westcott, *John*, 123. Cf. Zahn, *Johannes*, 399-400. The phrase ἐκ τῆς κοιλίας αὐτοῦ ('from within him') remains difficult for all proposed OT backgrounds (see Menken's recent valiant efforts to account for it [*Old Testament Quotations in the Fourth Gospel*, 199-201]). It seems best to conclude that this phrase is used to re-orient the OT expectations such that they fit into the realized eschatological framework required by 7:37-39. John does something similar, although less drastic, in 2:17 when he changes the tense of the verb to a future tense (Menken, *Old Testament Quotations in the Fourth Gospel*, 40-41; on this verse, see chapter 3).

[102] These prophetic expectations are consistent with the idealizations of the Temple found in the Psalms (see chapter two). The psalmists associate the Temple with plentiful resources to satisfy fully the needs of the righteous worshiper. These resources include life-sustaining water, light, and food. Cf. Pss 36:5-9 (MT vv. 6-10), 43:3, 46:4 (MT v. 5), 52:8 (MT v. 10), 65:4 (MT v. 5), 84:10-11 (MT vv. 11-12), 92:12-14 (MT vv. 13-15). It is also possible for the psalmist to encounter a sense of isolation from the abundant blessings associated with the Temple, especially during the feasts (Pss 42-43). In Ps 42:2, this sense of isolation is expressed in terms of thirst for God. Ezekiel 47:1-12, Zech 14:8, and Isa 44:3 make it clear that such thirst will not characterize the new age.

believers. This living water symbolizes the Spirit who mediates the blessings of the new age to believers (7:39).[103] Such blessings include spirit, truth, and eternal life.[104] The gifts of spirit and truth are necessary equipment for offering true worship (4:20-24). Further, in John's realized eschatology, the Spirit is the primary means by which Jesus continues to dwell in his followers after his ascension.[105] The Spirit therefore continues the ministry of the incarnate Word, which includes the task of revealing truth (1:14-18, 51). Clearly, the Spirit is the key gift that flows out from Jesus, the true Temple. It is the means by which believers experience the unique communion with Jesus and the Father that is the foretaste and guarantee of eternal life. This communion both fulfills and anticipates the ultimate fulfillment of the role of the Temple as the locus of God's provision for his people in the new age.[106]

Jesus' declaration that he is the light of the world (8:12) is also connected, at least in part, to God's provision for his people. It appears likely that the setting for 8:12 is the same as that for 7:37-39.[107] If so, then the lights in the Temple during the Feast of Tabernacles are probably at least one aspect of the background to Jesus' declaration in 8:12.[108] The location of these lights along with certain Old Testament passages regarding God's provision of light suggest that the Temple is regarded as a significant locus for the provision of light. When Jesus declares that he is the light of the world, it could be relevant for the theme of Jesus' fulfillment of the Temple.

In order to evaluate this connection, the Old Testament background for it requires attention as well as the evidence that this background is germane to

---

[103] Several interpreters contend that the living water that Jesus offers to the Samaritan woman symbolizes either revelation or the Spirit (4:10-14). In light of the clear statement in 7:39, it appears likely that the living water in 4:10-14 symbolizes the Spirit (perhaps it also symbolizes revelation) (Barrett, *John*, 195; Bernard, *John*, vol. 1, 141-2; Franz Mussner, *ZΩH: Die Anschauung vom 'Leben' im vierten Evangelium unter Berücksichtigung der Johannesbriefe* [München: Karl Zink, 1952], 112-5).

[104] John 3:5; 4:23-24 (spirit); 4:23-24; 14:17, 26; 15:26; 16:13-15 (truth); 3:6; 4:14; 6:63, 68 (eternal life).

[105] John 14:17; Brown, *John*, 1141; Ridderbos, *John*, 508; Schnackenburg, *John*, vol. 3, 197; Smith, *Theology of the Gospel of John*, 79, 142; cf. John 1:14; 14:20, 23; 15:4-5; 17:23, 26.

[106] John's theology contains a not-yet element with regard to Jesus' fulfillment of the Temple. Its full realization is anticipated when the disciples are able to join Jesus where he is (12:26, 14:3, 17:24). At this point, they will be able to be with Jesus and to behold his glory. They will also experience his abundant provision for them as Rev 22:1-5 shows.

[107] See, for example, Barrett, *John*, 277; Schlatter, *Johannes*, 205; cf. the cautions of Morris, *New Testament and the Jewish Lectionaries*, 64-65.

[108] Morris is careful to insist that the lighting of the candelabra at the Feast is only part of the background to 8:12 (*New Testament and the Jewish Lectionaries*, 65).

John 8:12. In the Old Testament, light is sometimes used figuratively to speak about the blessings that God bestows upon his people or the nations. In some cases, the exact nature of these blessings can be difficult to identify.[109] In other cases, the context clarifies what sort of blessing is in view; typical blessings include salvation and guidance.[110] Light is also found in idiomatic expressions where the access to light is a necessary quality of being alive.[111]

The figurative significance of light in the Old Testament fits with the significance of the visible manifestations of light that occur when God reveals himself to humans. These manifestations of light are commonly the means by which God reveals himself as his people's savior and guide.[112] Of particular significance is the pillar of fire that guides and protects Israel during the time of the Exodus.[113] It contributes to the pattern for the salvific events of the new age described by Isaiah. In Isaiah, God's salvific advent is associated with the manifestation of his presence in the form of light.[114] This light is bound up with the manifestation of God's glory in Jerusalem and is a key aspect of the attraction of the nations to it (Isa 60:3-17). When one places Isaiah 60:3 alongside 2:2-5, the nations are simultaneously drawn to the visible manifestation of light in Jerusalem and to the figurative manifestation of light concentrated there, that is, the teaching of the law or the word of the Lord.[115]

---

[109] For instance, Pss 89:15 (MT v. 16), 112:4.

[110] The blessing of guidance can be quite general (Job 22:28, 29:3; Ps 43:3; Isa 42:6, 49:6), or the law or decree of God can be the instrument of guidance (Pss 18:8 [in LXX]; 119:105, 130; Prov 6:23; Isa 2:5; 26:9 [in LXX]; 51:4). For the blessing of salvation, see Pss 27:1, 33:5 (in LXX), 36:9 (MT v. 10), 43:3, 44:3 (MT v. 4), 97:11. On these points, see Sverre Aalen, 'אוֹר,' trans. John T. Willis, in *TDOT*, ed. G. Johannes Botterweck et al., vol. 1 (Grand Rapids: Eerdmans, 1977), 160-2.

[111] Pss 49:19 (MT v. 20), 56:13 (MT v. 14); Job 33:28 (Aalen, 'אוֹר,' 158); probably also Ps 36:9 (MT v. 10) (Kraus, *Psalms 1-59*, 400).

[112] Sometimes, as in Ezek 1, the manifestation of God's light is connected with the revelation of God's judgment (Ezek 1:4-28, 4:1-17). A similar, beatific manifestation of light occurs at the time when God's glory returns to his Temple (43:2-3).

[113] Exod 13:21-22, 14:19-20; Neh 9:12, 19; Pss 78:14, 105:39 (Aalen, 'אוֹר,' 162); cf. Wis 18:3, 2 Macc 2:8.

[114] On the one hand, God manifests his presence on Mount Zion or in Jerusalem. In Isa 4:5-6, the manifestation clearly takes a form that recalls the pillar of cloud and fire (Childs, *Isaiah*, 36-37). On the other hand, just as the pillar of fire and cloud guided and protected the Israelites at the time of the Exodus, so also those returning from exile will experience similar divine guidance and protection (Isa 42:16, 52:12; Aalen, 'אוֹר,' 162, 166; Motyer, *Isaiah*, 422). Yet the light that shines in Jerusalem in Isa 60:1-2, 19-20 might recall the pillar of fire, but it also transcends it. It even renders the sun superfluous (60:19). Cf. Zech 14:8.

[115] Cf. Childs: 'The motif of the nations coming to the divine city of light [60:1-3] forms a background reminiscent of 2:2-5' (*Isaiah*, 496). Cf. Isa 51:4, which is also reminiscent of 2:2-5.

The above Old Testament background contains several elements that point to the Temple as a significant locus of light for the world. First, in several passages where light symbolizes God's blessings, the Temple is idealized as the place where one experiences these blessings.[116] Even in the case where the Law is presented as God's light, the Tabernacle and the Temple lie close at hand as prominent places where the Law is revealed.[117] Second, visible manifestations of divine light sometimes occur at the Tabernacle or the Temple.[118] Third, the Temple is presented as the place where the nations come for instruction in the new age (Isa 2:2-5). Such instruction enables them to 'walk in the light of the Lord' (Isa 2:5). In sum, based on the Old Testament evidence alone, the Temple's role as a locus of light appears to be at least a possible aspect of the Old Testament background to John 8:12.

The next task is to examine the evidence from the Fourth Gospel for a connection between the Temple as a locus of light and John 8:12. To begin with, John 8:12 and other passages on light make it clear that Jesus both is and provides the true light.[119] People accept the light that Jesus offers by following him or believing in him.[120] As a result, they emerge from the darkness in order to walk in the light that leads to life.[121] When Jesus comes into the world as the true light (1:9), he fulfills and replaces all other sources of God's light, including the Jerusalem Temple.[122] He becomes the place where Israel and the nations should expect to see God's light manifest itself. Given these general points, what specific indications does one find in the Fourth Gospel that the Temple is one of the sources of God's light that Jesus fulfills?

The context of John 8:12 provides several hints that one of the sources of light fulfilled by Jesus is the Temple. First, the lights placed in the Temple during the Feast of Tabernacles draw attention to the Temple as a place of light. Second, as seen above, Jesus' offer of water in 7:37-38 probably fulfills and replaces the Temple as the source of water in the new age. Perhaps the Temple is replaced again in 8:12. Third, if one regards 7:53-8:11 as a later addition to the Fourth Gospel, Jesus' next words after 7:37-38 are found in 8:12. Placing 7:37-38 and 8:12 side by side draws out the resemblance between what Jesus provides for believers and what God provides for his people at the Temple (Ps 36:8-9). In both cases, the blessed recipients are provided with plentiful drink, a

---

[116] Pss 27:1-10, 36:7-9 (MT vv. 8-10), 43:3-4; Isa 2:2-5. This includes the blessing of life itself (Ps 36:9).

[117] Lev 1:1, Ezek 43-44.

[118] Exod 40:38 (pillar of fire on Tabernacle), Isa 4:5 (fire on Mount Zion), Ezek 43:3 (return of glory to the Temple).

[119] Cf. John 1:9; 12:35-36, 46.

[120] John 8:12; 12:36, 46.

[121] John 3:21, 8:12, 12:36.

[122] Cf. Feuillet, *The Priesthood of Christ and His Ministers*, 150; Ladd, *Theology of the New Testament*, 267; Schnackenburg, *John*, vol. 1, 254.

river, and light.[123] It is also significant that in both cases the provision of drink and light are associated with the provision of life itself. Thus Jesus' offer of drink, light, and life at the Feast of Tabernacles could allude to Psalm 36:8-9.[124] If so, then this allusion suggests that the Temple is fulfilled by Jesus as a place where one seeks divine light. Fourth, 'I am the light of the world' (8:12) is a universal claim that makes Jesus the place where the nations should come to receive divine light. As such, he fulfills a role Isaiah envisions for the Temple.[125] Finally, Jesus' provision of light is closely related to his role as the revealer. Since Jesus fulfills and replaces the Temple as the place of revelation (1:14, 51), it is possible that the Temple is also replaced as a place for seeking God's light.[126]

The preceding evidence supports the conclusion that John could have had the Temple in mind as a place of light that is fulfilled and replaced by Jesus, the light of the world. In comparison to Jesus' provision of living water, Jesus' provision of light is admittedly more difficult to tie to his fulfillment and replacement of the Temple. As a result, Jesus' fulfillment of the Feast of Tabernacles and his fulfillment of the Temple probably are connected when it comes to Jesus' provision of living water. There could be a second connection between them with regard to his provision of light, but it remains tentative. In the first case, Jesus fulfills and replaces the Temple as the place out of which living water flows in the new age. In the second case, Jesus fulfills and replaces the Temple as a locus of divine light. In both cases, Jesus fulfills and replaces the Temple as the place of God's abundant provision for his people.

Fulfillment of the Feast of Dedication

The Feast of Dedication is mentioned once in the Fourth Gospel (10:22). It

---

[123] It should be noted that the strong thematic parallels between Ps 36:7-9 and John 7:37-38, 8:12 are not reinforced by verbal parallels in the LXX. Even so, several interpreters regard Ps 36:9 as a significant background passage for Jesus' provision of light (for example, see Barrett, *John*, 131; Bruce, *John*, 188; Dodd, *Interpretation of the Fourth Gospel*, 202).

[124] The Feast of Tabernacles would be a fitting occasion to make such a proclamation, since it is a time when people come to the Temple to celebrate God's blessings (Deut 16:15).

[125] Isa 2:2-5 (cf. 51:4-5, Mic 4:1-4). The Temple is referred to as the light of the world in a talmudic conversation between a rabbi and Herod where the rabbi alludes to Isa 2:2 (b. B. Bat., 4a; Hermann L. Strack and Paul Billerbeck, *Kommentar zum Neuen Testament aus Talmud und Midrasch*, vol. 1 [Munich: C. H. Beck'sche Verlagsbuchhandlung, 1922], 237). The suffering servant is also referred to as a light for the nations (Isa 42:6, 49:6).

[126] Cf. Culpepper's chiastic structure for the prologue where 1:9-10 corresponds to 1:14 ('Pivot of John's Prologue,' 13-14).

celebrates the rededication of the Temple under the leadership of Judas Maccabeus in 164 B.C. As seen in 2 Maccabees 1:18-2:18, the Feast also provides an opportunity to recall the miraculous events associated with the dedication of the Tabernacle and Temple under Moses, Solomon, and Nehemiah. These events are associated with certain well-established points of Temple theology. Of particular significance for John 10 is the fact that the dedication of the Temple under Solomon and Judas Maccabeus is carried out in recognition of God's election of the Temple in Jerusalem to be his consecrated sanctuary.[127] God confirmed his consecration of the Temple in Jerusalem by displaying his glory there at the time of its dedication.[128] Second Maccabees 2:8 shows that at least some Jews continued to anticipate the day when the Temple would again be dedicated in the likeness of its dedication in the days of Solomon. Given these considerations, Jesus' consecration could be relevant to his fulfillment of the Temple (John 10:36).[129] The likelihood of its relevance is enhanced when it is considered in the context of what is said about Jesus' fulfillment of the Temple elsewhere. The following section builds a case for the relevance of Jesus' consecration to his simultaneous fulfillment of the Feast of Dedication and the Temple. Then it suggests possible links between Jesus' consecration, his role as the locus of prayer, and his death on the cross.

Evidence for a viable connection between Jesus' consecration, the celebration of the Feast of Dedication, and the consecration of the Temple arises from considering John 10:36a in the context of the Fourth Gospel.[130] The first element of John 10:36a that deserves mention is how it fits within its immediate context (John 10:22-39). John 10:36 is located within Jesus' response to the Jews' claim that he is blaspheming (10:33). Interpreters commonly regard Jesus' response as making an argument from the lesser to the

---

[127] In the case of Solomon, full assurance of God's consecration of the sanctuary in Jerusalem only comes after the dedication (1 Kgs 9:3 / / 2 Chr 7:16, 2 Macc 2:8). Yet God's election of the place for his consecrated sanctuary is made clear in advance (1 Chr 22:1, 2 Chr 6:6). The dedication of the Temple under Judas Maccabeus assumes this doctrine of election and God's consecration of the Temple in Jerusalem (2 Chr 30:8; 1 Esd 1:49; 3 Macc 2:9, 16).

[128] Exod 29:43 (MT), 2 Macc 2:8, 3 Macc 2:9.

[129] For other works where Jesus' consecration is related to his fulfillment of the Feast of Dedication and the Temple, see Braun, 'In Spiritu et veritate,' 261-3; Coloe, *God Dwells with Us*, 145-55; Davies, *Gospel and the Land*, 294; Léon Dufour, 'Le signe du temple selon saint Jean,' 171; Hoskyns, *Fourth Gospel*, 385, 392; Kerr, *Temple of Jesus' Body*, 250-5; McCaffrey, *House with Many Rooms*, 232-5; Yee, *Jewish Feasts and the Gospel of John*, 91.

[130] John 10:36: (a) ὃν ὁ πατὴρ ἡγίασεν καὶ ἀπέστειλεν εἰς τὸν κόσμον ('what about the one whom the Father set apart as his very own [or sanctified] and sent into the world?') (b) ὑμεῖς λέγετε ὅτι βλασφημεῖς, ὅτι εἶπον· υἱὸς τοῦ θεοῦ εἰμι ('why then do you accuse me of blasphemy because I said, 'I am God's Son'?').

greater.[131] The lesser party (10:35) is difficult to identify, but the phrase 'to whom the word of God came' implies to some interpreters that Jesus understands the 'gods' of Psalm 82:6 in reference to the Israelites who received the Law at Mount Sinai.[132] Jesus then presents himself as the greater party, that is, 'the one whom the Father consecrated and sent into the world' (10:36a). Jesus is therefore comparing himself to other people whom the Scripture calls gods. Apart from the context, Jesus' consecration would sound similar to the consecration of Jeremiah or Moses to their prophetic offices.[133] Given Jesus' claims in the nearby context, Jesus' consecration is clearly that of the unique Son of God whose relationship with the Father is 'incomparably closer' than the relationship enjoyed by those who are called gods in Psalm 82:6.[134]

Although Jesus' consecration as God's Son is prominent in the argument of John 10:22-39, it probably does not exhaust the significance of Jesus' consecration. The mention of the Feast of Dedication suggests that John may once again be concerned to present Jesus as the fulfillment of Jewish worship.[135] Even if the immediate focus of the Feast of Dedication is the purification, consecration, and rededication of the Temple under Judas Maccabeus, these acts recall the analogous acts by which the Jerusalem Temple and the Tabernacle were previously dedicated (2 Macc 1:19-2:12).[136] These

---

[131] See, for instance, Barrett, *John*, 320; Johannes Schneider, *Das Evangelium nach Johannes*, THKNT (Berlin: Evangelische Verlagsanstalt, 1976), 208.

[132] For the various identifications of the lesser party and the arguments in favor of understanding it as the Israelites, see especially Jerome H. Neyrey, '"I Said: You Are Gods": Psalm 82:6 and John 10,' *JBL* 108 (1989): 647-63; cf. also Carson, *John*, 397-9. The identification of the lesser party is not essential for the task at hand.

[133] Jer 1:5; Sir 45:4, 49:7 (Forestell, *Word of the Cross*, 78). Of course, it could also be compared to the consecration of Aaron and his sons (Exod 29:44). Other significant consecrations include the consecration of the firstborn sons of Israel and the Levites as their replacements (Exod 13:2, Num 3:12-13; cf. Exod 4:22). Cf. the general promise of priesthood and holiness for Israel (Exod 19:6) (Potterie, *La vérité dans Saint Jean*, 737-8).

[134] Schnackenburg, *John*, vol. 2, 312; cf. John 10:25-30, 37-38. Carson points out that a typological relationship between Israel and Jesus may be relevant here (*John*, 398). Both are God's consecrated sons (Exod 4:21-22, John 10:36). Jesus affirms elsewhere that he is the genuine or true Son of God (8:36; ibid., 350). It follows that his consecration as the Son of God is the true consecration toward which Israel's consecration points.

[135] Cf. the above discussions of John 4:20-24, 7:37-39, 8:12.

[136] Purification, consecration, and dedication are all aspects of the dedication or consecration of the Tabernacle (Exod 29:36, 43-44; Lev 8:15; Num 7:1, 11). Consecration and dedication are explicitly mentioned in connection with the dedication of Solomon's Temple (1 Kgs 8:63-4, 9:3 // 2 Chr 7:5, 7, 16). Thus it is not surprising that one finds purification, consecration, and dedication mentioned in the accounts of the rededication of the Temple under Judas Maccabeus (1 Macc 4:36, 48; 2 Macc 1:18; 2:8; 10:3, 5, 7). In the LXX (see the above passages), the common words for dedication are

previous acts are ratified on two occasions by the Lord's expressions of approval. The Lord's approval is communicated in two ways. One way is by manifesting his glory there, which signifies that he consecrates it with his glory.[137] Another way is God's verbal expression of his consecration of the Temple.[138] Both of these expressions of approval were given to Solomon in association with the dedication of the Temple. According to Ezekiel 43:1-12, both of these forms of approval will also validate the consecration of the new Temple. Perhaps this is why the author of 2 Maccabees continues to anticipate a future manifestation of the glory of the Lord in his Temple (2 Macc 2:8). In short, the celebration of the Feast of Dedication relies upon the visual and verbal assurance given to Solomon that the Jerusalem Temple is God's chosen, consecrated sanctuary.[139] This assurance undergirds the significance of the rituals of rededication under Judas Maccabeus. It means that Judas was responsible for rededicating the chosen Temple of the Lord, which the Lord himself had consecrated. Against this background, Jesus' claim that the Father himself has consecrated him resonates with a fundamental belief undergirding the significance of the Feast of Dedication.

Jesus' consecration takes on further significance when one realizes that his consecration is ratified by both his own claim (10:36) and his works (10:25, 32, 37-38). If one rejects the testimony of the incarnate Word regarding his sanctification by the Father, then one can examine his works. At this point in the Fourth Gospel, Jesus' works have testified and will testify again that he is the locus for the manifestation of the glory of God.[140] Jesus therefore presents verbal and visual evidence of consecration that makes his claims to divine consecration just as strong as those of the Jerusalem Temple. As a result, the mention of the Feast of Dedication, Jesus' claim of consecration by the Father, and his reference to his works provide evidence that Jesus' consecration is being subtly presented as the act of consecration that sets apart the true Temple. The consecration of Jesus as the true Temple necessarily means that he takes the place of the Jerusalem Temple, for God only chooses one place at a time for his people to come and worship him.[141]

---

clearly related to the name of the Feast (ἐγκαίνια) (cf. John 10:22). Similarly, ἁγιάζω is the most common verb for the act of consecration (cf. John 10:36).

[137] Exod 29:43-44, 40:34-35; 1 Kgs 8:10-11 // 2 Chr 5:13-14. Cf. Lev 9:23-24 and 2 Chr 7:1-3.

[138] 1 Kgs 9:3 // 2 Chr 7:16; cf. Exod 29:44.

[139] This is supported by the rededication of Solomon's Temple under Hezekiah. Even though it was purified and consecrated at his direction (2 Chr 29:5, 15-19), he refers to its eternal consecration by God as its decisive claim to consecration (30:8; cf. 1 Esd 1:49). Similarly, the Second Temple was dedicated (Ezra 6:16-17) and mention is made of its eternal consecration by God (3 Macc 2:9, 16).

[140] Cf. John 1:14; 2:11; 11:4, 40; 12:23; 13:31-32; 17:1, 4-5.

[141] Cf. Deut 12:2-28, 26:1-11; John 4:20-24.

The preceding treatment of Jesus' consecration suggests that his consecration is significant for his fulfillment of the Feast of Dedication and the Temple. If its significance for his fulfillment of the Temple be accepted, then this opens up two additional possible connections. First, the Temple background for Jesus' consecration leads one to suspect that his replacement of the Temple could also be relevant to his teaching on prayer. Solomon's Temple dedication prayer places particular emphasis upon the Temple as the locus of prayer, that is, the place where God is attentive to the prayers of his people. Thus the Temple is the place toward which one prays and the ideal place in which to pray.[142] Solomon's prayer prepares the way for at least one aspect of the significance of prayer in Jesus' name.[143] Whatever else it means, praying in Jesus' name acknowledges that Jesus is the means by which those who pray have access to God.[144] It therefore is possible that prayer in Jesus' name is meant to fulfill and replace prayer in or toward the Temple.[145]

Another possible connection suggested by Jesus' consecration as the true Temple (10:36) is clarified in light of the second mention of Jesus' consecration (17:19). When one views 10:36 alongside 17:18-19, it becomes clear that consecration is consecration for mission. The Father set Jesus apart and Jesus sets himself apart for the purpose of accomplishing his mission.[146] The climax of that mission occurs in the events of Jesus' hour, which the entire

---

[142] Solomon asks the Lord to be attentive to the prayers offered toward or within the Temple, even those offered by a non-Israelite (1 Kgs 8:29-30 // 2 Chr 6:20-21; also, 1 Kgs 8:33-48 // 2 Chr 6:24-38). The Lord answers Solomon's prayer with a promise that his eyes and heart will always be present at his Temple, where he has placed his name (1 Kgs 9:3 // 2 Chr 7:16). The psalmists affirm this emphasis and even pray that God's deliverance of the petitioner would proceed from Zion (Pss 18:6 [MT v. 7], 20:1-9 [MT vv. 2-10], 28:2; cf. Ps 27:5).

[143] Cf. John 14:13-14; 15:16; 16:23-24, 26 (also, 15:7). See also Amsler, *L'Ancien Testament dans l'église*, 217-8.

[144] Carson, *John*, 497; cf. Brown, *John*, 636; Westcott, *John*, 204.

[145] Several parallels between 1 Kgs 8:28-48 // 2 Chr 6:19-38 and John 14:13-14, 15:16, 16:23-26 affirm the possibility of influence. First, the inclusive nature of possible requests is stressed in 3 Kgdms 8:37-38, 43 // 2 Chr 6:28-29, 33 (LXX) and John 14:13-14; 15:7, 16; 16:23. Second, the response from God is to do (ποιέω) or to give (δίδωμι) the thing requested (3 Kgdms 8:30, 32, 36, 39, 43, 45 [cf. 2 Chr 6:23, 25, 27, 30, 33, 35, 39]; John 14:13-14, 15:16, 16:23). Third, God's presence in his Temple is associated with the presence of his name there (for example, 1 Kgs 8:29, 43-44; 9:3). Similarly, Jesus' ministry manifests the Father's name to his followers (John 17:6). Fourth, in 3 Kgdms 8:44 (LXX), God's people are encouraged to pray both 'in the name of the Lord' (2 Chr 6:34 has 'to you') and toward the Temple.

[146] Barrett, *John*, 426; Forestell, *Word of the Cross*, 81. The Father's sending of the Son into the world (10:36, 17:18) is inseparable from the mission which the Son was sent to accomplish (3:17, 12:44-50, 17:3-4).

Gospel anticipates.[147] This means that Jesus' consecration should not be viewed in isolation from his death/resurrection/exaltation. As a result, interpreters commonly read 'I consecrate myself for them' (17:19) in light of Jesus' sacrificial death. Then, given the context of 17:19, his self-consecration suggests that he is consecrating himself as both priest and sacrifice.[148] If Jesus is both priest and sacrifice, it is not surprising that he is also the consecrated Temple, the designated house of sacrifice.[149] In this way, Jesus' consecration in John 10:36 anticipates his death on the cross so that his fulfillment of the Feast of Dedication coincides with his fulfillment of the Passover.[150] In accordance with the Father's will, Jesus offers himself as the one and only sacrifice that is offered in the true Temple.

It seems plausible to connect Jesus' consecration, his fulfillment of the Feast of Dedication, and his fulfillment of the Temple. Jesus' simultaneous fulfillment of the Feast of Dedication and the Temple provides a second instance where the fulfillment of a Jewish feast and the fulfillment of the Temple overlap. The overlap is strengthened by the fact that fulfillment of the Feast and the Temple work together to contribute to the portrayal of Jesus as the locus of God's abundant provision. Specifically, the Father's consecration sets apart the true Temple where the decisive vicarious sacrifice takes place; this sacrifice is a significant aspect of God's abundant provision for those who believe and fulfills the Passover.

---

[147] Cf. John 12:27, 17:1-5.

[148] Barrett, *John*, 426; Brown, *John*, 766-7; Feuillet, *Priesthood of Christ and His Ministers*, 97-98, 125; Hoskyns, *John*, 503; Meyer, *John*, 468-9; Schnackenburg, *John*, vol. 3, 187. Bultmann associates his self-sanctification only with his role as sacrifice (*John*, 510-1; cf. Chrysostom, *Hom. Jo.* 82). Loader is representative of those who reject the connection between self-consecration and sacrifice in 17:19 (*Christology of the Fourth Gospel*, 99-100). This is consistent with his tendency to minimize the significance of Jesus' sacrificial death for the Fourth Gospel's Christology (Ibid., 102). For a more balanced assessment of the place of vicarious sacrifice in the Fourth Gospel's Christology, see Smith, *Theology of the Gospel of John*, 116-9. The OT background for Jesus' self-consecration is drawn from the consecration of the first-born to God for sacrifice (Exod 13:2, Deut 15:19-21), the consecration of the priests by God (Exod 29:44), and the self-consecration of priests in preparation for performing their 'cultic duties' (Exod 19:22; 1 Chr 15:12, 14; 2 Chr 5:11; 29:5, 34; 30:3, 15, 24) (Jackie A. Naudé, 'קדש,' in *NIDOTTE*, ed. Willem A. VanGemeren, vol. 3 [Grand Rapids: Zondervan, 1997], 884-6).

[149] Cf. Coloe, *God Dwells with Us*, 203; Kerr, *Temple of Jesus' Body*, 255; McCaffrey, *House with Many Rooms*, 234. For the Temple as a 'house of sacrifice,' see 2 Chr 7:12 and Deut 12:6, 16:1-8.

[150] This will be discussed further below.

Fulfillment of the Passover

Given the number of references to the Passover, it is by far the most prevalent of the three feasts mentioned in the Fourth Gospel.[151] Jesus' fulfillment of the Passover is commonly related to his sacrificial death and its benefits for believers. Jesus' sacrificial death has possible implications for his replacement of the Temple, because it makes Jesus the true place of sacrifice. At the same time, Jesus' fulfillment of all three Jewish feasts and of the Temple converge at the moment of his death on the cross. It appears likely that the blood and water from Jesus' side symbolize such a convergence (19:34). In order to substantiate these points, attention must be given to the evidence for Jesus' fulfillment of the Passover and for the proposed convergence of the three Jewish feasts and the Temple.

Jesus' fulfillment of the Passover is a theme that interpreters find relevant for several passages of the Fourth Gospel.[152] It is alluded to initially in John 1:29 and 2:13-25. The Passover allusion in 1:29 is probably the most ambiguous since the Passover has not been mentioned yet. Even so, a number of interpreters regard the Passover lamb as part of the background to 'the lamb of God who takes away the sin of the world.'[153] The first Passover celebration in the Fourth Gospel provides the occasion for Jesus' cleansing of the Temple (2:13, 23). It anticipates a connection between the Passover and Jesus' death, since Jesus' promised sign (2:19) and John's interpretation of it (2:21-22) point to his death. John 2:19-22 also provides the first hint that Jesus' fulfillment of the Passover and the Temple may be connected.

The next hint of Jesus' fulfillment of the Passover occurs in chapter six, especially vv. 51-58. After the mention of the Passover in 6:4, Jesus presents himself as the 'true bread from heaven' (6:32) in contrast to the manna given to the Israelites under Moses. The true bread is further described as Jesus' flesh, which he 'will give for the life of the world' (6:51). If the sacrificial overtones

---

[151] The term πάσχα occurs in John 2:13, 23; 6:4; 11:55; 12:1; 13:1; 18:28, 39; 19:14. In addition, the term ἑορτή ('feast') is used in reference to the Passover in 2:23; 4:45; 6:4; 11:56; 12:12, 20; 13:1, 29 (Morris, *New Testament and the Jewish Lectionaries*, 67).

[152] For a fuller treatment of the relevant passages and their contribution to the Passover theme, see Bruce H. Grigsby, 'The Cross as an Expiatory Sacrifice in the Fourth Gospel,' *JSNT* 15 (1982): 53-59; J. K. Howard, 'Passover and Eucharist in the Fourth Gospel,' *SJT* 20 (1967): 329-37; Yee, *Jewish Feasts and the Gospel of John*, 59-69. Cf. also François-Marie Braun, *Jean le théologien: Sa théologie*, vol. 3, *Le mystère de Jésus-Christ*, EBib (Paris: J. Gabalda and Co., 1966), 160-4.

[153] It is difficult to know exactly what John the Baptist meant by the expression. Still, it is possible that it had a significance unknown to him (cf. 11:49-52). As a result, interpreters commonly suggest that the Passover lamb and the suffering servant both contribute to the background for the 'lamb of God' in 1:29 (Barrett, *John*, 146-7; Brown, *John*, 60-63; Schnackenburg, *John*, vol. 1, 298-300). Some favor the Passover lamb over the suffering servant (Bultmann, *John*, 96; Zahn, *Johannes*, 121-2).

of 6:51 are not strong enough, one finds further sacrificial overtones in 6:53-57, which makes several references to eating Jesus' flesh and drinking his blood.[154] Obviously this is metaphorical language that has to be interpreted in light of the context. The context supports the conclusion that eating Jesus' flesh and drinking his blood involves 'believing in him (cf. verse 35), appropriating him by faith.'[155] In essence, one eats Jesus' flesh and drinks his blood when one believes in Jesus and receives the benefits of his sacrificial death, including freedom from sin and the gift of life that goes along with this freedom (6:54).[156] The reference to Jesus' flesh and blood in 6:53-56 is therefore an anticipation of his death on the cross. As was the case in 2:13-25, the second Passover in the Fourth Gospel is linked with Jesus' death, but it adds to the impression created by 1:29 that Jesus will fulfill the Passover as a sacrificial victim.[157] As is the case with the flesh and blood of the Passover lamb, the flesh and blood of Jesus are both essential elements for participating in this new Passover.[158]

Although recent interpreters give it less attention in connection with John's Passover theme, John 8:31-47 contains some important Passover elements that suggest its relevance.[159] These Passover elements include freedom, slavery to sin, and the devil (elsewhere the 'ruler of this world').[160] John 8:34 is consistent with 1:29 in its mention of dealing with people's sin problem. It adds to one's understanding of people's sin problem by diagnosing the problem as involving slavery to sin and desiring to carry out the desires of the devil (8:34, 44). In order for people to escape from this slavery, Jesus must free them, which will make them sons who have an eternal place in the Father's house.[161] Thus John 8:31-47 provides important support for the idea that two of the benefits of Jesus' sacrificial death are freedom from sin and the gift of life that goes along with this freedom.

The final Passover in the Fourth Gospel is first mentioned in 11:55. This Passover coincides with the coming of Jesus' hour, which means that his death

---

[154] On the sacrificial overtones in 6:51-8, see especially Smith, *Theology of the Gospel of John*, 116. Cf. Bertil Gärtner, *John 6 and the Jewish Passover*, ConBNT, no. 17 (Lund: C. W. K. Gleerup, 1959), 23.

[155] Bruce, *John*, 159. Notice the similarities between 6:40 and 6:54 (Ibid.). Such a reading of the passage avoids equating eating Jesus' flesh and drinking his blood with celebrating the Eucharist. However, it does not deny that this passage is significant for one's understanding of the Eucharist's significance (Ibid., 160; Carson, *John*, 297-8; Ridderbos, *John*, 237). See Ridderbos for a summary of the treatment of these verses by recent interpreters (*John*, 236-8).

[156] Cf. Bruce, *John*, 159-60; Ridderbos, *John*, 242.

[157] Cf. Schlatter, *Johannes*, 164, 182.

[158] On the Passover lamb's flesh and blood, see Exod 12:1-13.

[159] A noteable exception is Coloe (*God Dwells with Us*, 195-6).

[160] John 8:32, 34-36, 44; 12:31; 16:11.

[161] John 8:35-36, 14:2-3.

is imminent.[162] Indeed it is the moment of Jesus' death on the cross that provides John with the opportunity to bring out most clearly the connection between Jesus and the Passover lamb. According to John 19:36, the fact that the soldier did not break Jesus' legs (19:33) was anticipated by the Old Testament passages concerning the Passover lamb, whose bones were not to be broken.[163] When it is viewed alongside 1:29, 2:19-22, 6:51-58, and 8:31-47, John 19:33-36 appears to be the culmination of John's presentation of Jesus as the fulfillment of the Passover. The main Passover emphasis in 19:33-36 falls upon Jesus' fulfillment of the Passover as the Passover lamb. If so, then the blood that pours from his side (19:34) complements the attention to Jesus' unbroken bones (19:33, 36). The flesh and the blood both have sacrificial import; it is therefore significant that both find a place in 6:51-58 and 19:33-36.[164] Indeed the mention of blood in 19:34 creates the impression that 19:33-36 should be read alongside 6:51-58, which contains the only comparable mention of blood in the Fourth Gospel and occurs in a Passover context.[165] As a result, the blood from the side of Jesus draws attention to his death on the cross as the climactic

---

[162] Cf. especially John 13:1, 27-33. Many contemporary interpreters insist that John's chronology places Jesus on the cross at the time when the Passover lambs were being slaughtered in the Temple (see, for instance, France, 'Chronological Aspects of "Gospel Harmony,"' 54; Grigsby, 'Cross as an Expiatory Sacrifice in the Fourth Gospel,' 54-56). This chronology is often appealed to as evidence that Jesus fulfills the Passover as the Passover lamb. Yet it appears to conflict with the time of Jesus' death in the Synoptics. The arguments for and against the possibility of harmonizing this apparent discrepancy are complex and cannot be reviewed adequately here. Even so, one should note that a minority voice continues to defend the possibility of a credible harmonization (esp. in light of 19:31), one which places Jesus on the cross on the day after the Passover meal (see Carson, *John*, 455-8 [esp. p. 458, n. 1]; Barry D. Smith, 'The Chronology of the Last Supper,' *WTJ* 53 (1991): 29-45; cf. the similar remarks of Tholuck, *John*, 302-18).
[163] Exod 12:10 (LXX), 46; Num 9:12. See, for example, Braun, *Jean le théologien*, vol. 3, 162; Bruce, *Time is Fulfilled*, 48; Chrysostom, *Hom. Jo.* 85; Reim, *Hintergrund des Johannesevangeliums*, 51-52. On the other hand, some authors contend that Ps 34:20 (MT v. 21) is the most likely source for the loose citation from Scripture in John 19:36 (Dodd, *Interpretation of the Fourth Gospel*, 424; Zahn, *Johannes*, 663-4). The majority of interpreters affirm that John 19:36 refers to the verses concerning the bones of the Passover lamb, although many also recognize the relevance of Ps 34:20 (Beasley-Murray, *John*, 355; Brown, *John*, 937-8; Pancaro, *Law in the Fourth Gospel*, 349-50; Schnackenburg, *John*, vol. 3, 291-2). The mention of the Passover (19:14) and hyssop (19:29, Exod 12:22) support the relevance of the Passover for the death of Jesus and especially for John 19:36 (Barrett, *John*, 464; Grigsby, 'Cross as an Expiatory Sacrifice in the Fourth Gospel,' 57).
[164] Brown, *John*, 951, 953; Howard, 'Passover and Eucharist in the Fourth Gospel,' 337.
[165] Donald Senior, *The Passion of Jesus in the Gospel of John* (Collegeville, Minn.: Michael Glazier, 1991), 125-6. The only other mention of blood (1:13) is not relevant. Cf. Barrett, *John*, 463; Carson, *John*, 624.

offering of his flesh and his blood for the life of the world (6:51-58).

Even though the main Passover emphasis of John 19:33-36 falls upon Jesus' sacrificial death, it is likely that his fulfillment of the Temple lies close at hand (2:19-22). If the proper place to sacrifice and eat the Passover lamb is at the Temple (Deut 16:2-7), the sacrifice of Jesus as the Passover lamb could indicate that he is also the true Temple, the designated place of sacrifice.[166] In addition, he is subtly presented as the place to partake of the Passover in that all those who would appropriate his sacrificial death and gain eternal life must come to him and receive these things from him.[167]

Additional evidence for the true Temple's relevance to 19:33-36 arises from the mention of water in 19:34. The significance of this water follows readily from the significance of the blood that accompanies it. If the blood signifies Jesus' offering of his own blood in order to give freedom from sin and life to believers (6:51-58, 8:31-36), then the water probably symbolizes the Spirit who makes it possible for believers to appropriate the benefits of Jesus' sacrificial death for them.[168] According to John 7:39 and 16:7, the gift of the Spirit comes after Jesus' departure and glorification. Thus John 19:34 anticipates the gift of the Spirit, who will bring the benefits of Jesus' sacrificial death to the one who believes.[169] One should recall that the giving of the Spirit brings about the fulfillment of the Feast of Tabernacles (7:37-39). It follows that the blood and water from Jesus' side symbolize the fulfillment of the Passover through Jesus' sacrificial death and the fulfillment of the Feast of Tabernacles through the gift of the Spirit.[170] Since Jesus' fulfillment of the Temple has already been

---

[166] Cf. Carson, *John*, 182; Pancaro, *Law in the Fourth Gospel*, 348. Also, Ezekiel's new Temple is clearly the site for Passover sacrifices (45:21-24); note that it is also the site for the sacrifices of the Feast of Tabernacles (45:25).

[167] John 6:27, 35-45, 7:37; cf. 6:51-58.

[168] John 6:63, 7:37-39. This would not be the first time where water symbolizes the Spirit (see especially 7:37-39, but also 3:5-8, 4:10-24). Cf. Barrett, *John*, 462-3; Carson, *John*, 624; Hoskyns, *Fourth Gospel*, 533; Malatesta, 'Blood and Water from the Pierced Side of Christ,' 175; Schnackenburg, *John*, vol. 3, 294.

[169] John 3:5-6. See especially Burge, *Anointed Community*, 95. It is important to remember at this point that Jesus is the one who gives the Spirit to believers no matter whose κοιλία ('innermost being') is in view in John 7:38 (cf. 4:10, 16:7).

[170] Cf. Kerr, *Temple of Jesus' Body*, 243. Many interpreters interpret the water from Jesus' side in connection with 7:37-39 and the fulfillment of the Feast of Tabernacles (Braun, 'In Spiritu et veritate,' 260; Reim, *Hintergrund des Johannesevangeliums*, 58-61). Others relate the blood to the fulfillment of the Passover (Howard, 'Passover and Eucharist in the Fourth Gospel,' 337; Yee, *Jewish Feasts and the Gospel of John*, 68). Interpreters seem strangely reluctant to mention both feasts in connection with the blood and water. In some instances, the inference that the blood and water symbolize the fulfillment of both feasts can readily be drawn based upon an interpreter's remarks (Barrett, *John*, 462-3; Brown, *John*, 949-51; Burge, *Anointed Community*, 94-95;

connected with his fulfillment of the Feast of Tabernacles in 7:37-39, it is probably also significant for the flow of water from Jesus' side.

As seen above, similar conclusions emerge based upon the fulfillment of the Feast of Dedication. Its fulfillment is associated with Jesus' sacrificial death, because Jesus' consecration by the Father anticipates the events of Jesus' hour, especially his death (17:19). Since Jesus' consecration includes consecration as true Temple and sacrifice (10:36, 17:19), it points to his sacrificial death as the sanctified sacrifice offered in the true, sanctified Temple. The blood from Jesus' side therefore points to the simultaneous fulfillment of the Feast of Dedication and the Passover.[171] Again, Jesus' fulfillment of the Temple appears relevant due to its relevance for the fulfillment of the Feast of Dedication.

The above remarks imply that Jesus' fulfillment of the three Jewish feasts is brought together in the symbolism of the blood and water from Jesus' side (19:34). This symbolism constitutes a vivid reminder of the essential connection between Jesus' sacrificial death and his giving of the Spirit. The Spirit is the means by which believers appropriate the true food and true drink, namely, the flesh and blood of Jesus (6:53-56, 63). This true food and true drink will never fail to sustain them (6:35).[172] Since Jesus is this true food and true drink as well as the one who gives them to believers (6:27, 51-58), he fulfills and replaces the Temple as the place in and from which God pours out his abundant provision upon his people.[173] He also surpasses it, because the true food and true drink that he provides mean eternal life for those who receive them (6:58).

In conclusion, the fulfillment of the Passover, Feast of Tabernacles, Feast of Dedication, and the Temple is brought to fruition in Jesus' sacrificial death and the sending of the Spirit. The Spirit is the means by which believers appropriate the salvific benefits of Jesus' sacrificial death. These salvific benefits include true, life-giving food and drink. They represent God's abundant provision for his people in the new age and the fulfillment toward which the three feasts and the Temple pointed.

Carson, *John*, 624; Grigsby, 'Cross as an Expiatory Sacrifice in the Fourth Gospel,' 59, 61-62; Schnackenburg, *John*, vol. 3, 294)

[171] As Chrysostom recognizes, the blood of Jesus is the antitype to the blood of the Paschal lamb and to all of the sacrificial blood poured out in the Temple (*Hom. Jo.*, 46).

[172] Cf. the Isaianic promises of abundant water and food in the new age (Isa 33:16, 41:17-20; 43:19-21; 49:10; 51:14; 55:1-2). As pointed out earlier, the provision of water and Spirit comes together in Isa 44:2-3.

[173] Pss 36:5-9 (MT vv. 6-10), 46:4 (MT v. 5), 52:8 (MT v. 10), 65:4 (MT v. 5), 84:10-11 (MT vv. 11-12), 92:12-14 (MT vv. 13-15); Ezek 47:1-12; Joel 3:18 [MT 4:18]; Zech 14:8.

Conclusion

The two sections of this chapter are complementary in that both lead to the conclusion that Jesus' replacement of the Temple is significant for John's portrayal of Jesus' death/resurrection/exaltation. According to the first section, the language of lifting up and glorification marks his death/resurrection/exaltation as the decisive event whereby God reveals himself for judgment and salvation. Focusing upon salvation, the lifting up and glorification of Jesus as the true Temple suggests the advent of the age of salvation in which God gathers his people, provides for them, and draws the nations to himself. Then, according to the second section, Jesus' fulfillment of the Jewish Feasts and the Temple dwells upon the nature and content of God's provision for all his people. Jesus is and gives the true food and true drink that deliver believers from thirst and hunger. He demonstrates this by offering his flesh and blood for the life of the world and sending the Spirit to enrich believers with the salvific benefits of his sacrificial death. Thus he simultaneously fulfills the Passover, Feast of Tabernacles, Feast of Dedication, and the Temple. With reference to the Temple in particular, he fulfills and replaces it as the place in and from which God pours out his abundant provision upon his people.

CHAPTER 5

A Proper Understanding of Jesus' Replacement of the Temple in the Fourth Gospel

The preceding two chapters present evidence for Jesus' replacement of the Temple drawn from the Fourth Gospel and its interpreters. The evidence leads to the conclusion that replacement of the Temple is only one aspect of the relationship between Jesus and the Temple. Indeed the evidence for Jesus' replacement of the Temple is also evidence for his fulfillment of patterns and prophecies associated with the Temple in the Old Testament. Jesus' ability to fulfill such prophecies and patterns means that some measure of continuity exists between him and the Temple. It is therefore possible to speak of Jesus as the 'true Temple.'[1]

At the same time, it is difficult to ignore the discontinuity between Jesus and the Temple. When Jesus fulfills the patterns and prophecies associated with the Temple, he does so in a way that surpasses or transcends them. As a result, the relationship between Jesus and the Temple can properly be described as typological. In support of these points, the following chapter reviews the best evidence that Jesus fulfills, surpasses, and replaces patterns and prophecies associated with the Temple. Then, it clarifies the appropriateness of understanding this fulfilling, surpassing, and replacing in terms of a typological relationship between Jesus and the Temple, one that is in line with a traditional conception of typology.

John sets up a correlation between Jesus and the Temple by presenting Jesus as the one who fulfills patterns and prophecies associated with the Temple or its antecedents. John 1:14 introduces the incarnate Word as the place where God dwells among his people. As such, he fulfills a primary role of the Temple.[2]

---

[1] It seems preferable to speak of Jesus as the 'true Temple' rather than the 'new Temple,' because John prefers to use ἀληθινός ('true,' 'genuine') to distinguish between OT types and NT antitypes (Brown, *John*, 500-1). Although he never uses this adjective with 'Temple,' he certainly implies its appropriateness by using it for those who benefit from the gifts that flow from Jesus (the 'true worshipers') or for the gifts that Jesus gives to believers (the 'true light' and 'true bread').

[2] John develops two aspects of this idea of Jesus as the dwelling place of God in the midst of his people. The first aspect can be described as the realized eschatological aspect. This finds initial expression in those verses where Jesus' physical presence with

That is not all. According to John 1:14, Jesus also fulfills two other patterns associated with the dwelling place of God among his people, namely, it is the place where God manifests his glory and where he reveals himself to his people. During his ministry, Jesus already begins to fulfill these two patterns.[3] Their fulfillment reaches its peak during the events of his hour, namely, his death, resurrection, and exaltation. John unifies these three events into one event, Jesus' lifting up or glorification. This event is the Fourth Gospel's climactic revelatory moment when Jesus completes his mission and thereby manifests his glory. It therefore is the most significant event that presents Jesus as the new place where God manifests his glory and reveals himself to his people.[4] At the same time, it reveals Jesus as the lifted up and glorified Temple, which Isaiah anticipated as a prominent aspect of the new age. As in Isaiah 2, people from all nations come to Jesus, the true Temple, in order to learn the ways of the Lord and experience his goodness.[5]

Besides being a place associated with glory and revelation, the Temple is also the locus for Jewish worship, including the feasts. This role of the Temple is consistent with the conception of the Temple as the designated dwelling place of God among his people. Since it is a special place of divine presence, the Temple is the preeminent place to worship God. The connection between the Jewish feasts and the Temple goes deeper than this in that both are associated with God's abundant provision for his people. Indeed the Temple itself is idealized in the Old Testament as the place in and from which God pours out his abundant blessings upon his people. The Fourth Gospel presents Jesus as the fulfillment of this role of the Temple. It does so primarily in connection with his fulfillment of the Passover, the Feast of Tabernacles, and the Feast of Dedication. He fulfills these feasts as the true Temple in which he offers himself as the sacrifice that takes away the sin of the world (1:29). As a result of this sacrifice, the gift of the Spirit proceeds from the true Temple.[6] By means of the Spirit, believers are able to appropriate the salvific benefits of Jesus' sacrificial death. This means that they receive the only food and drink capable of sustaining them forever, that is, of providing them with eternal life

---

his disciples is referred to (1:14; 14:17; 16:16, 22). Jesus' presence with his disciples continues after he has gone to the Father apparently by means of the Spirit within them (14:17, 23; 15:4-6; 17:26). The second aspect is the futuristic eschatological aspect when Jesus will once again dwell visibly and physically with his people (12:26, 14:2, 17:24).

[3] John 1:51; 2:11; 3:34; 8:26-28; 11:4, 40; 12:49; 17:8.

[4] Consequently, it is the most significant event anticipated by John 1:14 and 1:51. Jesus' death and resurrection is also connected with his role as the Temple in 2:19-22.

[5] See, for example, John 10:16, 11:52, 12:32.

[6] In the Fourth Gospel, the gift of living water symbolizes the gift of the Spirit. Living water is an image that points to a connection between the gift of the Spirit and the life-giving water that flows out of the new Temple in Ezek 47:1-12.

(6:51-58).

Given the preceding evidence that Jesus fulfills prophecies and patterns associated with the Temple in the Old Testament, one might emphasize Jesus' ability to fill the place of the Temple while neglecting or discounting the notion that Jesus surpasses these prophecies and patterns.[7] Thus Jesus is nothing more nor less than the new Temple that fulfills Old Testament prophecies and patterns formerly associated with the Temple in Jerusalem. Proceeding in this way may be expedient for avoiding the implication that Jesus is greater than the Temple, but it does not appear to do justice to the presentation of Jesus in the Fourth Gospel.

Two analogous examples provide initial evidence that Jesus is greater than the Temple. First, the Fourth Gospel presents Jesus as the true light who brings the definitive revelation, the grace and truth (1:9, 14-18). On the one hand, the grace and truth corresponds to truth found in the Mosaic Law, which points to Jesus and the salvation that he brings.[8] On the other hand, this revelation surpasses and replaces the Law given through Moses, because it is the goal or fulfillment to which the Law pointed.[9] Second, Jesus both is and gives the true bread from heaven (6:32-35, 49-51). No other bread, even the manna eaten during Israel's wilderness wanderings, can compare with this bread with respect to its life-giving power. No other bread can deliver those who partake of it from death, that is, it cannot sustain them eternally (6:49-50, 58).[10] This true bread from heaven turns out to be the flesh and blood of Jesus that he offers up on the cross for the life of the world (6:51-58, 19:34-36). Nevertheless, in spite of the surpassing greatness of the true bread from heaven, it was effectively prefigured by the manna and prophetic predictions of plentiful food and drink in the new age.[11] As with the definitive revelation, the true bread surpasses and replaces the manna as its fulfillment or goal. Since the locus for the definitive revelation and the provision of true bread from heaven is Jesus, they already suggest that he surpasses and replaces the Temple with respect to two of its roles, namely, the place of revelation and of abundant

---

[7] Cf. Simon, 'Retour du Christ et reconstruction du Temple,' 257; Smith, 'John,' 107; also, N. T. Wright, 'Jerusalem in the New Testament,' in *Jerusalem Past and Present in the Purposes of God*, ed. Peter W. L. Walker, 2nd ed. (Grand Rapids: Baker, 1994), 58, 62.

[8] See chapter three on John 1:16-17; also, John 5:46; Braun, 'In Spiritu et veritate,' 265; Carson, *John*, 133; Pancaro, *Law in the Fourth Gospel*, 228. Cf. Amsler, *L'Ancien Testament dans l'église*, 216; David E. Holwerda, *Jesus and Israel: One Covenant or Two?* (Grand Rapids: Eerdmans, 1995), 74; Smith, 'John,' 107.

[9] Cf. John 1:16-18; 3:13, 31; Pancaro, *Law in the Fourth Gospel*, 542; Meeks, *Prophet-King*, 288.

[10] Cf. Meeks, *Prophet-King*, 91-93, 291.

[11] Bruce, *John*, 44; Pancaro, *Law in the Fourth Gospel*, 471; cf. Brown, *John*, 500-1.

provision.¹²

As seen above, one form of evidence for the surpassing greatness of Jesus as the fulfillment and replacement of the Temple is the salvific gifts that proceed from him. Even more significant is the evidence provided by his lifting up and glorification. The lifting up and glorification of Jesus demonstrate his pre-eminence in relation to any other temple, including the Jerusalem Temple. In other words, the surpassing greatness of Jesus' exaltation and glorification means that his status and glory exceed that of any temple, even the new Temple described in Isaiah and Ezekiel.¹³

If Jesus fulfills the prophecies and patterns of the Temple in a way that surpasses them, then it is possible to see Jesus and the Temple as corresponding yet distinct entities. In terms of correspondence, this means that one aspect of the Temple's significance is its ability to point to Jesus.¹⁴ On the other hand, the contrast between Jesus and the Temple is evidence of the climactic, definitive nature of the revelation and salvation that Jesus brings. Given John's presentation of Jesus, he is clearly more excellent than the Old Testament events, persons, or institutions that anticipated him.¹⁵

In characterizing Jesus as the one who fulfills and replaces the Temple, John is setting up a relationship between Jesus and the Temple that can properly be described as typological.¹⁶ To begin with, it has three widely recognized marks of a typological relationship. First, the Old Testament type is an institution. Second, there is a significant correspondence between the type and its antitype. This means that the evidence for a correspondence between them does not consist of superficial details; rather, the evidence consists of substantive parallels. Third, the antitype does not merely recapitulate the type, but the movement from type to antitype is progressive in nature such that the antitype surpasses the type.¹⁷ Thus far the relationship between Jesus and the Temple

---

¹² Cf. Dubarle, 'Le signe du temple,' 39; Smith, 'John,' 107.

¹³ On the glory of Jesus as the true Temple, see the description of the Lamb in Rev 21:22-24. The glory with which Jesus was adorned at the time of his glorification could only be partially seen even by Moses, the greatest of the prophets.

¹⁴ John makes it explicit that Moses and the Prophets wrote about Jesus (1:45, 5:39-46). When he presents Jesus as the fulfillment of the Temple (and the Tabernacle), he is providing particular instances where Moses and the Prophets wrote about Jesus.

¹⁵ Cf. especially, Meeks, *Prophet-King*, 288, 291, 319; Pancaro, *Law in the Fourth Gospel*, 471, 542; Reim, *Hintergrund des Johannesevangeliums*, 268; Cornelius van der Waal, "The Gospel according to John and the Old Testament," *Neotestamentica* 6 (1972): 28-47.

¹⁶ For further description of typology and typological relationships, see chapter one.

¹⁷ On this point, see Amsler, *L'Ancien Testament dans l'église*, 216-7; Cothenet, 'Typologie de l'exode dans le IVe Évangile,' 250; Fairbairn, *Typology of Scripture*, vol. 1, 70, 81-83. Because they discount this aspect of typology, Meeks and Reim do not see the relationship between Jesus and Moses as typological, and generally see little room

conforms to characteristics that would be acceptable to both of the primary conceptions of typology. The next step is to determine whether one conception of typology describes John's Temple–Jesus typology better than the other.

A decisive point at which the two conceptions of typology part ways is their understanding of the antitype's fulfillment of the type. Proponents of a traditional conception of typology understand typology as prospective or predictive. In their view, one significance of the type is to predict the antitype so that God might display his 'Lordship in moulding and using history to reveal and illumine His purpose.'[18] The New Testament antitype fulfills the Old Testament type in that it is the goal or climactic fulfillment that was effectively prefigured or predicted by the type. On the other hand, proponents of a modern conception of typology can understand fulfillment to mean that the antitype brings the type to completion, because it is a more perfect embodiment of the same 'principles of God's working.'[19] Such an understanding of fulfillment guards the type from having an anticipatory import that was unknown to the Old Testament author.[20] Since the purpose of the current study is to clarify the relationship between Jesus and the Temple based upon the evidence of the Fourth Gospel, one must ask whether evidence from the Fourth Gospel tips the scales in favor of one understanding of fulfillment or the other.[21]

The Fourth Gospel provides two pieces of evidence that favor the first understanding of the antitype's fulfillment of the type. First, in two instances, it says that Moses wrote about Jesus (1:45, 5:46). This already suggests that Moses' writings have a predictive significance.[22] The chief instance where a

---

for typology in the Fourth Gospel (Meeks, *Prophet-King*, 291-2, 319; Reim, *Hintergrund des Johannesevangeliums*, 268). Stressing the correspondence between type and antitype at the expense of progression undercuts the progressive nature of salvation history (see Stek, 'Biblical Typology,' 162). It appears that John sees Jesus as the climax toward which the earlier revelation through Moses and the Prophets pointed. The earlier revelation anticipated Jesus, but the salvation and revelation that Jesus brings exceed OT expectations.

[18] Ellis, *Paul's Use of the Old Testament*, 128; cf. Davidson, *Typology in Scripture*, 418-9; Stek, 'Biblical Typology,' 162.

[19] France, *Jesus and the Old Testament*, 40. For more on this conception of typology, see chapter one.

[20] I.e., the type is not prospective. See France, *Jesus and the Old Testament*, 41-43; Baker, *Two Testaments*, 180-1, 190.

[21] The question is appropriate, because some proponents of a modern understanding of typology claim that their understanding of typology is also that of the biblical authors (France, *Jesus and the Old Testament*, 77; Baker, *Two Testaments*, 185-88). Others freely admit that their conception of typology does not line up with that of the biblical authors (Amsler, 'La typologie de l'Ancien Testament,' 78).

[22] Taken by itself, this piece of evidence could be read in a non-predictive sense; that is, Moses wrote about Jesus in the sense that he wrote about the OT models that correspond

writing of Moses is cited as being fulfilled by Jesus is found in John 19:36.[23] Second, John 19:36 says that these things happened in order to fulfill the Scripture. John appears to be claiming that Jesus' bones were spared from being broken *in order to* fulfill one aspect of the Old Testament type, the Passover lamb.[24] Hence this incident affirms the typological relationship between Jesus and the Passover lamb that is hinted at elsewhere in the Fourth Gospel. It also shows that God is at work 'in moulding and using history to reveal and illumine His purpose.'[25] Taken together, these pieces of evidence suggest that a regulation regarding the Passover lamb anticipates, even necessitates, the preservation of Jesus' bones from being broken; that is, when Moses was writing about the bones of the Passover lamb, he was also

---

to Jesus. When it is taken with the second piece of evidence, this first piece becomes the initial hint that Moses predicted aspects of the life of Jesus.

[23] As seen in chapter four, most commentators relate the citation in 19:36 to Exod 12:46 or Num 9:12. Some also see the relevance of Ps 34:20. The other instance in which a writing of Moses is cited has to do with the bread from heaven (6:31). In that case, Jesus is the true bread that comes from heaven (6:48-58).

[24] John 19:36 in its entirety says, "Ἐγένετο γὰρ ταῦτα ἵνα ἡ γραφὴ πληρωθῇ, Ὀστοῦν οὐ συντριβήσεται αὐτοῦ' ('For these things came to pass to fulfill the Scripture, "Not a bone of him shall be broken."' [NASB]). The use of ἵνα ('in order to' or 'so that') here is surely telic (purpose) rather than ecbatic (result), as it is in other cases where one finds the phrase ἵνα ἡ γραφὴ πληρωθῇ or its equivalent (Blass et al., *Greek Grammar*, sec. 391; Bernard, *John*, vol. 1, cliii-clv; Carson, 'John and the Johannine Epistles,' 250; Bruce M. Metzger, 'The Formulas Introducing Quotations of Scripture in the NT and the Mishnah,' *JBL* 70 [1951]: 306; for a list of similar phrases and where they can be found, see Moule, 'Fulfilment-Words in the New Testament,' 312-3).

[25] Ellis, *Paul's Use of the Old Testament*, 128; cf. Bernard, *John*, vol. 1, cliii-cliv; Moule, 'Fulfilment-Words,' 297. This is an important aspect of John 19:36 (and 19:24-25a, 28; cf. 12:38-40, 13:18, 15:25, 17:12, 20:9). In this scene, God does not merely work in ways that correspond to OT patterns. Rather John is pointing to the way in which events are 'providentially overruled' in order to fulfill OT patterns (Bruce, *John*, 377, 369, 372); i.e., the events happen the way they do in order to fulfill Scripture. Thus God's hand is presumed to be at work both in overruling the establishment of the OT type and in overruling the events that fulfill expectations associated with the type. In the case of Jesus' bones not being broken, John affirms that this event happens in order to fulfill the expectation found in Scripture. The prediction is not presented as any less of a prediction than the words from Zech 12:10 cited in 19:37. As a result, one finds in 19:36 an instance of a typological pattern that is treated as an explicit prediction of events (see two more examples in 19:24-25a, 28). Consequently France's notion of typological fulfillment is inadequate.

predicting one of the details of Jesus' death on the cross.[26] In terms of typology, then, a detail concerning the type, the Passover lamb, prefigures a corresponding detail concerning the antitype, Jesus.[27] By implication, John is comfortable with the idea that a type can predict or prefigure its antitype. Unlike some recent proponents of typology, John does not appear to be concerned with protecting Old Testament types from being prospective.[28]

If Moses prefigures Jesus in writing about the Passover lamb, then it is also possible for him to prefigure Jesus in writing about the Tabernacle. By extension, it is possible for other biblical authors to prefigure Jesus in writing about the Temple.[29] As seen in chapter one with reference to David, the canonical context for these institutions supports the notion that they have anticipatory import. In the case of the Passover lamb, it is a celebrated element of Israel's Exodus from Egypt. The anticipatory import of the Exodus events is proclaimed by Isaiah in his prophecies of a new and greater Exodus.[30] When John presents Jesus as the fulfillment of the Passover lamb, he confirms, and further clarifies, its anticipatory import. In the case of the Tabernacle, it is presented in Exodus as the initial dwelling place of God in the midst of his people. The Temple of Solomon, from its consecration to its destruction, is the Tabernacle's divinely approved successor. Yet the prophets point to an even more glorious Temple as one aspect of Israel's future hope.[31] In fulfillment of these expectations, John presents Jesus as the true Temple who fulfills and surpasses the prophetic expectations. Given this canonical context, one can see that one element of the meaning of the Passover lamb, the Tabernacle, and the Temple is to point beyond themselves to a climactic fulfillment or goal that is

---

[26] Thus John views these words of Moses as a 'prophetic ordinance' that 'pointed forward to the manner of the death of Him who was the true Paschal Lamb' (Bernard, *John*, vol. 2, 651; cf. Chrysostom, *Hom. Jo.* 85).

[27] The relationship between the Passover lamb and Jesus is widely recognized as typological. See, for instance, Bruce, *John*, 377; Fairbairn, *Typology*, 384; Goppelt, *Typos*, 190.

[28] For further evidence of this, a similar case could be made for the prospective import of David's experiences as seen in 19:24-25a, 28 (cf. Carson, 'John and the Johannine Epistles,' 249-50). David–Jesus typology validates the appropriateness of saying that Pss 22:18, 69:21 predict elements of Jesus' passion.

[29] Moses already connects the Passover sacrifice with the Temple (Deut 16:5-7). Then, Passover is one of the feasts explicitly mentioned in connection with sacrifices in the new Temple (Ezek 45:21-24). Thus it is not surprising that John presents Jesus as both the true Passover lamb and as the true Temple where that sacrifice takes place.

[30] Cf. Watts, *Isaiah's New Exodus in Mark*, 49, 79-81; with specific reference to the Passover connections, see 353-4, 362.

[31] Ps 102:16 (MT v. 17); Isa 2:2-3; 44:28; 56:6-7; 60:7, 13; 62:9; 66:18-23; Jer 31:23; 33:11; Ezek 20:40; 37:26-28; 40:1-47:12; Joel 3:17 (MT 4:17); Mic 4:1-2; Hag 2:9; Zech 1:16; 6:12-15; 8:3; 9:8; 14:16-21.

yet to come.³² Since that goal is Jesus, he abundantly fulfills the patterns and prophecies connected with the Passover lamb, the Tabernacle, and the Temple. When Jesus, its climactic fulfillment, comes, the Temple's anticipatory and provisional nature becomes clear.³³

As discussed in chapter one, if the antitype is the fulfillment or goal of the type as this is understood by a traditional conception of typology, then the fulfillment of the type entails its replacement. In other words, replacement of the type follows from the fact that the antitype is the climactic fulfillment or goal to which the type pointed. One basis for asserting that the antitype is the type's fulfillment is the antitype's correspondence to the type. Such correspondence includes the antitype's ability to fill the place of the type. In addition, as the climactic fulfillment or goal to which the type points, the antitype possesses qualities that make it more excellent than the type. Consequently, once the antitype comes, it both fills the place of the type and surpasses it. At this point, the type becomes obsolete for accomplishing the purposes of God in all ways except one, namely, it still acts as a pointer to its antitype. Such an understanding of fulfillment and replacement appears coherent with John's theology and his understanding of typology.³⁴

It is important to maintain a tight connection between fulfillment and replacement, because it leads to a proper understanding of replacement. It is inadequate to speak of replacement alone, because one risks leaving the impression that the Old Testament type is simply discarded, or replaced by something entirely new.³⁵ When they are kept together, fulfillment and replacement communicate that both continuity and discontinuity exist between the type and the antitype. Thus some of the ambiguity inherent in discussing Jesus' replacement of the Temple is alleviated by those who draw attention to

---

³² Cf. especially, Stek, 'Biblical Typology,' 161-2.

³³ As seen in chapter two, its anticipatory and provisional nature is already hinted at in the OT.

³⁴ For evidence that this line of reasoning is consistent with Johannine theology, see p. 184 and Braun, 'In Spiritu et veritate,' 254; Brown, *John*, 500-1; Bruce, *John*, 43-44; Carson, *John*, 133; Carson, 'John and the Johannine Epistles,' 255-6; Holwerda, *Jesus and Israel*, 74-75; Pancaro, *Law in the Fourth Gospel*, 539. For its agreement with other writings on typology, see Amsler, *L'Ancien Testament dans l'église*, 225-6; Ladd, 'Israel and the Church,' 209-10; Moule, 'Fulfilment-Words in the New Testament,' 298-9; Stek, 'Biblical Typology,' 161-2.

³⁵ Cf. Carson, 'John and the Johannine Epistles,' 256. Also, cf. Chris Wright's complaints against those who stress replacement at the expense of fulfillment ('A Christian Approach to Old Testament Prophecy concerning Israel,' in *Jerusalem Past and Present in the Purposes of God*, ed. Peter W. L. Walker, 2nd ed. [Grand Rapids: Baker, 1994], 18-19).

Jesus as the fulfillment and replacement of the Temple.³⁶

Maintaining a tight connection between fulfillment and replacement is one step toward clarifying the discussion of Jesus' relationship to the Temple. Another significant step toward clarification involves giving an explanation as to how Jesus can be the Temple's replacement. As seen in the above study of the relationship between Jesus and the Temple in the Fourth Gospel, the transition from the Temple to Jesus involves some obvious discontinuities. Thus it hardly seems adequate simply to say that Jesus is the new Temple who replaces the old Temple.³⁷ This would be more fitting if one were describing the Temple as the replacement for the Tabernacle. Traditionally, the way to explain the relationship between Jesus and the Temple was in terms of typology. Typology provides an adequate framework for discussing the transition from the Temple to Jesus. It is therefore significant that in almost all recent treatments of Jesus' fulfillment and replacement of the Temple one finds no mention of typology and very few attempts to provide an explanation for the transition from the Temple to Jesus.³⁸

As long as a clear definition of typology is provided for the reader, there are good reasons to describe the relationship between Jesus and the Temple as 'typological' rather than only saying that he fulfills and replaces the Temple. First, the descriptor 'typological' implies both of these actions and a proper understanding of typology ties these actions together in a coherent explanatory

---

³⁶ One often finds a loose connection between fulfillment and replacement in treatments of the relationship between Jesus and the Temple. In several instances, replacement is explicit and fulfillment is ambiguously implied (see Brown, *John*, 33, 124-5; Smith, 'John,' 107). Schnelle is one of the few authors who stresses replacement with no hint of fulfillment ('Tempelreinigung und die Christologie des Johannesevangeliums,' 368-9, 371). For examples of those who hold together fulfillment and replacement, see Carson, *John*, 182; McKelvey, *New Temple*, 84, 180; Spatafora, *From the 'Temple of God' to God as the Temple*, 106-7, 286-7.

³⁷ Cf. Spatafora, *From the 'Temple of God' to God as the Temple*, 286-7. McKelvey is somewhat more helpful, because he gives a reason why Christ replaces the Temple, namely, 'Christ fulfils what it [the old order] stands for so magnificently that it is necessary for it to have a completely new form' (*New Temple*, 84). He does not clarify, however, why Christ's magnificent fulfillment of the old order necessarily leads to its replacement by something new.

³⁸ It is particularly surprising that one finds no mention of typology in major studies on the topic, including Kerr, *Temple of Jesus' Body*; Coloe, *God Dwells with Us*; McKelvey, *New Temple*; and Spatafora, *From the 'Temple of God' to God as the Temple*. Spatafora mentions in passing that the transition from the Temple to Jesus is consistent with the movement from the old covenant to the new (*From the 'Temple of God' to God as the Temple*, 287). Coloe describes the relationship between Jesus and the Temple as both metaphorical and involving fulfillment and replacement of 'Israel's Temple traditions' (*God Dwells with Us*, 6, 219; see my comments on this in chapter one).

framework.³⁹ Second, saying that Jesus fulfills and replaces the Temple leaves too much room for ambiguity.⁴⁰ It is not clear whether or why these notions belong together. The reader might sense that something is being hinted at, but be quite unequipped to decipher the code. Third, it ties the relationship between Jesus and the Temple to larger discussions regarding the New Testament authors' use of the Old Testament and the relationship between the Testaments. 'Typology' or 'typological' carries more specific content than the terms 'replacement' or 'fulfillment.'⁴¹ Of course, the term 'replacement' is especially open to misunderstanding and is sometimes associated with radical supersessionism.⁴²

A proper appreciation for Temple typology enriches one's understanding of several passages in the Fourth Gospel, as seen in chapters three and four above. This is especially evident with regard to John 2:13-22. Given the results of the above study, it is possible to return once again to the significance of Temple typology for the interpretation of these verses. Jesus displays his zeal for the Temple by casting out those who are making the Temple into a market. In doing so, he is following the pattern set by David, who was zealous for the Temple in his day. The disciples later come to understand that just as zeal for the Temple consumed David so also it consumed his antitype, Jesus. David–Jesus typology makes another contribution in that Jesus, like David and Solomon, is the one who will raise up a Temple (2:19), the replacement for the Jerusalem Temple.⁴³ This Temple is Jesus himself (2:19, 21).⁴⁴

---

[39] This is also true, for example, with regard to the OT sacrifices. As the antitype to the OT sacrifices, Jesus' sacrificial death fulfills and replaces them (Ladd, 'Israel and the Church,' 209-10).

[40] See, for example, Bruce, *John*, 43; McKelvey, *New Temple*, 84, 180; Spatafora, *From the 'Temple of God' to God as the Temple*, 106-7, 286-7.

[41] Cf. Baker, *Two Testaments*, 180. Of course, it is possible to advance good reasons for avoiding 'typological,' 'typology,' or 'type.' The terms may carry with them connotations that some wish to avoid. Even so, it is insufficient to succumb to the common tendency to refer to Jesus as the new Temple or the replacement of the Temple without discussing the nature of the relationship between the two (see, for example, Brown, *John*, 124-5).

[42] Donald G. Bloesch, ' "All Israel Will Be Saved": Supersessionism and the Biblical Witness,' *Int* 43 (1989): 131; Holwerda, *Jesus and Israel*, 2; Ladd, 'Israel and the Church,' 206. 'Radical supersessionism' is my own way of describing supersessionist thought that stresses God's judgment on ethnic Israel, calls the church the new Israel, and does not pay adequate attention to God's continuing plan for the salvation of ethnic Israel. In contrast, Ladd, Bloesch, and Holwerda outline the biblical conception of the church's replacement of Israel, which leaves room for God's unfolding plan of salvation for ethnic Israel (see especially Romans 9-11).

[43] As seen in chapter two, Chronicles is especially careful to make David instrumental in paving the way for the building of the Temple by Solomon. Revelation to David provides the location and plan for the Temple, the replacement for the Tabernacle. As

As seen in chapter four, patterns and prophecies associated with the Temple anticipate the departure and return of God's glory and presence with respect to the body of Jesus.[45] The departure and return of God's presence demonstrate that Jesus is truly the eternal Temple which God is lifting up and glorifying through his death, resurrection, and exaltation. It will not be replaced by another. Is it not also interesting that these patterns and prophecies attribute God's departure to the sinfulness of God's people?[46] In this way, they play a significant role in the destruction of the Temple. Their sin is responsible for the withdrawal of God's protective presence from the Temple.[47] Similarly, the sinfulness of some of God's people leads them to 'destroy this Temple' as Jesus commanded (2:19). It is also due to the sin of God's people generally that God must withdraw his protective presence from the body of Jesus and thus allow this destruction to take place. As a result, the death of Jesus is a consequence of sin. As the true sacrifice offered in the true Temple, it is also the solution to the sin problem of God's people.[48]

Based on this study, it appears that Jesus' role as the true Temple points to a connection between 2:19 and Jesus' lifting up or glorification. When Jesus is lifted up and glorified through the events of his hour, his ability to fulfill and replace the Jerusalem Temple is vindicated. As a result, his disciples, including John, are able to see the connection between the Old Testament patterns and prophecies concerning the Temple and Jesus (2:19, 22). This means that the Scripture referred to in 2:22 probably encompasses more than the usual prophecies appealed to by interpreters.[49] As it turns out, the Old Testament

---

the recipient of such revelation, David prefigures his antitype who comes to reveal the location and nature of the true Temple, the replacement of the Jerusalem Temple. On this point, cf. Daly-Denton, *David in the Fourth Gospel*, 128-9; Coloe, *God Dwells with Us*, 186-90.

[44] Cf. John 20:9. The underlying David–Jesus typology could account for this unique instance in which Jesus says that he raises himself up (on this issue, cf. Meyer, *John*, 114).

[45] See p. 159.

[46] Jer 7:12-14, Ps 78:60, Ezek 8:6; cf. Ezek 43:7-9.

[47] On God's protective presence in the Temple, see chapter two.

[48] The OT anticipates this in the sense that God's people under the new covenant (or in the new age) are presented as righteous and therefore worthy of being blessed by God. Purification and heart change have to happen to make them righteous (see Ezekiel 36). Jesus' blood and the Spirit turn out to be the keys to the purification and heart change (John 3, 6).

[49] Contrary to many interpreters, the reference to 'the Scripture' in 2:22 is probably a reference to OT passages that are relevant to Jesus' death and resurrection rather than a reference back to the citation from Ps 69:9 in 2:17 (cf. 20:9; Bruce, *John*, 77; Meyer, *John*, 115; Morris, *John*, 204; Benedikt Schwank, *Evangelium nach Johannes*, 2nd ed. [St. Ottilien: EOS Verlag, 1998], 95). The reason for this can be found in 2:21-22, i.e.,

patterns and prophecies connected with the Temple predict the death, resurrection, and glorification of Jesus and thus should be counted as contributing to the pool of Old Testament predictions that are relevant to John 2:22 and 20:9.[50]

In conclusion, interpreters of the Fourth Gospel commonly recognize that one finds in it a relationship between Jesus and the Temple. While some emphasize Jesus' replacement of the Temple and others emphasize his fulfillment of the Temple, a balanced approach recognizes Jesus as the one who fulfills and replaces the Temple. Further, evidence from the Fourth Gospel demonstrates that Jesus fulfills and replaces the Temple in a manner consistent with a traditional conception of typology. Thus significant patterns and prophecies regarding the Temple prefigure Jesus who fulfills and surpasses these patterns and prophecies. In doing so, Jesus emerges as the Temple's antitype.

---

the disciples' remembrance of Jesus' saying (which has to do with his death and resurrection) is directly connected with their belief in the Scripture. Therefore the Scripture that they believe in probably has to do with his death and resurrection. The quote from Ps 69:9 could be relevant to Jesus' death, but not to his resurrection (cf. Haenchen, *John 1*, 185).

[50] Bruce is one of the few commentators who defines the scope of the reference to Scripture in 2:22 broadly enough to encompass Jesus' fulfillment of the Temple. He says, 'The "scripture" which the disciples believed might be the total corpus of prophecy which was fulfilled in Jesus' ministry and resurrection, not least those passages which are referred to, implicitly if not in express quotation, in John's account of this incident [the Temple cleansing]' (*John*, 77). Cf. Carson, *John*, 183.

CHAPTER 6

Conclusion

As the above study shows, Jesus' replacement of the Temple is a significant theme in the Fourth Gospel. It touches upon several significant Johannine themes like glory, revelation, death/resurrection/exaltation, divine presence, and fulfillment of Jewish feasts. In light of John's portrayal of this theme, replacement alone appears to be an inadequate characterization of the relationship between Jesus and the Temple. Jesus both fulfills and replaces the Temple. As a result, the relationship between Jesus and the Temple is properly characterized as typological. Chapters one to five present the case for these points.

This chapter reviews the main points made in chapters one to five and their contribution to clarifying the nature of the relationship between Jesus and the Temple in the Fourth Gospel. It also relates the findings of this study to the Temple typology evident in other New Testament writings, especially the Pauline letters and Revelation. Then it suggests some implications of the study for further study and theological reflection.

Review of Chapters 1 to 5

Chapter one states two objectives for the study, namely, to examine John's portrayal of Jesus as the fulfillment and replacement of the Temple and to explore the possibility that the relationship between Jesus and the Temple may properly be described as typological. In preparation for fulfilling these objectives, it lays some basic groundwork, including the study's methodological framework and a review of relevant scholarship. The review of scholarship covers both Jesus' replacement of the Temple in the Fourth Gospel and typology. It demonstrates that a number of interpreters acknowledge the Johannine theme of Jesus' replacement of the Temple. Yet few recent interpreters give attention to the nature of the relationship between Jesus and the Temple. Fewer still follow earlier interpreters in describing the relationship between Jesus and the Temple as typological, though several interpreters give examples of other typological correspondences in the Fourth Gospel. The typology section of the review of scholarship demonstrates that even those who talk about Temple–Jesus typology may not mean exactly the same thing, since two different conceptions of typology exist in contemporary biblical scholarship.

The second chapter looks to the Old Testament to discern what patterns it associates with the Temple. These patterns develop through the repetition of similar beliefs, events, and predictions. They link Solomon's Temple with its predecessor, the Tabernacle, and with its anticipated replacement, the new Temple. Four significant patterns emerge. First, the Temple is regarded as God's chosen dwelling place among his people. His presence there is visibly demonstrated by manifestations of his glory, especially at its consecration. Second, it is an ideal place closely associated with God's majesty and experience of his abundant provision. Third, a new, eternal, glorified Temple is a prominent part of prophetic hopes for the future of Israel. Fourth, in spite of the Temple's greatness, the Old Testament does recognize its limitations. These limitations may be hints that the Temple is not the ultimate dwelling place of God in the midst of his people. These patterns anticipate John's portrayal of Jesus as the one who fulfills and replaces the Temple.

Several verses of the Fourth Gospel are commonly associated with Jesus' replacement of the Temple, that is, 1:14, 1:51, 2:18-22, and 4:20-24. Chapter three examines these verses for initial evidence of Jesus' replacement of the Temple. John 1:14 and 1:51 suggest that Jesus' replacement of the Temple encompasses the replacement of its predecessors, namely, Bethel and the Tabernacle. According to 1:14, Jesus is presented as the fulfillment and replacement of the Tabernacle and the Temple as the place where God dwells among his people and manifests his glory to them. John 1:51 makes a similar point: Jesus fulfills and replaces Bethel, the Tabernacle, and the Temple as the place where God reveals himself to his people. These verses anticipate 4:20-24. In 4:20-24, Jesus describes the true worship that he inaugurates. First, it is not tied to the Jerusalem Temple (4:21). Second, it is worship in spirit and truth, which are aspects of God's abundant provision for his people. Examining John's treatment of spirit, truth, and Jewish feasts reveals that the true worship fulfills worship at the Jerusalem Temple. The cumulative evidence from 1:14, 1:51, and 4:20-24 leads one to posit that Jesus fulfills and replaces the Temple as the locus of God's presence, glory, revelation, and abundant provision.

Chapter three also examines John 2:18-22. These verses explicitly connect Jesus' body and the Temple. At the same time, they associate Jesus' role as the Temple with his death/resurrection/exaltation. It is therefore necessary to examine what Jesus' death/resurrection/exaltation contributes to one's understanding of his replacement of the Temple. Similarly, the relationship between worship in spirit and truth and worship at the Jerusalem Temple (4:20-24) becomes clearer in light of the Fourth Gospel's treatment of the Jewish feasts. John 2:18-22 and 4:20-24 indicate that Jesus' replacement of the Temple reaches beyond the four texts examined in chapter three.[1]

Chapter four follows up on the insights gained from chapter three. The two sections of this chapter are complementary in that both lead to the conclusion that Jesus' replacement of the Temple is significant for John's portrayal of Jesus' death/resurrection/exaltation. According to the first section, John's language of lifting up and glorification marks his death/resurrection/exaltation as the decisive event whereby God reveals himself for judgment and salvation. God reveals himself by lifting up and glorifying Jesus, the true Temple. The primary Old Testament background for the lifting up and glorification of Jesus as the true Temple is found in Isaiah. According to Isaiah, part of God's decisive action on behalf of his people, and for revealing himself to the nations, is the lifting up of the Temple above all other temples. This expectation finds its fulfillment in Jesus, the Temple's antitype. It follows that Jesus is superior to any other temple, including the Jerusalem Temple. The lifting up and glorification of Jesus as the true Temple suggests the advent of the age of salvation in which God gathers his people, provides for them, and draws the nations to himself.[2]

The second section of chapter four demonstrates that Jesus' fulfillment of the Jewish Feasts and the Temple are both connected with the nature and content of God's provision for all his people. Jesus is and gives the true food and true drink that deliver believers from thirst and hunger. He accomplishes this by offering his flesh and blood for the life of the world and sending the Spirit to enrich believers with the salvific benefits of his sacrificial death. Thus he simultaneously fulfills the Passover, Feast of Tabernacles, Feast of Dedication, and the Temple. Looking at the Temple in particular, he fulfills and replaces it as the place of sacrifice and the place from which God pours out his abundant provision upon his people.

Chapter five examines the nature of the relationship between Jesus and the Temple as portrayed in the Fourth Gospel. The evidence for such a relationship leads to the conclusion that replacement of the Temple is only one aspect of the relationship between Jesus and the Temple. Indeed the evidence for Jesus' replacement of the Temple is also evidence for his fulfillment of the Temple. As a result, a more balanced approach recognizes Jesus as the one who both fulfills and replaces the Temple. Jesus' ability to fulfill Old Testament prophecies and patterns associated with the Temple means that some measure of continuity exists between him and the Temple. At the same time, it is difficult to ignore the discontinuity between Jesus and the Temple. When Jesus fulfills the patterns and prophecies associated with the Temple, he does so in a

---

[1] Of course, one could argue that 1:14 and 1:51 also anticipate the development of themes that elucidate Jesus' replacement of the Temple. Yet 2:18-22 and 4:20-24 are singled out, because they announce the replacement of the Temple more clearly.

[2] Cf. John 12:32, 10:16, 11:52; also 6:44-58.

way that surpasses or transcends them. As seen in chapter one, this means that the relationship between Jesus and the Temple is consistent with a traditional conception of typology. Thus significant patterns and prophecies regarding the Temple prefigure Jesus who fulfills and surpasses these patterns and prophecies. In doing so, Jesus emerges as the Temple's antitype.

John's Temple Typology in New Testament Perspective

Having examined the Fourth Gospel's presentation of Jesus as the Temple's antitype, it seems appropriate to ask how this theme relates to the use of Temple typology elsewhere in the New Testament. The Temple typology found in Paul and Revelation is given special attention, since interpreters often relate the Temple typology found there to that of the Fourth Gospel. The Temple typology found in Paul is briefly surveyed first. Paul presents the church as the Temple of God. This use of Temple typology appears more divergent from Jesus as the Temple's antitype than the Temple typology that one finds in Revelation. It is also a preparatory step along the way to the ultimate fulfillment of the Temple in Revelation 21-22, which is the culmination anticipated by John's presentation of Jesus as the Temple's antitype. Therefore the final task of this section is to relate the Temple typology of the Fourth Gospel and that of Revelation.

The Temple typology found in Paul focuses particular attention upon the church as the dwelling place of God through the Spirit. Only in 2 Corinthians 6:16 does Paul neglect to mention the Spirit as the means by which God dwells in his Temple, the church.[3] Through the indwelling Holy Spirit, the church currently experiences an abundant measure of the fulfillment of God's promise that he would dwell among his people (2 Cor 6:16).[4]

Paul also sees further implications of the church's role as the Temple. First, God's Temple is to be a holy place.[5] Therefore one should beware of undermining its holiness by causing divisions (1 Cor 3:17), engaging in sexual immorality (1 Cor 6:19), or becoming unequally yoked with unbelievers (2 Cor

---

[3] The Spirit is mentioned in 1 Cor 3:16, 6:19; Eph 2:22. Even though the body of the individual Christian is the Temple of the Holy Spirit in 1 Cor 6:19, it is important to note that 'the apostle's point of departure is not the individual (as in Stoic anthropology) but the community. To his way of thinking, God the Spirit does not dwell in the individual *qua* individual but as a member of the Christian community' (McKevley, *New Temple*, 104, 106; cf. B. H. Throckmorton, 'The ναός in Paul,' in *SE*, ed. E. Livingstone, vol. 7 [Berlin: Akademie-Verlag, 1982], 501).

[4] 2 Cor 6:16 cites Lev 26:12 (cf. Zech 2:10; Ezek 37:27; 43: 7, 9). This climactic fulfillment in the church now is the guarantee and anticipation of the promise's ultimate fulfillment in the new Jerusalem (Rev 21:3) (cf. Stek, 'Biblical Typology,' 162). See below.

[5] Cf. Throckmorton, 'The ναός in Paul,' 498-501.

6:14-17).[6] Second, the Temple is a unified construction that includes all Christians, Jews and Gentiles (Eph 2:19-22).[7] In Christ, God is only building one Temple, just as there was in the Old Testament only one Tabernacle and then only one divinely consecrated Temple.[8]

The 'in Christ' element of this Temple is important for understanding the relationship between the church as the Temple and Christ as the Temple. This Temple is not only structurally dependent upon Christ its cornerstone, its very existence is also set forth as 'in Christ' (Eph 2:20-22).[9] In other words, the entire building is organically related to Christ and no part of it exists outside of him.[10] It is by union with Christ that believers are incorporated into this Temple, which is quite similar to another Pauline image for the church, namely, the body of Christ.[11] As God's Temple in Christ, the church is currently the special locus for the presence of God in the world.[12]

Although the Fourth Gospel does not refer to the church as the Temple of God, it contains the theological bases for this Pauline title.[13] John sometimes portrays the church in the world such that its continuity with Christ is apparent. For example, the church manifests the Father's glory in the world (15:4-10). In doing so, they are following Christ who manifested the Father's glory in the world through his obedient life (17:4).[14] Similarly, after Jesus goes away, he gives his disciples the Spirit so that it is in them. Previously, Jesus himself was

---

[6] One finds a number of examples in the OT and Jewish literature where God punishes people for desecrating or destroying his holy Temple (for example, Lev 10:1-3, 2 Chr 26:16-23, Jer 51:11, Dan 9:27, 2 Macc 3:22-40, 3 Macc 1:9-2:24).

[7] Cf. the related Petrine passage, 1 Peter 2:4-8. On the links between these two texts, see I. Howard Marshall, 'Church and Temple in the New Testament,' *TynBul* 40 (1989): 213-5.

[8] McKelvey, *New Temple*, 106-7; cf. Joseph Coppens, 'The Spiritual Temple in the Pauline Letters and Its Background,' in *SE*, ed. E. Livingstone, vol. 6 (Berlin: Akademie-Verlag, 1973), 56.

[9] Clowney, 'Final Temple,' 126-7; McKelvey, *New Temple*, 115-6; Franz Mussner, *Christus das All und die Kirche: Studien zur Theologie des Epheserbriefes*, 2nd ed., TThSt, vol. 5 (Trier: Paulinus Verlag, 1968), 114-5. Thus one Christ means one unified Temple.

[10] Edmund P. Clowney, 'Toward a Biblical Doctrine of the Church,' *WTJ* 31 (1968-69): 68; McKelvey, *New Temple*, 116.

[11] Ernest Best, *One Body in Christ: A Study in the Relationship of the Church to Christ in the Epistles of the Apostle Paul* (London: SPCK, 1955), 167; McKelvey, *New Temple*, 115-6; John A. T. Robinson, *The Body: A Study in Pauline Theology* (London: SCM, 1952), 64-65.

[12] Cf. McKelvey, *New Temple*, 117.

[13] Cf. Schnackenburg, *John*, vol. 1, 352.

[14] Other examples might include the church's activities of shepherding (10:14, 21:15-17) and humble, sacrificial service (13:3-17).

the locus of the Spirit.[15] Now the church is the special dwelling place of the Spirit in the world (14:16-17).[16] Having the Spirit in them also entails union with Jesus and the Father (14:20-23).[17] John and Paul therefore agree that the church is currently the special locus for the presence of God in the world. This is due to the Spirit dwelling in her through which she experiences union with Christ.

Though John and Paul agree that God already dwells in his church through the Spirit, both realize that God will one day dwell in the midst of his people in an even fuller measure. At that point, they will actually be with Jesus.[18] As a result, the church is the current manifestation of the Temple, but it awaits the advent of the final Temple.[19]

For the advent of the final Temple, one must look to the book of Revelation. Its advent is the climax of Revelation's Temple theme. The Temple theme of the book of Revelation presents three Temple images that converge in Revelation 21-22.[20] First, the book contains two announcements of the future Temple in which the saints will dwell forever (3:12, 7:15). Second, until Revelation 21-22, the dwelling place of God is in heaven and this dwelling place is called God's Temple on several occasions.[21] Third, prior to the advent of the new Jerusalem, the Temple is used as a symbol for God's protection of his people during their time of tribulation.[22]

The convergence of the second and third Temple images in Revelation 21-22 is straightforward. With respect to the second image, Revelation 21:2-3 introduces the descent of the new Jerusalem from heaven and announces that God has now come to dwell in the midst of his people. After the new Jerusalem's appearance, there is no longer any need to say that God dwells in

---

[15] Cf. 3:34, 7:37-39.

[16] Furthermore Jesus and the Father are said to dwell in the church, which affirms that it is truly the dwelling place of God in the world (14:23).

[17] Cf. 15:1-7, 17:21-26. Cf. Brown, *John*, 1141; Ridderbos, *John*, 508.

[18] John 12:26, 14:3, 17:24; 2 Cor 5:8.

[19] Cf. Clowney, 'Final Temple,' 129; McKelvey, *New Temple*, 178.

[20] While these three Temple images are central to Revelation's Temple theme, Temple imagery (or cultic imagery) is a significant contributor in a number of passages (William Riley, 'Temple Imagery and the Book of Revelation: Ancient Near Eastern Temple Ideology and Cultic Resonances in the Apocalypse,' *PIBA* 6 [1982]: 88-96).

[21] Rev 11:19; 14:15, 17; 15:5, 6, 8; 16:1, 17. God's Temple in heaven is also significant for a number of other passages where it is not specifically identified as such (like Revelation 4).

[22] Rev 11:1-2. Cf. George R. Beasley-Murray, *The Book of Revelation*, rev. ed., NCB (Grand Rapids: Eerdmans, 1981), 182. Rev 11:1-2 is a notoriously difficult passage. It is not clear whether the church is the Temple of God or is limited to the worshipers in the Temple. Either way, it is an anticipatory Temple that will be replaced by the new Jerusalem.

heaven, but also on earth in the Temple.[23] The description of the new Jerusalem confirms that it has the unique honor of being the replacement for the Temple in heaven. For example, it contains the throne of God, which was previously located in heaven or the Temple in heaven.[24] Next, with respect to the third image, the new Jerusalem is also the replacement for the symbolic Temple of 11:1-2; that is, it is a place of security and safety for the people of God.[25]

The first Temple image is more challenging, because it seems to stand in tension with the announcement that there is no Temple in the new Jerusalem (21:22). The tension is resolved by seeing 3:12 and 7:15 as initial hints that the new Jerusalem is appropriately understood as both city and Temple. Revelation 3:12 is particularly significant, because it associates the eternal dwelling place of the righteous with both the new Temple and the new Jerusalem. Revelation 7:15 points in the same direction, because the saints are described as being in God's Temple and before his throne. The saints' proximity to God's throne fits with the picture of the new Jerusalem in 22:1-3. From 3:12 and 7:15, it follows that the saints in the new Jerusalem must also be in God's Temple. In other words, John must mean for the reader to regard the entire city as God's Temple.

Fortunately, John provides further evidence for understanding the new Jerusalem as God's eternal Temple. One piece of evidence is the statement that there is no Temple in the city, because God and Jesus are its Temple (21:22). If the city is itself playing the role of God's Temple, then it has no need for another Temple. The most noteworthy evidence is probably found in 21:16, namely, the city is a cube like the holy of holies in the Temple (1 Kgs 6:20).[26] Hence its shape marks it as a most holy place fit for God's presence and his throne.[27] As such, the new Jerusalem is not merely a new Temple, but the

---

[23] As seen in chapter two, the OT and Jewish literature describe God's true dwelling place as 'heaven.' See, for instance, 1 Kgs 8:27, 9:3 // 2 Chr 6:18, 7:16; Pss 20:6 (MT v. 7), 33:13-14, 80:14 (MT v. 15), 102:19 (MT v. 20), 103:19, 113:5, 115:3, 123:1; Isa 66:1; 3 Macc 2:15.

[24] See, for instance, 4:1-2, 12:5, 16:17, 22:1-3. Cf. Richard Bauckham, *The Theology of the Book of Revelation*, New Testament Theology (Cambridge: Cambridge University Press, 1993), 140. In Heb 8-9, one finds something similar in that God's true Tabernacle is currently in heaven. Believers already have access to this holy place (10:19-22). Yet they still await the final revelation of the 'heavenly Jerusalem' (12:22, 26-28).

[25] Cf. 7:16-17; 21:4, 8, 25; 22:5. In these verses, note the city's freedom from mourning, pain, and immorality as well as the city's open gates and eternal light.

[26] Bauckham, *Theology of Revelation*, 136; Beasley-Murray, *Revelation*, 322; McKelvey, *New Temple*, 176.

[27] The throne of God was associated in the OT with the ark of the covenant in the holy of holies (1 Sam 4:4, 2 Sam 6:2 // 1 Chr 13:6; 1 Kgs 8:4-11 // 2 Chr 5:5-14; 2 Kgs 19:15). Similarly, in Ezek 43:7, the Temple is called the place of God's throne. In addition, Jer 3:17 is relevant to Rev 21-22, because it identifies Jerusalem as God's throne and as the replacement of the ark of the covenant (3:16).

Temple 'in its perfected and eternal' form.[28] Since the city has the character of the holy of holies, those who dwell in it behold both God's throne and God himself (22:3-4). In conclusion, God and Jesus take the place of the Temple in the city and the entire city is therefore the Temple of God anticipated by 3:12 and 7:15.[29]

It is now possible to fit the basic elements of the Fourth Gospel's Temple typology with that found in Paul and Revelation. According to the Fourth Gospel, Christ is the true Temple, the dwelling place of God in the midst of his people. Those who are with him during his ministry witness God dwelling among them (John 1:14). His death/resurrection/exaltation makes it possible for his disciples to continue to experience God dwelling among them, because it results in the gift of the Spirit. The Spirit enables his disciples to experience union with Jesus and the Father. This union will come to fruition when they eventually go to dwell with Jesus where he is (14:3). These points anticipate the Temple typology found in Paul and Revelation. When Paul calls the church the Temple of God, he is focusing upon the church as the current, already abundant realization of God's promise to dwell among his people. God dwells in this Temple through the Spirit. The entire Temple is 'in Christ,' that is, in union with Christ. Then, in the book of Revelation, one finds the consummation of God's promise to dwell among his people. As the Fourth Gospel anticipated, the union between Christ and the people of God comes to fruition in the New Jerusalem when God's people are finally with God in the city of God (21:3). In that city, they are able to behold Father and Son who are its Temple.

Some Implications for Further Study and Theological Reflection

The Fourth Gospel is a theologically rich book. It would be presumptuous to think that this study has brought to light all of its riches with regard to Temple–Jesus typology. Furthermore, given the interconnectedness of Johannine theology, one would expect the preceding study to uncover numerous possible avenues for further study and reflection. A few of these deserve special mention.

As pointed out in chapters one and five, it is common for interpreters of the Fourth Gospel to say that Jesus fulfills or replaces a given Old Testament person, event, or institution. It is much less common to find a discussion of how one is to understand such an instance of fulfillment or replacement. It seems

---

[28] McKelvey, *New Temple*, 176; cf. Beale, *Temple and the Church's Mission*, 350. Other evidence for the Temple-like character of the city can be found in its decorations. The pure gold of 21:18 recalls the pure gold that gilded Solomon's Temple, the ark, and other Tabernacle furnishings (Exod 25, 2 Chr 3:4-8). The precious stones of 21:19-20 recall the precious stones that adorned Solomon's Temple (cf. esp. 2 Chr 3:6 [LXX]).

[29] Stevenson, *Power and Place*, 270.

appropriate to ask how and why Jesus fulfills or replaces Old Testament persons, events, and institutions. In doing so, interpreters will present a clearer picture of the nature of the relationship between Jesus and his Old Testament predecessors.

One way to explain a relationship between Jesus and an Old Testament entity is in terms of typology. Yet typological explanations would benefit from further study of the typology evident in the biblical authors. Proponents of traditional typology have as much to learn from such observation as anyone else.[30] In particular, the characteristics of the typology evident in the Fourth Gospel have been given little attention.[31]

Given the number of works concerned with Moses and the Exodus events, one might be inclined to think that the major typological relationships of the Fourth Gospel have received sufficient treatment. Yet in reading the Fourth Gospel, one finds other possible types, including Jacob, Israel, David, the Temple, the feasts, and the Sabbath.[32] As seen above in the case of the Temple, consideration of these types can be fruitful for appreciating John's concern to portray the relationship between Jesus and the Old Testament types that point to him. The nature and significance of the typological relationships that John develops would benefit from further attention to several particular aspects, including (1) the nature of the relationship between Jesus and an Old Testament person, event, or institution; (2) the common characteristics of the typological relationships found in the Fourth Gospel; (3) the variety of Old Testament types that point to Jesus; (4) hints in the Old Testament about the predictive nature of the Old Testament types that Jesus fulfills; and (5) methodological guidelines for identifying viable, defensible typological relationships.

Some readers will be curious about the implications of this study for the future of the Temple in Christian thought, specifically about the rebuilding of the Temple in Jerusalem. This is a debated topic and it would not be fair to say any more about it than to summarize what the above study clearly supports. The Fourth Gospel does not appear to be anticipating another Temple in Jerusalem. According to John, Jesus is the true Temple and the future of this Temple is hinted at with the suggestion that believers will one day join Jesus where he is (John 14:3, 17:24).

---

[30] Cf. Davidson, *Typology in Scripture*, 421-3.
[31] Helpful treatments in this regard include Carson, 'John and the Johannine Epistles,' 245-63; Goppelt, *Typos*, 194-5; Longenecker, *Biblical Exegesis in the Apostolic Period*, 152-7.
[32] For these and other possible types, see the following treatments: François-Marie Braun, *Jean le théologien*, vol. 2, *Les grandes traditions d'Israël et l'accord des Écritures selon le quatrième évangile*, EBib (Paris: J. Gabalda and Co., 1964); Bruce, *Time Is Fulfilled*, 35-53; Carson, 'John and the Johannine Epistles,' 253-6; Westcott, *John*, lxvii-lxviii.

Related to this, since Jesus is the true Temple and the fulfillment of the Old Testament feasts, it might pay dividends for Christians to reflect upon the logic of these typological relationships. If the Temple and Old Testament feasts anticipate and reach their fullness through the blessings that Jesus brings, one wonders if we are doing an adequate job of celebrating what God has done for us. Do we celebrate in a way that is consistent with the fact that we have even more to celebrate about? Reading about celebrating these feasts in various Jewish sources made me wonder if we could learn something from the joy and wonder that celebrating them at the Temple appears to have created. Some Christians are now following the lead of Jewish Christians in celebrating the Old Testament feasts in such a way as to point to Christ. This is a good start, but a number of Christians are struggling to celebrate Christmas and Easter in winsome ways that draw people to Jesus and the gifts that he brings to all who believe. A void exists here that deserves theological reflection and attention to Christian teaching and practice. Celebration of the Old Testament feasts provides more helpful instruction than Christians often realize. At the very least, we need their encouragement to rejoice and celebrate together because of all that God has done for us.

Bibliography

Aalen, Sverre. 'אוֹר.' Translated by John T. Willis. In *Theological Dictionary of the Old Testament*, ed. G. Johannes Botterweck et al., vol. 1, 147-66. Grand Rapids: Eerdmans, 1977.

Abbott, Edwin A. *Johannine Grammar*. 2 vols. London: Adam and Charles Black, 1906.

Abelson, J. *The Immanence of God in Rabbinical Literature*. London: Macmillan, 1912.

Achtemeier, Elizabeth. 'Typology.' In *Interpreter's Dictionary of the Bible Supplement*, ed. Keith Crim, 926-7. Nashville: Abingdon, 1976.

Ackroyd, Peter R. *Exile and Restoration: A Study of Hebrew Thought of the Sixth Century B.C.* Old Testament Library. Philadelphia: Westminster, 1968.

—— 'The Temple Vessels – A Continuity Theme.' In *Studies in the Religions of Ancient Israel*, 166-81. Vetus Testamentum Supplements, vol. 23. Leiden: E. J. Brill, 1972.

Alexander, Philip S. 'Rabbinic Judaism and the New Testament.' *Zeitschrift für die neutestamentliche Wissenschaft* 74 (1983): 237-46.

Allen, Leslie C. *Ezekiel 1-19*. Word Biblical Commentary, vol. 28. Dallas: Word Books, 1994.

—— *Ezekiel 20-48*. Word Biblical Commentary, vol. 29. Dallas: Word Books, 1990.

Allison, Dale C., Jr. 'The Living Water (John 4:10-14; 6:35c; 7:37-39).' *St. Vladimir's Theological Quarterly* 30 (1986): 143-57.

Alsup, John E. 'Typology.' In *Anchor Bible Dictionary*, ed. D. N. Freedman, vol. 6, 682-5. New York: Doubleday, 1992.

Amsler, Samuel. *L'Ancien Testament dans l'église: Essai d'herméneutique chrétienne*. Neuchâtel, Switzerland: Delachaux and Niestlé, 1960.

—— 'Où en est la typologie de l'Ancien Testament?' *Etudes théologiques et religieuses* 27 (1952): 75-81.

—— 'Prophétie et typologie.' *Revue de théologie et de philosophie* 3 (1953): 139-48.

Anderson, Paul N. *The Christology of the Fourth Gospel: Its Unity and Disunity in the Light of John 6*. Valley Forge, Pa.: Trinity, 1996.

Ashton, John. *Studying John: Approaches to the Fourth Gospel*. Oxford: Clarendon, 1994.

—— *Understanding the Fourth Gospel*. Oxford: Clarendon, 1991.

Aune, David E. *Revelation 17-22*. Word Biblical Commentary, vol. 52c. Nashville: Thomas Nelson, 1998.

Averbeck, Richard E. 'מוֹעֵד.' In *New International Dictionary of Old Testament Theology and Exegesis*, ed. W. VanGemeren, vol. 2, 873-7. Grand Rapids: Zondervan, 1997.

—— 'מִקְדָּשׁ.' In *New International Dictionary of Old Testament Theology and*

Exegesis, ed. W. VanGemeren, vol. 2, 1078-87. Grand Rapids: Zondervan, 1997.
— 'מִשְׁכָּן.' In *New International Dictionary of Old Testament Theology and Exegesis*, ed. W. VanGemeren, vol. 2, 1130-4. Grand Rapids: Zondervan, 1997.
Baker, David L. *Two Testaments, One Bible: A Study of the Theological Relationship Between the Old & New Testaments*. Downers Grove, Ill.: InterVarsity, 1991.
Balfour, Glenn. 'The Jewishness of John's Use of the Scriptures in John 6:31 and 7:37-38.' *Tyndale Bulletin* 46 (1995): 357-80.
Ball, David Mark. *'I Am' in John's Gospel: Literary Function, Background and Theological Implications*. Journal for the Study of the New Testament, Supplement, no. 124. Sheffield: Journal for the Study of the Old Testament, 1996.
Barker, Margaret. *The Gate of Heaven: The History and Symbolism of the Temple in Jerusalem*. London: SPCK, 1991.
Barrett, Charles K. 'Attitudes to the Temple in the Acts of the Apostles.' In *Templum Amicitiae: Essays on the Second Temple Presented to Ernst Bammel*, ed. William Horbury, 345-67. Journal for the Study of the New Testament, Supplement, no. 48. Sheffield: Sheffield Academic Press, 1991.
— *The Gospel according to John: An Introduction with Commentary and Notes on the Greek Text*. 2nd ed. Philadelphia: Westminster, 1978.
— 'The House of Prayer and the Den of Thieves.' In *Jesus und Paulus: Festschrift für Werner Georg Kümmel zum 70. Geburtstag*, ed. E. Earle Ellis and Erich Grässer, 2nd ed., 13-20. Göttingen: Vandenhoeck and Ruprecht, 1978.
Bauckham, Richard. 'James and the Jerusalem Church.' In *The Book of Acts in Its First Century Setting*. Vol. 4, *The Book of Acts in Its Palestinian Setting*, ed. Richard Bauckham, 415-80. Grand Rapids: Eerdmans, 1995.
— 'Jesus' Demonstration in the Temple.' In *Law and Religion: Essays on the Place of the Law in Israel and Early Christianity*, ed. Barnabas Lindars, 72-89. Cambridge: James Clarke and Co., 1988.
— *The Theology of the Book of Revelation*. New Testament Theology. Cambridge: Cambridge University Press, 1993.
Beale, G. K. 'Did Jesus and His Followers Preach the Right Doctrine from the Wrong Texts? An Examination of the Presuppositions of Jesus' and the Apostles' Exegetical Method.' In *The Right Doctrine from the Wrong Texts: Essays on the Use of the Old Testament in the New*, ed. G. K. Beale, 387-404. Grand Rapids: Baker Books, 1994.
— *The Temple and the Church's Mission: A Biblical Theology of the Dwelling Place of God*. New Studies in Biblical Theology, vol. 17. Downers Grove, Ill.: InterVarsity Press, 2004.
Beasley-Murray, George R. *John*. Word Biblical Commentary, vol. 36. Waco: Word Books, 1987.
— *The Book of Revelation*. Rev. ed. New Century Bible. Grand Rapids: Eerdmans, 1981.
Becker, Jürgen. *Das Evangelium nach Johannes*. Ökumenischer Taschenbuch-

Kommentar, vol. 4, no. 1. Gütersloh: Gerd Mohn, 1979.
— 'Das Johannesevangelium im Streit der Methoden (1980-1984).' *Theologische Rundschau* 51 (1986): 1-78.
Belleville, Linda L. 'The Theological Significance of Ὕδωρ in the Johannine Writings.' M.A. thesis, Trinity Evangelical Divinity School, 1980.
Bengel, Johann Albrecht. *Gnomon of the New Testament: Pointing out from the Natural Force of the Words, the Simplicity, Depth, Harmony and Saving Power of Its Divine Thoughts*. Translated by Charlton T. Lewis and Marvin R. Vincent. Vol. 1. Philadelphia: Perkinpine and Higgins, 1860.
Bernard, J. H. *A Critical and Exegetical Commentary on the Gospel according to St. John*. International Critical Commentary, vol. 29, pt. 1. Edinburgh: T. and T. Clark, 1928.
Best, Ernest. *One Body in Christ: A Study in the Relationship of the Church to Christ in the Epistles of the Apostle Paul*. London: SPCK, 1955.
Betz, Otto. '"To Worship God in Spirit and Truth": Reflections on John 4:20-26.' Translated by Nora Quigley et al. In *Jesus der Messias Israels: Aufsätze zur biblischen Theologie*, 420-38. Wissenschaftliche Untersuchungen zum Neuen Testament, vol. 42. Tübingen: J.C.B. Mohr (Paul Siebeck), 1987.
Bieder, Werner. 'πνεῦμα.' Translated by G. Bromiley. In *Theological Dictionary of the New Testament*, ed. G. Friedrich, vol. 6, 368-75. Grand Rapids: Eerdmans, 1968.
Bietenhard, Hans. 'ὄνομα.' Translated by G. Bromiley. In *Theological Dictionary of the New Testament*, ed. G. Kittel and G. Friedrich, vol. 5, 242-83. Grand Rapids: Eerdmans, 1967.
Black, Matthew. *The Book of Enoch or I Enoch: A New English Edition*. Studia in Veteris Testamenti pseudepigraphica, no. 7. Leiden: E. J. Brill, 1985.
Blank, Josef. *Krisis: Untersuchungen zur johanneischen Christologie und Eschatologie*. Freiburg: Lambertus Verlag, 1964.
Blass, F., A. Debrunner, and R. Funk. *A Greek Grammar of the New Testament and Other Early Christian Literature*. Chicago: University of Chicago Press, 1961.
Blocher, Henri. 'The "Analogy of Faith" in the Study of Scripture: In Search of Justification and Guide-lines.' In *The Challenge of Evangelical Theology: Essays in Approach and Method*, ed. Nigel M. de S. Cameron, 17-38. Edinburgh: Rutherford House Books, 1987.
Block, Daniel I. *The Book of Ezekiel: Chapters 1-24*. New International Commentary on the Old Testament. Grand Rapids: Eerdmans, 1997.
— *The Book of Ezekiel: Chapters 25-48*. New International Commentary on the Old Testament. Grand Rapids: Eerdmans, 1998.
Bloesch, Donald G. '"All Israel Will Be Saved": Supersessionism and the Biblical Witness.' *Interpretation* 49 (1978): 130-42.
Blomberg, Craig L. 'Interpreting the Old Testament Prophetic Literature in Matthew: Double Fulfillment.' *Trinity Journal*, new series, 23 (2002): 17-33.
Boer, Martinus C. de. *Johannine Perspectives on the Death of Jesus*. Kampen: Kok Pharos, 1996.

Boers, Hendrikus. *Neither on This Mountain nor in Jerusalem: A Study of John 4*. SBL Monograph Series, vol. 35. Atlanta: Scholars Press, 1988.
Bockmuehl, Markus. '1QS and Salvation at Qumran.' In *The Complexities of Second Temple Judaism*, ed. D. A. Carson et al, vol. 1 of *Justification and Variegated Nomism*, 381-414. Wissenschaftliche Untersuchungen zum Neuen Testament, 2nd series, vol. 140. Grand Rapids: Baker, 2001.
— *This Jesus: Martyr, Lord, Messiah*. Downers Grove, Ill.: InterVarsity, 1994.
Boismard, Marie-Émile. *St. John's Prologue*. Translated by Carisbrooke Dominicans. Westminster, Md.: Newman, 1957.
— *Moïse ou Jésus: Essai de christologie johannique*. Bibliotheca ephemeridum theologicarum lovaniensium, no. 84. Leuven: Leuven University, 1988.
Botha, J. Eugene. *Jesus and the Samaritan Woman: A Speech Act Reading of John 4:1-42*. Novum Testamentum, Supplement, vol. 65. Leiden: E. J. Brill, 1991.
Braun, François-Marie. 'Avoir soif et boire (Jn 4,10-14; 7,37-39).' In *Mélanges bibliques en hommage au R. P. Béda Rigaux*, ed. A. Descamps and A. De Halleux, 247-58. Gembloux: Duculot, 1970.
— 'L'expulsion des vendeurs du temple (Mt., XXI, 12-17, 23-27; Mc., XI, 15-19, 27-33; Lc., XIX, 45-XX, 8; Jo., II, 13-22).' *Revue biblique* 38 (1929): 178-200.
— 'In Spiritu et veritate.' *Revue thomiste* 52 (1952): 245-74.
— *Jean le théologien*. Vol. 2, *Les grandes traditions d'Israël et l'accord des Écritures selon le quatrième évangile*. Etudes bibliques. Paris: J. Gabalda and Co., 1964.
— *Jean le théologien: Sa théologie*. Vol. 3, *Le mystère de Jésus-Christ*. Etudes bibliques. Paris: J. Gabalda and Co., 1966.
— 'Quatre 'signes' johanniques de l'unité chrétienne.' *New Testament Studies* 9 (1962-63): 147-55.
Braun, Roddy. *1 Chronicles*. Word Biblical Commentary, vol. 14. Waco: Word Books, 1986.
— 'Solomon, the Chosen Temple Builder: The Significance of 1 Chronicles 22, 28, and 29 for the Theology of Chronicles.' *Journal of Biblical Literature* 95 (1976): 581-90.
Breck, John. *Spirit of Truth: The Holy Spirit in Johannine Tradition*. Vol. 1, *The Origins of Johannine Pneumatology*. Crestwood, N.Y.: St. Vladimir's Seminary Press, 1991.
Brettler, Marc Z. *The Creation of History in Ancient Israel*. New York: Routledge, 1995.
Briggs, Robert A. *Jewish Temple Imagery in the Book of Revelation*. Studies in Biblical Literature, no. 10. New York: Peter Lang, 1999.
Brockington, L. H. 'The Greek Translator of Isaiah and His Interest in ΔΟΞΑ.' *Vetus Testamentum* 1 (1951): 23-32.
Brodie, Thomas L. *The Gospel according to John: A Literary and Theological Commentary*. New York: Oxford University, 1993.
Brooke, George J. 'The Temple Scroll and the New Testament.' In *Temple Scroll Studies: Papers Presented at the International Symposium on the Temple Scroll*, ed. George J. Brooke, 181-200. Journal for the Study of the

Pseudepigrapha: Supplement Series, no. 7. Sheffield: Sheffield Academic Press, 1989.
Brown, Raymond E. *The Gospel according to John*. Anchor Bible, vol. 29. New York: Doubleday, 1966.
Bruce, Frederick F. *The Gospel of John: Introduction, Exposition and Notes*. Grand Rapids: Eerdmans, 1983.
— *The Time is Fulfilled: Five Aspects of the Fulfilment of the Old Testament in the New*. Grand Rapids: Eerdmans, 1978.
Bryan, Christopher. 'Shall We Sing Hallel in the Days of the Messiah?: A Glance at John 2:1-3:21.' *St. Luke's Journal of Theology* 29 (1985): 25-36.
Buchanan, George W. *Typology and the Gospel*. New York: University Press of America, 1987.
— 'The Use of Rabbinic Literature for New Testament Research.' *Biblical Theology Bulletin* 3 (1977): 110-22.
Bultmann, Rudolf. *The Gospel of John: A Commentary*. Translated by G. R. Beasley-Murray et al. Philadelphia: Westminster, 1971.
— 'Ursprung und Sinn der Typologie als hermeneutische Methode.' *Theologische Literaturzeitung* (1950): 205-12.
— *Theology of the New Testament*. Translated by Kendrick Grobel. Vol. 2. New York: Charles Scribner's Sons, 1955.
Burge, Gary M. *The Anointed Community: The Holy Spirit in the Johannine Tradition*. Grand Rapids: Eerdmans, 1987.
Burkett, Delbert. *The Son of the Man in the Gospel of John*. Journal for the Study of the New Testament, Supplement, no. 56. Sheffield: Sheffield Academic Press, 1993.
Busink, T. A. *Der Tempel von Jerusalem von Salomo bis Herodes: Ein archäologisch-historische Studie unter Berücksichtigung des westsemitischen Tempelbaus*. Vol. 2, *Von Ezechiel bis Middot*. Leiden: E. J. Brill, 1980.
Bussche, Henri van den. 'Jésus, l'unique source d'eau vive, Jean 7, 37-39.' *Bible et vie chretienne* 65 (1965): 17-23.
Busse, Ulrich. 'Die Tempelmetaphorik als ein Beispiel von implizitem Rekurs auf die biblische Tradition im Johannesevangelium.' In *The Scripture in the Gospels*, ed. C. M. Tuckett, 395-428. Bibliotheca ephemeridum theologicarum lovaniensium, no. 131. Leuven: University Press, 1997.
Cadman, W. H. *The Open Heaven: The Revelation of God in the Johannine Sayings of Jesus*. Edited by G. B. Caird. Oxford: Basil Blackwell, 1969.
Caird, G. B. 'The Glory of God in the Fourth Gospel: An Exercise in Biblical Semantics.' *New Testament Studies* 15 (1969): 265-77.
Caldecott, W. Shaw. *Solomon's Temple: Its History and Its Structure*. London: Religious Tract Society, 1908.
Caldecott, W. Shaw and James Orr. 'Tabernacle.' In *International Standard Bible Dictionary*, ed. J. Orr, vol. 5, 2887-92. Chicago: Howard-Severance, 1915.
— 'Temple.' In *International Standard Bible Dictionary*, ed. J. Orr, vol. 5, 2930-40. Chicago: Howard-Severance, 1915.
Calvin, John. *The Gospel according to St. John 1-10*. Translated by T. Parker.

Grand Rapids: Eerdmans, 1959.
Carroll, Robert P. *Jeremiah: A Commentary*. Old Testament Library. Philadelphia: Westminster, 1986.
Carson, Donald A. 'Current Source Criticism of the Fourth Gospel: Some Methodological Questions.' *Journal of Biblical Literature* 97 (1978): 411-29.
— *Divine Sovereignty and Human Responsibility: Biblical Perspectives in Tension*. New Foundations Theological Library. Atlanta: John Knox, 1981.
— *Exegetical Fallacies*. 2nd ed. Grand Rapids: Baker, 1996.
— *The Gospel according to John*. Grand Rapids: Eerdmans, 1991.
— 'John and the Johannine Epistles.' In *It Is Written: Scripture Citing Scripture: Essays in Honour of Barnabas Lindars*, ed. D. A. Carson and H. G. M. Williamson, 245-63. Cambridge: Cambridge, 1988.
— *Matthew 1-12*. Expositor's Bible Commentary. Grand Rapids: Zondervan, 1995.
— 'New Testament Theology.' In *Dictionary of the Later New Testament and Its Developments*, ed. Ralph P. Martin and Peter H. Davids, 796-814. Downers Grove, Ill.: InterVarsity, 1997.
— 'The Role of Exegesis in Contemporary Theology.' In *Doing Theology in Today's World*, ed. John Woodbridge and Thomas McComiskey, 39-76. Grand Rapids: Zondervan, 1991.
— 'Understanding Misunderstandings in the Fourth Gospel.' *Tyndale Bulletin* 33 (1982): 59-91.
Cassuto, U. *A Commentary on the Book of Exodus*. Translated by Israel Abrahams. Jerusalem: Magnes, 1967.
Chalvon-Demersay, Guy. 'Le symbolisme du Temple et le nouveau Temple.' *Recherches de science religieuse* 82 (1994): 165-92.
Charlesworth, James H. 'From Messianology to Christology: Problems and Prospects.' In *The Messiah: Developments in Earliest Judaism and Christianity*, ed. James H. Charlesworth et al., 3-35. Minneapolis: Fortress, 1992.
Chary, Théophane. *Aggée – Zacharie – Malachie*. Sources bibliques. Paris: J. Gabalda and Co., 1969.
— *Les prophètes et le culte à partir de l'exil*. Bibliothèque de théologie. Tournai: Desclée and Co., 1955.
Chester, Andrew. 'The Sibyl and the Temple.' In *Templum Amicitiae: Essays on the Second Temple Presented to Ernst Bammel*, ed. William Horbury, 37-69. Journal for the Study of the New Testament, Supplement, no. 48. Sheffield: Sheffield Academic Press, 1991.
Childs, Brevard S. *The Book of Exodus: A Critical, Theological Commentary*. Old Testament Library. Philadelphia: Westminster, 1974.
— *Isaiah*. Old Testament Library. Louisville, Ky.: Westminster John Knox, 2001.
Chilton, Bruce. 'Reference to the Targumim in the Exegesis of the New Testament.' *Society of Biblical Literature Seminar Papers* (1995): 77-81.
— '[ὡς] φραγέλλιον ἐκ σχοινίων (John 2:15).' In *Templum Amicitiae: Essays on the Second Temple Presented to Ernst Bammel*, ed. William Horbury,

330-44. Journal for the Study of the New Testament, Supplement, no. 48. Sheffield: Sheffield Academic Press, 1991.

Chrysostom, John. *Commentary on Saint John the Apostle and Evangelist: Homilies 1-47.* Translated by Sister Thomas Aquinas Goggin. Fathers of the Church, vol. 33. New York: Fathers of the Church, Inc., 1957.

Chyutin, Michael. *The New Jerusalem Scroll from Qumran: A Comprehensive Resonstruction.* Journal for the Study of the Pseudepigrapha: Supplement Series, no. 25. Sheffield: Sheffield Academic Press, 1997.

Clements, R. E. *God and Temple.* Philadelphia: Fortress, 1965.

— *God's Chosen People: A Theological Interpretation of the Book of Deuteronomy.* London: SCM Press, 1968.

Clifford, Richard J. *The Cosmic Mountain in Canaan and the Old Testament.* Harvard Semitic Monographs, vol. 4. Cambridge: Harvard University Press, 1972.

— 'The Temple and the Holy Mountain.' In *The Temple in Antiquity: Ancient Records and Modern Perspectives*, ed. Truman G. Madsen, 107-24. Provo, Utah: Brigham Young University, 1984.

Clowney, Edmund P. 'The Final Temple.' In *Studying the New Testament Today*, ed. John H. Skilton, 97-132. Nutley, N.J.: Presbyterian and Reformed, 1974.

— 'Toward a Biblical Doctrine of the Church.' *Westminster Theological Journal* 31 (1968-69): 22-81.

Cohen, Shaye J. D. *From the Maccabees to the Mishnah.* Library of Early Christianity. Philadelphia: Westminster, 1987.

— 'The Temple and the Synagogue.' In *The Temple in Antiquity: Ancient Records and Modern Perspectives*, ed. Truman G. Madsen, 151-74. Provo, Utah: Brigham Young University, 1984.

Cole, Alan. *The New Temple: A Study in the Origins of the Catechetical 'Form' of the Church in the New Testament.* London: Tyndale, 1950.

Collins, John J. *The Apocalyptic Imagination: An Introduction to the Jewish Matrix of Christianity.* New York: Crossroad, 1989.

— *The Sibylline Oracles of Egyptian Judaism.* SBL Dissertation Series, no. 13. Missoula, Mont.: Society of Biblical Literature, 1972.

— *The Scepter and the Star: The Messiahs of the Dead Sea Scrolls and Other Ancient Literature.* Anchor Bible Reference Library. New York: Doubleday, 1995.

Collins, Raymond F. *These Things Have Been Written: Studies on the Fourth Gospel.* Grand Rapids: Eerdmans, 1990.

Coloe, Mary. *God Dwells with Us: Temple Symbolism in the Fourth Gospel.* Collegeville, Minn.: Liturgical Press, 2001.

— 'Raising the Johannine Temple (John 19:19-37).' *Australian Biblical Review* 48 (2000): 47-58.

Congar, Yves M.-J. *The Mystery of the Temple or the Manner of God's Presence to His Creatures from Genesis to the Apocalypse.* Translated by Reginald Trevett. Westminster, Md.: Newman, 1962.

Conybeare, F.C. and St. George Stock. *Grammar of Septuagint Greek with Selected Readings from the Septuagint according to the Text of Swete.*

Peabody, Mass.: Hendrickson, 1988.
Cooke, G. A. *A Critical and Exegetical Commentary on the Book of Ezekiel.* International Critical Commentary, vol. 21. Edinburgh: T. and T. Clark, 1936.
Coppens, Joseph. *Les Harmonies des deux Testaments: Essai sur les Divers Sens des Ecritures et sur l'Unité de la Révélation.* Paris: Casterman, 1949.
— 'The Spiritual Temple in the Pauline Letters and Its Background.' In *Studia evangelica*, ed. E. Livingstone, vol. 6, 53-66. Berlin: Akademie-Verlag, 1973.
Cortés, Juan B. 'Yet Another Look at Jn 7,37-38.' *Catholic Biblical Quarterly* 29 (1967): 75-86.
Cothenet, Édouard. 'Typologie de l'exode dans le IVe Évangile.' In *Tradició i Traducció de la Paraula: Miscellània Guiu Camps*, ed. Frederic Raurell et al., 243-54. Barcelona: Associació Bíblica de Catalunya, 1993.
Craigie, Peter C. *The Book of Deuteronomy.* New International Commentary on the Old Testament. Grand Rapids: Eerdmans, 1976.
— *Psalms 1-50.* Word Biblical Commentary, vol. 19. Waco: Word, 1983.
Cross, Frank Moore Jr. 'The Priestly Tabernacle.' In *The Biblical Archaeologist Reader*, ed. G. Ernest Wright and D. N. Freedman, 201-28. New York: Doubleday, 1961.
— 'The Priestly Tabernacle in the Light of Recent Research.' In *The Temple in Antiquity: Ancient Records and Modern Perspectives*, ed. Truman G. Madsen, 91-106. Provo, Utah: Brigham Young University, 1984.
Cullmann, Oscar. 'L'opposition contre le temple de Jérusalem, motif commun de la théologie johannique et du monde ambiant.' *New Testament Studies* 5 (1958-1959): 157-73.
— *Salvation in History.* Translated by Sidney G. Sowers. New Testament Library. London: SCM, 1967.
Culpepper, R. Alan. *Anatomy of the Fourth Gospel: A Study in Literary Design.* Philadelphia: Fortress, 1983.
— 'The Pivot of John's Prologue.' *New Testament Studies* 27 (1980-1981): 1-31.
Curtis, Edward Lewis and Albert A. Madsen. *A Critical and Exegetical Commentary on the Book of Chronicles.* International Critical Commentary. New York: Charles Scribner's Sons, 1910.
Cyril of Alexandria. *Commentary on the Gospel according to St. John.* Translated by members of the English church. Library of Fathers of the Holy Catholic Church, Anterior to the Division of the East and West. 2 vols. Oxford: James Parker and Co., 1874.
Daly-Denton, Margaret. *David in the Fourth Gospel: The Johannine Reception of the Psalms.* Arbeiten zur Geschichte des antiken Judentums und des Urchristentums, vol. 47. Leiden: Brill, 2000.
Daniélou, Jean. 'Joh. 7,38 et Ezéch. 47,1-11.' In *Studia evangelica*, ed. F.L. Cross, vol. 2. Berlin: Akademie-Verlag, 1964.
— *The Presence of God.* Translated by Walter Roberts. London: A.R. Mowbray, 1958.
Davenport, Gene L. *The Eschatology of the Book of Jubilees.* Studia

Postbiblica, no. 20. Leiden: E.J. Brill, 1971.

Davidson, Richard. *Typology in Scripture: A Study of Hermeneutical ΤΥΠΟΣ Structures*. Andrews University Seminary Doctoral Dissertation Series, vol. 2. Berrien Springs, Mich.: Andrews University, 1981.

Davies, G. Henton. 'Tabernacle.' In *Interpreter's Dictionary of the Bible*, ed. G.A. Buttrick, vol. 4, 498-506. New York: Abingdon, 1962.

Davies, G. I. 'The Presence of God in the Second Temple and Rabbinic Doctrine.' In *Templum Amicitiae: Essays on the Second Temple Presented to Ernst Bammel*, ed. William Horbury, 32-36. Journal for the Study of the New Testament, Supplement, no. 48. Sheffield: Sheffield Academic Press, 1991.

Davies, Margaret. *Rhetoric and Reference in the Fourth Gospel*. Journal for the Study of the New Testament, Supplement, no. 69. Sheffield: Journal for the Study of the Old Testament, 1992.

Davies, Philip R. 'The Ideology of the Temple in the Damascus Document.' *Journal of Jewish Studies* 33 (1982): 287-301.

Davies, Philip R. 'The Judaism(s) of the Damascus Document.' In *The Damascus Document: A Centennial of Discovery: Proceedings of the Third International Symposium of the Orion Center for the Study of the Dead Sea Scrolls and Associated Literature, 4-8 February, 1998*, ed. J. M. Baumgarten et al., 27-44. Leiden: Brill, 2000.

Davies, W. D. *The Gospel and the Land: Early Christianity and Jewish Territorial Doctrine*. Sheffield: Journal for the Study of the Old Testament Press, 1994.

Deeley, Mary Katherine. 'Ezekiel's Shepherd and John's Jesus: A Case Study in the Appropriation of Biblical Texts. In *The Early Christian Interpretation of the Scriptures of Israel: Investigations and Proposals*, ed. Craig A. Evans and James A. Sanders, 252-65. Journal for the Study of the New Testament, Supplement, vol. 148. Sheffield: Sheffield Academic Press, 1997.

De Lacey, D. R. 'οἵτινές ἐστε ὑμεῖς: The Function of a Metaphor in St. Paul.' In *Templum Amicitiae: Essays on the Second Temple Presented to Ernst Bammel*, ed. William Horbury, 391-409. Journal for the Study of the New Testament, Supplement, no. 48. Sheffield: Sheffield Academic Press, 1991.

Delitzsch, Franz. *Biblical Commentary on the Prophecies of Isaiah*. Translated by James Martin. 2 vols. Biblical Commentary on the Old Testament, vols. 17-18. Grand Rapids: Eerdmans, 1960 (vol. 1), 1965 (vol. 2).

— *Biblical Commentary on the Psalms*. Translated by Francis Bolton. 3 vols. Biblical Commentary on the Old Testament, vols. 11-13. Grand Rapids: Eerdmans, 1971.

DeVries, Simon J. *1 Kings*. Word Biblical Commentary, vol. 12. Waco: Word, 1985.

— 'Moses and David as Cult Founders in Chronicles.' *Journal of Biblical Literature* 107 (1988): 619-39.

De Young, James C. *Jerusalem in the New Testament: The Significance of the City in the History of Redemption and in Eschatology*. Kampen: J. H. Kok, 1960.

Dillard, Raymond B. *2 Chronicles*. Word Biblical Commentary, vol. 15. Waco: Word, 1987.
Dion, Hyacinthe-M. 'Quelques traits originaux de la conception johannique du Fils de l'Homme.' *Sciences ecclésiastiques* 19 (1967): 49-65.
Dockery, David S. 'Reading John 4:1-45: Some Diverse Hermeneutical Perspectives.' *Criswell Theological Review* 3 (1988): 127-40.
Dodd, Charles H. *According to the Scriptures: The Sub-Structure of New Testament Theology*. London: Nisbet & Co., 1952.
— *The Interpretation of the Fourth Gospel*. Cambridge: Cambridge University Press, 1953.
Donaldson, T. L. 'Parallels: Use, Misuse and Limitations.' *Evangelical Quarterly* 55 (1983): 193-210.
Driver, S. R. *A Critical and Exegetical Commentary on Deuteronomy*. 3rd ed. Edinburgh: T. and T. Clark, 1901.
Du Toit, A. B. 'The Incarnate Word: A Study of John 1:14.' *Neotestamentica* 2 (1968): 9-21.
Dubarle, André Marie. 'Des fleuves d'eau vive (S. Jean, VII, 37-39). *Revue biblique* 52 (1943-1944): 238-41.
— 'Le signe du temple (Jo. II, 19).' *Revue biblique* 48 (1939): 21-44.
Duguid, Iain M. *Ezekiel and the Leaders of Israel*. Vetus Testamentum Supplements, vol. 56. New York: E. J. Brill, 1994.
Dumbrell, William J. 'Grace and Truth: The Progress of the Argument of the Prologue of John's Gospel.' In *Doing Theology for the People of God: Studies in Honor of J. I. Packer*, ed. Donald Lewis and Alister McGrath, 105-22. Downers Grove, Ill.: InterVarsity, 1996.
Dumermuth, F. 'Zur deuteronomischen Kulttheologie und ihren Voraussetzungen,' *Zeitschrift für die alttestamentliche Wissenschaft* 70 (1958): 59-98.
Edersheim, Alfred. *The Temple: Its Ministry and Services as They Were at the Time of Jesus Christ*. New York: Fleming H. Revell, 1874.
Edwards, Ruth B. 'Χάριν ἀντὶ χάριτος (John 1:16): Grace and the Law in the Johannine Prologue.' *Journal for the Study of the New Testament* 32 (1988): 3-15.
Eichrodt, Walther. *Ezekiel: A Commentary*. Translated by Cosslett Quin. Old Testament Library. Philadelphia: Westminster, 1970.
— 'Der neue Tempel in der Heilshoffnung Hesekiels.' In *Das ferne und nahe Wort: Festschrift Leonhard Rost*, ed. Fritz Maass, 37-48. Berlin: Alfred Töpelmann, 1967.
— 'Is Typological Exegesis an Appropriate Method?' Translated by James Barr. In *Essays on Old Testament Hermeneutics*, ed. Claus Westermann, 224-45. Richmond, Va.: John Knox, 1963.
— *Theology of the Old Testament*. Vol. 1. Translated by J. A. Baker. Philadelphia: Westminster, 1961.
Eisemann, Moshe. *Yechezkel or The Book of Ezekiel: A New Translation with a Commentary Anthologized from Talmudic, Midrashic, and Rabbinic Sources*. 3 vols. ArtScroll Tanach Series. New York: Mesorah, 1977 (vol. 1), 1980 (vols. 2-3).

Ellis, E. Earle. *The Old Testament in Early Christianity: Canon and Interpretation in the Light of Modern Research*. Grand Rapids: Baker, 1991.
— *Paul's Use of the Old Testament*. Grand Rapids: Eerdmans, 1957.
— *Prophecy and Hermeneutic in Early Christianity: New Testament Essays*. Grand Rapids: Eerdmans, 1978.
Enz, Jacob J. 'The Book of Exodus as a Literary Type for the Gospel of John.' *Journal of Biblical Literature* 76 (1957): 208-15.
Eppstein, Victor. 'The Historicity of the Gospel Account of the Cleansing of the Temple.' *Zeitschrift für die neutestamentliche Wissenschaft* 55 (1964): 42-58.
Evans, Craig A. 'Early Rabbinic Sources and Jesus Research.' *Society of Biblical Literature Seminar Papers* (1995): 53-76.
— 'Jesus' Action in the Temple: Cleansing or Portent of Destruction?' *Catholic Biblical Quarterly* 51 (1989): 237-70.
— 'Obduracy and the Lord's Servant: Some Observations on the Use of the Old Testament in the Fourth Gospel.' In *Early Jewish and Christian Exegesis: Studies in Memory of William Hugh Brownless*, ed. Craig A. Evans and William F. Stinespring, 221-36. Atlanta: Scholars Press, 1987.
— *Word and Glory: On the Exegetical and Theological Background of John's Prologue*. Journal for the Study of the New Testament, Supplement, no. 89. Sheffield: Sheffield Academic Press, 1993.
Fairbairn, Patrick. *An Exposition of Ezekiel*. Grand Rapids: Zondervan, 1960.
— *The Typology of Scripture*. 2 vols. Grand Rapids: Zondervan, 1963.
Farrer, Austin M. *The Glass of Vision*. London: Dacre Press, 1948.
— *A Study in St. Mark*. New York: Oxford University, 1952.
Feinberg, Charles L. *The Prophecy of Ezekiel: The Glory of the Lord*. Chicago: Moody, 1969.
Feinberg, John, ed. *Continuity and Discontinuity: Perspectives on the Relationship between the Old and New Testaments*. Westchester, Ill.: Crossway Books, 1988.
Ferguson, Everett. *Backgrounds of Early Christianity*. 2nd ed. Grand Rapids: Eerdmans, 1993.
Feuillet, André. 'Les fleuves d'eau vive de Jo., 7, 38: Contribution à l'étude des rapports entre Quatrième Évangile et Apocalypse.' In *Parole de Dieu et sacerdoce*, ed. E. Fischer and L. Bouyer, 107-20. New York: Desclée et Cie, 1962.
— *The Priesthood of Christ and His Ministers*. Translated by Matthew J. O'Connell. Garden City, N.Y.: Doubleday, 1975.
— *Le prologue du quatrième évangile: étude de théologie johannique*. Paris: Desclée de Brouwer, 1968.
Fiorenza, Elisabeth Schüssler. 'Cultic Language in Qumran and in the New Testament.' *Catholic Biblical Quarterly* 38 (1976): 159-77.
Fisher, Eugene J. 'From Polemic to Objectivity? A Short History of the Use and Abuse of Hebrew Sources by Recent Christian New Testament Scholarship.' *Hebrew Studies* 20-21 (1979-1980): 199-207.
Ford, J. Massingberd. '"Mingled Blood" from the Side of Chirst (John XIX. 34).' *New Testament Studies* 15 (1968-69): 337-8.

Forestell, J. Terence. *The Word of the Cross: Salvation as Revelation in the Fourth Gospel*. Analecta biblica, no. 57. Rome: Biblical Institute Press, 1974.

Fortna, Robert Tomson. *The Fourth Gospel and Its Predecessor*. Philadelphia: Fortress, 1988.

— *The Gospel of Signs: A Reconstruction of the Narrative Source Underlying the Fourth Gospel*. Cambridge: Cambridge, 1970.

Foulkes, Francis. *The Acts of God: A Study of the Basis of Typology in the Old Testament*. London: Tyndale, 1958.

Fowler, Mervyn D. 'The Meaning of *lipnê* YHWH in the Old Testament.' *Zeitschrift für die alttestamentliche Wissenschaft* 99 (1987): 384-90.

Fowler, William G. 'The Influence of Ezekiel in the Fourth Gospel: Intertextuality and Interpretation.' Ph.D. diss., Golden Gate Baptist Theological Seminary, 1995.

France, R. T. 'Chronological Aspects of "Gospel Harmony."' *Vox evangelica* 16 (1986): 33-59.

— *Jesus and the Old Testament: His Application of Old Testament Passages to Himself and His Mission*. London: Tyndale, 1971.

Freed, Edwin D. 'The Manner of Worship in John 4:23f.' In *Search the Scriptures: New Testament Studies in Honor of Raymond T. Stamm*, ed. J. Myers et al., 33-48. Leiden: E. J. Brill, 1969.

— *Old Testament Quotations in the Gospel of John*. Novum Testamentum, Supplement, vol. 11. Leiden: E. J. Brill, 1965.

Friedman, Richard E. 'Tabernacle.' In *Anchor Bible Dictionary*, ed. D. N. Freedman, vol. 6, 292-300. New York: Doubleday, 1992.

Fritsch, Charles T. 'Biblical Typology.' *Bibliotheca Sacra* 103 (1946): 293-305, 418-30; 104 (1947): 87-100; 214-22.

— 'TO 'ANTITYΠON.' In *Studia Biblica et Semitica*, 100-107. Wageningen: H. Veenman and Zonen N. V., 1966.

Fritsch, Irénée. '"...videbitis ...angelos Dei ascendentes et descendentes super Filium hominis" (Io. 1,51).' *Verbum domini* 37 (1959): 3-11.

Frühwald-König, Johannes. *Tempel und Kult: Ein Beitrag zur Christologie des Johannesevangeliums*. Biblische Untersuchungen, vol. 27. Regensburg: Friedrich Pustet, 1998.

Gaebelin, Arno C. *The Prophet Ezekiel: An Analytical Exposition*. 2nd ed. Neptune, N.J.: Loizeaux Brothers, 1972.

Gaines, Elizabeth A. 'The Eschatological Jerusalem: The Function of the Image in the Literature of the Biblical Period.' Ph.D. diss., Princeton Theological Seminary, 1987.

Galambush, Julie. *Jerusalem in the Book of Ezekiel: The City as Yahweh's Wife*. SBL Dissertation Series, no. 130. Atlanta: Scholars Press, 1992.

García Martínez, Florentino. *The Dead Sea Scrolls Translated: The Qumran Texts in English*. Translated by Wilfred G. Watson. 2nd ed. Leiden: E. J. Brill, 1996.

— 'L'interprétation de la Torah d'Ézéchiel dans les mss. de Qumran.' *Revue de Qumran* 13 (1988): 441-52.

— *Qumran and Apocalyptic: Studies on the Aramaic Texts from Qumran*.

Studies on the Texts of the Desert of Judah, no. 9. New York: E. J. Brill, 1992.
Gärtner, Bertil. *John 6 and the Jewish Passover.* Coniectanea biblica: New Testament Series, no. 17. Lund: C. W. K. Gleerup, 1959.
— *The Temple and the Community in Qumran and the New Testament: A Comparative Study in the Temple Symbolism of the Qumran Texts and the New Testament.* Cambridge: Cambridge University Press, 1965.
Gaston, Lloyd. *No Stone on Another: Studies in the Significance of the Fall of Jerusalem in the Synoptic Gospels.* Novum Testamentum, Supplement, vol. 23. Leiden: E. J. Brill, 1970.
Glasson, T. Francis. *Moses in the Fourth Gospel.* Studies in Biblical Theology. Naperville, Ill.: Alec R. Allenson, 1963.
Godet, Frédéric L. *Commentary on the Gospel of John.* Translated by Timothy Dwight. 3rd French ed., 3rd English ed. 2 vols. Grand Rapids: Zondervan, 1969.
Goldingay, John. 'The Chronicler as a Theologian.' *Biblical Theology Bulletin* 5 (1975): 99-129.
Goldstein, Jonathan A. *I Maccabees.* Anchor Bible, vol. 41. Garden City, N.Y.: Doubleday, 1976.
— *II Maccabees.* Anchor Bible, vol. 41A. Garden City, N.Y.: Doubleday, 1983.
Goppelt, Leonhard. *Theology of the New Testament.* 2 vols. Translated by John E. Alsup. Grand Rapids: William B. Eerdmans, 1981.
— 'τύπος.' In *Theological Dictionary of the New Testament*, ed. G. Friedrich, trans. G. Bromiley, vol. 8, 246-59. Grand Rapids: Eerdmans, 1972.
— *Typos: The Typological Interpretation of the Old Testament in the New.* Translated by D. H. Madvig. Grand Rapids: Eerdmans, 1982.
Görg, Manfred. 'Fleischwerdung des Logos: Auslegungs- und religionsgeschichtliche Anmerkungen zu Joh 1,14a.' In *Von Jesus zum Christus: Christologische Studien*, ed. Rudolf Hoppe and Ulrich Busse, 467-84. Beihefte zur Zeitschrift für die neutestamentliche Wissenschaft, no. 93. Berlin: Walter de Gruyter, 1998.
— *Das Zelt der Begegnung: Untersuchung zur Gestalt der sakralen Zelttraditionen Altisraels.* Bonner biblische Beiträge, no. 27. Bonn: Peter Hanstein Verlag, 1967.
Goulder, Michael D. *Type and History in Acts.* London: SPCK, 1964.
Grabbe, Lester L. 'The Current State of the Dead Sea Scrolls: Are There More Answers than Questions?' In *The Scrolls and the Scriptures: Qumran Fifty Years After*, ed. Stanley Porter and Craig Evans, 54-67. Journal for the Study of the Pseudepigrapha: Supplement Series, vol. 3. Sheffield: Sheffield Academic Press, 1997.
Greenberg, Moshe. 'The Design and Themes of Ezekiel's Program of Restoration.' *Int* 38 (1984): 181-208.
— 'Idealism and Practicality in Numbers 35:4-5 and Ezekiel 48.' *Journal of the American Oriental Society* 88 (1968): 59-66.
Grelot, Pierre. 'A propos de Jean 7, 38.' *Revue biblique* 67 (1960): 224-5.
— '"De son ventre couleront des fleuves d'eau." La citation sriptuaire de Jean,

VII, 38.' *Revue biblique* 66 (1959): 369-74.
— 'Jean VII, 38: eau du rocher ou source du Temple.' *Revue biblique* 70 (1963): 43-51.
Grigsby, Bruce H. 'The Cross as an Expiatory Sacrifice in the Fourth Gospel.' *Journal for the Study of the New Testament* 15 (1982): 51-80.
Guilding, Aileen. *The Fourth Gospel and Jewish Worship: A study of the relation of St. John's Gospel to the ancient Jewish lectionary system*. Oxford: Clarendon, 1960.
Gundry, Robert H. '"In my Father's House are many Μοναί" (John 14:2).' *Zeitschrift für die neutestamentliche Wissenschaft* 58 (1967): 68-72.
Haacker, Klaus. 'Gottesdienst ohne Gotteserkenntnis: Joh 4,22 vor dem Hintergrund der jüdisch-samaritanischen Auseinandersetzungen.' In *Wort und Wirklichkeit: Studien zur Afrikanistik und Orientalistik*. Vol. 1, *Geschichte und Religionswissenschaft: Bibliographie*, ed. B. Benzing, O. Böcher, and G. Mayer, 67-84. Meisenheim: Verlag Anton Hain, 1976.
Haenchen, Ernst. *John 1: A Commentary on the Gospel of John Chapters 1-6*. Translated by Robert W. Funk. Edited by Robert W. Funk with Ulrich Busse. Hermeneia. Philadelphia: Fortress, 1984.
— *John 2: A Commentary on the Gospel of John Chapters 7-21*. Translated by Robert W. Funk. Edited by Robert W. Funk with Ulrich Busse. Hermeneia. Philadelphia: Fortress, 1984.
Hahn, Ferdinand. '"Das Heil kommt von den Juden": Erwägungen zu Joh 4,22b.' In *Wort und Wirklichkeit: Studien zur Afrikanistik und Orientalistik*. Vol. 1, *Geschichte und Religionswissenschaft: Bibliographie*, ed. B. Benzing, O. Böcher, and G. Mayer, 67-84. Meisenheim: Verlag Anton Hain, 1976.
Halpern, Baruch. 'The Centralization Formula in Deuteronomy.' *Vetus Testamentum* 31 (1981): 20-38.
Hamid-Khani, Saeed. *Revelation and Concealment of Christ: A Theological Inquiry into the Elusive Language of the Fourth Gospel*. Wissenschaftliche Untersuchungen zum Neuen Testament, 2nd series, no. 120. Tübingen: Mohr Siebeck, 2000.
Hamilton, Neill Q. 'Temple Cleansing and Temple Bank.' *Journal of Biblical Literature* 83 (1964): 365-72.
Hamilton, Victor P. *The Book of Genesis: Chapters 18-50*. New International Commentary on the Old Testament. Grand Rapids: Eerdmans, 1995.
Hammerton-Kelly, R. G. 'The Temple and the Origins of Jewish Apocalyptic.' *Vetus Testamentum* 20 (1970): 1-15.
Hanson, Anthony T. *Jesus Christ in the Old Testament*. London: SPCK, 1965.
— 'John's Technique in Using Scripture.' In *The New Testament Interpretation of Scripture*. London: SPCK, 1980.
— 'John I. 14-18 and Exodus XXXIV.' *New Testament Studies* 23 (1977): 90-101.
— 'John's Use of Scripture.' In *The Gospels and the Scriptures of Israel*, ed. Craig A. Evans and W. Richard Stegner, 358-79. Journal for the Study of the New Testament, Supplement, no. 104. Sheffield: Sheffield Academic, 1994.
— 'The Theme of Christ as the True Temple in the Fourth Gospel.' In *The New*

Testament Interpretation of Scripture, 110-21. London: SPCK, 1980.
Haran, Menahem. 'The Divine Presence in the Israelite Cult and the Cultic Institutions.' *Bib* 50 (1969): 251-67.
— 'The Law Code of Ezekiel XL-XLVIII and Its Relation to the Priestly School.' *Hebrew Union College Annual* 50 (1979): 45-72.
— *Temples and Temple-Service in Ancient Israel: An Inquiry into the Character of Cult Phenomena and the Historical Setting of the Priestly School*. Oxford: Clarendon, 1978.
Harrington, Hannah K. 'The Halakah and Religion of Qumran.' In *Religion in the Dead Sea Scrolls*, ed. John Collins and Robert Kugler, 74-89. Studies in the Dead Sea Scrolls and Related Literature. Grand Rapids: Eerdmans, 2000.
Harrison, Everett F. 'A Study of John 1:14.' In *Unity and Diversity in New Testament Theology: Essays in Honor of George E. Ladd*, ed. Robert A. Guelich, 23-36. Grand Rapids: Eerdmans, 1978.
Hartley, John E. *Leviticus*. Word Biblical Commentary, vol. 4. Dallas: Word Books, 1992.
Hartman, Lars. '"He Spoke of the Temple of His Body" (Jn 2:13-22).' *Svensk exegetisk årsbok* 54 (1989): 70-79.
Hayward, C. T. R. *The Jewish Temple: A non-biblical sourcebook*. New York: Routledge, 1996.
Heil, John Paul. 'The Narrative Strategy and Pragmatics of the Temple Theme in Mark.' *Catholic Biblical Quarterly* 59 (1997): 76-100.
Hempel, Charlotte. 'Qumran Communities: Beyond the Fringes of Second Temple Society.' In *The Scrolls and the Scriptures: Qumran Fifty Years After*, ed. Stanley Porter and Craig Evans, 43-53. Journal for the Study of the Pseudepigrapha: Supplement Series, vol. 3. Sheffield: Sheffield Academic Press, 1997.
Henderson, E. *The Book of the Prophet Ezekiel*. Andover, Mass.: Warren F. Draper, 1870.
Hengel, Martin. *Judaism and Hellenism: Studies in Their Encounter in Palestine during the Early Hellenistic Period*. Translated by John Bowden. 2 vols. Philadelphia: Fortress, 1974.
Hengstenberg, E. W. *Commentary on the Gospel of St. John*. Vol. 1. Edinburgh: T. and T. Clark, 1871.
— *The Prophecies of the Prophet Ezekiel Elucidated*. Translated by A. C. Murphy and J. G. Murphy. Clark's Foreign Theological Library, series 4, vol. 21. Edinburgh: T. and T. Clark, 1869.
Hiers, Richard H. 'Purification of the Temple: Preparation for the Kingdom of God.' *Journal of Biblical Literature* 90 (1971): 82-90.
Hildebrandt, Wilf. *An Old Testament Theology of the Spirit of God*. Peabody, Mass.: Hendrickson, 1995.
Hill, Andrew E. *Malachi: A New Translation with Introduction and Commentary*. Anchor Bible, vol. 25D. New York: Doubleday, 1998.
Hofmann, J. C. K. von. *Interpreting the Bible*. Translated by Christian Preus. Minneapolis: Augsburg, 1959.
Holladay, William L. *Jeremiah 1: A Commentary on the Book of the Prophet Jeremiah, Chapters 1-25*. Hermeneia. Philadelphia: Fortress, 1986.

— *Jeremiah 2: A Commentary on the Book of the Prophet Jeremiah, Chapters 26-52*. Hermeneia. Minneapolis: Fortress, 1989.

Hollander, H. W. and M. de Jonge. *The Testaments of the Twelve Patriarchs: A Commentary*. Studia in Veteris Testamenti pseudepigraphica, no. 8. Leiden: E. J. Brill, 1985.

Holwerda, David E. *The Holy Spirit and Eschatology in the Gospel of John: A Critique of Rudolf Bultmann's Present Eschatology*. Kampen: Kok, 1959.

— *Jesus and Israel: One Covenant or Two?* Grand Rapids: Eerdmans, 1995.

Horbury, William. 'Herod's Temple and "Herod's Days."' In *Templum Amicitiae: Essays on the Second Temple Presented to Ernst Bammel*, ed. William Horbury, 103-49. Journal for the Study of the New Testament, Supplement, no. 48. Sheffield: Sheffield Academic Press, 1991.

— 'Land, Sanctuary and Worship.' In *Early Christian Thought in Its Jewish Context*, ed. John Barclay and John Sweet, 207-24. Cambridge: Cambridge University Press, 1996.

Hoskyns, Edwyn Clement. *The Fourth Gospel*. Edited by Francis N. Davey. London: Faber and Faber, 1947.

House, Paul R. *Old Testament Theology*. Downers Grove, Ill.: InterVarsity, 1998.

Houtman, C. 'What Did Jacob See in His Dream at Bethel? *Some Remarks on Genesis xxviii 10-22*.' *Vetus Testamentum* 27 (1977): 337-51.

Howard, J. K. 'Passover and Eucharist in the Fourth Gospel.' *Scottish Journal of Theology* 20 (1967): 329-37.

Hudry-Clergeon, Charles. 'Jésus et le Sanctuaire: Étude de Jn 2, 12-22.' *La nouvelle revue théologique* 105 (1983): 535-48.

Hugenberger, G. P. 'Introductory Notes on Typology.' In *The Right Doctrine from the Wrong Texts: Essays on the Use of the Old Testament in the New*, ed. G. K. Beale, 331-41. Grand Rapids: Baker Books, 1994.

Hurowitz, Victor (Avigdor). *I Have Built You an Exalted House: Temple Building in the Bible in the Light of Mesopotamian and Northwest Semitic Writings*. Journal for the Study of the Old Testament, Supplement, no. 115. Sheffield: Journal for the Study of the Old Testament Press, 1992.

Ibuki, Yu. *Die Wahrheit im Johannesevangelium*. Bonner biblische Beiträge, vol. 38. Bonn: Peter Hanstein Verlag, 1972.

Japhet, Sara. *1 and 2 Chronicles: A Commentary*. Old Testament Library. Louisville: Westminster/John Knox, 1993.

— 'The Historical Reliability of Chronicles: The History of the Problem and Its Place in Biblical Research.' *Journal for the Study of the Old Testament* 33 (1985): 83-107.

— 'The Temple in the Restoration Period: Reality and Ideology.' Translated by Steven Weitzman. *Union Seminary Quarterly Review* 44 (1991): 195-251.

Jenson, Philip P. *Graded Holiness: A Key to the Priestly Conception of the World*. Journal for the Study of the Old Testament, Supplement, no. 106. Sheffield: Journal for the Study of the Old Testament Press, 1992.

Jeremias, Joachim. 'Die Berufung des Nathanael (Jo 1,45-51).' *Angelos* 3 (1928): 2-5.

— 'Golgotha und der heilige Felsen.' *Angelos* 2 (1926): 74-128.

— *Jesus als Weltvollender*. Beiträge zur Förderung christlicher Theologie, vol. 33, no. 4. Gütersloh: C. Bertelsmann, 1930.
— 'Zwei Miszellen: 1. Antik-Jüdische Münzdeutungen. 2. Zur Geschichtlichkeit der Tempelreinigung.' *New Testament Studies* 23 (1977): 177-80.
Johnson, Aubrey R. *Cultic Prophet and Israel's Psalmody*. Cardiff: University of Wales Press, 1979.
Johnson, David H. 'Our Father Jacob: The Role of the Jacob Narrative in the Fourth Gospel Compared to Its Role in the Jewish Bible and in the Writings of Early Judaism.' Ph.D. diss., Trinity Evangelical Divinity School, 1992.
Johnstone, William. *1 and 2 Chronicles*. Vol. 1, *1 Chronicles 1-2 Chronicles 9: Israel's Place among the Nations*. Journal for the Study of the Old Testament, Supplement, 253. Sheffield: Sheffield Academic, 1997.
Jones, Gwilym H. *1 and 2 Kings*. Vol. 1, *1 Kings 1-16:34*. New Century Bible. Grand Rapids: Eerdmans, 1984.
Jones, Larry Paul. *The Symbol of Water in the Gospel of John*. Journal for the Study of the New Testament, Supplement, no. 145. Sheffield: Journal for the Study of the Old Testament, 1997.
Juel, Donald. *Messiah and Temple: The Trial of Jesus in the Gospel of Mark*. SBL Dissertation Series, no. 31. Missoula, Mont.: Scholars Press, 1977.
Kaiser, Walter C. Jr. 'Inner Biblical Exegesis as a Model for Bridging the 'Then' And 'Now' Gap: Hos 12:1-6.' *Journal of the Evangelical Theological Society* 28 (1985): 33-46.
Kaufmann, Yehezkel. *History of the Religion of Israel*. Vol. 4, *From the Babylonian Captivity to the End of Prophecy*. Translated by C. W. Efroymson. New York: Ktav, 1977.
— *The Religion of Israel from Its Beginnings to the Babylonian Exile*. Translated and abridged by Moshe Greenberg. New York: Schocken Books, 1972.
Keener, Craig S. *The Spirit in the Gospels and Acts: Divine Purity and Power*. Peabody, Mass.: Hendrickson, 1997.
Keil, Carl F. *Biblical Commentary on the Prophecies of Ezekiel*. 2 vols. Translated by James Martin. Biblical Commentary on the Old Testament, vols. 21-22. Grand Rapids: Eerdmans, 1966.
— *The Books of the Chronicles*. Translated by Andrew Harper. Biblical Commentary on the Old Testament, vol. 7. Grand Rapids: Eerdmans, 1971.
— *The Books of the Kings*. Translated by James Martin. Biblical Commentary on the Old Testament, vol. 6. Grand Rapids: Eerdmans, 1950.
— *The Prophecies of Jeremiah*. Vol. 1. Translated by David Patrick. Biblical Commentary on the Old Testament, vol. 19. Grand Rapids: Eerdmans, 1967.
— *The Prophecies of Jeremiah*. Vol. 2. Translated by James Kennedy. Biblical Commentary on the Old Testament, vol. 20. Grand Rapids: Eerdmans, 1967.
Keil, Carl F. and F. Delitzsch. *The Books of Samuel*. Translated by James Martin. Biblical Commentary on the Old Testament, vol. 5. Grand Rapids: Eerdmans, 1960.
— *The Pentateuch*. Vol. 2. Translated by James Martin. Biblical Commentary on the Old Testament, vol. 2. Grand Rapids: Eerdmans, 1966.

— *The Twelve Minor Prophets*. 2 vols. Translated by James Martin. Biblical Commentary on the Old Testament, vols. 24-25. Grand Rapids: Eerdmans, 1961.

Kellermann, D. 'מִשְׁכָּן.' Translated by David E. Green. In *Theological Dictionary of the Old Testament*, ed. G. Johannes Botterweck et al., vol. 9, 58-64. Grand Rapids: Eerdmans, 1998.

Kempthorne, R. 'Incest and the Body of Christ: A Study of I Corinthians VI. 12-20.' *New Testament Studies* 14 (1967-68): 568-74.

Kerr, Alan R. *The Temple of Jesus' Body: The Temple Theme in the Gospel of John*. Journal for the Study of the New Testament, Supplement, no. 220. Sheffield: Sheffield Academic Press, 2002.

Kinzer, Mark. 'Temple Christology in the Gospel of John.' *Society of Biblical Literature Seminar Papers* (1998): 447-64.

Klein, William W., C. L. Blomberg, and Robert L. Hubbard, Jr. *Introduction to Biblical Interpretation*. Nashville: Nelson, 1993.

Klinzing, Georg. *Die Umdeutung des Kultus in der Qumrangemeinde und im Neuen Testament*. Studien zur Umwelt des Neuen Testaments, no. 7. Göttingen: Vandenhoeck and Ruprecht, 1971.

Knoppers, Gary N. *Two Nations under God: The Deuteronomistic History of Solomon and the Dual Monarchies*. Vol. 1, *The Reign of Solomon and the Rise of Jeroboam*. Atlanta: Scholars Press, 1993.

Koch, K. 'Ezra and the Origins of Judaism.' *Journal of Semitic Studies* 19 (1974): 173-97.

Koch, Klaus. 'אֹהֶל.' Translated by John T. Willis. In *Theological Dictionary of the Old Testament*, ed. G. J. Botterweck and H. Ringgren, vol. 1, rev ed., 118-30. Grand Rapids: Eerdmans, 1977.

Koester, Craig R. *The Dwelling of God: The Tabernacle in the Old Testament, Intertestamental Jewish Literature and the New Testament*. Catholic Biblical Quarterly Monograph Series, no. 22. Washington, D. C.: Catholic Biblical Association of America, 1989.

— 'Messianic Exegesis and the Call of Nathanael (John 1.45-51).' *Journal for the Study of the New Testament* 39 (1990): 23-34.

Kohler, Marc. 'Des fleuves d'eau vive: Exégèse de Jean 7:37-39.' *Revue de théologie et de philosophie* 10 (1960): 188-201.

Köstenberger, Andreas J. 'Jesus the Good Shepherd Who Will Also Bring Other Sheep (John 10:16): The Old Testament Background of a Familiar Metaphor.' *Bulletin for Biblical Research* 12 (2002): 67-96.

Kraus, Hans-Joachim. *Psalms 1-59: A Commentary*. Translated by Hilton C. Oswald. Continental Commentary. Minneapolis: Augsburg, 1988.

— *Psalms 60-150: A Commentary*. Translated by Hilton C. Oswald. Continental Commentary. Minneapolis: Augsburg, 1989.

— *Theology of the Psalms*. Translated by Keith Crim. Minneapolis: Augsburg, 1986.

Kreitzer, Larry J. 'The Temple Incident in John 2.13-25: A Preview of What Is to Come.' In *Understanding, Studying and Reading: New Testament Essays in Honour of John Ashton*, ed. Christopher Rowland and Crispin H. T. Fletcher-Louis. Journal for the Study of the New Testament, Supplement,

no. 153. Sheffield: Sheffield Academic Press, 1998.
Kugler, Robert A. 'Priesthood at Qumran.' In *The Dead Sea Scrolls after Fifty Years: A Comprehensive Assessment*, ed. Peter W. Flint and James C. VanderKam, vol. 2, 93-116. Leiden: Brill, 1999.
Kugler, Robert. 'Rewriting Rubrics: Sacrifice and the Religion of Qumran.' In *Religion in the Dead Sea Scrolls*, ed. John Collins and Robert Kugler, 90-112. Studies in the Dead Sea Scrolls and Related Literature. Grand Rapids: Eerdmans, 2000.
Kümmel, Werner G. *Introduction to the New Testament*. Translated by Howard Clark Kee. Rev. ed. Nashville: Abingdon, 1975.
Kysar, Robert. *The Fourth Evangelist and His Gospel: An Examination of Contemporary Scholarship*. Minneapolis: Augsburg, 1975.
La Potterie, Ignace de. '"Nous adorons, nous, ce que nous connaissons, car le salut vient des Juifs": Histoire de l'exégèse et interprétation de Jn 4,22.' *Biblica* 64 (1983): 74-115.
— *La vérité dans Saint Jean*. 2 vols. Analecta biblica, nos. 73-74. Rome: Biblical Institute Press, 1977.
Laberge, Léo. 'Le lieu que YHWH a choisi pour y mettre son Nom (TM, LXX, Vg et Targums). Contribution à la critique textuelle d'une formule deutéronomiste.' *Estudios bíblicos* 43 (1985): 209-36.
Lachs, Samuel Tobias. 'Rabbinic Sources for New Testament Studies-- Use and Misuse.' *Jewish Quarterly Review* 74 (1983): 159-73.
Ladd, George Eldon. 'Israel and the Church.' *EQ* 36 (1964): 206-13.
— *A Theology of the New Testament*. Rev. ed. Grand Rapids: Eerdmans, 1993.
Laetsch, Theo. *Bible Commentary: Jeremiah*. Saint Louis: Concordia, 1952.
Lampe, G. W. H. 'Hermeneutics and Typology.' *London Quarterly and Holborn Review* 190 (1965): 17-25.
— 'The Reasonableness of Typology.' In *Essays on Typology*, 9-38. Studies in Biblical Theology. Naperville, Ill.: Alec R. Allenson, 1957.
Lelong, M.-H. *Saint Jean parmi nous: Le prologue*. Paris: Les Éditions du Cerf, 1961.
L'Eplattenier, Charles. *L'Évangile de Jean*. La Bible, porte-Parole. Geneva: Labor et Fides, 1993.
Lenski, R. C. H. *The Interpretation of St. John's Gospel*. Minneapolis: Augsburg, 1942.
Léon-Dufour, Xavier. 'Bulletin d'exégèse du Nouveau Testament: L évangile de Jean.' *Recherches de science religieuse* 73 (1985): 245-80.
— 'Le signe du temple selon saint Jean.' *Recherches de science religieuse* 39 (1951-1952): 155-75.
Levenson, Jon D. *Sinai and Zion: An Entry into the Jewish Bible*. San Francisco: Harper and Row, 1985.
— 'The Temple and the World.' *Journal of Religion* 64 (1984): 275-98.
— *Theology of the Program of Restoration of Ezekiel 40-48*. Harvard Semitic Monographs, no. 10. Atlanta: Scholars Press, 1976.
Levine, Baruch A. *In the Presence of the Lord: A Study of Cult and Some Cultic Terms in Ancient Israel*. Leiden: E. J. Brill, 1974.
— 'On the Presence of God in Biblical Religion.' In *Religions in Antiquity:*

Essays in Memory of Erwin Ramsdell Goodenough, ed. Jacob Neusner, 71-87. Leiden: Brill, 1968.
Lieu, Judith. 'Temple and Synagogue in John.' *New Testament Studies* 45 (1999): 51-69.
Lightfoot, John. *A Commentary on the New Testament from the Talmud and Hebraica: Matthew – 1 Corinthians.* Vol. 3, *Luke – John.* Grand Rapids: Baker, 1979.
Lightfoot, Robert H. *St. John's Gospel: A Commentary.* Edited by C. F. Evans. Oxford: Clarendon Press, 1956.
Lindars, Barnabas. *The Gospel of John.* New Century Bible. Grand Rapids: Eerdmans, 1972.
—— 'The Son of Man in the Johannine Christology.' In *Christ and Spirit in the New Testament*, ed. Barnabas Lindars and Stephen Smalley, 43-60. Cambridge: Cambridge University Press, 1973.
Lipton, Diana. *Revisions of the Night: Politics and Promises in the Patriarchal Dreams of Genesis.* Journal for the Study of the Old Testament, Supplement, no. 288. Sheffield: Sheffield Academic Press, 1999.
Loader, William. *The Christology of the Fourth Gospel: Structure and Issues.* 2nd ed. New York: Peter Lang, 1992.
—— 'John 1:50-51 and the 'Greater Things' of Johannine Christology.' In *Anfänge der Christologie: Festschrift für Ferdinand Hahn zum 65. Geburtstag*, ed. Cilliers Breytenbach and Henning Paulsen, 255-74. Göttingen: Vandenhoeck and Ruprecht, 1991.
Lofthouse, W. F. *Ezekiel: Introduction, Revised Version with Notes, and Index.* Century Bible. Edinburgh: T. C. and E. C. Jack, [1900].
Lohfink, Norbert. 'Zur deuteronomischen Zentralisationsformel.' *Biblica* 65 (1984): 297-329.
Long, V. Philips. *The Art of Biblical History.* In *Foundations of Contemporary Interpretation*, ed. Moisés Silva, 281-429. Grand Rapids: Zondervan, 1996.
Longenecker, Richard N. *Biblical Exegesis in the Apostolic Period.* Grand Rapids: Eerdmans, 1975.
—— *The Christology of Early Jewish Christianity.* Studies in Biblical Theology, 2nd series, no. 17. London: SCM, 1970.
Longman, Tremper III. *Literary Approaches to Biblical Interpretation.* In *Foundations of Contemporary Interpretation*, ed. Moisés Silva, 90-192. Grand Rapids: Zondervan, 1996.
Losie, Lynn Allan. 'The Cleansing of the Temple: A History of a Gospel Tradition in Light of Its Background in the Old Testament and in Early Judaism.' Ph.D. diss., Fuller Theological Seminary, 1984.
Macdonald, John. *The Theology of the Samaritans.* Philadelphia: Westminster, 1964.
MacRae, George W. 'The Meaning and Evolution of the Feast of Tabernacles.' *Catholic Biblical Quarterly* 22 (1960): 251-76.
Maddox, Robert. 'The Function of the Son of Man in the Gospel of John.' In *Reconciliation and Hope: New Testament Essays on Atonement and Eschatology*, ed. Robert Banks, 186-204. Grand Rapids: Eerdmans, 1974.
Maier, Gerhard. *Biblical Hermeneutics.* Translated by Robert W. Yarbrough.

Wheaton, Ill.: Crossway Books, 1994.
Maier, Johann. 'Tempel und Tempelkult.' In *Literatur und Religion des Frühjudentums: Eine Einführung*, ed. Johann Maier and Josef Schreiner, 371-90. Würzburg: Echter Verlag, 1973.
— *The Temple Scroll: An Introduction, Translation and Commentary*. Translated by Richard T. White. Journal for the Study of the Old Testament, Supplement, no. 34. Sheffield: Journal for the Study of the Old Testament, 1985.
Malatesta, Edward. 'Blood and Water from the Pierced Side of Christ (Jn 19,34).' In *Segni e sacramenti nel Vangelo di Giovanni*, ed. P.-R. Tragan, Studia Anselmiana, no. 66, 165-81. Rome: Editrice Anselmiana, 1977.
Manns, Frédéric. *L'Evangile de Jean à la lumière du Judaïsme*. Studium Biblicum Franciscanum Analecta, no. 33. Jerusalem: Franciscan Printing Press, 1991.
Manson, T. W. 'The Cleansing of the Temple.' *Bulletin of the John Rylands Library* 33 (1951): 271-82.
Mare, W. Harold. 'Zion.' In *Anchor Bible Dictionary*, ed. D. N. Freedman, vol. 6, 1096-7. New York: Doubleday, 1992.
Marshall, I. Howard. 'An Assessment of Recent Developments.' In *It Is Written: Scripture Citing Scripture: Essays in Honour of Barnabas Lindars*, ed. D.A. Carson and H.G.M. Williamson, 1-21. Cambridge: Cambridge, 1988.
— 'Church and Temple in the New Testament.' *Tyndale Bulletin* 40 (1989): 203-22.
Mason, Rex. 'The Prophets of the Restoration.' In *Israel's Prophetic Tradition: Essays in Honour of Peter R. Ackroyd*, ed. Richard Coggins et al., 137-54. Cambridge: Cambridge University Press, 1982.
Mathews, Kenneth A. 'John, Jesus and the Essenes: Trouble at the Temple.' *Criswell Theological Review* 3 (1988): 101-26.
Matson, Mark A. 'The Contribution to the Temple Cleansing by the Fourth Gospel.' *Society of Biblical Literature Seminar Papers* (1992): 489-506.
McCaffrey, James. *The House with Many Rooms: The Temple Imagery of Jn. 14,2-3*. Analecta biblica, no. 114. Rome: Editrice Pontificio Instituto Biblico, 1988.
McCarter, P. Kyle Jr. *II Samuel: A New Translation with Introduction, Notes and Commentary*. Anchor Bible, vol. 9. Garden City, N.Y.: Doubleday, 1984.
McConville, J. Gordon. '1 Kings VIII 46-53 and the Deuteronomic Hope.' *Vetus Testamentum* 42 (1992): 67-79.
— 'Ezra-Nehemiah and the Fulfilment of Prophecy.' *Vetus Testamentum* 36 (1986): 205-24.
— 'God's "Name" and God's "Glory."' *Tyndale Bulletin* 30 (1979): 149-63.
— 'Jerusalem in the Old Testament.' In *Jerusalem Past and Present in the Purposes of God*, ed. Peter W. L. Walker, 2nd ed., 21-52. Grand Rapids: Baker, 1994.
— *Law and Theology in Deuteronomy*. Journal for the Study of the Old Testament, Supplement, no. 33. Sheffield: Journal for the Study of the Old

Testament Press, 1984.
— 'Priests and Levites in Ezekiel: A Crux in the Interpretation of Israel's History.' *Tyndale Bulletin* 34 (1983): 3-31.
McConville, J. Gordon and J. G. Millar. *Time and Place in Deuteronomy*. Journal for the Study of the Old Testament, Supplement, no. 179. Sheffield: Sheffield Academic Press, 1994.
McCool, Francis J. 'Living Water in John.' In *The Bible in Current Catholic Thought*, ed. John L. McKenzie, 226-33. New York: Herder and Herder, 1962.
McKelvey, R. J. *The New Temple*. Oxford: Oxford University Press, 1969.
Meagher, John C. 'John 1:14 and the New Temple.' *Journal of Biblical Literature* 88 (1969): 57-68.
Meeks, Wayne A. 'The Man from Heaven in Johannine Sectarianism.' *Journal of Biblical Literature* 91 (1972): 44-72.
— *Moses Traditions and the Johannine Christology*. Novum Testamentum, Supplement, vol. 14. Leiden: E. J. Brill, 1967.
Ménard, Jacques-E. 'L'interprétation patristique de Jean, VII, 38.' *Revue de l'université d'Ottawa* 25 (1955): 5-25.
Menken, Maarten J. J. 'The Christology of the Fourth Gospel: A Survey of Recent Research.' In *From Jesus to John: Essays on Jesus and New Testament Christology in Honour of Marinus de Jonge*, ed. Martinus C. De Boer, 292-320. Journal for the Study of the New Testament, Supplement, no. 84. Sheffield: Journal for the Study of the Old Testament, 1993.
— *Old Testament Quotations in the Fourth Gospel: Studies in Textual Form*. Contributions to Biblical Exegesis and Theology, no. 15. Kampen: Kok Pharos, 1996.
Metso, Sarianna. 'Constitutional Rules at Qumran.' In *The Dead Sea Scrolls after Fifty Years: A Comprehensive Assessment*, ed. Peter W. Flint and James C. Vanderkam, vol. 1, 186-210. Leiden: Brill, 1999.
— 'The Relationship between the Damascus Document and the Community Rule.' In *The Damascus Document: A Centennial of Discovery: Proceedings of the Third International Symposium of the Orion Center for the Study of the Dead Sea Scrolls and Associated Literature, 4-8 February, 1998*, ed. J.M. Baumgarten et al., 85-94. Leiden: Brill, 2000.
Mettinger, Tryggve N. D. *The Dethronement of Sabaoth: Studies in the Shem and Kabod Theologies*. Translated by Frederick H. Cryer. Coniectanea biblica: Old Testament Series, no. 18. Lund: CWK Gleerup, 1982.
Metzger, Bruce M. 'The Formulas Introducing Quotations of Scripture in the New Testament and the Mishnah.' *Journal of Biblical Literature* 70 (1951): 297-307.
Meyer, Heinrich A. W. *Critical and Exegetical Handbook to the Gospel of John*. Translated by William Urwick and Frederick Crombie, 5th German ed., 2nd English ed. Vol. 1. Edinburgh: T. and T. Clark, 1883.
Meyers, Carol L. *The Tabernacle Menorah: A Synthetic Study of a Symbol from the Biblical Cult*. American Schools of Oriental Research Dissertation Series, no. 2. Missoula, Mont.: Scholars Press for the American Schools of Oriental Research, 1976.

— 'Temple, Jerusalem.' In *Anchor Bible Dictionary*, ed. D. N. Freedman, vol. 6, 350-69. New York: Doubleday, 1992.
Meyers, Carol L. and Eric M. Meyers. *Haggai, Zechariah 1-8: A New Translation with Introduction and Commentary*. Anchor Bible, vol. 25B. New York: Doubleday, 1987.
— *Zechariah 9-14: A New Translation with Introduction and Commentary*. Anchor Bible, vol. 25C. New York: Doubleday, 1993.
Michaelis, Wilhelm. 'Joh. 1,51, Gen. 28,12 und das Menschensohn-Problem.' *Theologische Literaturzeitung* 85 (1960): 561-78.
— 'κατασκηνόω.' Translated by G. Bromiley. In *Theological Dictionary of the New Testament*, ed. G. Kittel and G. Friedrich, vol. 7, 387-9. Grand Rapids: Eerdmans, 1971.
— 'σκηνή.' Translated by G. Bromiley. In *Theological Dictionary of the New Testament*, ed. G. Kittel and G. Friedrich, vol. 7, 368-83. Grand Rapids: Eerdmans, 1971.
— 'σκηνόω.' Translated by G. Bromiley. In *Theological Dictionary of the New Testament*, ed. G. Kittel and G. Friedrich, vol. 7, 368-83. Grand Rapids: Eerdmans, 1971.
Michel, O. 'ναός.' Translated by G. Bromiley. In *Theological Dictionary of the New Testament*, ed. G. Kittel and G. Friedrich, vol. 4, 880-90. Grand Rapids: Eerdmans, 1967.
Milgrom, Jacob. *Studies in Cultic Theology and Terminology*. Leiden: E. J. Brill, 1983.
Miller, Robert J. 'Historical Method and the Deeds of Jesus: The Test Case of the Temple Demonstration.' *Foundations and Facets* 8 (1992): 5-30.
Moloney, Francis J. *The Johannine Son of Man*. Biblioteca di Scienze Religiose, no. 14. Rome: Libreria Ateneo Salesiano, 1976.
— 'Reading John 2:13-22: The Purification of the Temple.' *Revue biblique* 97 (1990): 432-52.
Moo, Douglas J. *The Epistle to the Romans*. New International Commentary on the New Testament. Grand Rapids: Eerdmans, 1996.
— *The Old Testament in the Gospel Passion Narratives*. Sheffield: Almond, 1983.
— 'The Problem of *Sensus Plenior*.' In *Hermeneutics, Authority, and Canon*, ed. D.A. Carson and John D. Woodbridge, 175-212. Grand Rapids: Zondervan, 1986.
Moore, Carey A. *Tobit: A New Translation and Commentary*. Anchor Bible, vol. 40A. New York: Doubleday, 1996.
Morgan, Richard. 'Fulfillment in the Fourth Gospel: The Old Testament Foundations.' *Interpretation* 11 (1957): 155-65.
Morgen, Michèle. 'La promesse de Jésus à Nathanaël (Jn 1,51) éclairée par la hagaddah de Jacob-Israel.' *Recherches de science religieuse* 67, no. 3 (1993): 3-21.
Morris, Leon. *The New Testament and the Jewish Lectionaries*. London: Tyndale Press, 1964.
— *The Gospel According to John*. New International Commentary on the New Testament. Grand Rapids: Eerdmans, 1971.

Mosis, Rudolf. *Untersuchungen zur Theologie des chronistischen Geschichtswerkes*. Freiburger theologische Studien, no. 92. Freiburg: Herder, 1973.

Motyer, J. Alec. *The Prophecy of Isaiah: An Introduction and Commentary*. Downers Grove, Ill.: InterVarsity, 1993.

Moule, C. F. D. 'Fulfilment-Words in the New Testament: Use and Abuse.' *New Testament Studies* 14 (1967-68): 293-320.

— 'Sanctuary and Sacrifice in the Church of the New Testament.' *Journal of Theological Studies*, new series (1950): 29-41.

Moulton, Mark. 'Jesus' Goal for Temple and Tree: A Thematic Revisit of Matt 21:12-22.' *Journal of the Evangelical Theological Society* 41 (1998): 561-72.

Mowinckel, Sigmund. *He That Cometh*. Translated by G. W. Anderson. New York: Abingdon, 1954.

Müller, Christoph Georg. *Gottes Pflanzung – Gottes Bau – Gottes Tempel: Die metaphorische Dimension paulinischer Gemeindetheologie in 1 Kor 3,5-17*. Fuldaer Studien, vol. 5. Frankfurt: Josef Knecht, 1995.

Mussner, Franz. *Christus das All und die Kirche: Studien zur Theologie des Epheserbriefes*. 2nd ed. Treierer theologische Studien, vol. 5. Treier: Paulinus Verlag, 1968.

— 'Jesus und "das Haus des Vaters"– Jesus als "Tempel."' In *Freude am Gottesdienst: Aspekte ursprünglicher Liturgie*, ed. Josef Schreiner, 267-76. Stuttgart: Verlag Katholisches Bibelwerk, 1983.

— *ZΩH: Die Anschauung vom 'Leben' im vierten Evangelium unter Berücksichtigung der Johannesbriefe*. Münchener theologische Studien. München: Karl Zink, 1952.

Myers, Jacob M. *Ezra, Nehemiah*. Anchor Bible. Garden City, N.Y.: Doubleday, 1965.

Naudé, Jackie A. 'קדש.' In *New International Dictionary of Old Testament Theology and Exegesis*, ed. W. VanGemeren, vol. 3, 877-87. Grand Rapids: Zondervan, 1997.

Neill, Stephen and Tom Wright. *The Interpretation of the New Testament 1861-1986*. 2nd ed. New York: Oxford University Press, 1988.

Nereparampil, Lucius. *Destroy This Temple: An Exegetic-Theological Study on the Meaning of Jesus' Temple-Logion in Jn 2:19*. Bangalore: Dharmaram Publications, 1978.

Neusner, Jacob. 'The Use of the Mishnah for the History of Judaism Prior to the Time of the Mishnah: A Methodological Note.' *Journal for the Study of Judaism in the Persian, Hellenistic, and Roman Periods* 11 (1980): 177-85.

Newsom, Carol. *Songs of the Sabbath Sacrifice: A Critical Edition*. Harvard Semitic Studies, no. 27. Atlanta: Scholars Press, 1985.

Neyrey, Jerome H. '"I Said: You Are Gods": Psalm 82:6 and John 10.' *Journal of Biblical Literature* 108 (1989): 647-63.

— 'The Jacob Allusions in John 1:51.' *Catholic Biblical Quarterly* 44 (1982): 586-605.

— 'Jacob Traditions and the Interpretation of John 4:10-26.' *Catholic Biblical Quarterly* 41 (1979): 419-37.

Nicholson, Godfrey C. *Death as Departure: The Johannine Descent-Ascent Schema.* SBL Dissertation Series, no. 63. Chico, Cal.: Scholars Press, 1983.

Nickelsburg, George W. E. *Jewish Literature between the Bible and the Mishnah: A Historical and Literary Introduction.* Philadelphia: Fortress, 1981.

Niditch, Susan. 'Ezekiel 40-48 in a Visionary Context.' *Catholic Biblical Quarterly* 48 (1986): 208-24.

Niehaus, Jeffrey. 'The Central Sanctuary: Where and When?' *Tyndale Bulletin* 43 (1992): 3-30.

Nordheim, Eckhard von. 'König und Tempel: Der Hintergrund des Tempelbauverbotes in 2 Samuel vii.' *Vetus Testamentum* 27 (1977): 434-53.

Obermann, Andreas. *Die christologische Erfüllung der Schrift im Johannesevangelium: Eine Untersuchung zur johanneischen Hermeneutik anhand der Schriftzitate.* Wissenschaftliche Untersuchungen zum Neuen Testament, 2nd series, no. 83. Tübingen: J.C.B. Mohr (Paul Siebeck), 1996.

O'Day, Gail R. *Revelation in the Fourth Gospel: Narrative Mode and Theological Claim.* Philadelphia: Fortress, 1986.

Odeberg, Hugo. *The Fourth Gospel Interpreted in Its Relation to Contemporaneous Religious Currents in Palestine and the Hellenistic Oriental World.* Uppsala: Almquist and Wiksell, 1929.

Ollenburger, Ben C. *Zion the City of the Great King: A Theological Symbol of the Jerusalem Cult.* Journal for the Study of the Old Testament, Supplement, no. 41. Sheffield: Journal for the Study of the Old Testament Press, 1987.

Olsson, Birger. *Structure and Meaning in the Fourth Gospel: A Text-Linguistic Analysis of John 2:1-11 and 4:1-42.* Translated by Jean Gray. Coniectanea biblica: New Testament Series, no. 6. Lund: CWK Gleerup, 1974.

O'Neill, J. C. 'The Desolate House and the New Kingdom of Jerusalem: Jewish Oracles of Ezra in 2 Esdras 1-2.' In *Templum Amicitiae: Essays on the Second Temple Presented to Ernst Bammel*, ed. William Horbury, 226-36. Journal for the Study of the New Testament, Supplement, no. 48. Sheffield: Sheffield Academic Press, 1991.

Osborne, Grant R. *The Hermeneutical Spiral: A Comprehensive Introduction to Biblical Interpretation.* Downers Grove, Ill.: InterVarsity, 1991.

— 'Type; Typology.' In *International Standard Bible Dictionary*, ed. G. Bromiley, vol. 4, 930-2. Grand Rapids: Eerdmans, 1988.

Østenstad, Gunnar H. *Patterns of Redemption in the Fourth Gospel: An Experiment in Structural Analysis.* Studies in the Bible and Early Christianity, vol. 38. Lewiston, N.Y.: Edwin Mellen, 1998.

Ostmeyer, Karl-Heinrich. *Taufe und Typos: Elemente und Theologie der Tauftypologien in 1. Korinther 10 und 1. Petrus 3.* Wissenschaftliche Untersuchungen zum Neuen Testament, 2nd series, no. 118. Tübingen: Mohr Siebeck, 2000.

Oswalt, John N. *The Book of Isaiah: Chapters 1-39.* New International Commentary on the Old Testament. Grand Rapids: Eerdmans, 1986.

— *The Book of Isaiah: Chapters 40-66.* New International Commentary on the Old Testament. Grand Rapids: Eerdmans, 1998.

Packer, J. I. *God Has Spoken: Revelation and the Bible.* 3rd ed. Grand Rapids:

Baker, 1993.
Paesler, Kurt. *Das Tempelwort Jesu: Die Traditionen von Tempelzerstörung und Tempelerneuerung im Neuen Testament*. Göttingen: Vandenhoeck and Ruprecht, 1999.
Painter, J. 'Christ and the Church in John 1,45-51.' In *L' Évangile de Jean: Sources, rédaction, théologie*, ed. M. De Jonge, 359-62. Bibliotheca ephemeridum theologicarum lovaniensium, no. 44. Leuven: University Press, 1977.
Pamment, Margaret. 'The Meaning of *Doxa* in the Fourth Gospel.' *Zeitschrift für die neutestamentliche Wissenschaft* 74 (1983): 12-16.
Pancaro, Severino. *The Law in the Fourth Gospel: The Torah and the Gospel, Moses and Jesus, Judaism and Christianity according to John*. Novum Testamentum, Supplement, vol. 42. Leiden: E. J. Brill, 1975.
Parsons, Mikeal C. 'The Critical Use of the Rabbinic Literature in New Testament Studies.' *Perspectives in Religious Studies* 12 (1985): 85-102.
Partner, Nancy. 'Historicity in an Age of Reality-Fictions.' In *A New Philosophy of History*, ed. Frank Ankersmit and Hans Kellner, 21-39. Chicago: University of Chicago, 1995.
Patai, Raphael. *Man and Temple: In Ancient Jewish Myth and Ritual*. 2nd ed. New York: Ktav, 1967.
Paulien, Jon. 'Elusive Allusions: The Problematic Use of the Old Testament in Revelation.' *Biblical Research* 33 (1988): 37-53.
Peter, Adalbert. 'Der Segensstrom des endzeitlichen Jerusalem – Herkunft und Bedeutung eines prophetischen Symbols.' In *Miscellanea Fuldensia*, ed. Franz Scholz, 109-34. Fulda: Verlag Parzeller and Co., 1966.
Petersen, David L. *Haggai and Zechariah 1-8: A Commentary*. Old Testament Library. Philadelphia: Westminster, 1984.
Poncelet, M. *Le mystère du sang et de l'eau dans l'évangile de saint Jean*. Paris: Les Éditions du Cerf, 1961.
Porsch, Felix. *Pneuma und Wort: Ein exegetischer Beitrag zur Pneumatologie des Johannesevangeliums*. Frankfurt: Josef Knecht, 1974.
Porteous, Norman W. 'Jerusalem–Zion: The Growth of a Symbol.' In *Living the Mystery: Collected Essays*, 93-112. Oxford: Basil Blackwell, 1967.
Porter, Stanley E. 'Can Traditional Exegesis Enlighten Literary Analysis of the Fourth Gospel? An Examination of the Old Testament Fulfilment Motif and the Passover Theme.' In *The Gospels and the Scriptures of Israel*, ed. Craig A. Evans and W. Richard Stegner, 396-428. Journal for the Study of the New Testament, Supplement, no. 104. Sheffield: Sheffield Academic, 1994.
— *Idioms of the Greek New Testament*. 2nd ed. Sheffield: Sheffield Academic Press, 1996.
— 'The Use of the Old Testament in the New Testament: A Brief Comment on Method and Terminology.' In *The Early Christian Interpretation of the Scriptures of Israel: Investigations and Proposals*, ed. Craig A. Evans and James A. Sanders, 79-97. Journal for the Study of the New Testament, Supplement, no. 148. Sheffield: Sheffield Academic, 1997.
Poythress, Vern S. *The Shadow of Christ in the Law of Moses*. Brentwood, Tenn.: Wolgemuth and Hyatt, 1991.

— 'Divine Meaning of Scripture.' In *The Right Doctrine from the Wrong Texts: Essays on the Use of the Old Testament in the New*, ed. G. K. Beale, 82-113. Grand Rapids: Baker Books, 1994.

Priest, J. 'Testament of Moses: A New Translation and Introduction.' In *The Old Testament Pseudepigrapha*, ed. James H. Charlesworth, vol. 1, 919-34. New York: Doubleday, 1983.

Pryor, John W. 'Covenant and Community in John's Gospel.' *Reformed Theological Review* 47 (1988): 44-51.

— *John: Evangelist of the Covenant People: The Narrative and Themes of the Fourth Gospel*. Downers Grove, Ill.: InterVarsity, 1992.

Quispel, Gilles. 'Nathanael und der Menschensohn (Joh 1:51).' *Zeitschrift für die neutestamentliche Wissenschaft* 47 (1956): 281-3.

Rad, Gerhard von. 'Deuteronomy's 'Name' Theology and the Priestly Document's 'Kabod' Theology.' Translated by David Stalker. In *Studies in Deuteronomy*, 37-44. Chicago: Henry Regnery, 1953.

— *Old Testament Theology*. Vol. 2, *The Theology of Israel's Prophetic Traditions*. Translated by D. M. G. Stalker. New York: Harper and Row, 1965.

— 'Typological Interpretation of the Old Testament.' Translated by John Bright. In *Essays on Old Testament Hermeneutics*, ed. Claus Westermann, 17-39. Richmond, Va.: John Knox, 1963.

Rahner, Hugo. 'Flumina de ventre Christi: Die patristische Auslegung von Joh 7, 37-38.' *Biblica* 22 (1941): 269-302, 367-403.

Rahner, Johanna. *'Er aber sprach vom Tempel seines Leibes': Jesus von Nazaret als Ort der Offenbarung Gottes im vierten Evangelium*, Bonner biblische Beiträge, no. 117. Bodenheim: Philo, 1998.

Reim, Günter. *Studien zum alttestamentlichen Hintergrund des Johannesevangeliums*. Society for New Testament Studies Monograph Series, no. 22. Cambridge: Cambridge University, 1974.

Renz, Thomas. 'The Use of the Zion Tradition in the Book of Ezekiel.' In *Zion, City of Our God*, ed. Richard S. Hess and Gordon J. Wenham, 77-104. Grand Rapids: Eerdmans, 1999.

Richardson, Peter. 'Why Turn the Tables? Jesus' Protest in the Temple Precincts.' *Society of Biblical Literature Seminar Papers* (1992): 507-23.

Riches, J. K. 'Apocalyptic– Strangely Relevant.' In *Templum Amicitiae: Essays on the Second Temple Presented to Ernst Bammel*, ed. William Horbury, 237-63. Journal for the Study of the New Testament, Supplement, no. 48. Sheffield: Sheffield Academic Press, 1991.

Ridderbos, Herman N. *The Gospel according to John: A Theological Commentary*. Translated by John Vriend. Grand Rapids: Eerdmans, 1997.

Riedl, Johannes. 'Wenn ihr den Menschensohn erhöht habt, werdet ihr erkennen (Joh 8,28).' In *Jesus und der Menschensohn: Für Anton Vögtle*, ed. Rudolf Pesch and Rudolf Schnackenburg, 355-70. Freiburg: Herder, 1975.

Riley, William. *King and Cultus in Chronicles: Worship and the Reinterpretation of History*. Journal for the Study of the Old Testament, Supplement, 160. Sheffield: Journal for the Study of the Old Testament, 1993.

— 'Temple Imagery and the Book of Revelation: Ancient Near Eastern Temple Ideology and Cultic Resonances in the Apocalypse.' *Proceedings of the Irish Biblical Association* 6 (1982): 81-102.
Robertson, A. T. *A Grammar of the Greek New Testament in the Light of Historical Research.* Nashville: Broadman, 1934.
Robinson, John A. T. *The Body: A Study in Pauline Theology.* London: SCM, 1952.
— '"His Witness Is True": A Test of the Johannine Claim.' In *Jesus and the Politics of His Day*, ed. Ernst Bammel and C. F. D. Moule, 453-76. Cambridge: Cambridge University Press, 1984.
Rordorf, Willy. 'Gen 28,10ff und Joh 1,51 in der patristischen Exegese.' In *Johannes-Studien: Interdisziplinäre Zugänge zum Johannes-Evangelium*, ed. Martin Rose, 39-46. Zürich: Theologischer Verlag, 1991.
Ross, Allen P. 'שׁם.' In *New International Dictionary of Old Testament Theology and Exegesis*, ed. W. VanGemeren, vol. 4, 147-51. Grand Rapids: Zondervan, 1997.
Roth, Cecil. 'The Cleansing of the Temple and Zechariah xiv 21.' *Novum Testamentum* 4 (1960): 174-81.
Rowland, Christopher. 'John 1.51, Jewish Apocalyptic and Targumic Tradition.' *New Testament Studies* 30 (1984): 498-507.
— 'The Second Temple: Focus of Ideological Struggle?' In *Templum Amicitiae: Essays on the Second Temple Presented to Ernst Bammel*, ed. William Horbury, 175-98. Journal for the Study of the New Testament, Supplement, no. 48. Sheffield: Sheffield Academic Press, 1991.
Ruckstuhl, Eugen. 'Abstieg und Erhöhung des johanneischen Menschensohns.' In *Jesus und der Menschensohn: Für Anton Vögtle*, ed. Rudolf Pesch and Rudolf Schnackenburg, 314-41. Freiburg: Herder, 1975.
— *Die literarische Einheit des Johannesevangeliums: Der gegenwärtige Stand der einschlägigen Forschungen.* Rev. ed. Novum Testamentum et Orbis Antiquus, no. 5. Göttingen: Vandenhoeck and Ruprecht, 1987.
Ruckstuhl, Eugen and P. Dschulnigg. *Stilkritik und Verfasserfrage im Johannesevangelium: Die johanneischen Sprachmerkmale auf dem Hintergrund des Neuen Testaments und des zeitgenössischen hellenistischen Schrifttums.* Novum Testamentum et Orbis Antiquus, no. 17. Göttingen: Vandenhoeck and Ruprecht, 1991.
Rudolph, Wilhelm. *Esra und Nehemia samt 3. Esra.* Handbuch zum Alten Testament, vol. 20. Tübingen: J. C. B. Mohr, 1949.
Safrai, Shmuel. 'Talmudic Literature as an Historical Sources for the Second Temple Period.' *Mishkan* 17-18 (1992-93): 121-37.
Sahlin, Harald. *Zur Typologie des Johannesevangeliums.* Uppsala Universitetsarskrift, no. 4. Uppsala: A.-B. Lundequistska Bokhandeln, 1950.
Saldarini, Anthony J. 'Rabbinic Literature and the New Testament.' In *Anchor Bible Dictionary*, ed. D. N. Freedman, vol. 5, 602-4. New York: Doubleday, 1992.
Salier, Bill. "The Temple in the Gospel according to John." In *Heaven on Earth*, ed. T. D. Alexander and S. Gathercole, 122-33. Carlisle: Paternoster, 2004.

Sanders, E. P. *Jesus and Judaism*. London: SCM Press, 1985.
— *Judaism: Practice and Belief 63 BCE–66 CE*. Philadelphia: Trinity Press International, 1992.
Sanders, J. N. *A Commentary on the Gospel according to St. John*. Edited and completed by B. A. Mastin. Harper's New Testament Commentaries. New York: Harper and Row, 1968.
Sandmel, Samuel. 'Parallelomania.' *Journal of Biblical Literature* 81 (1962): 1-13.
Schenke, Ludger. *Johannes Kommentar*. Düsseldorf: Patmos Verlag, 1998.
Schlatter, Adolf. *Der Evangelist Johannes: Wie er spricht, denkt und glaubt*. 3rd ed. Stuttgart: Calwer Verlag, 1960.
Schmidt, Martin. *Prophet und Tempel: Eine Studie zum Problem der Gottesnähe im Alten Testament*. Zürich: Evangelischer Verlag, 1948.
Schmitt, John W. and J. Carl Laney. *Messiah's Coming Temple: Ezekiel's Prophetic Vision of the Future Temple*. Grand Rapids: Kregel, 1997.
Schmitt, Rainer. *Zelt und Lade als Thema alttestamentlicher Wissenschaft: Eine kritische forschungsgeschichtliche Darstellung*. Gütersloh: Gütersloher Verlagshaus, 1972.
Schnackenburg, Rudolf. *The Gospel according to St. John*. Translated by Kevin Smyth. Vol. 1. Herders theologischer Kommentar zum Neuen Testament. New York: Herder and Herder, 1968.
— *The Gospel according to St. John*. Herders theologischer Kommentar zum Neuen Testament. Translated by Cecily Hastings et al. Vol. 2. Tunbridge Wells: Burns and Oates, 1979.
— *The Gospel according to St. John*. Translated by David Smith and G. A. Kon. Vol. 3. Herders theologischer Kommentar zum Neuen Testament. New York: Crossroad, 1982.
Schneider, Johannes. *Das Evangelium nach Johannes*. Theologischer Handkommentar zum Neuen Testament. Berlin: Evangelische Verlagsanstalt, 1976.
Schnelle, Udo. 'Die Tempelreinigung und die Christologie des Johannesevangeliums.' *New Testament Studies* 42 (1996): 359-73.
Schreiner, Josef. *Sion–Jerusalem Jahwes Königssitz: Theologie der Heiligen Stadt im Alten Testament*. München: Kösel Verlag, 1963.
Schrenk, Gottlob. 'τὸ ἱερόν.' Translated by G. Bromiley. In *Theological Dictionary of the New Testament*, ed. G. Kittel and G. Friedrich, vol. 3, 230-47. Grand Rapids: Eerdmans, 1965.
Schuchard, Bruce G. *Scripture within Scripture: The Interrelationship of Form and Function in the Explicit Old Testament Citations in the Gospel of John*. SBL Dissertation Series, no. 133. Atlanta: Scholars Press, 1992.
Schürer, Emil. *The History of the Jewish People in the Age of Jesus Christ (175 B.C.–A.D. 135)*. Revised and edited by Geza Vermes, Fergus Millar, and Matthew Black. 3 vols. Edinburgh: T. and T. Clark, 1973 (vol. 1), 1979 (vol. 2), 1986 (vol. 3.1), 1987 (vol. 3.2).
Schüssler Fiorenza, Elisabeth. 'Cultic Language in Qumran and in the New Testament.' *Catholic Biblical Quarterly* 38 (1976): 159-77.
Schwank, Benedikt. *Evangelium nach Johannes*. 2nd ed. St. Ottilien: EOS

Verlag, 1998.

Schwartz, Joshua. 'Jubilees, Bethel and the Temple of Jacob.' *Hebrew Union College Annual* 56 (1985): 63-86.

Schweizer, Eduard. 'πνεῦμα.' Translated by G. Bromiley. In *Theological Dictionary of the New Testament*, ed. G. Friedrich, vol. 6, 389-451. Grand Rapids: Eerdmans, 1968.

Scott, E. F. *The Crisis in the Life of Jesus: The Cleansing of the Temple and Its Significance*. New York: Charles Scribner's Sons, 1952.

Scott, J. Julius Jr. *Customs and Controversies: Intertestamental Jewish Backgrounds of the New Testament*. Grand Rapids: Baker, 1995.

Selman, Martin J. 'אוּר.' In *New International Dictionary of Old Testament Theology and Exegesis*, ed. W. VanGemeren, vol. 1, 324-9. Grand Rapids: Zondervan, 1997.

— 'Jerusalem in Chronicles.' In *Zion, City of Our God*, ed. Richard S. Hess and Gordon J. Wenham, 43-56. Grand Rapids: Eerdmans, 1999.

Senior, Donald. *The Passion of Jesus in the Gospel of John*. Collegeville, Minn.: Michael Glazier, 1991.

Shidemantle, C. Scott. 'The Use of the Old Testament in John 7:37-39.' Ph.D. diss., Trinity Evangelical Divinity School, 2001.

Sidebottom, E. M. 'The Ascent and Descent of the Son of Man in the Gospel of John.' *Anglican Theological Review* 39 (1957): 115-22.

Simon, Marcel. 'Retour du Christ et reconstruction du Temple dans la pensée chrétienne primitive.' In *Aux sources de la tradition chrétienne: Mélanges offerts à M. Maurice Goguel à l'occasion de son soixante-dixième anniversaire*, ed. J.-J. von Allmen, 247-57. Paris: Delachaux & Niestlé, 1950.

Skehan, Patrick W. and Alexander A. Di Lella. *The Wisdom of Ben Sira*. Anchor Bible, vol. 39. New York: Doubleday, 1987.

Skinner, John. *The Book of Ezekiel*. Expositor's Bible, vol. 13. New York: A. C. Armstrong and Son, 1908.

Sloyan, Gerard S. *What Are They Saying about John?* New York: Paulist, 1991.

Smalley, Stephen S. 'Johannes 1,51 und die Einleitung zum vierten Evangelium.' Translated by August Berz. In *Jesus und der Menschensohn: Für Anton Vögtle*, ed. Rudolf Pesch and Rudolf Schnackenburg, 300-13. Freiburg: Herder, 1975.

— 'The Johannine Son of Man Sayings.' *New Testament Studies* 15 (1968-1969): 278-301.

Smith, Barry D. "The Chronology of the Last Supper." *Westminster Theological Journal* 53 (1991): 29-45.

Smith, D. Moody Jr. 'Johannine Studies.' In *The New Testament and Its Modern Interpreters*, ed. Eldon J. Epp and George W. MacRae, 271-98. Atlanta: Scholars Press, 1989.

— 'John.' In *Early Christian Thought in Its Jewish Context*, ed. John Barclay and John Sweet, 96-111. Cambridge: Cambridge University Press, 1996.

— *The Theology of the Gospel of John*. New Testament Theology. Cambridge: Cambridge University Press, 1995.

Smith, Robert Houston. 'Exodus Typology in the Fourth Gospel.' *Journal of*

Biblical Literature 81 (1962): 329-42.
Spatafora, Andrea. *From the 'Temple of God' to God as the Temple: A Biblical Theological Study of the Temple in the Book of Revelation*. TESI Gregoriana Serie Teologia, no. 27. Rome: Editrice Pontificia Università Gregoriana, 1997.
Stather Hunt, B. P. W. *Some Johannine Problems*. London: Skeffington, 1958.
Stegemann, Ekkehard W. 'Zur Tempelreinigung im Johannesevangelium.' In *Die Hebräische Bibel und ihre zweifache Nachgeschichte: Festschrift für Rolf Rendtorff zum 65. Geburtstag*, ed. Erhard Blum et al., 503-516. Neukirchen-Vluyn: Neukirchener Verlag, 1990.
Stek, John H. 'Biblical Typology Yesterday and Today.' *Calvin Theological Journal* 5 (1970): 133-62.
Sternberg, Meir. *The Poetics of Biblical Narrative: Ideological Literature and the Drama of Reading*. Bloomington: Indiana University, 1985.
Stevenson, Gregory. *Power and Place: Temple and Identity in the Book of Revelation*. Beihefte zur Zeitschrift für die neutestamentliche Wissenschaft, no. 107. Berlin: Walter de Gruyter, 2001.
Stevenson, Kalinda R. *Vision of Transformation: The Territorial Rhetoric of Ezekiel 40-48*. SBL Dissertation Series, no. 154. Atlanta: Scholars Press, 1996.
Stinespring, W. F. 'Temple, Jerusalem.' In *Interpreter's Dictionary of the Bible*, ed. G. A. Buttrick, vol. 4, 534-60. New York: Abingdon, 1962.
Strack, Hermann L. and Paul Billerbeck. *Kommentar zum Neuen Testament aus Talmud und Midrasch*. 6 vols. Munich: C. H. Beck'sche Verlagsbuchhandlung, 1922-61.
Strauss, David F. *The Life of Jesus Critically Examined*. Edited by Peter C. Hodgson. Translated by George Eliot. 4th German ed. Philadelphia: Fortress Press, 1972.
Sweet, J. P. M. 'A House Not Made with Hands.' In *Templum Amicitiae: Essays on the Second Temple Presented to Ernst Bammel*, ed. William Horbury, 368-90. Journal for the Study of the New Testament, Supplement, no. 48. Sheffield: Sheffield Academic Press, 1991.
Terrien, Samuel. *The Elusive Presence: Toward a New Biblical Theology*. New York: Harper and Row, 1978.
Terry, Milton S. *Biblical Hermeneutics: A Treatise on the Interpretation of the Old and New Testaments*. 2nd ed. Grand Rapids: Zondervan, 1974.
Thayer, Joseph Henry. *Greek-English Lexicon of the New Testament*. Grand Rapids: Baker Book House, 1977.
Theobald, Michael. *Die Fleischwerdung des Logos: Studien zum Verhältnis des Johannesprologs zum Corpus des Evangeliums und zu 1 Joh*. Neutestamentliche Abhandlungen, vol. 20. Münster: Aschendorff, 1988.
Thiering, B. E. '*Mebaqqer* and *Episkopos* in the Light of the Temple Scroll.' *Journal of Biblical Literature* 100 (1981): 59-74.
Thiselton, Anthony C. *New Horizons in Hermeneutics: The Theory and Practice of Transforming Biblical Reading*. Grand Rapids: Zondervan, 1992.
Thompson, John A. *The Book of Jeremiah*. New International Commentary on the Old Testament. Grand Rapids: Eerdmans, 1980.

Throckmorton, B. H. 'The ναός in Paul.' In *Studia evangelica*, ed. E. Livingstone, vol. 7, 497-504. Berlin: Akademie-Verlag, 1982.
Thüsing, Wilhelm. *Die Erhöhung und Verherrlichung Jesu im Johannesevangelium*. Neutestamentliche Abhandlungen, vol. 21. Westfalen: Aschendorffsche, 1960.
Tiller, Patrick A. *A Commentary on the Animal Apocalypse of I Enoch*. SBL Early Judaism and Its Literature, no. 4. Atlanta: Scholars Press, 1993.
Torrey, Charles C. '"When I Am Lifted up from the Earth," John 12:32.' *Journal of Biblical Literature* 51 (1932): 320-2.
Tovey, Derek. *Narrative Art and Act in the Fourth Gospel*. Journal for the Study of the New Testament, Supplement, no. 151. Sheffield: Journal for the Study of the Old Testament, 1997.
Townsend, John T. 'The Jerusalem Temple in New Testament Thought.' Th.D. diss., Harvard University, 1958.
Trocmé, Étienne. 'L'expulsion des marchands du Temple.' *New Testament Studies* 15 (1968): 1-22.
Trudinger, Paul. 'The Cleansing of the Temple: St. John's Independent, Subtle Reflections.' *Expository Times* 108 (1997): 329-30.
Tuell, Steven S. *The Law of the Temple in Ezekiel 40-48*. Harvard Semitic Monographs, no. 49. Atlanta: Scholars Press, 1992.
Ulfgard, Håkan. *The Story of Sukkot: The Setting, Shaping, and Sequel of the Biblical Feast of Tabernacles*. Beiträge zur Geschichte der biblischen Exegese, no. 34. Tübingen: J. C. B. Mohr (Paul Siebeck), 1998.
Umoh, Camillus. 'The Temple in the Fourth Gospel.' In *Israel und seine Heilstradition im Johannesevangelium: Festgabe für Johannes Beutler*, ed. Michael Labahn et al., 314-33. Paderborn: Ferdinand Schöningh, 2004.
Unger, Merrill F. 'The Temple Vision of Ezekiel.' *Bibliotheca Sacra* 105 (1948): 418-32; 106 (1949): 48-64, 169-77.
VanderKam, James C. *The Dead Sea Scrolls Today*. Grand Rapids: Eerdmans, 1994.
— 'Identity and History of the Community.' In *The Dead Sea Scrolls after Fifty Years: A Comprehensive Assessment*, ed. Peter W. Flint and James C. Vanderkam, vol. 2, 487-533. Leiden: Brill, 1999.
— 'John 10 and the Feast of the Dedication.' In *Of Scribes and Scrolls: Studies on the Hebrew Bible, Intertestamental Judaism, and Christian Origins*, ed. H. W. Attridge, J. J. Collins, T. H. Tobin, 203-14. New York: University Press of America, 1990.
VanGemeren, Willem A. *Interpreting the Prophetic Word*. Grand Rapids: Zondervan, 1990.
— 'The Spirit of Restoration.' *Westminster Theological Journal* 50 (1988): 81-102.
Vanhoozer, Kevin J. 'The Semantics of Biblical Literature: Truth and Scripture's Diverse Literary Forms.' In *Hermeneutics, Authority, and Canon*, ed. D.A. Carson and John D. Woodbridge, 49-104. Grand Rapids: Zondervan, 1986.
Van Seters, John. 'The Chronicler's Account of Solomon's Temple-Building: A Continuity Theme.' In *The Chronicler as Historian*, ed. M. P. Graham,

K.G. Hoglund, and S. L. McKenzie, 283-300. Journal for the Study of the Old Testament, Supplement, no. 238. Sheffield: Journal for the Study of the Old Testament, 1997.

Vaux, Roland de. *Ancient Israel: Its Life and Institutions*. Translated by John McHugh. New York: McGraw-Hill, 1961.

— 'Le lieu que Yahvé a choisi pour y établir son nom.' In *Das ferne und nahe Wort: Festschrift Leonhard Rost*, ed. Fritz Maass, 219-28. Berlin: Alfred Töpelmann, 1967.

— 'The Presence and Absence of God in History according to the Old Testament.' Translated by Theodore L. Westow. In *The Presence of God*, ed. Pierre Benoit et al., 7-20. Concilium, vol. 50. New York: Paulist Press, 1969.

Vergote, A. 'L'exaltation du Christ en croix selon le quatrième Evangile.' *Ephemerides theologicae lovanienses* 28 (1952): 5-23.

Vermes, Geza. 'Jewish Literature and New Testament Exegesis: Reflections on Methodology.' *Journal of Jewish Studies* 33 (1982): 361-76.

— 'Jewish Studies and New Testament Interpretation.' *Journal of Jewish Studies* 31 (1980): 1-17.

— 'Methodology in the Study of Jewish Literature in the Greco-Roman Period.' *Journal of Jewish Studies* 36 (1985): 143-58.

Vischer, Wilhelm. *The Witness of the Old Testament to Christ*. Translated from the third German edition by A. B. Crabtree. Vol. 1, *The Pentateuch*. London: Lutterworth, 1949.

Vogels, Heinrich. 'Die Tempelreinigung und Golgotha (Joh 2, 19-22).' *Biblische Zeitscbrift* 6 (1962): 102-7.

Volz, Paul. *Der Prophet Jeremia*. 2nd ed. Kommentar zum Alten Testament, vol. 10. Zürich: Georg Olms, 1983.

Vos, Geerhardus. *Biblical Theology: Old and New Testaments*. Grand Rapids: Eerdmans, 1954.

Waal, Cornelius Van Der. "The Gospel according to John and the Old Testament." *Neotestamentica* 6 (1972): 28-47.

Wacholder, Ben Zion. *The Dawn of Qumran: The Sectarian Torah and the Teacher of Righteousness*. Monographs of the Hebrew Union College, no. 8. Cincinnati: Hebrew Union College Press, 1983.

Walker, Peter W.L. *Jesus and the Holy City: New Testament Perspectives on Jerusalem*. Grand Rapids: Eerdmans, 1996.

Watts, Rikki E. *Isaiah's New Exodus and Mark*. Wissenschaftliche Untersuchungen zum Neuen Testament, 2nd series, no. 88. Tübingen: Mohr Siebeck, 1997.

Watty, William W. 'Jesus and the Temple–Cleansing or Cursing?' *Expository Times* 93 (1982): 235-9.

Weinfeld, Moshe. *Deuteronomy and the Deuteronomic School*. Winona Lake, Ind.: Eisenbrauns, 1992.

Weiser, Artur. *The Psalms: A Commentary*. Translated by Herbert Hartwell. Old Testament Library. Philadelphia: Westminster, 1962.

Wenham, Gordon J. 'Deuteronomy and the Central Sanctuary.' *Tyndale Bulletin* 22 (1971): 103-18.

— *The Book of Leviticus*. New International Commentary on the Old

Testament. Grand Rapids: Eerdmans, 1979.

— 'Sanctuary Symbolism in the Garden of Eden Story.' In *'I Studied Inscriptions from before the Flood': Ancient Near Eastern, Literary, and Linguistic Approaches to Genesis 1-11*, ed. Richard S. Hess and David T. Tsumura, 399-404. Winona Lake, Ind.: Eisenbrauns, 1994.

Wenschkewitz, Hans. *Die Spiritualisierung der Kultusbegriffe: Tempel, Priester und Opfer im Neuen Testament*. Angelos, no. 4. Leipzig: Eduard Pfeiffer, 1932.

Westcott, Brooke F. *The Gospel according to St. John: The Authorized Version with Introduction and Notes*. Grand Rapids: Eerdmans, 1971.

Westerholm, Stephen. 'Tabernacle.' In *International Standard Bible Dictionary*, ed. G. Bromiley, vol. 4, 698-706. Grand Rapids: Eerdmans, 1988.

— 'Temple.' In *International Standard Bible Dictionary*, ed. G. Bromiley, vol. 4, 759-76. Grand Rapids: Eerdmans, 1988.

Westermann, Claus. *Genesis 12-36: A Commentary*. Translated by John J. Scullion. Minneapolis: Augsburg, 1981.

— *The Gospel of John in the Light of the Old Testament*. Translated by Siegfried S. Schatzmann. Peabody, Ma.: Hendrickson, 1998.

Wevers, John W. *Ezekiel*. New Century Bible. London: Oliphants, 1969.

Whirley, Carl F. 'The Significance of the Temple Cultus in the Background of the Gospel of John.' Th.D. diss., Southern Baptist Theological Seminary, 1957.

Whitelaw, L. 'Tabernacle.' In *International Standard Bible Dictionary*, ed. J. Orr, vol. 5, 2893-8. Chicago: Howard-Severance, 1915.

— 'Temple.' In *International Standard Bible Dictionary*, ed. J. Orr, vol. 5, 2940-2. Chicago: Howard-Severance, 1915.

Wildberger, Hans. *Isaiah 1-12: A Commentary*. Translated by Thomas H. Trapp. CC. Minneapolis: Fortress, 1991.

Williamson, H. G. M. *1 and 2 Chronicles*. New Century Bible. Grand Rapids: Eerdmans, 1982.

— *Ezra, Nehemiah*. Word Biblical Commentary, vol. 16. Waco, Tex.: Word, 1985.

— 'The Temple in the Books of Chronicles.' In *Templum Amicitiae: Essays on the Second Temple Presented to Ernst Bammel*, ed. William Horbury, 15-31. Journal for the Study of the New Testament, Supplement, no. 48. Sheffield: Sheffield Academic Press, 1991.

Wilson, Ian. *Out of the Midst of the Fire: Divine Presence in Deuteronomy*. SBL Dissertation Series, no. 151. Atlanta: Scholars Press, 1995.

Windisch, Hans. 'Angelophanien um den Menschensohn auf Erden. Ein Kommentar zu Joh 1,51.' *Zeitschrift für die neutestamentliche Wissenschaft* 30 (1931): 215-33.

— 'Joh 1,51 und die Auferstehung Jesu. Ein Nachtrag zu dem Aufsatz: Angelophanien um den Menschensohn auf Erden (*Zeitschrift für die neutestamentliche Wissenschaft* 1931, 215ff.).' *Zeitschrift für die neutestamentliche Wissenschaft* 31 (1932): 199-204.

Wise, Michael Owen. *A Critical Study of the Temple Scroll from Qumran Cave*

11. Studies in Ancient Oriental Civilization, no. 49. Chicago: Oriental Institute of the University of Chicago, 1990.
Wolff, Hans Walter. *Haggai: A Commentary*. Translated by Margaret Kohl. Minneapolis: Augsburg, 1988.
— 'The Hermeneutics of the Old Testament.' Translated by Keith Crim. In *Essays on Old Testament Hermeneutics*, ed. Claus Westermann, 160-99. Richmond, Va.: John Knox, 1963.
Woollcombe, K. J. 'The Biblical Origins and Patristic Development of Typology.' In *Essays on Typology*, 39-75. Studies in Biblical Theology. Naperville, Ill.: Alec R. Allenson, 1957.
Wright, Chris. 'A Christian Approach to Old Testament Prophecy Concerning Israel.' In *Jerusalem Past and Present in the Purposes of God*, ed. Peter W.L. Walker, 2nd ed., 1-20. Grand Rapids: Baker, 1994.
Wright, G. Ernest. *The Rule of God: Essays in Biblical Theology*. Garden City, N.Y.: Doubleday, 1960.
Wright, N. T. 'Jerusalem in the New Testament.' In *Jerusalem Past and Present in the Purposes of God*, ed. Peter W. L. Walker, 2nd ed., 53-78. Grand Rapids: Baker, 1994.
— 'Jesus.' In *Early Christian Thought in Its Jewish Context*, ed. John Barclay and John Sweet, 43-58. Cambridge: Cambridge University Press, 1996.
Yadin, Yigael. *The Temple Scroll*. 3 vols. Jerusalem: Israel Exploration Society, 1983.
Yarbrough, Robert W. 'The *heilsgeschichtliche* Perspective in Modern New Testament Theology.' Ph.D. diss., University of Aberdeen, 1985.
Yee, Gale A. *Jewish Feasts and the Gospel of John*. Wilmington, Del.: Michael Glazier, 1989.
Young, Edward J. *The Book of Isaiah: The English Text, with Introduction, Exposition, and Notes*. 3 vols. New International Commentary on the Old Testament. Grand Rapids: Eerdmans, 1965 (vol. 1), 1969 (vol. 2), 1972 (vol. 3).
Young, Franklin W. 'A Study of the Relation of Isaiah to the Fourth Gospel.' *Zeitschrift für die neutestamentliche Wissenschaft* 46 (1955): 215-33.
Younger, K. Lawson., Jr. *Ancient Conquest Accounts: A Study in Ancient Near Eastern and Biblical History Writing*. Journal for the Study of the Old Testament, Supplement, no. 98. Sheffield: Journal for the Study of the Old Testament, 1990.
Zahn, Theodor. *Das Evangelium des Johannes*. Wuppertal: Brockhaus, 1983.
Zimmerli, Walther. *Ezekiel 1: A Commentary on the Book of the Prophet Ezekiel, Chapters 1-24*. Translated by Ronald E. Clements. Hermeneia. Philadelphia: Fortress, 1979.
— *Ezekiel 2: A Commentary on the Book of the Prophet Ezekiel, Chapters 25-48*. Translated by James D. Martin. Hermeneia. Philadelphia: Fortress, 1983.

Author Index

Aalen, S. 168
Abbott, E.A. 115, 121
Abelson, J. 97
Achtemeier, E. 19, 20
Ackroyd, P.R. 83-85, 88
Alexander, T.D. 16
Allen, L.C. 74, 78, 128
Alsup, J.E. 32
Amsler, S. 2, 19-20, 27-28, 30, 36, 38, 174, 184-186, 189
Anderson, G.W. 88
Anderson, P. 4, 5
Ashton, J. 3, 4
Aune, D.E. 128
Baker, D.L. 19-20, 27-29, 93, 186, 191
Balfour, G. 162
Ball, D.M. 5
Banks, R. 135
Barclay, J. 123
Barrett, C.K. 111-113, 120-122, 124, 127, 132-133, 136, 140, 142-143, 161, 165, 167, 170, 172, 174-176, 178-179
Bauckham, R. 109, 200
Baumgarten, M. 92
Beale, G.K. 21, 23, 26, 81-82, 103, 201
Beasley-Murray, G. 7, 13, 113, 178, 199, 200
Becker, J. 3, 8
Bengel, J. 2
Benzing, B. 140
Bernard, J.H. 113, 115, 117-118, 132, 158, 167, 187, 188
Berz, A. 126
Best, E. 198
Betz, O. 138-139
Black, M. 91, 96
Blank, J. 149, 151

Blass, F. 14, 187
Blocher, H. 24
Block, D.I. 70, 73
Bloesch, D.G. 191
Blomberg, C. 21, 23
Böcher, O. 140
Bockmuehl, M. 93
Boer, M. de 6, 149, 151, 152
Boers, H. 138
Boismard, M.-É. 33, 117-118, 120-121
Botha, J.E. 140
Botterweck, G.J. 168
Bouyer, L. 162
Braun, F.-M. 10, 11, 67, 109, 119, 123-124, 141, 158, 160, 166, 171, 176, 178-179, 184, 189, 202
Braun, R. 49, 54-56
Brettler, M.Z. 7
Breytenbach, C. 129
Brockington, L.H. 152
Brodie, T. 4, 6, 9, 158
Bromiley, G. 20, 117-118, 143
Brooke, G.J. 131, 151
Brown, R. 18, 112, 114, 118-124, 126-127, 140-143, 148, 151, 162, 166-167, 174-176, 178-179, 182, 184, 189-191, 199
Bruce, F.F. 13, 23, 111, 123, 126-127, 136-137, 157, 170, 176-178, 184, 187, 188-189, 191-193, 202
Buchanan, G.W. 31, 34, 35
Bultmann, R. 13, 112, 121-122, 134, 140, 142, 175, 176
Burge, G.M. 143, 179
Burkett, D. 131-133
Busink, T. 102
Busse, U. 11, 36
Caird, G.B. 150-153

Caldecott, W.S. 39
Calvin, J. 111, 121
Cameron, N. 24
Carson, D.A. 1-6, 7, 9, 13-14, 16, 18-, 20, 25-26, 28, 34-36, 85-87, 104, 109, 111-114, 120-121, 123, 127, 129, 142-143, 147, 151-152, 157, 163, 165, 172, 174, 177-180, 184, 187-190, 193, 202
Cassuto, U. 40, 42
Charlesworth, J.H. 95
Chary, T. 84
Chester, A. 95, 98-99
Childs, B.S. 39, 40, 104, 154, 157, 168
Chilton, B. 109
Chyutin, M. 101
Clements, R.E. 46, 49, 52, 54, 76
Clifford, R.J. 64
Clowney, E.P. 11, 23, 81, 198, 199
Coggins, R. 88
Cohen, S.J.D. 102
Cole, A. 115
Collins, J. 93, 94, 101
Collins, R.F. 125, 135, 158
Coloe, M. 16-18, 113, 116, 157, 160, 171, 175, 177, 190, 192
Congar, Y. 11, 44, 79
Conybeare, F.C. 153
Coppens, J. 24, 198
Cortés, J.B. 162
Cothenet, E. 34, 185
Crabtree, A.B. 26
Craigie, P.C. 63
Cullmann, O. 10, 11, 20, 126, 132
Culpepper, R.A. 3, 6, 113, 119, 134, 140, 170
Curtis, E.L. 67
Cyril of Alexandria 121
Daly-Denton, M. 35, 192
Davey, F.N. 18
Davids, P.H. 9
Davidson, R. 19-22, 30-32, 186, 202
Davies, G.I. 97
Davies, M. 4, 5, 9, 12, 126

Davies, P. 91-94, 99, 137, 171
Davies, W.D. 12
De Young, J.C. 47, 57, 62
Debrunner, A. 14
Delitzsch, F. 41, 42, 49, 52, 64, 153
DeVries, S.J. 54, 55
Dillard, R.B. 58
Dion, H. 147, 149
Dodd, C.H. 114, 123, 130, 132, 134, 151, 156, 170, 178
Dubarle, A.M. 10, 113, 114, 185
Duguid, I.M. 77
Dumbrell, W.J. 117, 124
Dwight, T. 111
Edwards, R.B. 120, 121
Eichrodt, W. 19, 20, 27, 29-30, 39, 46, 78, 79, 81, 82
Eisemann, M. 75, 77, 78, 80, 82, 102
Ellis, E.E. 2, 21-22, 104, 186, 187
Enz, J.J. 32, 33
Epp, E.J. 1
Eppstein, V. 110
Evans, C. 5, 35, 91, 109, 110, 118, 120-121, 157, 158
Fairbairn, P. 2, 36, 81, 82, 185, 188
Farrer, A.M. 30
Feinberg, C.L. 80
Feuillet, A. 118-121, 124, 140, 162, 165, 169, 175
Fischer, E. 162
Fletcher-Louis, C. 109
Flint, P.W. 92
Forestell, J.T. 142, 151, 156, 172, 174
Foulkes, F. 19, 20, 28
Fowler, M. 40
Fowler, W.G. 11, 12
France, R.T. 19, 21, 27, 28, 29, 109, 178, 186
Freed, E. 111, 140
Frühwald-König, J. 15, 113
Funk, R. 14, 109
Gaebelein, A.C. 80
García Martínez, F. 91, 94, 99-101, 104

Gärtner, B. 34, 93, 177
Gaston, L. 11
Gathercole, S. 16
Glasson, T.F. 33, 36
Godet, F.L. 111, 113-114, 121, 134
Goldstein, J.A. 90
Goppelt, L. 2, 20-21, 27, 30, 34, 36, 123, 144, 188, 202
Görg, M. 42
Goulder, M.D. 31
Grabbe, L.L. 91
Graham, M.P. 55
Green, D.E. 117
Greenberg, M. 73, 75-78, 80
Grelot, P. 163, 165, 166
Grigsby, B.H. 176, 178, 180
Guilding, A. 11, 12
Gundry, R.H. 18
Haenchen, E. 109, 110, 151, 193
Hahn, F. 129, 139
Halpern, B. 45
Hamid-Khani, S. 10
Hamilton, V.P. 127, 129, 131, 133
Hanson, A.T. 11, 31, 35, 36, 38, 120, 126
Haran, M. 40, 47, 49, 59, 62, 75, 76
Harrington, H.K. 93
Hartman, L. 11, 116
Hartwell, H. 65
Heil, J.P. 115
Hempel, C. 91
Henderson, E. 80
Hengel, M. 92, 93
Hengstenberg, E.W. 2, 80
Hess, R.S. 62, 65
Hiers, R.H. 110
Hildebrandt, W. 144, 164
Hill, A.E. 86
Hofmann, J.C.K. von 21-22
Hoglund, K.G. 55
Hollander, H.W. 98
Holwerda, D. 23, 142, 143, 149, 184, 189, 191
Horbury, W. 54, 95-96, 98, 110

Hoskyns, E.C. 18, 113, 119, 124, 126, 134, 136, 139, 157, 171, 175, 179
Houtman, C. 129-131
Howard, J.K. 176, 178, 179
Hubbard, R.L. 23
Hunt, S. 33
Hurowitz, V. 51-52
Ibuki, Y. 166
Japhet, S. 56-58, 67, 83, 85, 104
Jenson, P.P. 40-41, 48, 60
Jerome 115
John Chrysostom 121-122, 138, 175, 178, 180, 188
Johnson, A.R. 63
Jonge, M. de 6, 98, 127
Juel, D. 114-115
Kaiser, Jr., W.C. 130
Kaufmann, Y. 75, 88
Keener, C.S. 161, 166
Keil, C.F. 41-42, 52-53, 58, 61, 70, 74, 77, 81, 82
Kellermann, D. 117
Kerr, A. 16-18, 123, 132, 160, 171, 175, 179, 190
Kinzer, M. 13
Klein, W.W. 23
Klinzing, G. 93
Koch, K. 85
Koester, C.R. 11, 38, 117-118, 120, 124
Köstenberger, A.J. 35, 111
Kraus, H. 62-65, 168
Kreitzer, L.J. 109
Kugler, R. 92, 93, 94
L'Eplattenier, C. 111
La Potterie, I. de 136, 139, 140, 143, 172
Labahn, M. 12
Laberge, L. 42
Ladd, G.E. 23, 81, 104, 140-143, 169, 189, 191
Lampe, G.W.H. 20, 24, 27, 30, 31
Lane, W.L. 110
Laney, J.C. 80

Léon-Dufour, X. 3, 10, 113, 160, 162, 171
Levenson, J. 62-65, 75-76, 78-80, 98, 144
Levine, B.A. 41
Lewis, D. 118
Lightfoot, J. 2
Lindars, B. 109-110, 115, 120-121, 126, 132, 134-135, 140, 142, 158, 163, 166
Livingstone, E. 197, 198
Loader, W. 129, 149, 150, 151, 152, 175
Lofthouse, W.F. 80
Lohfink, N. 45, 48
Longenecker, R.N. 2, 36, 160, 202
Losie, L.A. 11
Maass, F. 47
Macdonald, J. 137
MacRae, G.W. 1
Maddox, R. 135
Madsen, A.A. 67, 102
Maier, J. 99, 100-101
Malatesta, E. 163, 179
Marshall, I. H. 19, 198
Martin, J. 41, 52, 61, 70, 73-74, 153
Martin, R.P. 9
Mason, R. 88
Mayer, G. 140
McCaffrey, J. 12-15, 18, 157, 160, 162, 171, 175
McCarter, P.K. 51, 52, 56, 57
McConville, J.G. 45-49, 51, 61, 75-76, 85, 87
McCool, F.J. 142
McGrath, A. 118
McKelvey, R.J. 11, 36, 93, 96, 99, 190, 191, 197-201
McKenzie, J.L. 142
McKenzie, S.L. 55
Meeks, W.A. 33-34, 123, 148, 184, 185, 186
Menken, M. 6, 33, 111, 161-162, 164, 165, 166

Mettinger, T. 48
Metzger, M. 187
Meyer, H. 2, 13, 109, 112, 114, 115, 118, 121-122, 134, 175, 192
Meyers, C.L. and Meyers, E.M. 85, 88, 89
Michaelis, W. 117-118, 126-128
Milgrom, J. 41
Millar, F. 91
Millar, J.G. 45-46, 48, 49
Moloney, F.J. 126, 128, 134, 135, 151, 156, 158
Moo, D.J. 20, 25-26, 28, 111, 122
Morgen, M. 126, 129-130, 133
Morris, L. 2, 12, 36, 110, 160, 167, 176, 192
Mosis, R. 54, 56, 58-59, 66
Motyer, J.A. 153, 154, 168
Moule, C.F.D. 10, 21, 22, 108, 187, 189
Mowinckel, S. 88, 111
Murphy, A.C. 80
Murphy, J.G. 80
Mussner, F. 11, 167, 198
Naudé, J.A. 175
Neill, S. 1
Nereparampil, L. 10
Neyrey, J.H. 127, 129, 130-131, 133, 137, 172
Nicholson, G.C. 148-150
Nickelsburg, G.W.E. 95-96, 98-99
Niehaus, J. 46, 49-50
Nordheim, E. von 51
O'Connell, M.J. 140
O'Day, G.R. 136, 140-141
Odeberg, H. 130
Olsson, B. 165-166
Orr, J. 39, 49
Osborne, G.R. 9, 20, 23
Østenstad, G.H. 15
Ostmeyer, K.H. 31
Oswald, H.C. 62, 65
Oswalt, J.N. 104
Packer, J.I. 25

Author Index

Pamment, M. 147, 149
Pancaro, S. 34, 121, 123-124, 126-127, 131, 143, 178-179, 184-185, 189
Parker, T. 111
Paulien, J. 120, 128
Paulsen, H. 129
Pesch, R. 126, 149
Peter, A. 79, 81
Petersen, D.L. 84, 85
Porsch, F. 140-141, 143
Porter, S.E. 5, 14, 91
Poythress, V.S. 23, 25, 40
Priest, J. 95
Pryor, J.W. 123
Quispel, G. 129
Rad, G. von 20, 24-25, 27, 29-30, 46-48
Rahner, J. 10, 116
Raurell, F. 34
Reim, G. 33-34, 178-179, 185-186
Ridderbos, H.N. 116, 120-121, 124, 127, 132, 134, 167, 177, 199
Riley, W. 52, 199
Robertson, A.T. 14
Robinson, J.A.T. 198
Roth, C. 110
Rowland, C. 96, 99, 109, 130, 132, 133
Ruckstuhl, E. 4, 149
Rudolph, W. 85
Sahlin, H. 2, 32, 33, 36
Salier, B. 16
Sanders, E.P. 90, 91, 92, 93, 94, 95, 96, 121, 124
Schenke, L. 134
Schlatter, A. 118, 120, 124, 134, 158, 166, 167, 177
Schmidt, M. 56, 79, 81, 82
Schmitt, J.W. 80
Schmitt, R. 40
Schnackenburg, R. 18, 113, 121, 124, 126, 134, 136, 142-143, 149-151, 161-163, 166-167, 169, 172, 175-176, 178-180, 198
Schneider, J. 172

Schnelle, U. 112, 116, 190
Scholz, F. 79
Schreiner, J. 11, 45, 47, 50, 53, 60, 64
Schürer, E. 91-93, 95-97, 99
Schüssler Fiorenza, E. 90, 93
Schwank, B. 192
Schwartz, J. 130
Scott, C. 161
Scott, Jr., J.J. 102
Scullion, J.J. 131
Selman, M.J. 62
Senior, D. 178
Shidemantle, C.S. 161
Simon, M. 10-11, 184
Skilton, J.H. 11
Skinner, J. 73
Smalley, S.S. 126, 128, 134, 135
Smith, B.D. 178
Smith, D.M. 1, 123, 152, 167, 175, 177, 184, 185, 190
Smith, R. 32, 33
Spatafora, A. 11, 99, 190, 191
Stegner, W.R. 5, 35
Stek, J.H. 21-22, 24-25, 27-29, 186, 189, 197
Sternberg, M. 4-8
Stevenson, G. 82
Stevenson, K. 73, 201
Stock, G. 153
Sweet, J. 123
Terrien, S. 46
Terry, M.S. 22, 24
Thiering, B.E. 99-100
Thiselton, A. 3
Tholuck, 178
Thompson, J.A. 86
Throckmorton, B.H. 197
Thüsing, W. 12, 148, 152
Tiller, P.A. 95
Townsend, J. 11
Tragan, P.R. 163
Trocmé, E. 110
Tsumura, D.T. 65
Tuckett, C.M. 11

Ulfgard, H. 163
Umoh, C. 12
Unger, M.F. 80-81
Van Seters, J. 55, 58, 60
VanderKam, J.C. 91, 92
VanGemeren, W.A. 88, 144, 175
Vaux, R. de 47, 48
Vergote, A. 149
Vermes, G. 91
Vischer, W. 26
Vriend, J. 116
Wacholder, B.Z. 99-100
Walker, P.W.L. 12-13, 184, 189
Walker, W.L. 51
Watts, R. 26, 164, 188
Weiser, A. 65
Wenham, G.J. 41, 45-47, 49, 62, 65
Wenschkewitz, H. 10, 113, 115
Westcott, B.F. 151, 166, 174, 202
Westermann, C. 19, 131
White, R.T. 99
Whitelaw, L. 49
Williamson, H.G.M. 1, 19, 54, 55, 57, 58, 61, 68
Wilson, I. 40, 47, 48, 61
Windisch, H. 133
Woollcombe, K.J. 30, 31
Wright, C. 189
Wright, N.T. 1, 184
Yadin, Y. 94, 99, 100, 101
Yarbrough, R.W. 30
Yee, G.A. 161, 171, 176, 179
Young, E.J. 102, 104, 164
Younger, Jr., K.L. 7, 8
Zahn, T. 18, 114, 117-118, 121-122, 124, 134, 139, 157, 166, 176, 178
Zimmerli, W. 73-74, 78-7

Scripture Index

Genesis

1:2	144
2:8-10	79
2:10	64
2:13	64
2:16	65
3:17-19	65
3:8	65
12:6	137
17:8	45
18	129
22	57
27:35	126
27:35-36	126
28:12	126, 128, 129, 130, 131, 132, 133
28:12-17	130
28:13a	129
28:13-15	129
28:16	129
28:17	129, 132
32:24-30	129
32:26-29	127
32:28	126
33:19-20	137
35:2-4	139
35:10	126
35:10-12	129

Exodus

2:23-12:51	32
4:21-22	172
4:22	172
9:8-12	32
12:1-13	177
12:10	178
12:22	178
12:43-49	77
12:46	187
12:49	77
13:2	172, 175
13:21	43, 44
13:21-22	44, 168
14:4, 17, 18	153
14:19-20	168
15:1, 6, 11, 21	153
15:2	149
15:17	56, 57, 99
15:23-26	33
15:26	85
16:10	43, 44, 105, 117
17:1-7	163
19-20	43
19:2	44
19:6	172
19:9	60, 124
19:9-13	43
19:12-13, 23	43
19:16	43
19:16, 18	43, 44
19:17-24	61
19:20	43
19:22	175
20:18	43
20:21	60, 61, 124
20:22	61
20:24	48
24	43
24:1, 10	43
24:3-8	144
24:12	43
24:15-16	42
24:15-18	44, 73
24:16-17	43, 105, 119
25	54, 73, 201
25-31	39, 54, 105
25:1-9	51
25:2-7	55
25:8	39, 57, 74, 105, 117, 118, 125
25:9	39, 55, 73
25:10-22	39, 53
25:22	39, 58, 59, 105, 125
25:30	40
25:40	41
26:33-34	39
27:21	40
28:1	77
29:1-46	41
29:36	76
29:36, 43-44	172
29:42-43	39, 105, 125
29:43	42, 60, 74, 105, 125, 171
29:43-44	173
29:44	172, 173, 175
29:45	40, 45, 74, 104, 117, 118, 125
29:45-46	39
30:20	41
30:22-33	41
31:1-5	54
33:7	44
33:7-11	117
33:12-34:9	117
33:18-19	120
33:18-23	47, 61
33:18-34:7	120
33:19-23	124
33:20-23	120
34:1-4	120
34:5-6	61
34:5-7	120

34:6	120	17:11	41	19:9	97
35	54	19:2	44	19:13	41
35-40	54	24:5-9	101	20:2-13	163
35:4-29	55	25	73	20:6	43, 44, 117, 125
35:30-33	54	25:10	73	20:6-8	105, 125
36:8-39:32	54	26	45, 63, 70, 87	21:16-18	163
37:1	55	26:1-3	144	21:17-18	164
38:22	55	26:1-12, 30-33	69	25:11-13	77
40:9-13	41	26:3-13	71	33:2	8
40:33-35	58	26:5	78	35:34	118, 125
40:34	42	26:11	65, 74, 125		
40:34-35	42, 58, 74, 105, 173	26:11-12	45, 104	**Deuteronomy**	
		26:12	65, 197	1:33	48
40:34-38	42, 44, 117	26:14	85	4:8	122
40:38	169	26:14-39	70	4:11	60, 124
		26:28	70	4:12, 15, 33, 36	48
Leviticus		26:40-45	87	4:29	86
1:1	44, 105, 125, 169	26:45	45	4:29-30	87
1:3	77			4:36, 39	61
1:5-6	77	**Numbers**		5	43
3	64	2	44	5:4	48
4	41	2:1-31	78	5:4, 22, 23, 24, 26	48
4:1-6:7	41	3:12-13	172	5:22	60, 124
8-9	41	3:23, 29, 35, 38	78	6:20-25	8
8:2	77	4	54, 76	8:1-20	8
8:15	172	5:3	118, 125	8:15	163
9	42, 43, 117	7:1, 11	172	9:10, 21	48
9:1-24	44	7:89	39	10:4	48
9:2-4, 7-22	42	9:12	178, 187	11:13	85
9:3-4	42	9:15	42	11:29	137
9:6	42	9:15-23	44	11:30	137
9:23-24	43, 58, 105, 173	11:25-29	144	12	47, 48, 137
		12	44	12-26	50
9:24	43, 54, 74	14:10	42, 43, 117, 125	12:1	47
10:1-2	77	14:10-35	105, 125	12:2	47
10:1-3	198	14:14	44	12:2-3	47
10:3	153	15:14-16	77	12:2-28	173
11:1-15:33	41	16	44	12:3	67
15:31	41	16:19	125	12:5	45, 47, 56, 62, 105
16	41, 77	16:19, 42	42, 43, 117		
16:11-17	58	16:19-24, 42-44	105, 125	12:5, 11, 14, 18, 21	137
16:12, 14	124				
16:13	39	16:35	44	12:5, 21	45
16:16, 19	41	18:7	77	12:5-6	105, 137

Scripture Index

12:5-7	106	31:15	48, 125	**2 Samuel**	
12:6	175			5:6-12	53
12:6, 11	46	**Joshua**		5:7	57
12:7, 12, 18	48	1:13	56	5:10	52
12:9-10	56	1:13, 15	78	6	50, 53
12:10	47, 49, 56, 78, 83	6:4	50	6:2	39, 47, 53, 58, 59, 74, 200
12:11	45	8:33-34	137	6:12	53
12:18, 26	45	11:23	56	6:17-18	50
14:23	45	18:1	49, 56, 78	7:1	56
14:23, 26	48	21:44	49, 56, 78	7:1, 11	56, 78
14:24	45	22:4	49, 56, 78	7:2	51, 52, 53
14:25	45	23:1	56, 78	7:2, 7	53
15:19-21	175	24:4, 14	139	7:2-16	52
15:20	45, 48			7:5	61
16	46	**Judges**		7:5-7	51, 52
16:11, 16	48	18:31	49, 50, 59	7:5-16	61
16:15	170	21:19-21	49	7:6	49, 57
17:8, 10	45			7:6-11	57
17:8-9	76	**1 Samuel**		7:7	52
18:6	45	1:3	49	7:8-9	52
18:7	48	1:7	49	7:8-16	52
23:18	49	1:7, 24	49, 59	7:10	56
26:1-11	173	1:9	49, 60	7:10-11	57
26:2	45	2:22	49	7:11	63
26:5, 10	61	2:27-36	50	7:13	50, 51, 52, 55, 57
26:5, 10, 13	48	3:3	49, 60	7:15	66
26:10	137	3:11-14	50	12:20	49
26:15	61	3:12-14	77		
27:2-7	137	3:15	49	**1 Kings**	
27:4	137	4	56	1:32-39	77
27:12	137	4:4	39, 50, 200	2:3	60
28	63, 70, 85, 87	4:4, 21-22	74	3:2	50
28:1	85, 144	4:11	50	5:3-5	52
28:2-13	71	4:21-22	69, 103, 106, 159	5:4	56, 67, 78
28:15-57	70	4:22	50	5:4-5	83
30:1-4	85	6:8	97	5:18	56
30:2-5	87	7:1	50	6	73
30:2-10	87	8	51, 52	6-7	54
30:3-10	87	8:5	51	6:2	98, 105
30:6-10	87	8:11-18	52	6:12-13	105
31:11	45	21:1-6	50	6:13	45, 57, 118, 125
31:14-15	44, 48			6:20	200
31:14-21	105, 125			7:49	60

8:4-11	53, 74, 200
8:9	58
8:10-11	58, 60, 74, 119, 173
8:10-12	47
8:10-13	105
8:12	60
8:12-13	60, 61, 74, 105, 124
8:12-61	75
8:13	61, 62, 125
8:13, 29-30, 43	90
8:16-19	52
8:17	61
8:18	52, 55
8:20-21	61
8:22, 54	77
8:25-26	61
8:27	61, 90, 103, 107, 200
8:27-53	61
8:28-48	174
8:29, 43-44	174
8:29-30	61, 174
8:29-30, 35, 38, 42, 44, 47	62
8:30, 32, 36, 39, 43, 45 LXX	174
8:30, 39, 43, 49	62
8:31-32	61
8:32, 34, 36, 45	62
8:33	62
8:33-48	61, 174
8:37-38, 43	174
8:44	57
8:44 LXX	174
8:56	56, 63, 78
8:63-4, 9:3	172
9:3	59, 62, 66, 75, 90, 103, 107, 171, 172, 173, 174, 200
9:3-9	67
9:4-9	66
10:23-25	72
10:25	68
11:4-13	66
11:9-14, 23, 26	57
11:36	57
12:28-33	67
13:28-33	138
14:9-10, 15-16	66
14:11-14	66
18:7-8	67
19:32-34	67
21:1	59

2 Kings

5:1-19	72
6:20, 22	153
14:10 LXX	153
16:10-16	77
17	139
17:7-20	138
17:21-23	66
17:24-26	138
17:24-41	138
17:26-28	138
17:32-41	138
17:34	139
17:34-41	144
17:35-39	139
17:39	139
18:3	68
18:4	68
18:5-6	68
19	68
19:15	39, 74
1915	200
20:1-11	68
21:5, 7	67
21:7-8	67
21:11-15	66
22:2	67, 68
22:20	67
23:25	144
23:26-27	68
24:3-4	66

1 Chronicles

6:12-15	77
6:49	60
11:9	52
13	53
13:3	53
13:6	39, 53, 58, 59, 74, 200
15	53
15:12, 14	175
16	50, 53
16:39	50
17	52
17:1	53
17:4	61
17:4-14	61
17:7-8	52
17:9	56
17:10	63
17:12	55
17:12, 14	52
18-20	72
21:1	53
21:18	55
21:18-22:1	53, 57
21:18-25	53
21:26	53, 58
21:26-22:1	73
21:29	50
22	49
22-29	54
22:1	53, 78, 105, 171
22:2-5	54
22:6-16	54
22:6-19	54
22:7-11	52, 61
22:9	56
22:9, 18	56, 67, 78
22:9-10	56
22:9-10, 18-19	83
22:13	54, 60
22:17-19	54
22:18	63
23-26	54, 76

23:25	56, 78	6:7-9	52	14:6-7	56, 67, 78
23:26	54	6:8	52, 55	15:15	56, 67, 78
28	49, 54	6:10-11	61	17:10-11	72
28:2	56, 57, 62	6:12	77	20:30	56, 67, 78
28:2-6	52	6:16-17	61	23:18	54, 60, 76
28:2-10	61	6:18	61, 90, 103, 107, 200	24:6, 9	60
28:3	56			26:16	77
28:6, 10-21	105	6:18-39	61	26:16-23	91, 198
28:11-19	55, 73	6:19-38	174	29	68
28:19	55	6:20-21	61, 174	29:5, 15-19	173
28:20-21	54	6:20-21, 26, 29, 32, 34, 38	62	29:5, 34	175
29	49, 54			29:25	54, 55, 76
29:1-5	55	6:21, 30, 33, 39	62	30:3, 15, 24	175
29:1-9	55	6:22-23	61	30:8	171, 173
29:29-30	8	6:23, 25, 27, 30, 33, 35, 39	174	30:16	60
				30:26	68
2 Chronicles		6:23, 25, 27, 35	62	32:1-22	68
2:6	61	6:24	62	32:22	56, 67, 68
3	73	6:24-38	174	32:23	68, 72, 84
3-4	54	6:24-38:1	61	32:24	68
3:1	55, 57	6:28-29, 33	174	32:27-29	68
3:3	54	6:34	174	32:30	64
3:4-8	201	6:41	59	33:5, 7	67
3:6	156, 201	7:1	54, 58	33:7-8	67
3:8	54	7:1-2	105	33:11-13	66
3:11-16	54	7:1-3	58, 60, 74, 119, 173	34:2	67
4:7-8, 19-20	60			34:28	67
4:18-22	54	7:2	58	35:4, 15	54, 76
5:4-14	53	7:3	58, 74	35:6, 12	60
5:5-14	74, 200	7:5, 7, 16	172	36:22-23	83
5:10	58	7:12	60, 105, 175		
5:11	175	7:12-15	66	**Ezra**	
5:11-14	58	7:14-15	62	1:1-8	83
5:13-14	60, 74, 119, 173	7:15-16	90	1:4	83
		7:16	59, 62, 66, 75, 90, 103, 105, 107, 171, 173, 174, 200	3:2	80
5:13-6:2	105			3:10-4:24	83
6:1-2	60, 61, 74, 105, 124			3:12	84
		7:16-22	67	5:1-2	83
6:1-42	75	7:17-22	66	6:4	83
6:2	61, 125	8:13	39, 60, 68	6:14	83
6:2, 20-21, 33	90	9:3	105	6:16-17	173
6:5-6	137	9:22-24	72	6:18	80
6:6	105, 171	9:24	68	9:1-3	87
6:7	61	11:13-15	67	9:4	87

9:14-15	85	
10:2-4	85	
10:3	87	

Nehemiah

1:8-9	85
8:14	80
9:9-31	164
9:12, 19	168
9:14-15, 20	163
9:15, 20	163
9:20	164
9:34	144
9:36-38	85
10	85
10:29	85
10:30-39	85
12:24, 45	54, 76, 80
13:10-30	85
13:31	87

Job

22:28	168
29:3	168
33:4	144
33:28	168
34:14-15	144

Psalms

2	24, 68, 72
2:6-9	25
5	106
5:7	106, 138
7:6	153
11:4	62
12:2	153
15	63, 104, 144
15:1	63
15:1-5	69
15:2-5	63, 65
18:6	62, 66, 106, 174
18:8	168
18:16-29	63
18:43-50	25
20:1-9	62, 106, 174
20:2	66
20:6	62, 103, 107, 200
20:13	153
22:18	188
23:6	65, 106
24	63, 104
24:1-6	69
24:3	63
24:3-6	144
24:4	63, 65, 106
24:4-5	104
24:5	65
26:1-12	69
26:6	77
26:8	62, 63, 106
27:1	168
27:1-10	169
27:4	63, 64, 65, 105, 106, 125, 134
27:5	63, 174
28:2	62, 106, 174
33:5	168
33:13-14	62, 103, 107, 200
34:20	178, 187
36:1-4, 12	66
36:5-9	64, 65, 79, 106, 166, 180
36:7-9	64, 65, 169, 170
36:8	64, 79, 106
36:8-9	64, 169, 170
36:9	134, 168, 169, 170
36:20	149, 153
37	70, 86
37:7-10, 22	66
37:22	87
37:27	87
42-43	166
42:1-4	63, 65, 106
42:2	166
42:2-4	64
43:3	62, 134, 166, 168
43:3-4	63, 65, 106, 169
44:3	168
46	63, 106
46:4	62, 64, 79, 106, 166, 180
48	63, 106
48:1-2	106
48:2	63, 78
49:19	168
50:2	63, 64, 66, 106
50:16-22	63
50:16-23	66
51:7-12	142
51:14-17	104
52:1-9	69
52:8	65, 79, 106, 166, 180
56:5, 11	153
56:13	168
61:3-4	64
61:4	63, 65, 106
63:1	63
63:1-5	65, 106
63:2	62, 64
65:4	64, 65, 79, 106, 166, 180
65:7	153
68:24	62
69	110
69:4	110
69:9	110, 111, 192, 193
69:9b	110
69:21	110, 188
69:25	110
72:8-11	25
72:10	68
74:2-4	62
76	63, 98, 106
76:2	62
78:9-33	164
78:14	168
78:16, 20	163

Scripture Index

78:20	164	
78:56-59	50	
78:60	50, 69, 103, 106, 159, 192	
78:68	57	
78:69	98, 99, 105	
80:1	62	
80:14	62, 103, 107, 200	
81:11-16	63	
82:6	172	
84	63	
84:1-4	64	
84:1-12	65, 106	
84:4	106	
84:10	63	
84:10-11	64, 79, 106, 166, 180	
88:13	153	
89:15	168	
89:27	25	
92:7-14	69	
92:12-14	65, 79, 106, 166, 180	
93:2	153	
97:11	168	
99:1-2, 5	62	
99:5	62, 74, 106	
99:5, 9	106, 138	
101	87	
102:15, 22	72	
102:16	71, 97, 105, 119, 188	
102:19	62, 103, 107, 200	
103:19	62, 103, 107, 200	
104:30	144	
105:1	163	
105:25-45	164	
105:39	168	
105:41	164	
112:4	168	
113:5	62, 103, 107, 200	
115:3	62, 103, 107, 200	
116	68	
119:105, 130	168	
123:1	62, 103, 107, 200	
132:5, 7, 13-14	62	
132:7	62, 106, 138	
132:8	59	
132:13-14	57	
135:21	62, 98	
137	71	
138:2	106, 138	
147:19-20	122	

Proverbs
6:23	168

Isaiah
1:10-20	144
2	153, 154, 155, 183
2:1	154
2:1, 11, 17	155
2:1-5	157
2:1-5, 12-22	148
2:2	72, 82, 154, 156, 157, 170
2:2-3	71, 72, 98, 157, 188
2:2-4	89, 139, 154, 157
2:2-5	134, 168, 169, 170
2:3	78, 156, 157
2:4	72
2:5	164, 168
2:6-22	153
2:7-22	156
2:9-21	154
2:10	153
2:10-11, 17, 19, 21	154
2:11	153, 155
2:11, 17	153, 154
2:14	154
2:17	153
4:2	149, 155
4:5	164, 169
4:5-6	70, 168
5:16	149, 155
5:16, 17	153
6	105, 125
6:1-2	125
6:1-13	158
9:2	164
9:6-7	25, 71, 72
9:7	25
10:15	149, 153, 156
11:1-5	25, 71
11:2	164
11:4	72
11:6-9	71
11:12	71, 157
12:3	164
12:6	153, 155
14:4-20	156
24:23	153, 155
26:9	164, 168
27:12-13	71
27:13	106, 138
30:18	153, 155
30:18, 23-25	159
30:23	164
30:23-25	164
30:23-26	71
30:26	164
31:3	141
32:15	71, 164
32:15-17	144
33	154, 155
33:10	149, 153, 154, 155, 156
33:10, 16, 21	159
33:15-16	156
33:16	164, 180
33:16, 21	164
33:20-21	79

Reference	Pages
33:20-24	71, 89
33:21	164
35:6-7	79, 164
40:11	157
41:17-20	79, 164, 180
42:1	164
42:6	164, 168, 170
42:16	168
43:5	157
43:5-7	71
43:19-20	79
43:19-21	164, 180
44:2-3	180
44:3	164, 166
44:3-4	79, 164
44:3-5	144
44:28	71, 83, 188
48:20-21	164
48:21	165
49:3	132, 153, 155, 156
49:3, 10	159
49:5	155
49:5-6	71, 156, 157
49:6	164, 168, 170
49:10	164, 180
50:10	164
51:3	79, 106
51:4	164, 168
51:4-5	170
51:5	164
51:14	164, 180
52	147
52:7-53:12	158
52:12	168
52:13	147, 149, 155, 156
53:11	164
53:11-12	155
54:10	71
54:11-17	71, 89
54:12	101
54:14-15	71
55:1	164
55:1-2	180
55:2	164
55:5	155, 157
56:6-7	71, 98, 188
56:6-8	157
56:7	72, 106
56:8	71, 157
57:15	104
58:10	164
58:11	164
59:20	86
59:21	164
60	106
60:1, 3, 19-20	164
60:1-2, 19-20	168
60:3	168
60:3-17	168
60:5-13	71
60:5-14	72
60:7	72, 98, 158
60:7, 13	71, 89, 148, 155, 156, 188
60:7, 13, 19	159
60:13	74
61:1	164
61:6-9	71
61:8	71
62:1	164
62:1-12	71, 89
62:8-9	71
62:9	71, 188
63:8-14	164
65:8-16	86
65:17-20	71, 89
65:20-24	71
66:1	74, 103, 107, 200
66:1-2	103, 141
66:1-6	144
66:2	107, 156
66:3	104
66:7-24	154
66:12-14	71
66:18-19	97, 105, 119
66:18-21	72
66:18-23	71, 98, 188
66:18-24	134
66:20	71
66:23	72, 106, 138, 157

Jeremiah

Reference	Pages
1:5	172
2:13	79
3:14, 18	71
3:16	71, 74, 97, 201
3:17	72, 74, 106, 201
7	51, 69, 70, 71, 144
7:1-15	69
7:2	106, 138
7:2-3	69
7:4-8	70
7:5-6, 9-10	69
7:9-11	71
7:10	90
7:11	69
7:12	49, 56
7:12-14	69, 103, 106, 137, 159, 192
7:12-15	51
7:14-15	69, 70
7:21-23	104
7:23	86
14:21	74
17:12	74
17:24	86
17:24-27	86, 88
18:1-10	86
18:9-10	87
18:11	86
22:2-5	86, 88
22:3	86
23:3	71
23:5-6	25, 71
24:7	45
26:1-6	69
26:2	106, 138
29:10-14	86
30:3, 10	71

Scripture Index

30:9	25, 71	11:16	70, 103, 104, 107	37:24-28	25, 71
30:18	71	11:17	70	37:24b	87
30:19	71	11:17-21	71	37:25-28	89
31:5, 12	71	11:22	70	37:26	89, 103
31:8-11	71	11:22-23	103, 106, 159	37:26-27	71, 104, 159
31:16-20	86	11:23	74	37:26-28	71, 98, 105, 188
31:23	71, 188	16:61-63	75	37:27	45, 74, 118, 125, 197
31:31-37	71	17:3-24	80	38:8, 11, 14	78
31:33	45	17:22-23	78	38:23	154
31:38-40	71, 89	19:10-14	80	39:10	71
32:37	71	20:10-12	75	39:25	71
32:38	45	20:34-38	87	39:26	78, 89
32:38-41	71	20:39-40	86	39:29	144
33:6-9	71	20:40	71, 78, 188	40	75
33:9-11	71	20:41	71	40-42	72, 73
33:11	71, 188	21:27	25, 71	40-46	105
33:15-22	25, 71	22:26	78	40-47	12
33:18	77	28:13-14	79	40-48	38, 69, 72, 73, 75, 76, 78, 80, 81, 82, 89, 101
51:11	198	28:22	154	40:1	72
		28:25-26	71	40:1-47:12	71, 188
Lamentations		28:26	78	40:2	73, 78, 82, 156
2:1	62, 74, 106	31:3-18	80	40:39-41	77
		34:11-16	71	42:20	78
Ezekiel		34:23-24	25, 71	43	75
1	168	34:24	45	43-44	169
1:1	128	34:25	71	43-46	72, 76
1:4-28	168	34:25, 27, 28	78	43-48	105, 125
1:28	74	34:25-31	89	43:1-5	74
4:1-17	168	34:26-27	71, 79	43:1-12	173
8-11	69, 70	36	192	43:2-4	97, 105, 119, 159
8:3-17	70	36:8-12, 29-30, 35	71	43:2-6	105, 125
8:6	70, 71, 192	36:11, 37-38	71	43:3	74, 169
9	86	36:24-28	71	43:4	125
9:1-10:7	70	36:25-27	103, 104, 142, 144	43:7	74, 106, 200
9:4-6	70	36:25-28	81	43:7, 9	45, 105, 118, 125, 197
9:4-10:6	71	36:27	76	43:7-9	77, 192
9:9	70	36:31-32	75	43:7-11	81
10:18	70	36:35	79, 106	43:7b, 9	77
10:18-19	103, 106, 159	37:14	142, 144		
10:19-11:12	70	37:15-23	71		
11:7	70	37:23	45		
11:15	70, 103				
11:15-16	141				

43:7b-9	75	
43:9	86, 98, 103, 118	
43:10	73, 75	
43:11	75, 76	
43:12	77	
43:18-27	75	
44	75	
44:1-4	74	
44:2	74	
44:3	77	
44:4	74, 97, 105, 119, 125, 159	
44:5	75, 76	
44:5-9	75	
44:7-8	76	
44:9	76, 89	
44:10-16	76	
44:10-31	75	
44:11	77	
44:15	77	
44:23	78	
44:24a	76	
45:1-4	77	
45:1-6	78	
45:3	77	
45:5	78	
45:6	71, 89, 101	
45:8-9	77	
45:9-46:15	75	
45:18-20	77	
45:21-24	179, 188	
45:24	76	
45:25	179	
46:2, 3, 9	106, 138	
46:2, 8, 12	77	
46:3	77, 100	
47	165, 166	
47:1-12	78, 79, 81, 106, 164, 165, 166, 180, 183	
47:2	89	
47:3-5	78	
47:5	164	
47:7, 12	79	
47:8	89	
47:8-10	79	
47:9	165	
47:12	79	
48:9-12	77	
48:9-20	78	
48:13-14	78	
48:15	89, 101	
48:15-17, 30-35	71	
48:16	101	
48:31	82, 101	
48:31-34	101	

Daniel
4	72
9:27	198
9:4-11	144
11:36	153

Hosea
1:10-11	71
2:16-20, 23	71
2:18	71
2:22	71
2:23	45
3:5	25, 71
6:6	104
11:12-12:14	126
12:1	126
12:4	129
12:5	130

Joel
2:19, 23-24	71
2:20	71
2:28	164
2:28-29	144
3:17	71, 98, 118, 188
3:17, 20	71, 89
3:18	71, 82, 106, 164, 165, 180
4:18	79

Amos
5:21-24	144
5:21-25	104
9:11	25, 71
9:13-15	71

Micah
3	71
3:12	71
4:1	72, 82, 154
4:1-2	71, 72, 188
4:1-3	89, 98, 157
4:1-4	134, 154, 170
4:2	78
4:4	72
4:6-7	71
5:2-4	25, 71
5:2-15	72
5:3	71
5:4	25
5:4-6	71

Zephaniah
3:13, 15	71
3:19-20	71

Haggai
1:2	83
1:5-11	84
1:8	154
1:13-15	83
2:3	84
2:6-9	84
2:7	72
2:7-8	71
2:7-9	156
2:9	71, 89, 98, 106, 188
2:15-19	84
2:18-19	106
2:23	25, 71, 84
2:24	84

Zechariah

1-8	84
1:2-6	84
1:3	86
1:16	71, 84, 188
1:19-21	84
2	118
2:1-5	71, 89
2:4-6, 11-12	84
2:5	97, 119
2:8-11	84
2:10	118, 125, 197
2:10-11	45
2:11	72
2:14	118
3:1-7	85
3:8	25, 71
4:10	84
5	85
5:1-11	85
5:2-4	87
6:11-12	25, 71
6:12-15	71, 188
6:15	85
7:8-14	84
7:9-10	85
8:3	71, 98, 118, 188
8:3-5, 22	71, 89
8:3-8, 14-15	84
8:4-5	71
8:7-8	71
8:8	45
8:9-11	84
8:9-12	106
8:12	71
8:12-13	84
8:16-17	85
8:20-23	72, 84, 89
9:8	71, 98, 188
9:8, 13-17	71
9:9	25, 71, 165
9:9-10	72
9:9-16	84
9:11	71
9:17	71, 84
10:4	25, 71, 84
10:8-12	84
10:9-12	71
12:1-9	71, 89
12:2-9	84
12:7-9	84
12:8	25, 71
12:10	165, 187
13:1	25, 164, 165
13:1, 9	84
13:8-9	86, 88
13:9	87
14	89
14:1, 14	89
14:1-21	88
14:2-5, 12-19	84
14:6-11, 20-21	84
14:8	79, 82, 89, 106, 164, 165, 166, 168, 180
14:8, 10	89
14:8-11, 16-21	71
14:10	82, 156
14:11	71
14:11, 21	89
14:14	71
14:16	89, 98, 157
14:16-17	106, 138
14:16-19	89, 165
14:16-19, 21	89
14:16-21	71, 188
14:17-18	165
14:17-19	72
14:20	89
14:21b	110

Malachi

1:8	86
1:10	94
1:11	72
2:8	86
2:11, 14	86
2:13	69, 86
3:1-5	86, 110
3:2-3	88
3:7	86
3:8-9	86
3:10-12	86
3:13-15	87
3:16-18	87
3:17-4:3	86
3:18-4:3	88
4:5-6	11

Matthew

3:16	128
12:39-40	111, 116
12:40	114
13:32	117
16:21	114
17:23	114
20:19	114
23:21	98
26:61	114, 115
27:34	110
27:40	114, 115
27:63	114

Mark

1:10	128
4:32	117
8:31	114
9:31	114
9:32	114
10:34	114
14:58	114, 115
15:29	114, 115

Luke

1:8-20	105, 125
3:21	128
9:22	114
13	114
13:19	117
18:33	114
23:36	110
24:7, 46	114

John

Reference	Pages
1	12, 17
1:1	118, 157
1:1, 18	124
1:1-18	16
1:9	169
1:9, 14-18	184
1:9-10	170
1:12-13	142, 143
1:14	12, 13, 108, 116, 117-119, 123-125, 131, 133, 135, 145, 146-147, 150-151, 155, 158, 167, 170, 173, 182, 183, 195, 196, 201
1:14, 16-18	135
1:14, 17-18	120, 143
1:14, 51	136, 145, 170
1:14-18	133
1:14-18, 51	167
1:14a	117, 121
1:14b	118, 119, 121
1:14b-d	124
1:14b-e	120
1:14c	118
1:14c-d	117, 119, 120, 125
1:14c-d	119
1:14e	119, 120, 122
1:14e, 16-18	122, 125
1:15	119
1:16	120, 121, 122
1:16-17	119, 122, 123, 125, 184
1:16-18	122, 184
1:16b	122, 123
1:17	121, 122
1:17-18	143
1:17a	120, 121, 122
1:17b	121
1:18	122, 124, 131
1:18a	120
1:29	176, 177, 178, 183
1:31, 49	126
1:32	141, 142
1:33	141, 163
1:38, 41-42	118
1:39	148
1:41	134
1:41, 49	111
1:45	1, 75, 123, 185, 186
1:45-51	126, 127, 136
1:47	126, 127
1:48-50	134
1:49	134, 136
1:50	127
1:51	16-18, 108, 116, 125-135, 145-147, 158, 183, 195, 196
1:51a	127
1:51b	127
2	115, 176
2:1-11	33
2:4	148
2:11	150, 151, 155, 173, 183
2:13	108, 109, 145
2:13, 23	160, 176
2:13-17	108
2:13-22	15, 16, 116, 158, 191
2:13-25	16, 109, 176, 177
2:14-17	16
2:15	109
2:15-16	110
2:16	109, 110
2:17	110-111, 113, 116, 166, 192
2:18	111, 115
2:18-19	158
2:18-22	108, 112, 135-136, 145-147, 158, 195, 196
2:19	2, 16, 111-116, 176, 191, 192
2:19, 20	115
2:19, 21	116, 191
2:19, 21-22	116
2:19, 22	192
2:19-21	131
2:19-22	2, 10, 12, 159, 178, 179, 183
2:20	16, 111, 112
2:21	111-115
2:21-22	112-113, 116, 176, 192
2:22	110-111, 113-14, 116, 163, 192, 193
2:23	176
3	142, 143, 156, 192
3:5	141, 142, 167
3:5, 16, 36	142
3:5-6	104, 141, 142, 143, 179
3:5-8	179
3:6	142, 167
3:7, 11-12	127
3:10	126
3:11, 31-34	131
3:13	128, 135
3:13, 31	131, 184
3:13-19	135
3:14	34, 148, 149
3:14-15	135
3:15	149
3:17	174
3:18	156
3:18-21	156
3:19-21	135
3:21	169
3:34	124, 131, 132, 141, 142, 183, 199
3:36	143
4	131
4:1-24	12
4:1-26	15
4:1-45	16
4:5-19	136

4:6, 52-53 148	5:24 156	7:18 150, 151
4:9 139	5:24-27 135	7:30 148
4:10-14 139, 142, 144, 149, 162-163, 165, 167	5:25 140, 142	7:33-36 113
	5:25, 28-29 148	7:37 162, 166, 179
	5:31-47 123	7:37-38 169, 170
4:10-24 166-167, 179	5:36 150, 151	7:37-39 82, 139, 141-145, 149, 159-161, 164, 166-168, 172, 179, 180, 199
4:10-26 137	5:37-47 143, 144	
4:12 136	5:38-47 123	
4:14 141-142, 162, 167	5:39-46 185	
	5:39-47 1	7:37b-38a 161
4:16-17 199	5:41-44 150	7:38 161, 162, 166, 179
4:16-24 16	5:46 139, 184, 186	
4:18 136	6 4, 5, 34, 192	7:38c 161, 162, 163, 166
4:19 136	6:4 109, 145, 160, 176	
4:19, 29, 39 136	6:27, 35-45 179	7:38c-39 163
4:20 136-137	6:27, 51-58 180	7:39 113, 142, 151, 152, 167, 179
4:20-16 138	6:31 187	
4:20-23 199	6:32 176	7:53-8:11 169
4:20-24 108, 116, 125, 135, 136, 141, 145-147, 158, 172, 173, 195, 196	6:32-35, 49-51 184	8:5 33
	6:35 159, 162, 180	8:12 139, 143, 151, 160, 167, 168, 169, 170, 172
	6:40 177	
	6:44-45 157	
4:20a 136	6:44-58 196	8:20 148
4:21 136-138, 140, 145, 146, 157, 195	6:45 143	8:21-36 144
	6:46 124, 131	8:24, 31-36 143
4:21, 23 140, 148	6:48-58 187	8:26, 38, 40 131
4:21, 23-24 140	6:49-50, 58 184	8:26-28 131, 132, 183
4:21-24 137, 157	6:51 177	8:28 135, 148, 149
4:22 138-140, 157	6:51-58 176, 177, 178, 179, 184	8:31 140
4:22-24 157		8:31-32 143, 156
4:22b 139, 140	6:53-56 177	8:31-36 143, 179
4:23 140	6:53-56, 63 180	8:31-47 177, 178
4:23-24 136, 138, 140-143, 167	6:53-57 177	8:32, 34-36, 44 177
	6:53-62 128	8:34 177
4:24 141, 143	6:54 177	8:34, 44 177
4:24b 141	6:58 180	8:35-36 177
4:31-34 112	6:62 135	8:36 172
4:42 139	6:63 142, 144, 163, 179	8:49 150
4:45 176		8:49-50, 54 150
5:1 109, 145, 160	6:63, 68 167	8:50, 54-55 159
5:1-18 15	7 7	8:54 150, 151
5:2-9 32	7:1-52 15	8:54-55 151
5:19 159	7:1-8:59 16	9:5, 35, 39 135
5:22-30, 41-44 156	7:2 145, 160	9:7 118

10	171, 172		199	14:13	151, 152
10:14	198	12:27	175	14:13-14	174
10:16	35, 183, 196	12:27-28	151	14:16-17, 26	142
10:22	145, 160, 170, 173	12:28	151	14:16-23	142
10:22-39	171, 172	12:31	157, 177	14:17	13, 142, 143, 167, 183
10:22-42	16	12:31, 37-49	156	14:17, 23	183
10:25, 32, 37-38	173	12:31-32	157	14:17, 26	167
10:25, 37-38	150	12:31-36	135	14:17-23	143
10:25-30, 37-38	172	12:32	148, 149, 157, 158, 183, 196	14:20, 23	13, 167
10:33	171	12:33	113, 148, 149	14:20, 26	112
10:35	172	12:34	148	14:23	124, 199
10:36	171-175, 180	12:34-36	135	14:26	113, 142
10:36a	171	12:35-36	149	14:28	132
11	137, 150	12:35-36, 46	169	15:1	131
11:4	151	12:36	169	15:1-7	199
11:4, 40	150, 173, 183	12:43	150	15:4-5	167
11:26	142	12:44-50	174	15:4-6	13, 183
11:40	155	12:49	131, 132, 183	15:4-10	198
11:45	140	12:49-50	131	15:7	174
11:46-53	150	13	16	15:7, 16	174
11:48	137	13:1	148, 160, 176	15:8	151, 152
11:49-52	176	13:1, 27-33	178	15:14-15	143
11:51-52	113	13:1, 29	176	15:16	174
11:52	156, 157, 158, 183, 196	13:3-17	198	15:25	25, 110, 111, 187
11:55	109, 145, 160, 176, 177	13:18	25, 111, 187	15:26	142, 163, 167
		13:21-31	151	16:2, 25, 32	148
11:56	176	13:28-29	113	16:7	142, 163, 179
12	125, 149, 151, 156, 158	13:31	148, 151, 156	16:7, 12-15	112, 143
		13:31-32	135, 151, 155, 156, 173	16:7-15	142
12:1	160, 176	13:32	148, 151, 156	16:11	177
12:12, 20	176	14	14, 16, 18, 124	16:12-15	143
12:13	126	14:1-31	16	16:13	142
12:15	165	14:2	18, 183	16:13-15	167
12:16	113	14:2-3	12, 13, 14, 15, 18, 124, 177	16:14	151, 152
12:18	150	14:3	13, 14, 18, 167, 199, 201, 203	16:16, 19-22	159
12:20-23	157			16:16, 22	13, 183
12:23	148, 151, 173	14:6	143	16:23	174
12:23, 27	148	14:9-10	124	16:23-24, 26	174
12:23, 31	157	14:10	131	16:23-26	174
12:23, 32-34	135	14:10-11	134	17	16, 151
12:23-24	151	14:11	150	17:1	148, 151
12:26	13, 167, 183,			17:1, 4	155

Scripture Index

17:1, 4, 22	151	19:34-36	184	**2 Corinthians**	
17:1, 4-5	173	19:35	8	5:1, 4	117
17:1, 5	156	19:36	163, 178, 187	5:8	199
17:1-3	156	19:37	165, 187	6:14-17	198
17:1-5	151, 175	20:9	113, 163, 187, 192, 193	6:16	45, 104, 197
17:2-3	144	20:16	118	**Ephesians**	
17:3	142	20:17	148	2:19-22	198
17:3-4	174	20:18-29	159	2:20-22	198
17:4	150, 151, 159, 198	20:22	142, 163	2:22	197
17:4-5	148, 151	20:30-31	8		
17:5	151	21:3	201	**Colossians**	
17:5, 24	151, 156, 159	21:7-14	159	2:17	22
17:6	174	21:15-17	198		
17:8	131, 132, 183	21:19	113, 151	**Hebrews**	
17:10, 22	151	21:23	113	7-10	104
17:12	187	21:24	8	8-9	20, 200
17:18	174			8:1-6	104
17:18-19	174	**Acts**		8:10	45
17:19	174, 175, 180	1:20	110	8:13	23
17:21, 26	13	2:26	117	9-10	23
17:21-24	13	2:33	149	9:1-14, 23-25	104
17:21-26	199	4:25	24	10	23
17:22	118	5:31	149	10:1	22
17:23, 26	167	7:45-47	50	10:19-22	104
17:24	13, 18, 167, 183, 199, 203	7:56	128		
		10:11	128	**1 Peter**	
17:26	183	10:40	114	2:4-8	198
18:1-19:42	16	26:22	75	3:21	31
18:28, 39	160, 176				
19:14	160, 176, 178	**Romans**		**2 Peter**	
19:14, 27	148	3:2	122	1:13-14	117
19:24-25a	111	6:14	122		
19:24-25a, 28	187, 188	9:4	122	**1 John**	
		15:3	110	1:5	141
19:28	110			4:8, 16	141
19:29	178	**1 Corinthians**			
19:30	159	3:16	197	**Revelation**	
19:31	178	3:17	197	3:12	104, 199, 200, 201
19:33	178	6:19	197	4	199
19:33, 36	178	10:11	21	4:1	128
19:33-36	178, 179	15:4	114	4:1-2	200
19:34	162, 163, 176, 178, 179, 180			6	82

7:15	117, 199, 200, 201
7:16-17	200
10:19-22	200
11:1-2	199, 200
11:19	199
12:5	200
12:12	117
12:22, 26-28	200
13:6	117
14:15, 17	199
15:5, 6, 8	199
16:1, 17	199
16:17	200
19-22	82
19:11	128
21	99
21-22	82, 197, 199, 201
21:1-22:5	104
21:2-3	199
21:3	45, 117, 197
21:3, 22-23	15
21:4, 8, 25	200
21:12-14	82
21:16	200
21:18	201
21:19-20	201
21:22	18, 82, 200
21:22-23	157
21:22-24	185
22:1-2	166
22:1-3	200
22:1-5	167
22:3-4	15, 201
22:5	200

Index for Other Ancient Sources

Aprocrypha

1 Esdras
1:49	171, 173
8:25, 67	156

2 Esdras
7:27	156
8:36	156

1 Maccabees
2:64	153
3:14	153
4:36, 48	172
7:37	90, 106
14:15	91
14:30, 41	95

2 Maccabees
1:18	172
1:18-2:18	171
1:19-2:12	172
1:20-23, 31-34	90
2:4-5	97
2:4-8	97
2:7-8	97, 119
2:8	105, 168, 171, 172, 173
3:1-3	91
3:22-40	91, 198
5:15-20	91
5:19-20	96
10:3, 5, 7	172
14:35	105
14:35-36	90

3 Maccabees
1:9-2:24	90, 198
2:9	156
2:9, 16	173
2:9-16	90
2:15	90, 103, 107, 200
2:9	171
2:9, 16	171
2:9-16	137
6:18	128

Sirach
36:16-19	96
36:19	119
36:20	99
36:20-21	96
43:30	149
45:4	172
49:7	172
49:12	91

Tobit
13	96
13:10-11	98
13:11	98, 156
14:4-7	96
14:5	97, 98, 99, 106
14:5-7	96, 98
14:6-7	157

Wisdom
18:3	168

Pseudepigrapha

Apocalypse of Abraham
29:17-18	98

2 Baruch
4:2-7	99
6:5-9	97
22:1	128
32:3-4	98
32:4	97
68:5-6	98

1 Enoch
89:28-29	96
89:36	95
89:40	95
89:50, 73	96
89:51	96
89:54, 56, 67	96
89:72-73	96
89:73	95, 98
90:28	96
90:28-36	98
90:29	95, 96, 98, 99, 106
91:13	96, 98

4 Ezra
7:26	98, 99
8:52	98, 99
10:27, 41-55	98, 99
10:46	99
13:32-50	97
13:36	98, 99

Jubilees
1	96
1:15-17	96
1:17	98
1:17, 26-29	98, 105
1:23	142
1:26-29	100
27:21	128
28:20-21	133

Letter of Aristeas
84-99   91

Psalms of Solomon
2   95
2:3-13   95
8   95
8:8-22   95
17   95
17:5-10   95
17:21-42   96
17:21-44   95
17:23-24   25
17:30-31   98
17:30b   110
17:31   98
18:5   110

Sibylline Oracles
3:287-294   91
3:652-795   97
3:657-672   98
3:657-673, 702-704, 718-720, 772-779   98
3:657-795   97
3:715-720, 772-77398,   157
3:772-773   156
3:773-775, 785-787   98
3:785-787   105
4:6-11, 27-30   95
4:116   95
5:247-255, 397-434   98
5:247-285, 414-434   97
5:414-434   98, 99

Testament of Benjamin
9:2   96, 98, 106

Testament of Daniel
5:12-13   98

Testament of Levi
2:8   128
5:1   128
14   95
17:10-11   95
18   95

Testament of Moses
5:1-6:1   95
9:1-10:10   95

Dead Sea Scrolls
(titles based on F. García Martínez)

Apocryphal Psalm
11QPs^a XXII: 1-5   98

Community Rule
1QS I, 2-3   100
1QS II, 19-20   101
1QS II, 24-III, 9   92, 93
1QS IV, 18-26   142
1QS IV, 20-22   103
1QS V, 4-7   93, 104
1QS V, 8-10   100
1QS V, 8-12   92
1QS V, 8-13   92, 93
1QS VIII, 4-10   93, 104
1QS VIII, 5   93
1QS VIII, 5-9   93
1QS IX, 3-6   93, 104
1QS IX, 4-5   94
4QS^d 2 I, 1-3   93
4QS^d 2 II, 6   93
4QS^e II, 11-16   93
4QS^e IX, 6   93

Damascus Document
CD I, 11   92, 93
CD III, 18-IV, 10   93
CD IV, 17   95
CD V, 6-7   95
CD VI, 11-14   94
CD VI, 12   94
CD VI, 12-14   94
CD VIII, 3-13   92, 95
CD IX, 13-14   94
CD XI, 17-XII, 2   94
CD XIV, 5-6   101
CD XVI, 13   94
CD XX, 22-23   95
CD XX, 27-33   93

1 Enoch
4QEn^g ar IV, 18   96

Florilegium
4QFlor I, 1-7   93
4QFlor I, 1-7   98
4QFlor I, 3   99
4QFlor I, 4-6   98
4QFlor I, 5   98, 119

Habakkuk Pesher
1QpHab VIII, 8-13   92
1QpHab IX, 4-15   92
1QpHab IX, 9-11   92
1QpHab XI, 4-8   92
1QpHab XI, 4-15   92
1QpHab XII, 7-9   92

Halakhic Letter
4QMMT   92

Isaiah Pesher
4QpIsa^a 8-10 III, 25   101

New Jerusalem
2QNJ ar 4   94, 101
4QNJ^a ar 1 I, 12-II, 11   101
4QNJ^a ar 1 II, 18   101
4QNJ^a ar 2 II, 13-15   101

4QNJ^a ar 2 III, 16-18
    100
5QNJ ar 1 I, 3-4   101
11QNJ ar   94
11QNJ ar 13   101
11QNJ ar 13 I, 3   101

Psalms Pesher
4QpPs II, 19   92
4QpPs III, 15   92

Temple Scroll
11QT^a XIII-XXIX   94
11QT^a XXIX, 7-9   98, 99
11QT^a XXIX, 8   105
11QT^a XXIX, 9   98, 131
11QT^a XXXV, 1-9
    100
11QT^a XL, 5-8   100
11QT^a XLVI, 9-12
    101

Reworked Pentateuch
4QRP^{b,c} 28 II, 1-4   101

War Scroll
1QM I, 1-2   100
1QM II, 1-6   100
1QM II, 1-6   94

Philo

Special Laws
1.9-2:24   91
1.68-69   91
1.71-74   91
1.77   91

Josephus

Jewish Antiquities
9.289   138
11.82   91
11.297-301   91
12.10   136, 137
12.237-256   91
13.74-79   137
14.69-79   91, 95
15.380-387   97
15.420-1   16
18.19   94
18.29-30, 85-87   137

Jewish War
6.299   98

Rabbinic Writings

Babylonian Talmud
Baba Batra 4a   170
Yoma 21b, 52b   97

Jerusalem Talmud
Sukkah 5:1   164
Ta'anit 4:5   110

Midrashim
Canticles Rabbah
8:9,3   97
Genesis Rabbah
68:12   130-132
Numbers Rabbah
15:10   97

Mishnah
Middot 2:6   165
Sheqalim 6:3   165
Sukkah 5:4   98

Targums
Isaiah
53:5   98
Zechariah
6:12   98

Tosefta Sukkah
3:3   165
3:3-8   165
3:6-8   164
3:18   165

Ancient Christian Writings

(John Chrysostom, Cyril of Alexandria, Jerome in author index)

1 Clement 12:7   20

Paternoster Biblical Monographs

(All titles uniform with this volume)
Dates in bold are of projected publication

Joseph Abraham
Eve: Accused or Acquitted?
A Reconsideration of Feminist Readings of the Creation Narrative Texts in Genesis 1–3
Two contrary views dominate contemporary feminist biblical scholarship. One finds in the Bible an unequivocal equality between the sexes from the very creation of humanity, whilst the other sees the biblical text as irredeemably patriarchal and androcentric. Dr Abraham enters into dialogue with both camps as well as introducing his own method of approach. An invaluable tool for any one who is interested in this contemporary debate.
2002 / 0-85364-971-5 / xxiv + 272pp

Octavian D. Baban
Mimesis and Luke's on the Road Encounters in Luke-Acts
Luke's Theology of the Way and its Literary Representation
The book argues on theological and literary (mimetic) grounds that Luke's on-the-road encounters, especially those belonging to the post-Easter period, are part of his complex theology of the Way. Jesus' teaching and that of the apostles is presented by Luke as a challenging answer to the Hellenistic reader's thirst for adventure, good literature, and existential paradigms.
2005 */ 1-84227-253-5 / approx. 374pp*

Paul Barker
The Triumph of Grace in Deuteronomy
This book is a textual and theological analysis of the interaction between the sin and faithlessness of Israel and the grace of Yahweh in response, looking especially at Deuteronomy chapters 1–3, 8–10 and 29–30. The author argues that the grace of Yahweh is determinative for the ongoing relationship between Yahweh and Israel and that Deuteronomy anticipates and fully expects Israel to be faithless.
2004 / 1-84227-226-8 / xxii + 270pp

Jonathan F. Bayes
The Weakness of the Law
God's Law and the Christian in New Testament Perspective
A study of the four New Testament books which refer to the law as weak (Acts, Romans, Galatians, Hebrews) leads to a defence of the third use in the Reformed debate about the law in the life of the believer.
2000 / 0-85364-957-X / xii + 244pp

Mark Bonnington
The Antioch Episode of Galatians 2:11-14 in Historical and Cultural Context

The Galatians 2 'incident' in Antioch over table-fellowship suggests significant disagreement between the leading apostles. This book analyses the background to the disagreement by locating the incident within the dynamics of social interaction between Jews and Gentiles. It proposes a new way of understanding the relationship between the individuals and issues involved.

2005 / 1-84227-050-8 / approx. 350pp

David Bostock
A Portrayal of Trust
The Theme of Faith in the Hezekiah Narratives

This study provides detailed and sensitive readings of the Hezekiah narratives (2 Kings 18–20 and Isaiah 36–39) from a theological perspective. It concentrates on the theme of faith, using narrative criticism as its methodology. Attention is paid especially to setting, plot, point of view and characterization within the narratives. A largely positive portrayal of Hezekiah emerges that underlines the importance and relevance of scripture.

2005 / 1-84227-314-0 / approx. 300pp

Mark Bredin
Jesus, Revolutionary of Peace
A Non-violent Christology in the Book of Revelation

This book aims to demonstrate that the figure of Jesus in the Book of Revelation can best be understood as an active non-violent revolutionary.

2003 / 1-84227-153-9 / xviii + 262pp

Robinson Butarbutar
Paul and Conflict Resolution
An Exegetical Study of Paul's Apostolic Paradigm in 1 Corinthians 9

The author sees the apostolic paradigm in 1 Corinthians 9 as part of Paul's unified arguments in 1 Corinthians 8–10 in which he seeks to mediate in the dispute over the issue of food offered to idols. The book also sees its relevance for dispute-resolution today, taking the conflict within the author's church as an example.

2006 / 1-84227-315-9 / approx. 280pp

Daniel J-S Chae
Paul as Apostle to the Gentiles
His Apostolic Self-awareness and its Influence on the Soteriological Argument in Romans
Opposing 'the post-Holocaust interpretation of Romans', Daniel Chae competently demonstrates that Paul argues for the equality of Jew and Gentile in Romans. Chae's fresh exegetical interpretation is academically outstanding and spiritually encouraging.
1997 / 0-85364-829-8 / xiv + 378pp

Luke L. Cheung
The Genre, Composition and Hermeneutics of the Epistle of James
The present work examines the employment of the wisdom genre with a certain compositional structure and the interpretation of the law through the Jesus tradition of the double love command by the author of the Epistle of James to serve his purpose in promoting perfection and warning against doubleness among the eschatologically renewed people of God in the Diaspora.
2003 / 1-84227-062-1 / xvi + 372pp

Youngmo Cho
Spirit and Kingdom in the Writings of Luke and Paul
The relationship between Spirit and Kingdom is a relatively unexplored area in Lukan and Pauline studies. This book offers a fresh perspective of two biblical writers on the subject. It explores the difference between Luke's and Paul's understanding of the Spirit by examining the specific question of the relationship of the concept of the Spirit to the concept of the Kingdom of God in each writer.
2005 / 1-84227-316-7 / approx. 270pp

Andrew C. Clark
Parallel Lives
The Relation of Paul to the Apostles in the Lucan Perspective
This study of the Peter-Paul parallels in Acts argues that their purpose was to emphasize the themes of continuity in salvation history and the unity of the Jewish and Gentile missions. New light is shed on Luke's literary techniques, partly through a comparison with Plutarch.
2001 / 1-84227-035-4 / xviii + 386pp

Andrew D. Clarke
Secular and Christian Leadership in Corinth
A Socio-Historical and Exegetical Study of 1 Corinthians 1–6

This volume is an investigation into the leadership structures and dynamics of first-century Roman Corinth. These are compared with the practice of leadership in the Corinthian Christian community which are reflected in 1 Corinthians 1–6, and contrasted with Paul's own principles of Christian leadership.

2005 / 1-84227-229-2 / 200pp

Stephen Finamore
God, Order and Chaos
René Girard and the Apocalypse

Readers are often disturbed by the images of destruction in the book of Revelation and unsure why they are unleashed after the exaltation of Jesus. This book examines past approaches to these texts and uses René Girard's theories to revive some old ideas and propose some new ones.

2005 / 1-84227-197-0 / approx. 344pp

David G. Firth
Surrendering Retribution in the Psalms
Responses to Violence in the Individual Complaints

In *Surrendering Retribution in the Psalms*, David Firth examines the ways in which the book of Psalms inculcates a model response to violence through the repetition of standard patterns of prayer. Rather than seeking justification for retributive violence, Psalms encourages not only a surrender of the right of retribution to Yahweh, but also sets limits on the retribution that can be sought in imprecations. Arising initially from the author's experience in South Africa, the possibilities of this model to a particular context of violence is then briefly explored.

2005 / 1-84227-337-X / xviii + 154pp

Scott J. Hafemann
Suffering and Ministry in the Spirit
Paul's Defence of His Ministry in II Corinthians 2:14–3:3

Shedding new light on the way Paul defended his apostleship, the author offers a careful, detailed study of 2 Corinthians 2:14–3:3 linked with other key passages throughout 1 and 2 Corinthians. Demonstrating the unity and coherence of Paul's argument in this passage, the author shows that Paul's suffering served as the vehicle for revealing God's power and glory through the Spirit.

2000 / 0-85364-967-7 / xiv + 262pp

Scott J. Hafemann
Paul, Moses and the History of Israel
The Letter/Spirit Contrast and the Argument from Scripture in 2 Corinthians 3
An exegetical study of the call of Moses, the second giving of the Law (Exodus 32–34), the new covenant, and the prophetic understanding of the history of Israel in 2 Corinthians 3. Hafemann's work demonstrates Paul's contextual use of the Old Testament and the essential unity between the Law and the Gospel within the context of the distinctive ministries of Moses and Paul.
2005 / 1-84227-317-5 / xii + 498pp

Douglas S. McComiskey
Lukan Theology in the Light of the Gospel's Literary Structure
Luke's Gospel was purposefully written with theology embedded in its patterned literary structure. A critical analysis of this cyclical structure provides new windows into Luke's interpretation of the individual pericopes comprising the Gospel and illuminates several of his theological interests.
2004 / 1-84227-148-2 / xviii + 388pp

Stephen Motyer
Your Father the Devil?
A New Approach to John and 'The Jews'
Who are 'the Jews' in John's Gospel? Defending John against the charge of antisemitism, Motyer argues that, far from demonising the Jews, the Gospel seeks to present Jesus as 'Good News for Jews' in a late first century setting.
1997 / 0-85364-832-8 / xiv + 260pp

Esther Ng
Reconstructing Christian Origins?
The Feminist Theology of Elizabeth Schüssler Fiorenza: An Evaluation
In a detailed evaluation, the author challenges Elizabeth Schüssler Fiorenza's reconstruction of early Christian origins and her underlying presuppositions. The author also presents her own views on women's roles both then and now.
2002 / 1-84227-055-9 / xxiv + 468pp

Robin Parry
Old Testament Story and Christian Ethics
The Rape of Dinah as a Case Study

What is the role of story in ethics and, more particularly, what is the role of Old Testament story in Christian ethics? This book, drawing on the work of contemporary philosophers, argues that narrative is crucial in the ethical shaping of people and, drawing on the work of contemporary Old Testament scholars, that story plays a key role in Old Testament ethics. Parry then argues that when situated in canonical context Old Testament stories can be reappropriated by Christian readers in their own ethical formation. The shocking story of the rape of Dinah and the massacre of the Shechemites provides a fascinating case study for exploring the parameters within which Christian ethical appropriations of Old Testament stories can live.

2004 / 1-84227-210-1 / xx + 350pp

Ian Paul
Power to See the World Anew
The Value of Paul Ricoeur's Hermeneutic of Metaphor in Interpreting the Symbolism of Revelation 12 and 13

This book is a study of the hermeneutics of metaphor of Paul Ricoeur, one of the most important writers on hermeneutics and metaphor of the last century. It sets out the key points of his theory, important criticisms of his work, and how his approach, modified in the light of these criticisms, offers a methodological framework for reading apocalyptic texts.

2006 / 1-84227-056-7 / approx. 350pp

Robert L. Plummer
Paul's Understanding of the Church's Mission
Did the Apostle Paul Expect the Early Christian Communities to Evangelize?

This book engages in a careful study of Paul's letters to determine if the apostle expected the communities to which he wrote to engage in missionary activity. It helpfully summarizes the discussion on this debated issue, judiciously handling contested texts, and provides a way forward in addressing this critical question. While admitting that Paul rarely explicitly commands the communities he founded to evangelize, Plummer amasses significant incidental data to provide a convincing case that Paul did indeed expect his churches to engage in mission activity. Throughout the study, Plummer progressively builds a theological basis for the church's mission that is both distinctively Pauline and compelling.

2006 / 1-84227-333-7 / approx. 324pp

David Powys
'Hell': A Hard Look at a Hard Question
The Fate of the Unrighteous in New Testament Thought
This comprehensive treatment seeks to unlock the original meaning of terms and phrases long thought to support the traditional doctrine of hell. It concludes that there is an alternative—one which is more biblical, and which can positively revive the rationale for Christian mission.

1997 / 0-85364-831-X / xxii + 478pp

Sorin Sabou
Between Horror and Hope
Paul's Metaphorical Language of Death in Romans 6.1-11
This book argues that Paul's metaphorical language of death in Romans 6.1-11 conveys two aspects: horror and hope. The 'horror' aspect is conveyed by the 'crucifixion' language, and the 'hope' aspect by 'burial' language. The life of the Christian believer is understood, as relationship with sin is concerned ('death to sin'), between these two realities: horror and hope.

2005 / 1-84227-322-1 / approx. 224pp

Rosalind Selby
The Comical Doctrine
The Epistemology of New Testament Hermeneutics
This book argues that the gospel breaks through postmodernity's critique of truth and the referential possibilities of textuality with its gift of grace. With a rigorous, philosophical challenge to modernist and postmodernist assumptions, Selby offers an alternative epistemology to all who would still read with faith *and* with academic credibility.

2005 / 1-84227-212-8 / approx. 350pp

Kiwoong Son
Zion Symbolism in Hebrews
Hebrews 12.18-24 as a Hermeneutical Key to the Epistle
This book challenges the general tendency of understanding the Epistle to the Hebrews against a Hellenistic background and suggests that the Epistle should be understood in the light of the Jewish apocalyptic tradition. The author especially argues for the importance of the theological symbolism of Sinai and Zion (Heb. 12:18-24) as it provides the Epistle's theological background as well as the rhetorical basis of the superiority motif of Jesus throughout the Epistle.

2005 / 1-84227-368-X / approx. 280pp

Kevin Walton
Thou Traveller Unknown
The Presence and Absence of God in the Jacob Narrative
The author offers a fresh reading of the story of Jacob in the book of Genesis through the paradox of divine presence and absence. The work also seeks to make a contribution to Pentateuchal studies by bringing together a close reading of the final text with historical critical insights, doing justice to the text's historical depth, final form and canonical status.
2003 / 1-84227-059-1 / xvi + 238pp

George M. Wieland
The Significance of Salvation
A Study of Salvation Language in the Pastoral Epistles
The language and ideas of salvation pervade the three Pastoral Epistles. This study offers a close examination of their soteriological statements. In all three letters the idea of salvation is found to play a vital paraenetic role, but each also exhibits distinctive soteriological emphases. The results challenge common assumptions about the Pastoral Epistles as a corpus.
2005 / 1-84227-257-8 / approx. 324pp

Alistair Wilson
When Will These Things Happen?
A Study of Jesus as Judge in Matthew 21–25
This study seeks to allow Matthew's carefully constructed presentation of Jesus to be given full weight in the modern evaluation of Jesus' eschatology. Careful analysis of the text of Matthew 21–25 reveals Jesus to be standing firmly in the Jewish prophetic and wisdom traditions as he proclaims and enacts imminent judgement on the Jewish authorities then boldly claims the central role in the final and universal judgement.
2004 / 1-84227-146-6 / xxii + 272pp

Lindsay Wilson
Joseph Wise and Otherwise
The Intersection of Covenant and Wisdom in Genesis 37–50
This book offers a careful literary reading of Genesis 37–50 that argues that the Joseph story contains both strong covenant themes and many wisdom-like elements. The connections between the two helps to explore how covenant and wisdom might intersect in an integrated biblical theology.
2004 / 1-84227-140-7 / xvi + 340pp

Stephen I. Wright
The Voice of Jesus
Studies in the Interpretation of Six Gospel Parables
This literary study considers how the 'voice' of Jesus has been heard in different periods of parable interpretation, and how the categories of figure and trope may help us towards a sensitive reading of the parables today.
2000 / 0-85364-975-8 / xiv + 280pp

Paternoster
9 Holdom Avenue,
Bletchley,
Milton Keynes MK1 1QR,
United Kingdom
Web: www.authenticmedia.co.uk/paternoster

Paternoster Theological Monographs
(All titles uniform with this volume)
Dates in bold are of projected publication

Emil Bartos
Deification in Eastern Orthodox Theology
An Evaluation and Critique of the Theology of Dumitru Staniloae
Bartos studies a fundamental yet neglected aspect of Orthodox theology: deification. By examining the doctrines of anthropology, christology, soteriology and ecclesiology as they relate to deification, he provides an important contribution to contemporary dialogue between Eastern and Western theologians.

1999 / 0-85364-956-1 / xii + 370pp

Graham Buxton
The Trinity, Creation and Pastoral Ministry
Imaging the Perichoretic God
In this book the author proposes a three-way conversation between theology, science and pastoral ministry. His approach draws on a Trinitarian understanding of God as a relational being of love, whose life 'spills over' into all created reality, human and non-human. By locating human meaning and purpose within God's 'creation-community' this book offers the possibility of a transforming engagement between those in pastoral ministry and the scientific community.

***2005** / 1-84227-369-8 / approx. 380 pp*

Iain D. Campbell
Fixing the Indemnity
The Life and Work of George Adam Smith
When Old Testament scholar George Adam Smith (1856–1942) delivered the Lyman Beecher lectures at Yale University in 1899, he confidently declared that 'modern criticism has won its war against traditional theories. It only remains to fix the amount of the indemnity.' In this biography, Iain D. Campbell assesses Smith's critical approach to the Old Testament and evaluates its consequences, showing that Smith's life and work still raises questions about the relationship between biblical scholarship and evangelical faith.

2004 / 1-84227-228-4 / xx + 256pp

Tim Chester
Mission and the Coming of God
Eschatology, the Trinity and Mission in the Theology of Jürgen Moltmann
This book explores the theology and missiology of the influential contemporary theologian, Jürgen Moltmann. It highlights the important contribution Moltmann has made while offering a critique of his thought from an evangelical perspective. In so doing, it touches on pertinent issues for evangelical missiology. The conclusion takes Calvin as a starting point, proposing 'an eschatology of the cross' which offers a critique of the over-realised eschatologies in liberation theology and certain forms of evangelicalism.
2006 / 1-84227-320-5 / approx. 224pp

Sylvia Wilkey Collinson
Making Disciples
The Significance of Jesus' Educational Strategy for Today's Church
This study examines the biblical practice of discipling, formulates a definition, and makes comparisons with modern models of education. A recommendation is made for greater attention to its practice today.
2004 / 1-84227-116-4 / xiv + 278pp

Darrell Cosden
A Theology of Work
Work and the New Creation
Through dialogue with Moltmann, Pope John Paul II and others, this book develops a genitive 'theology of work', presenting a theological definition of work and a model for a theological ethics of work that shows work's nature, value and meaning now and eschatologically. Work is shown to be a transformative activity consisting of three dynamically inter-related dimensions: the instrumental, relational and ontological.
2005 / 1-84227-332-9 / xvi + 208pp

Stephen M. Dunning
The Crisis and the Quest
A Kierkegaardian Reading of Charles Williams
Employing Kierkegaardian categories and analysis, this study investigates both the central crisis in Charles Williams's authorship between hermetism and Christianity (Kierkegaard's Religions A and B), and the quest to resolve this crisis, a quest that ultimately presses the bounds of orthodoxy.
2000 / 0-85364-985-5 / xxiv + 254pp

Keith Ferdinando
The Triumph of Christ in African Perspective
A Study of Demonology and Redemption in the African Context
The book explores the implications of the gospel for traditional African fears of occult aggression. It analyses such traditional approaches to suffering and biblical responses to fears of demonic evil, concluding with an evaluation of African beliefs from the perspective of the gospel.
1999 / 0-85364-830-1 / xviii + 450pp

Andrew Goddard
Living the Word, Resisting the World
The Life and Thought of Jacques Ellul
This work offers a definitive study of both the life and thought of the French Reformed thinker Jacques Ellul (1912-1994). It will prove an indispensable resource for those interested in this influential theologian and sociologist and for Christian ethics and political thought generally.
2002 / 1-84227-053-2 / xxiv + 378pp

David Hilborn
The Words of our Lips
Language-Use in Free Church Worship
Studies of liturgical language have tended to focus on the written canons of Roman Catholic and Anglican communities. By contrast, David Hilborn analyses the more extemporary approach of English Nonconformity. Drawing on recent developments in linguistic pragmatics, he explores similarities and differences between 'fixed' and 'free' worship, and argues for the interdependence of each.
2006 / 0-85364-977-4 / approx. 350pp

Roger Hitching
The Church and Deaf People
A Study of Identity, Communication and Relationships with Special Reference to the Ecclesiology of Jürgen Moltmann
In *The Church and Deaf People* Roger Hitching sensitively examines the history and present experience of deaf people and finds similarities between aspects of sign language and Moltmann's theological method that 'open up' new ways of understanding theological concepts.
2003 / 1-84227-222-5 / xxii + 236pp

John G. Kelly
One God, One People
The Differentiated Unity of the People of God in the Theology of Jürgen Moltmann
The author expounds and critiques Moltmann's doctrine of God and highlights the systematic connections between it and Moltmann's influential discussion of Israel. He then proposes a fresh approach to Jewish–Christian relations building on Moltmann's work using insights from Habermas and Rawls.
2005 / 0-85346-969-3 / approx. 350pp

Mark F.W. Lovatt
Confronting the Will-to-Power
A Reconsideration of the Theology of Reinhold Niebuhr
Confronting the Will-to-Power is an analysis of the theology of Reinhold Niebuhr, arguing that his work is an attempt to identify, and provide a practical theological answer to, the existence and nature of human evil.
2001 / 1-84227-054-0 / xviii + 216pp

Neil B. MacDonald
Karl Barth and the Strange New World within the Bible
Barth, Wittgenstein, and the Metadilemmas of the Enlightenment
Barth's discovery of the strange new world within the Bible is examined in the context of Kant, Hume, Overbeck, and, most importantly, Wittgenstein. MacDonald covers some fundamental issues in theology today: epistemology, the final form of the text and biblical truth-claims.
2000 / 0-85364-970-7 / xxvi + 374pp

Keith A. Mascord
Alvin Plantinga and Christian Apologetics
This book draws together the contributions of the philosopher Alvin Plantinga to the major contemporary challenges to Christian belief, highlighting in particular his ground-breaking work in epistemology and the problem of evil. Plantinga's theory that both theistic and Christian belief is warrantedly basic is explored and critiqued, and an assessment offered as to the significance of his work for apologetic theory and practice.
2005 / 1-84227-256-X / approx. 304pp

Gillian McCulloch
The Deconstruction of Dualism in Theology
With Reference to Ecofeminist Theology and New Age Spirituality
This book challenges eco-theological anti-dualism in Christian theology, arguing that dualism has a twofold function in Christian religious discourse. Firstly, it enables us to express the discontinuities and divisions that are part of the process of reality. Secondly, dualistic language allows us to express the mysteries of divine transcendence/immanence and the survival of the soul without collapsing into monism and materialism, both of which are problematic for Christian epistemology.

2002 / 1-84227-044-3 / xii + 282pp

Leslie McCurdy
Attributes and Atonement
The Holy Love of God in the Theology of P.T. Forsyth
Attributes and Atonement is an intriguing full-length study of P.T. Forsyth's doctrine of the cross as it relates particularly to God's holy love. It includes an unparalleled bibliography of both primary and secondary material relating to Forsyth.

1999 / 0-85364-833-6 / xiv + 328pp

Nozomu Miyahira
Towards a Theology of the Concord of God
A Japanese Perspective on the Trinity
This book introduces a new Japanese theology and a unique Trinitarian formula based on the Japanese intellectual climate: three betweennesses and one concord. It also presents a new interpretation of the Trinity, a co-subordinationism, which is in line with orthodox Trinitarianism; each single person of the Trinity is eternally and equally subordinate (or serviceable) to the other persons, so that they retain the mutual dynamic equality.

2000 / 0-85364-863-8 / xiv + 256pp

Eddy José Muskus
The Origins and Early Development of Liberation Theology in Latin America
With Particular Reference to Gustavo Gutiérrez
This work challenges the fundamental premise of Liberation Theology, 'opting for the poor', and its claim that Christ is found in them. It also argues that Liberation Theology emerged as a direct result of the failure of the Roman Catholic Church in Latin America.

2002 / 0-85364-974-X / xiv + 296pp

Jim Purves
The Triune God and the Charismatic Movement
A Critical Appraisal from a Scottish Perspective
All emotion and no theology? Or a fundamental challenge to reappraise and realign our trinitarian theology in the light of Christian experience? This study of charismatic renewal as it found expression within Scotland at the end of the twentieth century evaluates the use of Patristic, Reformed and contemporary models of the Trinity in explaining the workings of the Holy Spirit.
2004 / 1-84227-321-3 / xxiv + 246pp

Anna Robbins
Methods in the Madness
Diversity in Twentieth-Century Christian Social Ethics
The author compares the ethical methods of Walter Rauschenbusch, Reinhold Niebuhr and others. She argues that unless Christians are clear about the ways that theology and philosophy are expressed practically they may lose the ability to discuss social ethics across contexts, let alone reach effective agreements.
2004 / 1-84227-211-X / xx + 294pp

Ed Rybarczyk
Beyond Salvation
Eastern Orthodoxy and Classical Pentecostalism on Becoming Like Christ
At first glance eastern Orthodoxy and classical Pentecostalism seem quite distinct. This ground-breaking study shows they share much in common, especially as it concerns the experiential elements of following Christ. Both traditions assert that authentic Christianity transcends the wooden categories of modernism.
2004 / 1-84227-144-X / xii + 356pp

Signe Sandsmark
Is World View Neutral Education Possible and Desirable?
A Christian Response to Liberal Arguments
(Published jointly with The Stapleford Centre)
This book discusses reasons for belief in world view neutrality, and argues that 'neutral' education will have a hidden, but strong world view influence. It discusses the place for Christian education in the common school.
2000 / 0-85364-973-1 / xiv + 182pp

Hazel Sherman
Reading Zechariah
The Allegorical Tradition of Biblical Interpretation through the Commentary of Didymus the Blind and Theodore of Mopsuestia
A close reading of the commentary on Zechariah by Didymus the Blind alongside that of Theodore of Mopsuestia suggests that popular categorising of Antiochene and Alexandrian biblical exegesis as 'historical' or 'allegorical' is inadequate and misleading.
2005 / 1-84227-213-6 / approx. 280pp

Andrew Sloane
On Being a Christian in the Academy
Nicholas Wolterstorff and the Practice of Christian Scholarship
An exposition and critical appraisal of Nicholas Wolterstorff's epistemology in the light of the philosophy of science, and an application of his thought to the practice of Christian scholarship.
2003 / 1-84227-058-3 / xvi + 274pp

Damon W.K. So
Jesus' Revelation of His Father
A Narrative-Conceptual Study of the Trinity with Special Reference to Karl Barth
This book explores the trinitarian dynamics in the context of Jesus' revelation of his Father in his earthly ministry with references to key passages in Matthew's Gospel. It develops from the exegeses of these passages a non-linear concept of revelation which links Jesus' communion with his Father to his revelatory words and actions through a nuanced understanding of the Holy Spirit, with references to K. Barth, G.W.H. Lampe, J.D.G. Dunn and E. Irving.
2005 / 1-84227-323-X / approx. 380pp

Daniel Strange
The Possibility of Salvation Among the Unevangelised
An Analysis of Inclusivism in Recent Evangelical Theology
For evangelical theologians the 'fate of the unevangelised' impinges upon fundamental tenets of evangelical identity. The position known as 'inclusivism', defined by the belief that the unevangelised can be ontologically saved by Christ whilst being epistemologically unaware of him, has been defended most vigorously by the Canadian evangelical Clark H. Pinnock. Through a detailed analysis and critique of Pinnock's work, this book examines a cluster of issues surrounding the unevangelised and its implications for christology, soteriology and the doctrine of revelation.
2002 / 1-84227-047-8 / xviii + 362pp

Scott Swain
God According to the Gospel
Biblical Narrative and the Identity of God in the Theology of Robert W. Jenson
Robert W. Jenson is one of the leading voices in contemporary Trinitarian theology. His boldest contribution in this area concerns his use of biblical narrative both to ground and explicate the Christian doctrine of God. *God According to the Gospel* critically examines Jenson's proposal and suggests an alternative way of reading the biblical portrayal of the triune God.
2006 / 1-84227-258-6 / approx. 180pp

Justyn Terry
The Justifying Judgement of God
A Reassessment of the Place of Judgement in the Saving Work of Christ
The argument of this book is that judgement, understood as the whole process of bringing justice, is the primary metaphor of atonement, with others, such as victory, redemption and sacrifice, subordinate to it. Judgement also provides the proper context for understanding penal substitution and the call to repentance, baptism, eucharist and holiness.
2005 / 1-84227-370-1 / approx. 274 pp

Graham Tomlin
The Power of the Cross
Theology and the Death of Christ in Paul, Luther and Pascal
This book explores the theology of the cross in St Paul, Luther and Pascal. It offers new perspectives on the theology of each, and some implications for the nature of power, apologetics, theology and church life in a postmodern context.
1999 / 0-85364-984-7 / xiv + 344pp

Adonis Vidu
Postliberal Theological Method
A Critical Study
The postliberal theology of Hans Frei, George Lindbeck, Ronald Thiemann, John Milbank and others is one of the more influential contemporary options. This book focuses on several aspects pertaining to its theological method, specifically its understanding of background, hermeneutics, epistemic justification, ontology, the nature of doctrine and, finally, Christological method.
2005 / 1-84227-395-7 / approx. 324pp

Graham J. Watts
Revelation and the Spirit
A Comparative Study of the Relationship between the Doctrine of Revelation and Pneumatology in the Theology of Eberhard Jüngel and of Wolfhart Pannenberg

The relationship between revelation and pneumatology is relatively unexplored. This approach offers a fresh angle on two important twentieth century theologians and raises pneumatological questions which are theologically crucial and relevant to mission in a postmodern culture.

2005 / 1-84227-104-0 / xxii + 232pp

Nigel G. Wright
Disavowing Constantine
Mission, Church and the Social Order in the Theologies of John Howard Yoder and Jürgen Moltmann

This book is a timely restatement of a radical theology of church and state in the Anabaptist and Baptist tradition. Dr Wright constructs his argument in dialogue and debate with Yoder and Moltmann, major contributors to a free church perspective.

2000 / 0-85364-978-2 / xvi + 252pp

Paternoster
9 Holdom Avenue,
Bletchley,
Milton Keynes MK1 1QR,
United Kingdom
Web: www.authenticmedia.co.uk/paternoster

July 2005

www.ingramcontent.com/pod-product-compliance
Lightning Source LLC
Chambersburg PA
CBHW061432300426
44114CB00014B/1656